**Praise for Dick Lord's books:**

"*Vlamgat* deserves a place of pride in the lor air force in the world."—Lt-Gen Willem H African Air Force

"*Vlamgat* is a superb book … my congratulations to Brigadier Dick Lord for the outstanding work he has done."—**Serge Dassault** (builder of the Mirage) in a letter to General Willem Hechter, former commander of the SAAF

"Should *Vlamgat* have been written three years earlier, I would have made it compulsory reading for my pilots … I was CO of Sqn 2/33 from September '96 to May '99, after getting my wings in 1982. I flew in the Gulf, and I had some experience of Africa in Chad, Central Africa … but we French were not fighting there for our country, as you did in SWA."—Vincent Gojon, former F1 pilot and squadron CO in the French Air Force

"I wanted to tell you that I thoroughly enjoyed reading *From Tailhooker to Mudmover*. As a former tailhooker in the U.S. Navy, it made me break out the old logbooks and review some mutual South China Sea dates."—**Thomas A. Kamm**, Rear Admiral U.S. Naval Reserve (Ret.)

"I read *From Tailhooker to Mudmover* from cover to cover over the weekend and really enjoyed it. It is a superb book."— **William Hare**, former Fleet Air Arm pilot, UK

"As a former Officer of the Reserve of the Netherlands Air Force I have to congratulate you on writing this fine book [*Fire, Flood and Ice*], which I have been reading with great pleasure and interest."—W. P. J. Schuiten, Holland

"*Vlamgat* is outstanding! If you have any interest in air combat this book is a must-read … this is the best book I have read about the South African Air Force."—E. Burke Lauderhill, Florida, USA

"*Vlamgat* is an eye opener on the skills, professionalism and training of the South African Air Force. If you thought that all African air forces were 'Third-World', then this book shows you are mistaken. Air-to-air combat, ground strikes far away from home base into the hornets' nest, SAMs chasing your tail, AAA fire from hell, odds 100-to-1 against you—you'll find it all here."—Michiel Erasmus, Netherlands

# VLAMGAT

The Story of the Mirage F1 in the
South African Air Force

## Brig-Gen Dick Lord

**Also by Dick Lord**

*Fire, Flood and Ice—Search and Rescue Missions of the South African Air Force*

*From Tailhooker to Mudmover—An Aviation Career in the Royal Naval Fleet Air Arm, United States Navy, and South African Air*

*From Fledgling to Eagle—The South African Air Force during the Border War*

Published in 2008 by 30° South Publishers (Pty) Ltd.
28, Ninth Street, Newlands
Johannesburg 2092, South Africa
www.30degreessouth.co.za
info@30degreessouth.co.za

First published in 2000 by Covos Day

Maps and diagrams by Genevieve Edwards

Copyright © Dick Lord, 2000 and 2008
dicklord@mweb.co.za

Design and origination by 30° South Publishers (Pty) Ltd.

Printed and bound by Pinetown Printers, Durban

All rights reserved. No part of this publication may be reproduced, stored, manipulated in any retrieval system, or transmitted in any mechanical, electronic form or by any other means, without the prior written authority of the publishers. Any person who engages in any unauthorized activity in relation to this publication shall be liable to criminal prosecution and claims for civil and criminal damages.

ISBN 978-1-920143-36-7

**Brigadier-General Dick Lord** was born in Johannesburg where he grew up. He joined the Royal Navy as an air cadet in 1958, where he qualified as a fighter pilot. Flying Sea Venoms and Sea Vixens, he served on board the aircraft carriers *Centaur*, *Victorious*, *Hermes* and *Ark Royal* on cruises around the world. In the mid 1960s, he was selected for a two-year exchange tour with the US Navy, flying A4 Skyhawks and F4 Phantoms out of San Diego, California. He completed tours of air warfare instruction, flying Hunters out of the naval air stations at Lossiemouth, Scotland and Brawdy, Wales.

He returned to South Africa in early 1970s and joined the South African Air Force (SAAF), flying Impalas, Sabres and Mirage IIIs. During the Border War, he commanded 1 Squadron, flying Mirage F1AZs into Angola, followed by running air force operations out of Oshakati, Windhoek and SAAF Headquarters in Pretoria. He was mentioned in dispatches for his role in the remarkable rescue of all 581 people from the ill-fated liner *Oceanos*. A highlight of his career was organizing the successful flypast of 76 aircraft for Nelson Mandela's inauguration as President of South Africa in 1994.

He retired to Somerset West near Cape Town with his wife June. He is author of *Fire, Flood and Ice*, which chronicles some of the SAAF's spectacular search and rescue operations; *Vlamgat—The Story of the Mirage F1 in the South African Air Force* and *From Tailhooker to Mudmover*, an autobiographical account of his service in the Royal Naval Fleet Air Arm, the US Navy and the SAAF. He has just written his fourth book, *From Fledgling to Eagle—The South African Air Force in the Border War*.

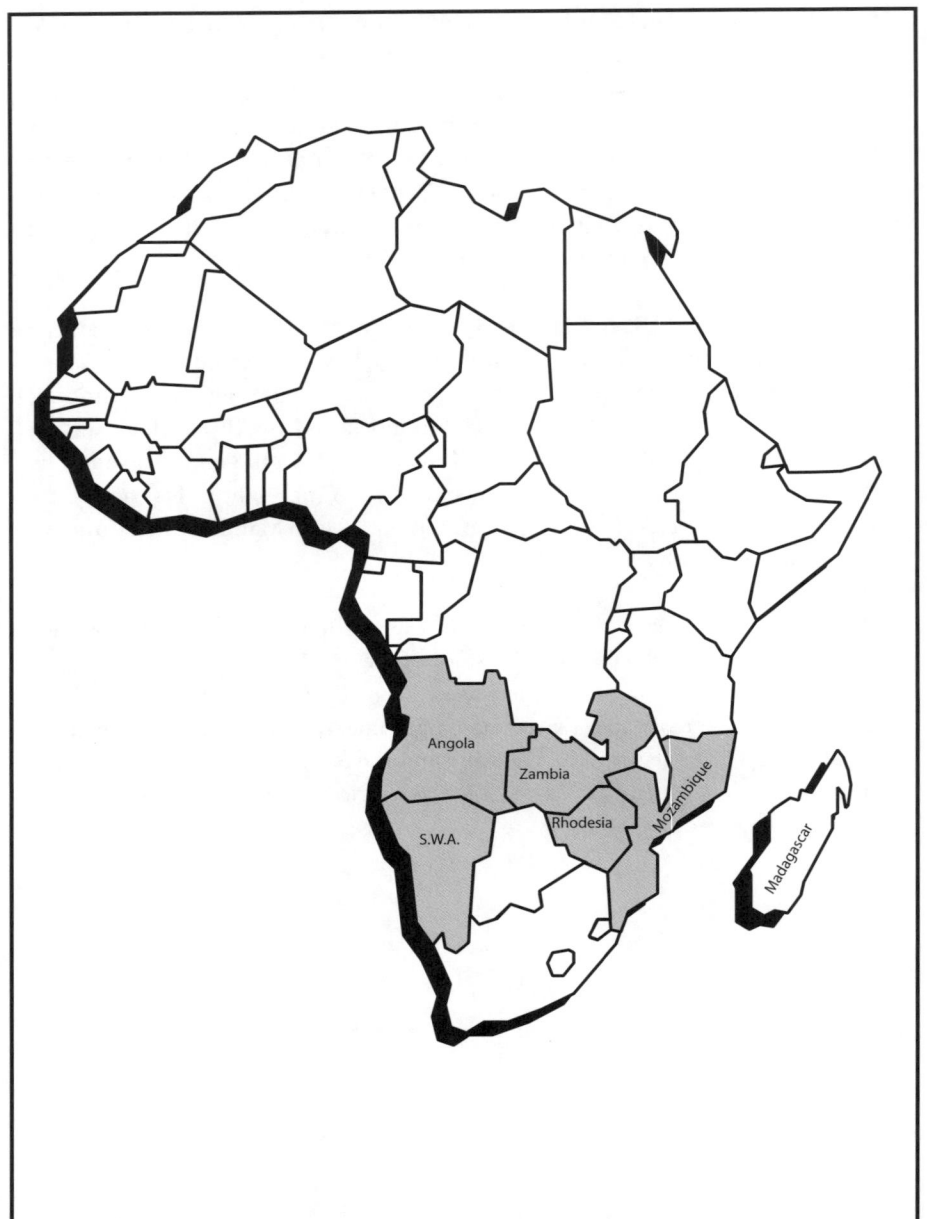

**AREA OF BORDER WAR OPERATIONS**

*This book is dedicated to*

Chris Brits, Ed Every, Willie van Coppenhagen and Louis Joubert

They shall not grow old, as we that are left grow old:
Age shall not weary them, nor the years condemn.
At the going down of the sun and in the morning
We will remember them.
*Ibid*

# CONTENTS

| | | |
|---|---|---|
| List of maps and diagrams | | 9 |
| Foreword by Lt-Gen W. H. Hechter | | 11 |
| Author's note | | 12 |
| Introduction | They are flying again in the morning | 15 |
| Chapter 1 | 1969–1974: Acquisition of a legend | 24 |
| Chapter 2 | 1975: Return to South Africa | 33 |
| Chapter 3 | 1976: 13 Squadron | 42 |
| Chapter 4 | 1977: Laying foundations | 51 |
| Chapter 5 | 1978: Border war escalation | 60 |
| Chapter 6 | 1979: The rising storm | 67 |
| Chapter 7 | 1980: Nearing boiling point | 80 |
| Chapter 8 | 1981: The pot boils over | 102 |
| Chapter 9 | 1982: Stoking the fire | 127 |
| Chapter 10 | 1983: Paradigm shift | 144 |
| Chapter 11 | 1984: An uneasy peace | 151 |
| Chapter 12 | 1985: Internationalization of the conflict | 158 |
| Chapter 13 | 1986: The lull before the storm | 171 |
| Chapter 14 | 1987: All hell breaks loose | 178 |
| Chapter 15 | 1988: Stalemate | 194 |
| Chapter 16 | 1989–1992: Beginning of the end—3 Squadron | 205 |
| Chapter 17 | 1989–1991: Return to peace | 214 |
| Chapter 18 | 1992–1994: Hanging on a thread | 224 |
| Chapter 19 | 1995–1997: End of an era | 237 |
| Glossary | | 246 |
| Appendix 1 | A day on the flight line | 258 |
| Appendix 2 | The Billy Boys' song | 262 |
| Appendix 3 | Commanding officers | 264 |
| Appendix 4 | Technical and Intelligence officers | 265 |
| Appendix 5 | Mirage FI pilots and potted biographies | 267 |
| Appendix 6 | Honours and awards | 292 |
| Appendix 7 | "One of our aircraft is missing"—SAAF aircraft and crew losses to enemy action during the bush war | 294 |
| Appendix 8 | Mirage F1 losses | 304 |
| Appendix 9 | V3 air-to-air missiles | 307 |
| Bibliography | | 308 |
| Index | | 309 |

## List of maps and diagrams

| | |
|---|---|
| Area of border war operations | 6 |
| Southern Africa | 23 |
| Air-to-air target firing pattern | 40 |
| South West Africa/Namibia | 59 |
| Angola and South West Africa/Namibia | 109 |
| First MiG kill | 123 |
| Armed recce | 125 |
| Diagram illustrating a strike out of the sun | 133 |
| Second MiG | 141 |
| The *Vergooi* (long toss) bombing profile | 169 |
| *Gatup* (day) or *Nagup* (night) | 175 |
| MiG surprise | 185 |

Lieutenant-General W. H. Hechter SSAS, SD, SM, MMM
Chief of the South African Air Force, 1999

# Foreword

It is both a pleasure and an honour to write the foreword for Dick Lord's second book—because I am also proud to be known as a *Vlamgat*. Reflecting on my long career in the South African Air Force, I think perhaps my happiest years were those spent in the fighter fraternity.

During the period covered in this book, the SAAF grew from fledgling to eagle. From peacetime in the early 1970s, the fighter-bomber capability expanded dramatically to cater for the requirements of a long bush war. Almost overnight new aircraft, radar systems, squadrons and aircrew numbers trebled. Despite this, the standards required to operate efficiently never suffered. In fact, quite the opposite occurred. I can state that the SAAF answered its call to duty whenever the situation demanded.

This book is about the Mirage F1 aircraft and the men and women who flew and supported it throughout its 22 years of service to the nation. It is a proud history which the author, having flown the aircraft in war and peace, relates with accuracy and authority.

Reading this book has recalled bittersweet memories of incidents and friends, some of them long gone. *Vlamgat* deserves a place of pride in the long history of this, the second oldest air force in the world.

Lieutenant-General W. H. Hechter SSAS, SD, SM, MMM
Chief of the South African Air Force
Pretoria, 1999

# Author's note

Air force people the world over love a party. Any and every excuse is used for a get-together. The SAAF is no exception. On 5 July 1996, 1 Squadron hosted a reunion at AFB Hoedspruit to celebrate the 21st anniversary of Mirage F1 service in the South African Air Force.

The gathering, like most air force activities, was well organized and well attended. 'Old' jet-jocks and spanner tiffies arrived from all over the country to observe the flying display with professional interest, and partake of the golden beverages with abandon.

While enjoying the evening function, I realized that a vital element was missing from the festivities. General Bossie Huyser, the archetypal party lover had recently died and his presence was sorely missed. He had been the father of the F1 project and with his passing a chapter of history was lost. Bossie had a marvellous brain, which was just as well because his handwriting was appalling. Consequently, precious anecdotes were stored only in his head and not on paper.

Being of the school that believes military history and traditions are the very essence of military service, I decided to document the F1 history before more aviators depart on their last flight.

While the task has been laborious it has been filled with pleasure. Both the AZ and CZ derivatives of the Mirage F1 were beautiful aircraft. This fact becomes abundantly clear when one talks at length to those who flew and maintained them. The presence of the aircraft in the inventory united these people into a spontaneous F1 fan club and it is the people around whom the proud history of the aircraft has been built.

No attempt has been made to re-colour or desensitize events to enable them to suit the new dispensation in the country. Events and operations have been recorded as they occurred in the three decades covering the aircrafts' service life. Like paying one's TV licence, it is the right thing to do. Research is continuous, but at some stage a line has to be drawn to allow a book like this to be completed. If, therefore, errors or omissions do exist, the fault is clearly mine. My plea in mitigation is that it was not done intentionally.

Among the appendices I have included a list of all SAAF aircraft losses as a direct result of enemy fire, under the title "One of our aircraft is missing"—a statement that still today sends shivers down one's spine. The reason for including this appendix in a book on the F1 is purely author indulgence.

During my research, I have read Angolan and Cuban documentation, wherein they claim to have shot down scores of SAAF fixed-wing aircraft and helicopters. For example, in their glossy coffee-table book, *FAPLA: Bulwark of Peace in Angola*, they state, "From October 1987 to March 1988, Angolan anti-aircraft defence shot down more than forty aircrafts and helicopters from the South African air force." (sic)

I hasten to add the Angolans did at least have the decency to print at the back of this good-looking book: "This book was manufactured by the Agitation and Propaganda section of the National Political Department of FAPLA". Hopefully, my appendix will dispel once and for all, this type of manufactured propaganda because, as a historian, it really 'agitates' me.

In the book I have included two short stories, both of which were published in the SAAF Safety Magazine, *Nyala*. I wrote the introduction 'They are flying again in the morning' to while away the long hours spent on operational standby during Operation *Daisy* in 1981. I tried to capture the essence of wartime flying from the pilots' point of view. Appendix 1, 'A day on the flight line', was written by Warrant Officer W. J. 'Sparky Doep' du Plessis to cover the same situation, but this time from the ground crews' perspective. His story is brilliant and displays extraordinary insight. Together, these tales encapsulate border-war operations as experienced by the men in the air force.

Finally, the title! The author makes no apology for this. *Vlamgat* is an air force term of endearment for a jet-fighter pilot. The literal, much watered-down translation from the Afrikaans is 'burning backside', indicating the flaming jet pipe at the tail of the aircraft.

*Vlamgat* evolved into a most satisfying project for me. Not a week goes by without someone contacting me about the book. Mostly they want to know where they can obtain a copy; therefore I am very pleased that this updated reprint is now available. I always ask people why they want *Vlamgat* and if they have any involvement with the SAAF. Invariably, the people are not connected with the SAAF; they simply have a fascination and, in some cases, an obsession with aviation. I have had contact with people from as far afield as Korea, North America, UK, France, Holland, Germany, Australia and New Zealand.

Please take time to read the biographies in appendix 1 included in this edition. The history and tradition of the Mirage F1 force was created by these men and their colleagues. In her hour of need, South Africa once again produced airmen of the highest calibre.

To Louis du Plessis and Dave Klopper, whom I somehow omitted from the list of F1 pilots in the original edition, please accept my apologies.

And now some thank-yous:

To Dassault for producing a thoroughbred.

To the SAAF, for their wisdom in using the aircraft in the correct role.

To the maintenance people who kept the aircraft flying and the pilots safe throughout 22 years of service.

To the men and women of the Atlas Aircraft Company, and the countless other aviation industries, for the superb support they gave to the aircraft and the SAAF—often during times of great stress.

To the men and women of the SAAF who without hesitation related their stories and willingly lent me their own precious photographs for this book.

To Lieutenant-Colonel Rassie Erasmus for being my right-hand man, gathering obscure information.

To Sergeant Edwin Graaff who willingly waded through mountains of documentation.

To Warrant Officer Andy Andersen and the personnel of the Central Photographic Unit at AFB Waterkloof for their assistance in compiling the photographs used in this book; in particular Sergeant Johnny Snodgrass who spent hours of his own time ensuring my every request was satisfied.

To Peggy and John who made the draft understandable for 'civvy' readers.

For Michael, Richard, Heather and Courtney for their love and support.

Most of all to June who made this draft readable and particularly for her patience and encouragement throughout the last three decades.

For Keegan and Tayla—my expanding support team.

For Marius Whittle who suggested the format for this revised edition.

For Chris and Kerrin Cocks, my publishers, whose business association over the last decade has grown into a firm friendship.

My gratitude for the response I received from all the 'old and bolds' of the Mirage F1 force.

Thank you all.

Dick Lord
Somerset West
September 2008
dicklord@mweb.co.za

# Introduction

# The are flying again in the morning

---

It is remarkable how cold it can become in the early hours of the morning in the arid semi-desert regions of the world, the tremendous heat of the previous day having radiated out into the clear dry atmosphere during the hours of darkness.

Perhaps it is the early morning chill that awakens them, for they are most certainly awake. The steady, slow breathing and the rhythmic half-snores have been replaced by the absolute silence of the fully alert. Men strive to remain silent so as not to disturb their fellow occupants in the tent, displaying the consideration that comes with the comradeship developed during moments of shared danger. *They are flying again in the morning.*

It may be the rising and falling rumble of aircraft engine noise that awakens them—the testing and servicing of aircraft and engines that has gone on throughout the night. Audible evidence that the hard-working ground crew are giving of their utmost to ensure that the aeroplanes are fully prepared for the tasks that lie ahead in the morning.

The subconscious thoughts that pass through each pilot's mind as he lies in his tent, coupled with the engine noise, probably brings each one out of his slumber. "Is my fuel gauge over-reading? I must get them to check my headset for that loose connection! Why is my number two hydraulic pressure low?" *They are flying again in the morning.*

As the long minutes of silence pass, the sky begins to lighten in the east. It is with relief that the men rise from their beds at the beginning of another day. Relief, because the anxiety and tension of the early morning thought session can be replaced by the routine chores of washing and dressing. In a war environment, too much time spent thinking and imagining is not always conducive to maintaining a relaxed state of mind. It is always worst in the dark hours.

They are mostly young men, active and healthy, with flair and enthusiasm for their chosen profession. But that morning, their normal boisterousness has been replaced by a more sombre mood. Although young in years, these men display maturity achieved only by those who have experienced actual combat. To shoot and be shot at in anger is a maturing process that can change a youth into an adult virtually overnight.

These pilots have been in combat before—some more often than others have—and the novelty of war has long since eroded. The seriousness of the job and the consequences of making mistakes are well understood. The knowledge and the balancing of the odds of each operation are mental exercises that are never far from a pilot's mind—*and they are flying again in the morning.*

The morning ablutions have become almost a ritual with most of the aviators. A good clean shave—no one wants to look scruffy if brought down on the other side. A long, refreshing shower, the running water having a soothing therapeutic effect. No one talks much, each man preferring to keep his own council. The odd, ribald remark from the squadron joker receives a polite laugh or is even totally ignored. On other occasions the same remark would have brought forth loud guffaws and salvos of repartee.

Breakfast also takes on an almost ceremonial atmosphere, with the ceremony differing for each individual. A good, hearty breakfast is devoured by some; who knows when the next meal will be taken? A strong cup of coffee is sufficient for others, the tension making the swallowing of fried eggs impossible. One or two cannot stomach anything at all, the stress bringing them close to nausea. *They are flying again that morning.*

At last it is time to suit-up. The modern-day jet pilot needs to bedeck himself with the special clothing and equipment that enables him to perform his job

Carrying out an external check of the aircraft and missiles before take-off on an operation from AFB Ondangwa in South West Africa, now Namibia.

efficiently. There is a remarkable similarity to the knights of old donning their armour before joining battle. The pilot's mind is at last fully occupied with this complicated procedure. Cotton underclothes; no nylon in case of fire. Good strong boots to protect the toes on bailout, and the ankles during a parachute landing. A Nomex flying overall full of zips and pockets, adorned with badges of rank and squadron emblems, and heat resistant in case of a cockpit fire. Then the anti-G suit. This is zipped on around the abdomen, thighs and legs to inflate as the pilot pulls G. This G is the insidious effect of gravity that drains the blood from a pilot's eyes and brain when he pulls out of an attack dive, or while dog-fighting.

The combat jacket is next—an over-large canvas waistcoat covered in pockets of all shapes and sizes. Contained in these pockets are all the survival aids a pilot might need in the event of his having to eject from his aircraft: day and night flares, signalling mirrors, emergency radio, pocket knives and rations. A pistol and ammunition are included in case he has to fight his way out—and bottles of water. Always water. The dangers of dehydration in the furnace-like temperatures of the operational area are possibly greater than the dangers from the enemy.

On completion of the suiting-up procedure, the pilot forgets the anxieties and tension of the early-morning hours. The professional has emerged from the mere mortal of the morning. The concentration of the briefing is complete. Routes in and out, navigation, target recognition, attack parameters, switch selection, formations and radio procedures are noted and digested. Finally, a time check is given to synchronize all the watches. Exact timing is a prerequisite for the successful joint strike. The briefing is over and *they will be flying again in 30 minutes.*

Bombing-up at AFB Ondangwa during Operation *Askari* in December 1983.

There is a last flurry of activity as the maps and target photographs prepared the night before are studied and rearranged. Helmets, gloves, gun, cameras, and emergency booklets are collected and balanced on kneeboards, as the pilots prepare to leave the tent that serves as the operations room. Calls across the room of 'Good luck' and 'Fly safely' are given with an intensity and sincerity matching the situation.

Magically the operations tent empties. Cups of coffee—some only half-finished—empty cold drink bottles and discarded sections of maps litter the floor. The recently occupied chairs are left in disarray. Alongside some of them the ashtrays are abnormally full.

The pilots walk out to another tent which houses all the aircraft-servicing documents. They have to check the signatures of the ground crew who have signed to certify that the aircraft are serviceable to fly, that sufficient fuel, oil and oxygen are on board and that all weapons have been correctly loaded. Here the ground crew are particularly polite and solicitous. They, too, are professionals and can read the telltale signs. This is going to be a tough one, *and their pilots are flying again this morning.*

Fifteen minutes before take-off and the pilots arrive at their aircraft. An external check of their aeroplanes and weapons is carried out. Practised eyes search for any abnormality that may indicate something wrong. They can't take any chances that a panel or a door may come loose at 600 knots. The results could be catastrophic. A moment of tension flares as a pilot discovers that his windscreen hasn't been cleaned. The short temper and the caustic remark indicate the inner

F1AZ aircraft being prepared for operations at AFB Ondangwa. The protective revetments were covered with layers of wire netting to detonate mortars before they could penetrate the revetments.

stress that that man is undergoing—*for they are flying again in ten minutes.*

Time to climb aboard—always a poignant moment as the pilot steps onto the bottom rung of the aircraft ladder. The words of a song made famous by the Rolling Stones passes through his head: 'This may be the last time'.

As he snuggles his way into the familiar and trusty ejection seat the tension dissipates. Here he is at home, relaxed in the surroundings he knows intimately. His hands and eyes flash about the cockpit with the ease that comes from practice. He methodically checks the multitude of switches, knobs and gauges, knowing the use and function of each.

A momentary hush descends on the flight line. All the pilots are strapped securely into their cockpits. Attendant ground crews wait patiently for the next act in the drama to begin. The pilots' eyes on their cockpit clocks watch the remaining minutes and seconds tick away.

Like the opening tattoo of a military band the peace of the morning is shattered by the rising crescendo of engine noise, as the jets begin the long wind-up to idling power. Like marionettes, the ground crew dance around and under their aircraft, performing the functional checks on flight controls and aircraft systems. At last the chocks are removed and the aircraft are freed to start the long taxi out to the waiting runway.

Always an impressive sight, the long line of attack aircraft, fully armed, taxiies—sheep-like—one after the other, out to the threshold of the runway. Each pilot gives a little wave or salute, or the pilots' well-known thumbs-up sign. These gestures are avidly answered by all the ground crew, willing the pilots to

Mirage F1AZ on operations over southern Angola.

realize that their thoughts and best wishes are with them for a safe return.

The rumbling growl of the idling engines increases sharply as the pilots prepare for take-off. The decibel level exceeds the pain threshold, forcing the onlooker to protect his ears with his hands. After finally checking temperatures and pressures, the pilots select the engine into afterburner and release the brakes. The aircraft jerks forward as the power is unleashed. With temperatures approaching 800°C in the white-hot jet pipe and a noise that reverberates through their bodies, the aircraft accelerate quickly to the over 160 knots that they require to get airborne. *They are flying this morning.*

Inside the cockpits the pilots are performing the routine tasks required to carry out a precision attack sortie. Watches, compasses, headings, airspeeds and heights are constantly monitored. Navigation charts are consulted, power is adjusted to keep in the proper battle formation. Heads are constantly turning to keep a lookout for any enemy aircraft that may be in the area.

At a precise time and position over the ground all the aircraft pitch-up into a steep climbing attitude and rise rapidly to the altitude they require for rolling into the attack. At altitude a last, quick check is done to ensure that all the necessary armament switches are selected 'on'. A quick study of the photograph for orientation purposes, a look down to visually acquire the target, a quick thought that it looks exactly like the target photos studied the night before.

Five seconds to go before rolling into the attack. The defenders down below will be waiting for them. The intelligence officer said that heavy anti-aircraft

68mm rocket pods hung under the wing of an F1AZ standing in a hardened revetment at AFB Hoedspruit. These pods are fitted with frangible nose cones to reduce drag en route to the target.

fire could be expected and nowadays the chances of SAM-7 missiles being launched are pretty good. The pilots notice that their hands inside their gloves are sweating. Their grip on the stick and throttle is extraordinarily firm. The next instant they are rolling into the steep dive down upon the waiting target.

The next 20 seconds seem like an eternity. Eyes in the sight, hands keeping the aircraft firmly aimed at the target, ears picking up the warning cries from other pilots of anti-aircraft fire at 9 o'clock low. A SAM launched from 7 o'clock. Everybody glances quickly in that direction to pick up the telltale trail of smoke. They take valuable seconds to decide whether that missile was aimed at them or not.

The bombs are released. The aircraft shudder then rise rapidly as if glad to be free of the burden of bombs. Afterburners are lit and the aircraft claw their way back up to a safe altitude, where the ack-ack and the SAMs can no longer reach them. A quick radio call from the leader and, thankfully, all the aircraft check in. Formations are resumed as the squadron sets course for base.

As each pilot settles back in the cockpit, he notices that his mouth is so very dry that his tongue seems to stick to his palate. He notices that the oxygen consumption is greater than normal and realizes that his breathing rate had increased significantly. The base comes into view and the aircraft trail one another into the circuit and land. *They have been flying again that morning.*

As the pilots climb down from the aircraft the sombre mood of the morning disappears. In its place an adrenaline-charged atmosphere has affected everyone. Ground crew crowd round the pilots, eagerly waiting to hear if the target has been demolished, the strike a success and if their beloved aeroplanes are still in one piece. The pilots themselves talk and demonstrate with their hands, recounting exactly what happened, where and how. If one looks carefully at the gesticulating hands, one might notice that some of them are shaking ever so slightly. *They have been flying that morning.*

The signing in of the aircraft and the reporting of any defects, the intelligence debriefing plus the flight leader's debriefing and the returning of helmets and other equipment to the flying lockers completely fill the following hour and a half. After a cup of coffee or a cold drink to remove the dryness of throats, the adrenaline flow once more returns to normal. The aviators slump into chairs to relax, suddenly overcome by fatigue.

With no scheduled flights for the rest of the day, the squadron relaxes. After refuelling and re-arming the aircraft, the ground crew disperse to a selected corner here, or a patch of shade there, anywhere where they can lie down to sleep. They have been up very early preparing their aircraft.

Just before the evening meal the base loudspeaker interrupts all activities. Everybody listens attentively.

"Will the officer commanding X Squadron and his flight commanders please report to base operations immediately. I repeat, will the officer commanding X Squadron and his flight commanders please report to base operations immediately."

Not a word is spoken for the next minute. The relaxed mood of the afternoon dissipates, to be replaced instantly by one charged with tension. They are all experienced personnel and they know that *they will be flying again in the morning.*

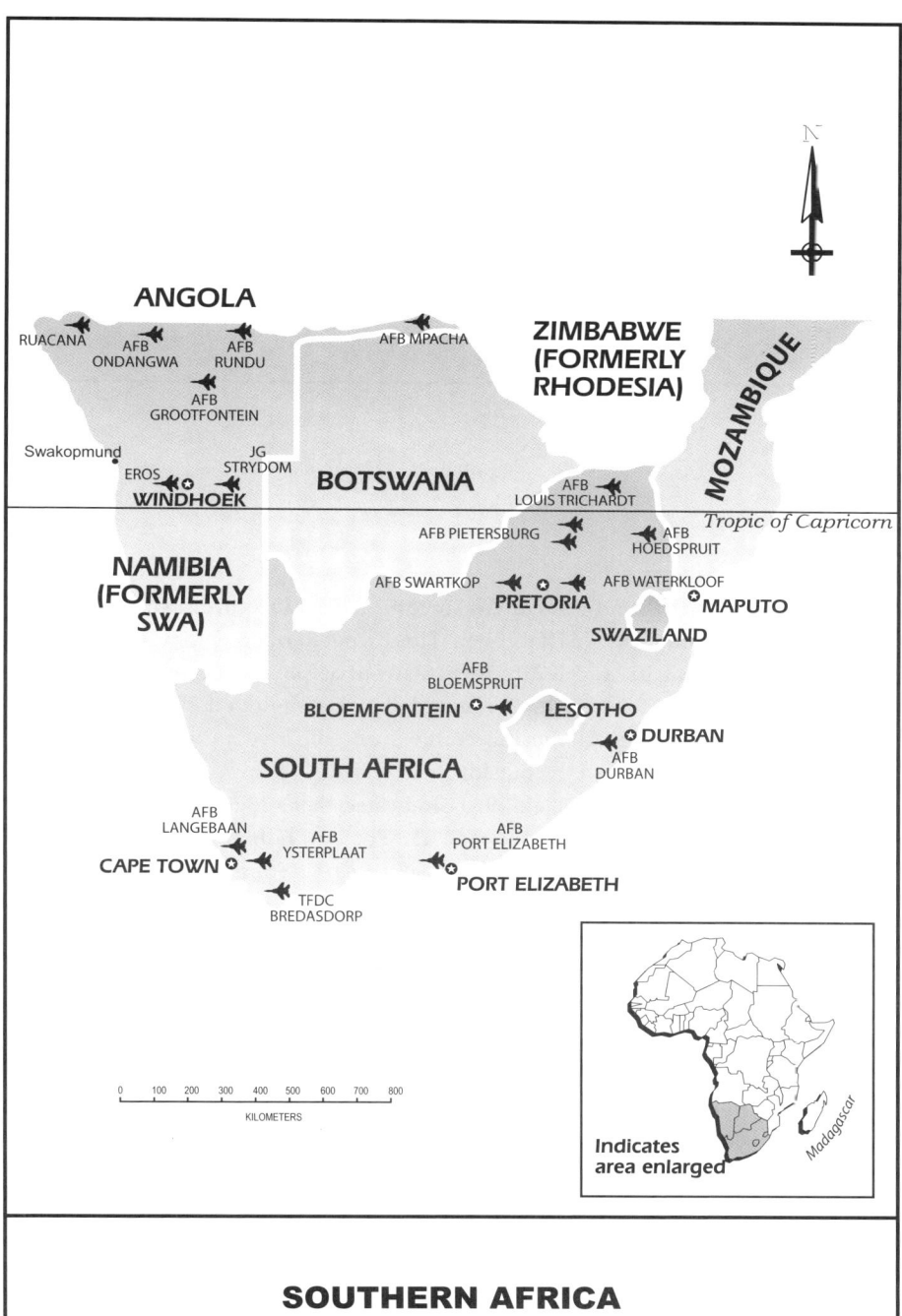

# Chapter 1

# 1969–1974: Acquisition of a legend

## Defence requirements

By the early 1960s, the South African Air Force (SAAF) had acquired a considerable fleet of Dassault-built Mirage III fighters. This included interceptor CZ, ground-attack EZ, dual-seat BZ and DZ trainers, as well as photo-reconnaissance RZ versions of the aircraft. The letter Z was added by Dassault to designate aircraft destined for South Africa. All these aircraft were on the inventory of 2 Squadron based at AFB Waterkloof, on the outskirts of Pretoria.

Strategic studies, during the late 1960s, indicated that additional aircraft were required to complement the older Mirage IIIs. The new fighter was needed to be able to defend the industrial heartland of South Africa from any air or ground threat emanating from neighbouring countries. Communist imperialism had spread southwards through Africa during the 1950s and '60s, filling the vacuum left by the collapse of colonialism. Ominous revolutionary indications were perceived in the Portuguese states of Angola and Mozambique.

Minister of Defence P. W. Botha announced in December 1969, that South Africa would be buying new jet fighters early in the 1970s. The SAAF started looking at a number of alternative aircraft, which included the Mirage V, Milan, Jaguar and Dassault-Breguet Mirage F1. While all the aircraft were good options, the F1 offered the technological advance the SAAF was seeking.

Brigadier Jan Blaauw, a Korean War and 2 Squadron veteran and Officer Commanding Strike Command at the time, placed the original requirement for 100 new aircraft. After refinement, this figure was adjusted to 48 Mirage F1s, four PR Mirage III R2Zs and eleven dual-seat Mirage III D2Z trainers. The initial sales package included French corvettes for the South African Navy, also national acceptance of the French TV system. Television broadcasting was planned to start in South Africa during 1975. In the event, the corvettes never materialized and the country adopted the German PAL TV system. The aircraft package cost over R500 million, but was considered to be an excellent deal, as South Africa was accepted as a launch customer for the F1.

## Evaluation team

In October 1971, commandants Piet Bosman ('Bossie') Huyser and Zach Repsold, both top-class Mirage III pilots, visited France to evaluate the new aircraft. Huyser was the senior staff officer (Fighters) at SAAF headquarters, while Repsold commanded 2 Squadron. At the French Air Force base, Istres, they were given a one-day technical course on the F1, followed by an oral exam later in the afternoon, which they successfully completed.

That night, they noticed that the Dassault team, under their test pilot Jean-Maurice Saget, attempted to prevent the South Africans from indulging in any form of alcohol. Two weeks earlier, prospective buyers from a Middle Eastern country nearly wrote off the prototype after freely enjoying the products of the French vineyards. The French wanted to eliminate that risk. However, they underestimated Huyser's ingenuity and both pilots enjoyed a nightcap.

The next day, 6 October 1971, Repsold flew Dassault's Mirage F1 prototype 04, on a one-hour, 45-minute familiarization sortie. This aircraft's wing shape differed from later production models. The sawtooth vortex generator, on the wing leading-edge, was positioned far out near the wingtip. On service models, the sawtooth was moved closer to the fuselage.

Repsold's first impression was extremely favourable. The Atar 9K50 engine produced great sea-level performance. Well-balanced flying controls gave the F1 the same positive feel as experienced in the much-loved Sabre. The weather, as usual in Europe during autumn, was partly cloudy with tops up 25,000 feet. Finding an open patch, Repsold got the feel of the aircraft before climbing to 30,000 feet to carry out ground-controlled intercepts (GCIs) against a French Air Force F1. Although unused to the controls, he was impressed with the capability of the Cyrano IV radar, achieving good pick-up and lock-on ranges, from on-the-beam and head-on attack profiles.

After the GCIs, Repsold's sequence of aerobatics was interrupted by the warning panel sounding off, indicating a slat/flap problem, which he rectified. These technical problems were largely cured by the time the F1 entered service. He then flew a radar let-down, followed by a short landing, using the flight path indicator in the head-up display. In fewer than 1,000 metres the almost empty aircraft was brought to a very impressive stop. This was a half the distance it took to bring a Mirage III to a halt on a hot day at AFB Waterkloof, 5,000 feet above sea level. Later that day, Huyser flew a similar sortie on the same aircraft.

The following day they had lunch in the officers' mess at Istres with the Falcon pilot who was to fly them to Cazaux after the meal. Not being used to drinking and flying, both South Africans were amazed at the amount of wine the French pilot consumed with his lunch. After placing Repsold in the co-pilot's seat, the Frenchman took off. As soon as the wheels and flaps were up he handed control to Repsold, who flew the rest of the flight and landed the aircraft.

At Cazaux, both pilots carried out air-to-ground weapon sorties, firing the 30mm Defa cannons. Out of 250 rounds fired Huyser scored 209 hits and Repsold 198—results that excited their French hosts. After two sorties each, the pilots returned to South Africa to compile an evaluation report. It was realized, from those first flights in the French prototype, that the Mirage F1 would be an excellent fighter for the SAAF.

The F1CZ was similar to the F1C model in service in the French Air Force. However, the F1AZ was a South African concept and requirement. The design and development of the roller map and the navigation and weapon systems were largely funded by South Africa. In the ground-attack role the AZ demonstrated a considerable improvement over the earlier Mirage III EZs. The combat range had doubled, the bomb load dramatically improved with the aircraft capable of carrying two infrared missiles on the wingtips. Later, Bossie Huyser was responsible for the cockpit layouts of both models.

Since receiving them in 1963, 2 Squadron had operated all Mirage III aircraft. It was a multi-role squadron, responsible for ground attack, interception and photographic reconnaissance. In addition, it was responsible for ab-initio training on the supersonic aircraft. This training task was considered all important, as flying safety has always carried a high premium in the SAAF. However, as a result, operational aspects were often neglected. The acquisition of new aircraft allowed the SAAF force structure to be improved to eliminate this problem.

2 Squadron kept the Mirage III CZ interceptors, BZ two-seat trainers and RZ photographic aircraft. The four new R2Zs greatly strengthened the photographic reconnaissance capabilities of the operational squadron. Squadron roles were restricted to daytime interceptions, air-combat manoeuvring and photographic reconnaissance. Unreliability of the Cyrano II radar precluded night-time and bad weather interceptions.

85 Advanced Flying School, at AFB Pietersburg, became the fighter school of the SAAF. In addition to their Impala and Sabre aircraft, the school received the Mirage III EZ and trainer DZs from 2 Squadron. The eleven new two-seater D2Zs allowed the training capacity at the school to be substantially increased. Pilots destined for Canberra and Buccaneer squadrons received the benefit of advanced fighter training on the Mirage before being posted to the bomber squadrons.

The new Mirage IIIs had much-improved, on-board avionics compared to the older aircraft. A number of the systems, particularly those in the sophisticated

R2Z, were also incorporated in the avionics suite of the Mirage F1. The SAAF selected a group of experienced technicians, mainly from 2 Squadron, to attend courses in France during September 1973. These technical courses covered the head-up display, navigation computer and VOR/ILS—avionics equipment new to the fighter community. Included in this group was Commandant Daantjie Retief, an electronics officer from AFB Waterkloof staff. When the group returned to South Africa, Retief stayed on in Paris, to become a founder member of the F1 project support team.

## SAAF project team in France

Early in 1974, Commandant Bossie Huyser, appointed to oversee the Mirage F1 programme, flew to France with his wife Ebeth, where they settled in an apartment in Paris. Here, he joined up with Daantjie Retief, Eric Esterhuise from Armscor and Major Frikkie Bolton, the project maintenance officer, to form the F1 project team.

At the same time a special posting list was brought out. Newly promoted Major Chris Lombard, Captain Jack Gründling and Captain 'Mitz' Maritz, all serving pilots in 2 Squadron, were appointed to form the nucleus of aircrew for the F1 project. Their first step in this direction was to attend a French language course, presented by the Department of Education. Every morning, from 8 to 12 o'clock, the three students would labour under the instructions of a French woman who refused to speak one word of English, let alone Afrikaans. However, her tuition paid dividends when, at the end of July, the three pilots flew to Paris to meet up

South African contingent in France in 1974.

with Bossie Huyser to undergo the technical course on the F1.

After an exhausting 12-hour night flight from Johannesburg, the three musketeers arrived in Paris to be met at the airport by Commandant Bossie Huyser, then resident in Paris. He immediately drove them to the South African embassy to pay a courtesy call on Brigadier Ed Pienaar, the air force attaché. Afterwards, Huyser stopped off at a bistro on the Champs Élysées to allow them to view Paris by day. By the time they had caught up on all their news and eaten, night had fallen. He then introduced them to Paris by night with a visit to the famous Pigalle, but was quite peeved when, halfway through the show, with semi-naked girls prancing all over the stage he noticed his young bloods were asleep.

Usually, Dassault arranged for foreign customers to be presented with the Mirage course by factory personnel. However, Huyser, a dedicated air force man, told Dassault he would prefer air force personnel because he felt they understood the military environment better than civvies. This was certainly true but, whereas the industry presented their course in English, the French Air Force instructors presented theirs in French.

The four pilots attended the course at the French Air Force base at Rheims. From day one language was a problem. Huyser did not speak any French and Jack Gründling and Mitz Maritz were better pilots than linguists—so it was left to Chris Lombard to use his 'streetwise' French to interact with the instructors. After two days of struggle, Huyser arranged with the project office in Paris to hire professional interpreters. These men were excellent at translating French into academic English, but their knowledge of aviation terminology was non-existent. After a further two days of struggle, Huyser banned the interpreters from speaking so they sat at the back of the class and only translated when requested. The pilots, all experienced and current Mirage III operators, concentrated on the diagrams of the engine, hydraulic and electrical systems of the F1. After three weeks, they wrote the technical exams and passed with flying colours.

They returned to Paris to visit Dassault's main sub-contractors, including Thomson CSF for the gun sight, and Mesier who built the undercarriage. This glorious two-week period did serious damage to the men's waistlines. The visits took place in the mornings, always followed by sumptuous meals that lasted the rest of the afternoon. It was with regret that the three pilots took leave of Huyser and returned to 2 Squadron at AFB Waterkloof.

In July 1974, the original team of airframe technicians, drawn mostly from 2 Squadron, also left for F1 training in France. A second ten-man team of engine specialists joined forces at Rheims for the eleven-week technical course.

Initially, the French Air Force instructors treated the South Africans with reserve. However, after the excellent results of the first technical examinations were published, the French attitude changed completely. They realized these foreigners were there to learn. The theory, presented by the French Air Force instructors, was excellent, even if most of them sounded like Peter Sellers in his famous role as Inspector Clouseau. Where language difficulties did occur, Warrant Officer Geoff Boyd was used as the interpreter. He had learned the language in France when the original Mirage IIIs were collected early in 1960.

Throughout France, wherever the men were accommodated, in hotels and air force bases, the local population made them very welcome. At a number of the hotels, as a friendly gesture, the managers even put up additional signboards proclaiming 'Hôtel Afrique du Sud'.

Every Sunday, yearnings for home were eased by the holding of a traditional South African *braai* (barbecue). The first braai, at the Hôtel de Famille in Paris, caused a certain amount of concern for the manageress. She was relieved to find that the cloud of smoke billowing from her backyard was actually under control. She was a lovely lady who won the hearts of all the South Africans. She received her salary weekly and on these evenings would entertain her guests to champagne in the lounge. These splendid gatherings turned into singalongs with Sergeant Francois Potgieter leading the group with his guitar.

On completion of the technical phase, the technicians attended lectures at factories that manufactured components for the F1. The engine technicians attended a course at the engine factory, Snecma, and short tours were undertaken to Bordeaux and Toulouse to visit Turbomeca, the manufacturers of the engine starter motors.

At the end of October 1974, Captain Mitz Maritz returned to France for a week specifically to carry out the acceptance tests on the F1CZ simulator. Once again, he was met at the airport by the dynamic Bossie Huyser, who took him to the hotel, arriving there late Friday afternoon. He gave Maritz three thick prototype Mirage F1CZ technical manuals and instructed him to study them by Monday morning, when they were due at the simulator factory.

Then, Huyser took Maritz to Commandant Daantjie Retief's apartment for drinks, where they stayed until 02h00. At 06h00 the next morning, Huyser arrived at the hotel, picked up Maritz and set off for a weekend in Holland. At 22h00 Sunday evening, he offloaded an exhausted Maritz at his hotel. During the drive to the simulator factory at 07h00 the following morning, Huyser asked Maritz why he had not studied the books!

At 10h00, Huyser climbed into the simulator, with Maritz sitting outside as scribe. Before take-off, Huyser had found 35 errors in settings, instrumentation, inscriptions and readings. By the time he landed the simulator, the total had risen to fifty-five. They finally left the factory at 22h30, after discussing the required changes with the manufacturers, who immediately made all the corrections. That simulator remained a superb training machine throughout its service life in the SAAF.

In November, the three pilots returned to Paris to be kitted out with flying equipment, before travelling to the French Air Force base, Mont de Marsan, near Bordeaux in the south of France. Here they joined up with Huyser, Daantjie Retief, Alan Nelson, in charge of radios and radar, and the 30-strong South African ground crew contingent.

Close to the base, a small hotel had been rented for the exclusive use of the South Africans. This ideal arrangement was the foundation on which the spirit of the F1 community was built and which lasted throughout the F1's twenty-two years of service in the SAAF. The whole contingent, acting as a unit in a foreign country, combined to produce results that greatly impressed their French hosts.

This feeling of unity was strengthened on the base where the French had thoughtfully arranged a special South African flight line and crewroom. The South Africans operated autonomously under the guidance of Captain Reboul, a wonderful French liaison officer for whom nothing was too much trouble.

French pilots delivered F1CZs 201, 202 and 203 to Mont de Marsan, so operations could begin. Aircraft 200, the first South African aircraft, had been the project aircraft and had been returned to the factory for modification back to service standard. All the aircrew underwent training in the French simulator before they were ready for their first flights on 2 December 1974. At that time the weather was awful, with total cloud cover and poor visibility. The flights were to be radar monitored throughout, with an English-speaking air traffic control officer handling the sorties.

## First flights

Huyser, using the old acronym RHIP (rank has its privileges), was adamant he would fly the first sortie in Mirage 202. Major Chris Lombard in 201, was briefed to fly the same mission, but had been warned by Huyser that he was only to take off second. With a French instructor pilot standing on the ladder to oversee the strap-in procedures, the two pilots were ready to start engines. At a designated position along the taxiway, both aircraft stopped to check the serviceability of their transponders. In France, no aircraft is allowed to fly without this equipment.

Lombard's transponder was serviceable, but Huyser's, despite being switched on and off repeatedly, would not work. The air traffic controller refused to let Huyser take off and this created a dilemma for Lombard, who had been told that he was to be second. Then Lombard asked Huyser, over the radio, whether he should fly or not. After a deathly hush, a bitterly disappointed Huyser came onto the air and said in Afrikaans, *"Ag man, fokof!"*

Not waiting for a change of mind, Lombard taxiied past the stricken Huyser and was airborne at 14h50. Entering clouds at 700 feet he was soon through the 8,000 feet thick cloud layer and into the clear for a perfect radar-vectored, general flying sortie. The return was via an accurate ground-controlled approach (GCA) for a visual landing. Meanwhile, Huyser had had his problem attended to and was airborne on his first flight. The next day, 3 December, Jack Gründling and then Mitz Maritz flew their solo sorties, followed later that evening by a grand solo party in the 'South African' hotel.

Maritz, being the junior pilot, had ended up at the back of the queue when the solo flights were flown. Adverse weather during the day had delayed Gründling's flight and it was 17h00 before Maritz climbed into the F1 cockpit for the first time. Cloud base was a mere 300 feet with a solid overcast. In Europe, darkness comes early that late in the year and it was pretty gloomy when Maritz entered the cloud. Forty-five minutes later, still in cloud, with cockpit and navigation lights on, Maritz was fed into the approach pattern by the competent French controllers. His landing, in total darkness, off an actual GCA became the first night landing of a South African F1—an eventful first solo.

Between 2 and 18 December, each of the four pilots flew about ten sorties on those aircraft, testimony to the good serviceability of the new type. One of these flights was a formation flight, when Chris Lombard and Jack Gründling flew in company with a French Air Force photographic aircraft. The French pilot led them close to the Spanish border so the snow-covered Pyrenees mountains would act as a back-drop to the formation of F1s. Everything worked out well and the photos were magnificent, except that the formation drifted over the border into Spain. Frantic calls by the air traffic controller managed to bring the formation back into France before Spanish fighters could intercept. The culminating flight in France was the ferry to Bordeaux on 18 December, so the aircraft could be prepared for shipment to South Africa.

Huyser, a previous commander of 2 Squadron, had secretly hoped the F1CZs would be commissioned as 2 Squadron. However, Air Force Headquarters decided to keep 2 Squadron as a front-line Mirage III squadron, while commissioning the F1CZs as 3 Squadron. During December, Huyser made a long international telephone call to General Bob Rogers, Chief of the Air Force, trying to change his mind. This was one battle Huyser lost. Nevertheless, when he broke the news to his men that they would be forming 3 Squadron, there was yet another huge celebration.

Mirage III R2Z of 2 Squadron being towed through revetments at AFB Hoedspruit.

Blackburn Buccaneer on hardstanding at sunset.

# Chapter 2

# 1975: Return to South Africa

## F1CZ deliveries

By mid-January 1975, all the personnel were back in South Africa awaiting the arrival of the F1s. The aircraft were shipped directly to Atlas Aircraft Corporation at Jan Smuts airport, just outside Johannesburg. The first aircraft to be assembled was 204, as 200 was being standardized in the Dassault factory and 201, 202 and 203 were being disassembled at Bordeaux for shipping.

On the afternoon of 4 April, Commandant Bossie Huyser and Major Chris Lombard delivered 204 and 205 to 3 Squadron at AFB Waterkloof—Huyser ensuring that this time he did take off first. As on their first solo flights in France, the weather was poor. On this occasion it was low cloud and rain, associated with a highveld summer thunderstorm. Huyser briefed for a ten-second-stream take-off on runway 03 at Jan Smuts. He would throttle back, stay below cloud, turn 20° left and set up for a straight-in approach to runway 01 at AFB Waterkloof. Meanwhile, Lombard was to join up in echelon for the landing.

When airborne, Huyser changed his mind and ordered Lombard into close line-astern. He decided to do a flypast at Waterkloof, instead of the straight-in approach they had briefed on. Staying underneath the rapidly decreasing cloud base, the two F1s hurtled over the 3 Squadron hangar. Lombard became more and more anxious as Huyser flew lower and lower. Eventually, with a grunt, Huyser pulled up and disappeared into the cloud, with Lombard doing the same moments later. Both aircraft required radar vectors and GCAs to return them safely to the ground.

The pilots were met outside 3 Squadron by Chief of the Air Force, General Bob Rogers, who officially received the first Mirage F1s into SAAF service. Among the welcoming dignitaries were General Ed Pienaar, ex-attaché from Paris and

Foundation members of the Mirage F1 fraternity. Standing from left: Gandi van Heerden (T/O), Gawie Winterbach, Mitz Maritz, André van der Heever. Sitting: Frank O'Connor (T/O), Chris Lombard, Bossie Huyser, Daantjie Retief, Jack Gründling, Jan Coetzee (T/O).

the base commander, Colonel P. P. Potgieter. The 4th of April 1975 became the official re-commissioning date of 3 Squadron, equipped with Mirage F1CZ aircraft. 3 Squadron had served with distinction during World War II. Later that afternoon, captains Jack Gründling and Mitz Maritz took to the air in the two aircraft. That evening, a party in the NCOs' mess celebrated the formation of the new squadron in grand style. The function was attended by all the dignitaries including the French Air Force attaché, Colonel le Guen.

Carrying on where they had left off in France, 3 Squadron personnel were soon hard at work. On 8 April, squadron flying commenced, albeit with only two aircraft. The Atlas assembly line was busy assembling the remaining CZs and the pilots were commuting to Jan Smuts to perform the necessary test and acceptance flights. On 17 April, 206 was ferried to Waterkloof, starting the flow of accepted aircraft which finally ended in 1977 when 200, the project demonstrator, eventually completed 3 Squadron's full complement of sixteen F1CZs.

Apart from numerous test flights, the pilots started using the aircraft in its primary role as an interceptor. Fighter controllers sitting deep underground in a bunker at the Northern Air Defence Sector (NADS) near Devon put the pilots through their paces. It was soon apparent that the operational capability of the SAAF had increased dramatically. The Cyrano IV radar, although still awkward to operate like its predecessor the Cyrano II, produced much better results. Camaraderie between pilots and radar controllers reached new heights, which remained throughout the F1's service in the SAAF.

If the flying was new, so too were the conditions in the new, very empty hangar. The quartermaster's stores could not provide all the equipment needed by the new squadron. Tables, chairs, carpets and curtaining were required to furnish offices and crewrooms. To alleviate the problem Huyser decided to hold a grand concert in the Pretoria City Hall.

Maritz, still the junior officer, was given the awesome task of arranging the entire evening. With his natural charm he soon organized a comprehensive programme with performers and stars lined up for the evening. Attracting a large enough audience to cover the costs worried Maritz —until he referred the problem to his boss. Huyser immediately tasked his brother, Commandant John Huyser of the South African Army, to fill the empty seats with army personnel at 50 cents a seat. The hall overflowed, the concert was a great success and the squadron raised R2,000—a considerable sum in 1974.

When 3 Squadron was barely out of the starting blocks they were given an additional task. In France, the F1AZ programme was gathering momentum and pilots were needed to begin preparations for receiving the ground-attack aircraft. 3 Squadron were given the responsibility to train these new pilots, while adjusting to new aircraft themselves. This mutual assistance between the F1 squadrons became a feature of their co-existence throughout the entire period F1s remained in SAAF service.

## F1AZ project officers join 3 Squadron

Early in 1975, the Mirage Operational Conversion Unit (OCC) of 85 Advanced Flying School at AFB Pietersburg had just begun operational training. Captain André van der Heever ('Neefy' to his Afrikaans friends and Andrew to his English associates) was one of the instructors. He had just had the satisfaction of sending his first student solo in a Mirage III, when he was called to the officer commanding's office. Commandant Zach Repsold opened the conversation with the words, "Do you want the good news or the bad news?" Van der Heever opted for the bad news first and was told to start packing his belongings as he had been posted. The good news was that he had been selected to start the F1AZ programme.

A brand-new advanced aircraft is a challenge to any pilot, so the good news was excellent. However, it was not so easy to break the bad news to Sammy, his wife. They had just succeeded in selling their Pretoria house, having been assured by air force personnel planners that they could expect a long tour at AFB Pietersburg. Now they had to return to Preoria—the Jacaranda City. Air force wives are expected to put up with quite a lot during their husbands' careers.

Captain Gawie Winterbach, cricketer Brian MacMillan's lookalike, was an old 1 Squadron veteran, having flown Sabres in 1971 when the squadron was based at AFB Pietersburg. He was flying Mirage IIIs at 2 Squadron when selected to start the F1AZ programme with van der Heever. They were posted to 3 Squadron on 4 April 1975 to become the first CZ students. Major Lombard and captains Gründling and Maritz presented the technical course, after which they started flying the F1CZ early in May. At the end of the month, after 25 hours' flying, they headed off to Paris to spend a month with the Dassault personnel, who presented the technical course on the AZ navigation–weapon system. Upon completion they returned to Waterkloof where they were responsible for editing the F1AZ navigation–weapon manual from French into understandable English—only the SAAF would give this task to two Afrikaans-speaking pilots.

In October, the two AZ pioneers flew back to France, where they accepted the AZ simulator. At Istres, in the south of France, Winterbach had the honour of flying the first acceptance test flight on F1AZ 216. His first impression, in the cool European temperature and operating from near sea level, was of very impressive performance. His second impression was that the bomb-line in the head-up display (HUD) was very unstable—the first alteration to the system to suit South African conditions.

This particular sortie was one of van der Heever's most memorable. Not many pilots fly their first sortie in a brand-new aircraft, in a foreign country, on a navigational acceptance test flight.

The French ensured that an English-speaking controller was on duty in the tower and the flight was monitored under positive radar control from take-off to touchdown. At the first turning point van der Heever, flying F1AZ 216, decided to perform a tear-drop before setting heading for the next leg, to enable him to check the accuracy of the navigation system. When he did not turn immediately onto heading for his second leg, the radar controller started vectoring him in case he had lost his way. In truth, they were more worried that this South African might abscond with the as yet unpaid-for aircraft.

Meanwhile, 3 Squadron continued with the task of solving teething problems associated with introducing a new aircraft into service.

The fighter community at AFB Pietersburg, anxious to pit their skills against the Mirage F1, threw down the gauntlet to 3 Squadron. They issued an invitation to meet over Ebenezer Dam at 20,000 feet. Captain Jack Gründling, accepting the challenge, flew north in his F1CZ. Unfortunately, his aircraft was configured with an underbelly tank; he had previously only flown 'clean' aircraft.

The Mirage III and the F1 met as planned and an engagement ensued over Magoebaskloof. With fuel still in the belly tank, Gründling found the F1 very unstable. From a low-speed scissors manoeuvre Gründling's F1 departed into the incipient stage of an inverted spin, at about 12,000 feet above the ground.

He recovered by releasing the controls, which slowed the rotation rate. Then he pulled the nose down to pick up flying speed before rolling wings level to recover out of the steep dive, a much wiser pilot.

On 12 May, when three aircraft became available, Commandant Bossie Huyser led Chris Lombard and Jack Gründling in a three-ship formation to show off the new acquisition to the fighter community of AFB Pietersburg. Escorted by two Mirage IIIs from 85 ADFS they overflew the base. Huyser, forever the showman, had planned to impress the onlookers by demonstrating the short field-landing capability of the new F1.

The graphs had been studied to ensure the aircraft were below the required landing weight so that, on touchdown, full brakes could be applied. The knowledgeable audience, used to the long, high-speed, drag-'chute rollouts of the Mirage IIIs, was suitably impressed. All the F1s stopped a long way before the end of the runway.

The F1s taxiied into dispersal and shut down. As the pilots descended their cockpit ladders, the overheat plug in one of the tyres of Chris's aircraft blew out and the tyre deflated. Huyser was in the middle of berating Chris when all the main-wheel tyres on Huyser's aircraft deflated with a loud hiss. Overheated brakes initiated the deflation system to avoid tyre explosions, eventually leaving all three aircraft stranded on flat wheels. Red faces remained in place until replacement wheels were flown up from Waterkloof. Two factors overlooked in the graphs were the difference in ambient temperature and the height above sea level between Pietersburg and Europe.

This situation had an amusing sequel in Paris in 1976. Huyser, as overall project supervisor for the F1 programme, was seated in the Dassault boardroom at a meeting chaired by Serge Dassault, son of Marcel, founder of the famous company. The meeting was F1AZ-related so Gawie Winterbach was present.

Huyser, an immensely talented, dynamic man had one failing—his use of English. It was not considered one of his strong points. As the AZ meeting came to a close, Serge Dassault asked politely if the South Africans had experienced any other problems with the aircraft.

Huyser then pushed back his chair, looked directly at the French representatives and stated, "You know, your F1's brakes is shitter than a Tiger Moth's!"

There is an old proverb that states: 'If you want a job done, give it to a busy man'. The powers that be in Air Force Headquarters recognized that in Bossie Huyser they had an asset. Busy he certainly was, but he had such a dynamic personality that he could be, and often was, given three or more jobs at a time—and he could handle them all. By the end of June 1975, Huyser had acquired the additional job as project officer for the proposed Hoedspruit air force base. He became responsible for the two biggest projects running in the SAAF at that time. He was not posted away from 3 Squadron but, apart from returning to fly a sortie every now and then, he was to become permanently involved with the activities at Hoedspruit.

Although Huyser never flew operationally, his presence influenced not only the F1 community in South Africa, but probably Dassault and the French aircraft industry as well. Dassault had two major projects on the go in the early 1970s. One was the F1 and the other the Milan programme—both good aircraft with worldwide potential. Huyser influenced the SAAF to invest in the F1 project. This probably influenced Dassault to favour the F1 rather than the Milan.

The SAAF was not the first overseas buyer of the F1. Spain and Turkey had also decided on the aircraft, but the SAAF was the biggest buyer and the 32 F1AZs were developed specifically for their requirements. Huyser's business acumen and brain were needle-sharp; this made him a valued customer who was held in high esteem by the French aircraft industry. Huyser's dealings with everyone were blunt and straightforward—he never hesitated to call a spade a spade. This trait was not appreciated by some, particularly his seniors, who often felt threatened, but the French loved him for it.

With Huyser's services needed at Hoedspruit, Chris Lombard, as a young major, was left in temporary command of 3 Squadron. His responsibility was ensuring the smooth transition of the F1 into SAAF service. He was ably assisted by Captain Jack Gründling who performed legendary feats, producing procedures and documentation for the squadron.

At one stage during Lombard's tenure as the acting officer commanding, firecrackers became the 'flavour of the month'. One of the pilots had obtained a packet of squibs, with long pull-leads attached. The booby traps were tied to locker doors, flying helmets, toilet seats and anything that was moveable. Blasts were two a penny and everyone became conditioned to carefully studying anything they touched.

Lombard was in the officer commanding's office, deep in conversation with very senior, foreign air force officers, when his telephone rang. Reaching for the instrument he detected a telltale string, so decided to leave the phone ringing. He then needed some information for his guests, but as he started opening his desk drawer, once again he noticed the string. Remembering he had the information in a document in his in-tray, he reached for the file. Once again, his now alerted eye noticed the attached cord, so he left it. The phone rang again. The administration clerk, seated just outside the office, then rushed in and answered the persistent phone. To this day Chris still believes that Captain Darryl Lee was the perpetrator of the explosions that followed. In fact, his office had been sabotaged by captains Dick Warncke and Philip Rosseaux of the rival Buccaneer squadron.

Two flights in the Mirage F1CZ stick in Chris Lombard's mind: his first solo in France and a flight from Waterkloof to AFB Langebaanweg in the Cape for a weapons deployment. The weather was atrocious with large thunderstorms and an active cold front to traverse en route. The F1 was configured with two large underwing ferry tanks. The cloudbase at Waterkloof was 200 feet. Immediately after lifting the undercarriage, Lombard engaged the autopilot and only touched the stick again on round-out for landing at Langebaan. The F1 had introduced a degree of technological sophistication into the fighter community of the SAAF, unknown until then.

Brigadier Jan Blaauw, Officer Commanding Strike Command, decided that the F1s could carry out formation flypasts and give solo displays at airshows. Formation aerobatics were to be the preserve of the Silver Falcons based at AFB Langebaan. 3 Squadron deployed to AFB Ysterplaat to display their aircraft at the air show on 17 October 1975. Captain Mitz Maritz, the solo pilot, achieved fame and notoriety for his display. The airshow audience was thrilled—not so the punters at the Milnerton horse races. Maritz's low-level, high-speed pass caused the favourite to bolt and the race was won by one of the donkeys.

## First air-to-air camp

Early in November 1975, 3 Squadron deployed to AFB Langebaan on the first of many subsequent air-to-air camps. Impala jets towed flag targets between Cape Columbine and Dassen Island, at 10,000 feet above the sea. The F1s flew a pattern on the landward side of the target, which allowed the high-speed jets to fire inert rounds of 30mm ammunition, while pointing out to sea. Each belt of ammunition had the tips of the rounds painted different colours. When these rounds passed through the flag target, the hole would be edged with paint.

At the end of each firing sortie, the target tugs would drop off their flags on the airfield to be collected by the recovery crew. These flags, spread out on the concrete outside the crewroom were then scrutinized by an adjudicator. This scrutiny included counting and plotting all the holes, deciding how many of each colour had hit the target and looking at the length of the holes for safety reasons. The optimum firing position would be when the angle between the target and the nose of the firing aircraft was about 25 degrees. If the angle decreased it indicated the pilot was firing dangerously close to the towing aircraft. This tendency could be picked up from the shape of the holes on the flag. Extremely long holes resulted in a severe penalty.

During that first F1 deployment the highest score obtained was 38/100—clearly more homework was needed. The exercise is a measure of the pilots' skill as well as an indication of the efficiency of the man–machine harmonization. To hit a moving target from a moving platform requires integration of the sighting system, radar ranging system and proper harmonization of the cannon barrels. As expertise increased over the years, so did the number of hits on the flag.

On one of these firing sorties, Major Lombard suffered a hydraulic 1 failure—

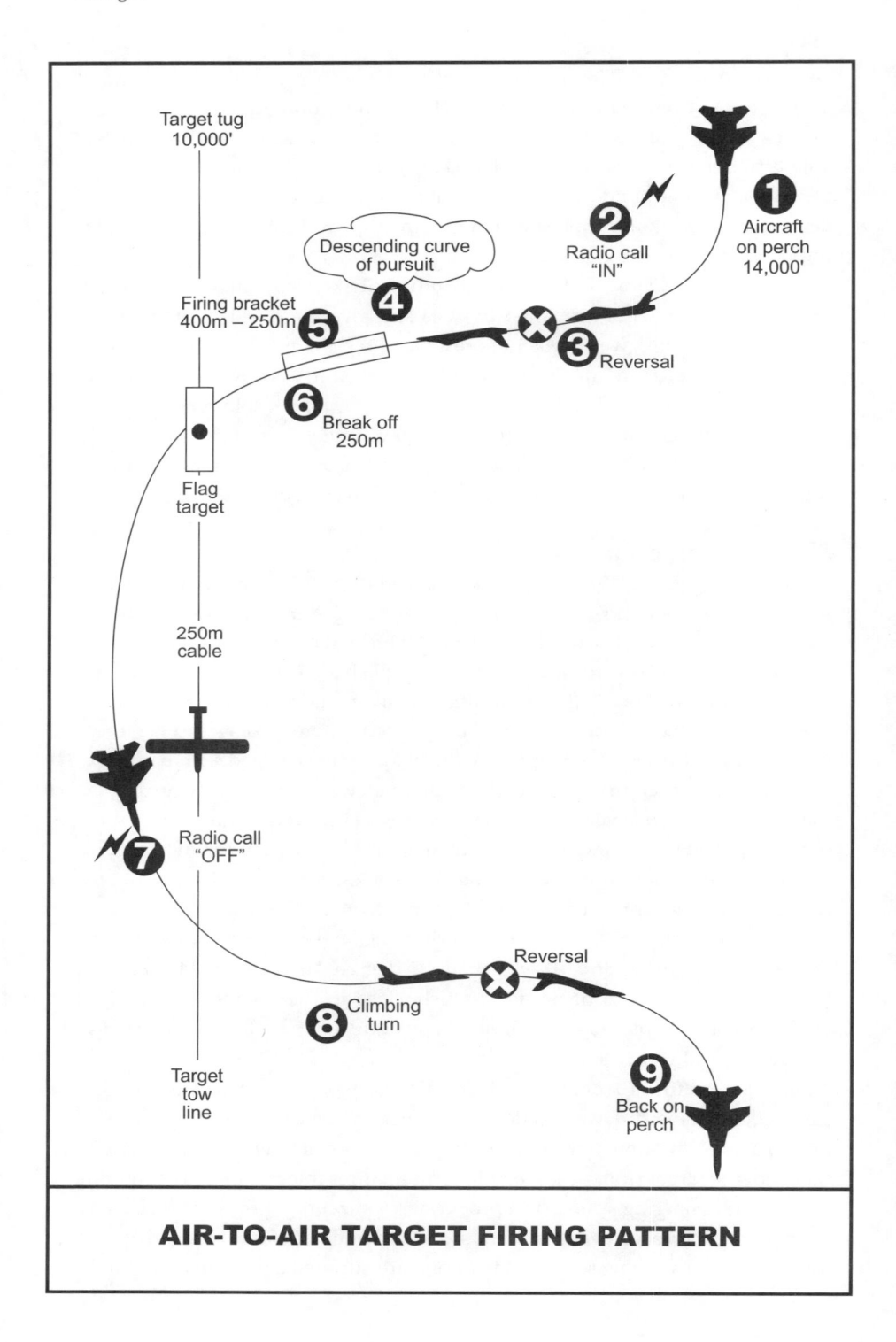

Vlamgat

Target tug
10,000'

① Aircraft on perch 14,000'
② Radio call "IN"
③ Reversal
④ Descending curve of pursuit
⑤ Firing bracket 400m – 250m
⑥ Break off 250m
Flag target
250m cable
⑦ Radio call "OFF"
⑧ Climbing turn
Reversal
⑨ Back on perch
Target tow line

**AIR-TO-AIR TARGET FIRING PATTERN**

the only serious mechanical fault he ever experienced flying the F1. He returned to Langebaan and landed without high-lift devices at 210 knots, but stopped safely. The aircraft was needed on the flag the following morning, but the necessary spare part was at Waterkloof. Captain Maritz took off from Langebaan in an F1 at 17h03 that afternoon to fetch the tiny part from AFB Waterkloof. He landed back at Langebaan at exactly 20h00—two hours and 57 minutes for the 2,400-kilometre round trip. Little wonder that he earned the nickname 'Mitz Blitz'.

During Maritz's two-year tour on 3 Squadron he amassed 500 hours on the F1. Perhaps his only incident of note was a lightning strike after taking off from Waterkloof in bad weather. Recovering from the shock of the blinding flash he was dismayed to find that the fire-warning light had illuminated. After carrying out the correct emergency procedures he diverted to AFB Pietersburg, where the prevailing weather was much better.

Oryx casevac scene.

# Chapter 3

# 1976:
# 13 Squadron

## Command confusion

Commandant Fred du Toit's name appeared on the December 1975 officers' appointments list, transferring him from OC AFB Durban to OC 1 Squadron. He had been told 3 Squadron, but the list said 1 Squadron, AFB Waterkloof. Whichever way it was, Fred was happy to be chosen to fly the new Mirage F1.

Commandant Fred du Toit with AZ and CZ pilots of the mythical '13' Squadron. Standing from left: Lt Havelaar (T/O), Pierre du Plessis, Carlo Gagiano, Mitz Maritz, Dries Wehmeyer, Lt Alan Norrie, Capt Kitley. Sitting: Roelf Beukes, Gawie Winterbach, Jack Gründling, Fred du Toit, Chris Lombard, Capt Wasserman, André van der Heever, Mossie Basson.

He had previously flown Sabres on 1 Squadron, Mirage IIIs on 2 Squadron and, while in Durban, Impalas with 5 Squadron.

Upon arrival at Waterkloof early in January 1976, he was handed command of 3 Squadron from Major Chris Lombard, despite the notification on the posting signal. Then he discovered that all the F1s, and a sprinkling of pilots for the proposed 1 Squadron, were also under his command. He settled the confusion quite happily by calling himself OC 1-3 Squadron.

Du Toit's conversion-course colleagues were also a mixed bunch. Captains Dries Wehmeyer, Peter Cooke and Carlo Gagiano were to fly F1CZs in 3 Squadron while majors Roelf Beukes and ('Mossie') Basson were destined for 1 Squadron, after completing the CZ course. After their solo flights the pilots all agreed that "the F1 performed like a Mirage but handled like a Sabre"—high praise indeed.

Du Toit saw his prime task as commander to be the preparation of the Mirage F1 system for active service. This huge responsibility involved marrying the aircraft, equipment and personnel into a cohesive fighting unit. 1976 was a period of organized chaos, when the foundations were laid for both squadrons.

## Arrival of F1AZs

Captains Winterbach and van der Heever had returned to 3 Squadron from France. While awaiting the delivery of the first AZ aircraft, they prepared an AZ acceptance flight test programme. This programme called for a taxi test and three flights before acceptance. Flight 1 checked the aircraft systems. Flight 2 was the navigation–weapon system check and on the third flight, aircraft performance at Mach 2 was checked.

During March 1976, the first F1AZs began arriving at Atlas Aircraft Corporation for assembly. On 24 March, Captain Gawie Winterbach flew the first F1AZ in African skies. Coincidentally, this was the same aircraft, 216, in which he had flown the first AZ sortie in France on 7 October 1975. Winterbach in 216 and André van der Heever flying 217 took off from Jan Smuts on the delivery flight to AFB Waterkloof. To celebrate the occasion, they were joined by two Sabres and two F1CZs for a combined flypast over the base. On shut-down the pilots were welcomed by General Bob Rogers, General Ed Pienaar and Brigadier Mike Muller.

1976 became the year of the test flight. All thirt-two AZs were subjected to the laid-down test programme. Fortunately, pilot strength was increased to cope with the test schedule, with the arrival on 1 Squadron of Major Roelf Beukes and Captain Mossie Basson. A few aircraft were accepted after the proposed three flights, but most needed four or five. The real 'problem' aircraft needed up to 12 flights to attain the laid-down standards. The Mach 2 run consisted of a climb to altitude via Hartebeespoort to Swartwater and then acceleration to twice the speed of sound on the return flight to Pretoria. Among the four men they must have had more Mach 2 flying than all the other SAAF pilots put together.

As the novelty of these repetitious sessions wore off, the pilots decided to spice up the flights. After completion of each test flight, two pilots would dogfight with each other, until low fuel states forced them to land. Flying together so often, they developed into formidable air-combat teams—despite the fact that the AZ was a designated ground-attack aircraft. Becoming bored with fighting each other, their attention became focused on the activities of the 3 Squadron pilots, whose primary role was air supremacy. Soon the intrepid four were 'attacking' the CZs when and where they came across them. To add insult to injury, the ground-attack pilots invariably ended up the victors.

## Destruction at Rust de Winter

To defend the Pretoria–Johannesburg area against air attack a combined exercise was set up: the AZs would attack and 3 Squadron would defend. 1 Squadron's success rate was causing great annoyance in 3 Squadron's crewroom and the fighter pilots were becoming desperate for a victory. Their frustration reached boiling point on a flight where Winterbach and van der Heever, who had been detected by the air defence radar system, descended to low level on their run-in to simulate an attack on Pretoria.

Radar controllers had vectored Captain Jack Gründling and Lieutenant Des Steinhobel in F1CZs, onto the bogeys as the AZs plunged. Realizing that the CZs

The once-peaceful hamlet of Rust de Winter, north of Pretoria, after a supersonic, low-level pass by two 3 Squadron F1CZs.

were behind them, Winterbach and van der Heever held their speed at M.95, 100 feet above the ground, knowing that to catch them the CZs would have to go supersonic, which was banned below 30,000 feet. Well, catch them they did, even though Gründling had to take his formation down to 50 feet to keep the AZs in sight.

However, 3 Squadron had very little time in which to celebrate their 'kill'. The telephone system at AFB Waterkloof was inundated with calls from irate farmers living in the Rust de Winter area, claiming damages for the trail of destruction left under the flight path of the interceptors. A rapidly arranged visit by helicopter revealed a pathway of broken windows, shattered lights, hanging ceilings, buckled advertising boards and road signs, which resulted in considerable work for the air force's legal and finance departments.

In April 1976, 13 Squadron deployed to AFB Langebaan for their second air-to-air weapon's camp. The 'lessons learned' from the first camp had been heeded and generally good scores were recorded on the flag. Pete Cooke shot a 75/100 and Chris Lombard 38/50. The camp's highest combined flag total was 158/300 made up by Gawie Winterbach's 18/50, Pete Cooke's 53/100, Carlo Gagiano's 31/50 and Jack Gründling's 56/100.

During May, 3 Squadron tested their aircraft in the air-combat manoeuvring (ACM) arena. The first one-vs-one sorties were flown against Sabres operating out of AFB Pietersburg. In almost every engagement the Sabre, with its better slow-speed turning ability, emerged the victor. Once again valuable lessons were learned in how to and particularly how *not* to fly the F1.

The introduction to service of any new aircraft involves sorting out the numerous teething problems that arise. In this case, the hasty arrival of untested and underdeveloped F1AZs before the imposition of the arms embargo against South Africa increased the difficulties. Hard work and long hours became the order of the day and, initially, relatively few hours were flown. In spite of this, the F1 remained the 'flavour of the month' and was displayed to the public and the rest of the air force.

Over the years, Fred du Toit had accumulated many hours of aerobatic experience. This background gave him the confidence to adopt the mantle of F1 display pilot, showing off the new aircraft at displays around the country. Low-level displays require thought and practice if the aircraft is to be demonstrated effectively. Central Flying School Dunnottar had requested a show one afternoon after all their Harvards had landed.

In the morning, du Toit took off in an F1CZ to practise his display using the *dammetjies* (little dams) north of Bronkhorstspruit as his display point. His routine included an inverted run at 400 feet above ground level. On completion of this pass, he snap-rolled the Mirage upright with the intention of entering the next manoeuvre, but the aircraft had other ideas. As he started the roll the engine flamed-out. Gliding inverted at 400 feet, he moved the throttle to the stop position, then opened it to idle, while pressing the relight button. As advertised the engine re-lit.

Discontinuing his practice, du Toit flew back to Waterkloof. He snagged the offending aircraft in the F700 and asked the maintainers to prepare another aircraft for the afternoon show. After a cup of coffee a slightly greyer-haired pilot took off for Dunnottar. Du Toit left 3 Squadron at the end of 1979 but continued to fly the F1. He performed his low-level aerobatic sequence at the AFB Waterkloof Air Day in 1980.

July brought to an end the long and distinguished career of Admiral Bierman, the last navy Chief of the Defence Force. To mark the occasion 3 Squadron led a combined F1 and Mirage III formation over the farewell parade. As a goodwill gesture, du Toit formed the aircraft into a large, impressive B. Utilizing the privileges of formation leader, du Toit allowed the F1s to fly in line-astern, forming the vertical line of the B. The Mirage IIIs had to fly the difficult positions forming the curves of the letter B. RHIP—rank has its privileges.

The spring of 1976 belonged to Major Dries Wehmeyer. For some unknown, but often guessed-at reason, he was known as 'Mealie' in the 3 Squadron crewroom. However, at the squadron's annual musketry training, he was re-christened 'Major Caprivi', when he let rip across the firing range with his Uzi sub-machine gun. Instead of single shot he had inadvertently selected automatic.

The F1s were forbidden to perform formation aerobatics. For the AFB Waterkloof Air Day in 1976, it was decided 3 Squadron would fly a five-ship formation from which Captain Maritz would detach to perform solo aerobatics in a synchronized display with the remaining four. Maritz developed his own display routine and introduced the stunning 'knife-edge' manoeuvre to South Africa. This entailed holding the F1 in a 90° bank, applying full top rudder and negative G for the aircraft to maintain a straight line. This uncomfortable attitude allowed his aircraft to streak down the display line as if balanced on a knife-edge.

## Inter-squadron rivalry

Squadron rivalry is traditional and no opportunity is missed to outdo another squadron. After the completion of the 1976 Cape Town airshow, all the aircraft ferried back to their home bases. Major Johan Nieuwoudt, flying a Buccaneer of 24 Squadron, took off five minutes before the formation of F1CZs. Sixty-five minutes after take-off, the Mirages touched down at AFB Waterkloof before the Buccaneer arrived, proof of the supersonic capability of the F1.

On 18 August 1976, Commandant du Toit in a CZ led Major Beukes and Captain Basson in AZs, on a flight up to AFB Pietersburg. The F1s were escorted over the base by two Sabres flown by Captains 'Toekie' Snyman and Graham Rochat. A

Dakota carrying squadron ground crew also made the flight northwards. Their task was to officially take over the 1 Squadron memorabilia that was stored at that base, after 1 Squadron had decommissioned. Included among the honours boards and diaries was the historical 1 Squadron ostrich egg.

The Air Operational School, forerunner of 85 Advanced Flying School, was based at AFB Langebaan. On a visit to Oudtshoorn they had bought a stuffed baby ostrich, which was displayed in their pilots' crewroom. On an air-to-air deployment, 1 Squadron stole the ostrich and took it back to their crewroom at AFB Waterkloof. On a subsequent visit to the Transvaal, Air Ops personnel reclaimed their ostrich, only to have it stolen again by 1 Squadron members. Eventually, Air Operations School members solved the problem by buying an ostrich egg and having 1 Squadron's badge painted on it. This they presented officially to 1 Squadron with a fervent plea to "go and hatch your own bloody ostrich and leave ours alone!"

Lieutenant Pierre du Plessis, the first lieutenant to fly the F1 in the SAAF, went solo in a CZ on 13 August. He had previously flown Sabres and Mirage IIIs at AFB Pietersburg. Du Plessis was used as a guinea-pig to establish how well young pilots could cope with the new aircraft and new technology. Formerly, flying hours were used as a criterion for judging skill. Pierre did extremely well and secured the road ahead for young aspiring fighter pilots in the SAAF. In his first month he flew 36 hours on the F1CZ—a record which was probably not exceeded by any other pilot on an F1 course. He felt the F1 handled like a Sabre—only better. The stick did not have the dead spot in the neutral position common to the Sabre.

## In-flight refuelling

In-flight refuelling (IFR) began for the F1AZs on 23 August 1976. 24 Squadron supplied the tanker Buccaneer, while Roelf Beukes, Mossie Basson, Gawie Winterbach and André van der Heever attempted their first plugs. Like most bridegrooms 'first-night' nerves were initially apparent, as the pilots worked on their technique. However, after the first successful 'dry' plugs, the task became reasonably easy—testimony to the positive handling of the Mirage F1.

A 'dry' plug is a practice coupling when the fighter's probe is pushed into the tanker's trailing basket but no fuel is actually transferred. The following afternoon, the pilots performed the first 'wet' plugs, taking on sufficient fuel to complete a two-hour tactical navigation sortie, which ended with a dusk attack on a target at Roodewaal bombing range.

In-flight refuelling is a classic force-multiplier, where the capability of the refuelled aircraft can be greatly enhanced in several ways. By topping up the fuel tanks en route, combat range can be tremendously increased. Fighters can end up in a combat arena with sufficient fuel to allow full use of the fuel-guzzling afterburner if engaged by enemy aircraft. As fuel runs low at the end of a combat air patrol, fighters can return to a tanker to top up and then return to station. The alternative is to return to base, land, refuel and probably rebrief, before taking off again.

Fighter-bombers, operating on short runways or in high ambient temperatures, are often critical during take-off. Bomb loads often have to be reduced to allow the aircraft to lift off safely. Using IFR the aircraft can take off with a reduced fuel load. Once safely airborne, full fuel loads can be taken on board as the formation heads towards the target.

New pilots invariably suffer 'first-night' nerves on their first practice IFR sorties. Throughout his entire flying career a pilot is taught to avoid all obstacles—or suffer dire consequences. However, on an IFR sortie, they are instructed to fly their aircraft until part of it collides with a foreign object! Little wonder nerves are initially on edge.

When the exercise is ready to commence the tanker streams his hose, making sure no aircraft is directly astern. The hose unwinds to its full extent. At the end of the hose is a conical-shaped metal basket. A canvas strip, secured around the tips of the basket, ensure that the cone opens up properly after the basket slips out of the tanker's housing.

In the F1AZ, the pilot extends his refuelling probe by selecting the appropriate switch in the cockpit. The probe extends from a position on the right of the pilot's canopy. The tip of the probe sits ahead of the pilot, just to the right of the canopy. Then the fighter pilot flies his aircraft astern of the tanker and lines up behind the hose. He formats on the tanker, ensuring that their speeds are the same and his aircraft is about five metres behind the basket.

He commences his attempt by applying positive throttle, causing his aircraft to accelerate towards the basket and tanker. This is the moment that tests the pilot's nerves. With a positive overtaking speed he has to keep the probe of his aircraft lined up with the centre of the basket. On a good approach the windflow over the fighter's nose will sweep the basket neatly over the tip of the probe. A firm connection will be felt and the momentum of the fighter will allow the extended hose to start reeling in. The fighter pilot must push the hose in until a yellow-coloured section of the hose reaches the tanker pod. He now reduces his throttle to maintain that position.

On the trailing edge of the tanker's pod are three lights. When the red is illuminated the fighter must not make an approach. On amber, the approach can be started. The lights turn to green when the yellow section of the hose is positioned correctly and fuel will start to transfer. Keeping station directly behind the tanker, once a successful plug has been achieved, is not too difficult. It is plain-formation flying, which all military pilots practice. However, during a 'wet' plug, there are inherent difficulties.

As fuel is taken on board, the fighter becomes heavier and heavier. More and more throttle is required to remain in position. It has also happened that pilots flying aircraft carrying a heavy bomb load have had to light their afterburners just to keep in the basket. The other difficulty is that, as the fighter's weight increases the centre of gravity of the aircraft tends to alter. Changes to trim and control settings have to be made to counteract the effects.

Under operational conditions, the light signals on the pod allow refuelling to take place in complete radio silence. Surprise is a safety factor in any strike and an alert enemy scans the radio frequencies hoping to pick up any pre-warning of an impending strike. These lights also make night refuelling a viable option. During the years in service the F1AZ pilots used the in-flight refuelling facility to great effect.

Early in September, Captain Dries Wehmeyer was pulling 5G in a training dogfight when the trim-box came loose and dropped in front of the stick. To his consternation, when he released the G pressure the stick did not return to its normal central position, leaving the aircraft in a 3G turn. Under these G forces, 'Captain Caprivi' had to unstrap himself from his ejection seat so he could carry out running repairs to his circling Mirage.

## Supersonic air-combat manoeuvring (ACM)

Between 13 and 23 September, six CZs and four AZs were deployed to Air Force Base Durban to take part in the annual supersonic air-combat manoeuvring (ACM) camp. Mirage IIIs from 2 Squadron and the Mirage course from 85 Advanced Fighter School were also present.

It had long been realized that a special technique was required to extract the maximum performance from thin-winged, high-speed jet fighters. Below Mach 0.9, the thicker-winged, transonic fighters like the Sabre and even the subsonic Impala could easily out-turn the Mirage family of fighters. However, at high Mach numbers, if the machines were handled correctly, supersonic fighters ruled supreme.

The ACM camp at AFB Durban afforded the pilots the opportunity of flying to the edge of the envelope. Supersonic flight below 30,000 feet is forbidden over South African soil. Because most dogfights occur well below this height, training overland was severely restricted. Operating out to sea, these restrictions were lifted and the full potential of the Mirages could be exploited. At the end of the camp the opinion was that in aerial combat the Mirage III and F1 compared favourably, with the F1 having advantages in fuel specifics and when fighting in the vertical plane. The zoom capability of the F1 allowed the pilot to outclimb his opponent to make positioning for a firing pass a little easier.

70 Mobile Radar Unit (MRU) deployed from their home base at AFB Pietersburg in a huge convoy of vehicles. They set up their camp and their mobile radar

stations on the hill outside Umhlanga Rocks. This site provided excellent radar coverage seawards. The aircraft operating out of AFB Durban would, therefore, have positive radar coverage throughout the sortie even out to 100 nautical miles from the coast. Sonic booms were two a penny, but only shipping was affected. In later years, the mobile radar set-up was increased with an additional station being deployed outside Scottburgh, south of Durban. Helicopters from 17 Squadron and strike craft of the South African Navy participated in the search and rescue (SAR) role.

During October 1976, 13 Squadron concentrated on weaponry sorties flown to Roodewaal bombing range. Captains Winterbach and Basson filmed each attack through the sight camera, to get factual footage to take to France. The AZ bombline, which Winterbach complained about in his first sortie in France, was still too sensitive, but this problem took years to sort out.

3 Squadron experienced a bad day on the range on 27 October. Captain Maritz bent the rocket launchers on his aircraft, Captain Wehmeyer picked up shrapnel damage to his F1 and Major Gründling lost the range en route to the target owing to variation problems in his compass.

During November, war games between the CZ and AZ pilots began, with the Buccaneers of 24 Squadron joining forces with the AZs. Late one afternoon, the terrible AZ quadruplets, Gawie Winterbach, André van de Heever, Roelf Beukes and Mossie Basson, were returning to Pretoria in a four-ship formation, flying into the bright, setting sun. All four pilots had their darkened visors down when they were jumped by a pair of F1CZs. Immediately they nosed down to dive underneath a cloud layer while applying full throttle to get up to fighting speed as the four-versus-two dogfight started. At a combined closing speed of well over 1,000 miles per hour, events occurred at breakneck speed. It appeared to get exceptionally dark as they descended, and it was only after several near misses in the space of a few seconds that someone called out over the radio to remind the AZ pilots to lift their dark visors. 3 Squadron claimed a moral victory.

The 'war' extended into December when the F1s did battle against the Impalas of 4 Squadron. Captain Basson learned not to come down into the 250–300 knot regime, especially if Major Peter Cooke, an ACM specialist, was flying the Impala.

# Chapter 4

# 1977: Laying foundations

## 1 Squadron nucleus

At the beginning of 1977, six new pilots arrived from 85 ADFS for conversion to the F1: Commandant Willem Hechter and Lieutenant Thys Muller for 1 Squadron, and lieutenants Darryl Lee and Des Steinhobel for 3 Squadron. Also on the course were commandants Jan Marais and Bob Masson, test pilots attached to the Test Flight Development Centre (TFDC). These men and this unit were to play an important role in developing the largely untested AZ for operational service.

All the men agreed that the F1 was a delight to fly. Darryl's only problem was to get the flaps up after take-off, before exceeding the flap limiting speed. At this early stage the aircraft's flaps and slats were not stressed for combat.

Willem Hechter's solo flight was disappointing because, after take-off, his undercarriage refused to retract. He had to burn off fuel before returning to land. However, throughout the rest of his F1 career he never had a serious emergency. Of all the aircraft he flew it became his favourite. In those days, the F1AZ was a modern fighter at the cutting edge of technology. It was a forgiving aircraft that could be pushed past the edge of the envelope without worries. It was not as demanding to fly as the delta-winged Mirage III and had 'fuel for Africa'.

Three-year postings are the norm for aircrew in the SAAF. Hechter had spent just one year as commanding officer of the fighter school at AFB Pietersburg when, to his complete surprise, he was appointed Officer Commanding 1 Squadron. Within three days of arriving at AFB Waterkloof, Willem Hechter set an objective for himself. In the shortest possible time, he would divorce the AZs from the CZs to become a fully autonomous squadron.

This was by no means an easy task, especially as the logisticians informed him that the ground support equipment had been bought for the F1s as a whole, not as individual units. So much for planning. With the assistance of Lieutenant Alan Norrie, the new squadron's first technical officer, an action plan to disentangle 13 Squadron was developed.

His second objective concerned the AZs. The aircraft were arriving in droves from France, so a plan was made to test fly them and get them into service as quickly as possible. All the F1s arrived at Atlas Aircraft Corporation by sea and road, except the last nine (239 to 247). These aircraft were crated and flown out by C-130s of 28 Squadron, to circumvent the rapidly approaching international arms boycott.

How times had changed. One of the first F1s being transported by road was refused passage through the Orange Free State. In those days, provincial law forbade heavy-duty vehicles from driving on a Sunday.

## Squatter status

Fred du Toit and Willem Hechter had been friends all their service lives. However, both men recognized the potential for conflict when two commanders had to share the same office space. Willem moved, with his small core of pilots, across 3 Squadron's hangar. 1 Squadron was established, under very inauspicious circumstances, as squatters in a vacated storeroom. Whenever Hechter called his men together they had to use his table to sit on because space was so limited.

Hechter asked Colonel Bossie Huyser to define the role the SAAF had set for 1 Squadron. The answer he received was typical of Huyser: "CZ interceptors, AZ ground-attack."

With that clear directive Willem Hechter set his men to writing a ground-attack syllabus that would develop tactics to cater for the performance of the technologically advanced aircraft.

During his conversion course, one simulated rocket projectile (RP) strike set the standard for what he wanted the AZ to achieve operationally. With André van der Heever as wingman, they climbed out of AFB Waterkloof. After a high-level navigation leg, they carried out a rapid operational descent to low level. Flying fast and low, they followed the Kuruman River before pitching in to a simulated RP attack on information derived from the navigational computer. The chosen target, a rural shop at a place called Koop Pan Suid, west of Kuruman, was perfectly positioned under the nose of the attacking aircraft. Egress from the 'target' was for 80 nautical miles at low level, before climbing to altitude and returning to base. The entire flight, in clean aircraft, was on minimum ('bingo') fuel limits and after one hour and 40 minutes the aircraft landed.

Because of the workload on the small core of personnel in 1 Squadron, Commandant Hechter decided to limit flying to one sortie per pilot per day. All the other tasks involved in getting the squadron operational had to be kept up to date. To ensure efficiency was maintained, low-level tactical sorties, culminating in a live-weapon strike at Roodewal, were carried out.

During January and February 1977, F1 weapon results showed promise. On the first automatic bomb-release sortie, Captain André van der Heever achieved five out of six bombs within 30 metres of the target; the other bomb fell 69 metres away. Sixteen F1s from 3 and 1 Squadrons deployed to AFB Langebaan for an air-to-air camp. 1 Squadron achieved an average of 34.6 per cent and 3 Squadron 34.5 per cent hits. Poor mean-time-between-failure (MTBF) rates were experienced with the radars. Lieutenant Thys Muller landed safely after a hydraulic pipe burst in his AZ.

## Close shave 1

Air-combat manoeuvring (ACM) formed a large part of 3 Squadron's training syllabus. Captain Carlo Gagiano and Lieutenant Darryl Lee were involved in a one-vs-one dogfight in the military flying area, northeast of Pretoria. The high speeds and varying G forces required total concentration from the pilots and they watched each other like hawks. Lee came out of a vertical manoeuvre with his aircraft pointing straight down. Momentarily taking his eyes off Gagiano's threatening fighter, Lee glanced out of his front screen and received the biggest fright of his entire life. There, filling his windscreen was the plan form of a civilian Fokker F27 transport plane. By pulling back on his control column Lee managed to flash past the nose of the airliner, in the closest of near misses.

The unexpected is often the cause of these incidents. Gagiano and Lee were legally exercising in a restricted military flying area. To save time and fuel, the airline pilot—not anticipating other aircraft in the same air space—nearly caused a disaster by sneaking across a corner of the area.

Ironically, potentially hazardous low-level flying was considered the biggest safety factor when flying in heavily defended combat arenas. The F1 training syllabus emphasized this aspect and a great deal of low flying was practised. From his experience at the fighter school, Willem Hechter realized that most pilots turn naturally to the left. However, when turning right at extremely low altitudes, pilots tend to allow the aircraft to gain height in the turn. 3 Squadron confirmed this fact, as often it was only when turning that low-flying aircraft were visually picked up by the interceptors.

For the same reason crossing ridges, if flown incorrectly, exposes the aircraft and its hot exhaust to possible enemy fire. Ridge-crossing techniques were, therefore, incorporated into the training. Concentration on these fine details ensured that very low-level operations could be flown safely.

Early in April 1 Squadron organized an ACM 'war' against 4 Squadron. Once again, the F1 pilots lost the first round convincingly by trying to manoeuvre at the same speed as the Impalas. Days two and three were much better—the lesson had been learned.

\*\*\*\*\*

On 29 April, the new course of pilots attempted their first IFR sorties behind the Buccaneer tankers, with usual first-time results. 'Wassie' Wasserman achieved the distinction of becoming the squadron's first, but not last, 'panty-ripper'. On one dirty dart with his F1, the probe completely removed the canvas strip (the 'panty') from the edge of the basket. Hechter achieved a creditable 8/10 plugs—good for a first attempt. A problem was experienced when it was found that the belly tanks refused to top up correctly, sending the engineers scurrying back to their drawing boards.

The rapid departure of the AZs from France meant they were largely untested on assembly at Atlas. Some of the aircraft had not even been painted owing to the hasty exodus. Configuration trials, carrying different permutations of armament and underwing stores, required exhaustive testing. Speeds, power settings, fuel consumption figures, time to climb readings and a host of other data had to be compiled and checked against performance manuals. Each variation had to be checked while aircraft handling under different external loads was noted.

## Close shave 2

After many months the ultimate sortie was reached when eight inert 460kg bombs were loaded—four under the belly and two under each wing. Claiming commander's perks, Willem Hechter elected to fly the sortie and drop the bombs on Roodewal bombing range. During planning, Hechter was assured by the armourers that inert bombs weighed only half the weight of live bombs. Oops!

Taxiing out for an 11h00 take-off on a hot, sunny day, Hechter had the feeling the aircraft was quite heavy. Taking off on runway 01 towards Pretoria, he realized that the acceleration was terrible and started sweating. The thought of aborting flashed through his mind but, with eight large bombs on board, his chances of stopping successfully were minimal. On the concrete at the end of the runway he rotated the aircraft and it lifted sluggishly into the air. Unfortunately, with the drag from the undercarriage and flaps it would not accelerate.

Rapidly approaching the rising ground of Waterkloof ridge, Hechter made his decision. Using gentle applications of rudder, he slewed the aircraft to the left to allow his labouring Mirage to enter the length of the valley immediately before the ridge. The extra 200 feet enabled him to bunt gently forward to allow the speed to increase while he lifted the wheels. The aircraft, responding to the decrease in drag started to accelerate slowly. With the buildings of Unisa University towering above the right-hand wing, the Mirage caused consternation among vehicle drivers speeding around the well-known Fountains Circle. By the time the aircraft reached the centre of downtown Pretoria, Hechter had managed to raise flaps and had started a gentle climb en route to Roodewal. This

# 1977: Laying foundations

F1AZ armed with eight 460kg inert bombs. With this load Commandant Willem Hechter only just scraped into the air. The all-up-weight had been calculated in pounds.

exciting take-off was not the fault of the F1—it was purely a human error. The inert bombs were double the planned-for weight.

At that time, a 14-bomb configuration for the AZ had been proposed. Substantial modification and strengthening of the undercarriage were required and Dassault concentrated much of their factory's attention on achieving a satisfactory solution. Unfortunately, this shift of emphasis was to the detriment of 1 Squadron. It took years of development before the bomb racks and bombing computer worked satisfactorily when the bomb load varied. When bombs are dropped from an aircraft the centre of gravity (C of G) changes very rapidly. One of the functions of the bombing computer was to ensure correct sequencing when the bombs were released, to keep the C of G within controlled limits.

*****

April was flypast month. On the 20th, Captain Winterbach led three F1s and four Mirage IIIs for the Freedom of Kimberley parade. He found Kimberley but led his formation down the wrong street! On the 30th, Commandant Hechter led a four-ship formation over Vereeniging to celebrate Republic Day.

During the month of May, combined strikes were flown, with CZ fighters acting as escorts for the ground-attack AZs. The missions were not too successful and resulted in long discussions on tactics to improve results.

In June 1977, 3 Squadron presented another conversion course for captains Bill Einkamerer, I. C. ('IC') du Plessis, Wassie Wasserman and Lieutenant Neil de Villiers. All four pilots were destined for 1 Squadron. The F1AZs were 'out-the-box' new aircraft causing Wasserman, used to flying the older Mirage IIIs, to comment that pilots should fly AZs wearing top hats, bow-ties and tails. They all found the aircraft comparatively easy to fly, especially in the circuit where everything happened at 20 knots slower than in the III. The flaps and leading-edge slats allowed the pilots to see the runway with ease. Gone was the problem of peering around the left-hand side of the highly raised nose of the Mirage III on final approach. Engaging nose-wheel steering made taxiing a delight, after the differential braking of the older Mirage type.

Before training as a pilot, Captain Wasserman had been a navigator on Shackeltons and C-130s. Therefore, he was very impressed with the AZ's on-board systems. Because of his enthusiasm he became an expert on the nav–weapon system. While serving on the squadron, he gladly undertook the role of instructor on these subjects to future conversion courses.

3 Squadron must receive acknowledgement for the help and assistance it gave in those early years that allowed 1 Squadron to develop. It was only in January 1978, when lieutenants Dieter Ortmann, Les Bennett and 'Tinkie' Jones were posted in, that 3 Squadron could grow.

Test pilot Commandant Jan Marais, who had completed the technical course in January, finally went solo on 14 June. The delay was caused by a long battle to get the simulator serviceable.

Late in June 1977, all three Mirage Squadrons attended the supersonic ACM camp in Durban. Competition between the Mirage IIIs of 2 Squadron and both types of F1 was intense. Initially, the IIIs tended to win the low-speed fights. Discussion on the problem proved beneficial after the F1s used high-speed approaches and made ample use of the vertical plane. At the end of the camp, there were eight 'kills' claimed against the F1s and 58 against the Mirage IIIs.

This camp was interrupted on 28 April, when all three squadrons, plus Mirage IIIs from 85 ADFS, flew a 27-ship Mirage formation for the turning-of-the-sod ceremony at Hoedspruit. In 1979, AFB Hoedspruit became the home base of 2 Squadron. 1 Squadron followed during December 1980.

By mid-September, Commandant Jan Marais finally cleared the strengthened rocket pods for use, after the incident the previous year.

## Weaponry

During the last three months of 1977, hard work was put in trying to solve problems in the bombing computer. In October Commandant Hechter, using the auto-release mode, tossed bombs far off target. Major Beukes did the same when firing rockets. A glimmer of hope was achieved in November when Commandant Hechter and Lieutenant Thys Muller demolished Alpha 'coke', and Captain van der Heever achieved a centre of error possibility (CEP) of nine metres for eight individual bombs.

There were three main targets on Roodewal bombing range. Alpha and Bravo were identically marked circular targets on either side of the range control hut, used only for inert weapons. Charlie target, used for live weapons training, was two miles farther down range, safely outside the effective range of the exploding weapons. The centre of each target was marked by a triangular raised structure, referred to as the 'coke'.

The programme was completed by 8 December, with some good and some dreadful results. Captain Wasserman achieved the best rocket results with 7/8 rockets under ten metres. The best air-to-ground score was 35/50 by Captain van der Heever.

During one of these range sorties Captain Wasserman's aircraft suffered a hydraulic failure. He burned off excess fuel and returned to carry out a flapless landing at AFB Waterkloof. He deployed the drag 'chute on touchdown and, within the laid-down emergency brake applications, he managed to slow down the Mirage and turn off at the end of the runway. Here all the base emergency vehicles greeted him and he should have stopped. However, the brakes still had pressure and the separate nose-wheel accumulator allowed the aircraft to manoeuvre properly, so Wasserman headed back to the line. The 3 Squadron hardstanding slopes gently down towards the main runway. He was marshalled into a position between the parked F1s. Everything worked as planned until the ground marshal, standing directly in front of the aircraft, indicated to Wasserman to stop. By now, pressure in the emergency brake accumulator had been depleted. Although he applied both brakes, the aircraft kept rolling gently down the slope. The nimble-footed marshal dived to his right just in time—the pilot probe would have impaled him between the eyes. Fortunately, the nose-wheel steering accumulator had sufficient pressure to allow Wasserman to turn through another 180°, which left his aircraft facing up the slight, uphill slope. Applying a little power, he stopped the aircraft from rolling backwards down the slope, while calling the ground crew to chock the Mirage—something he should have done at the end of the runway. This was a lesson that could have had serious consequences.

On 19 December, lieutenants Piet Truter and Ed Deschamps joined 1 Squadron from the fighter school. On the same day, the squadron received its first practice V3 air-to-air missile.

The author after his solo flight in the F-86 Sabre.

**NAMIBIA**

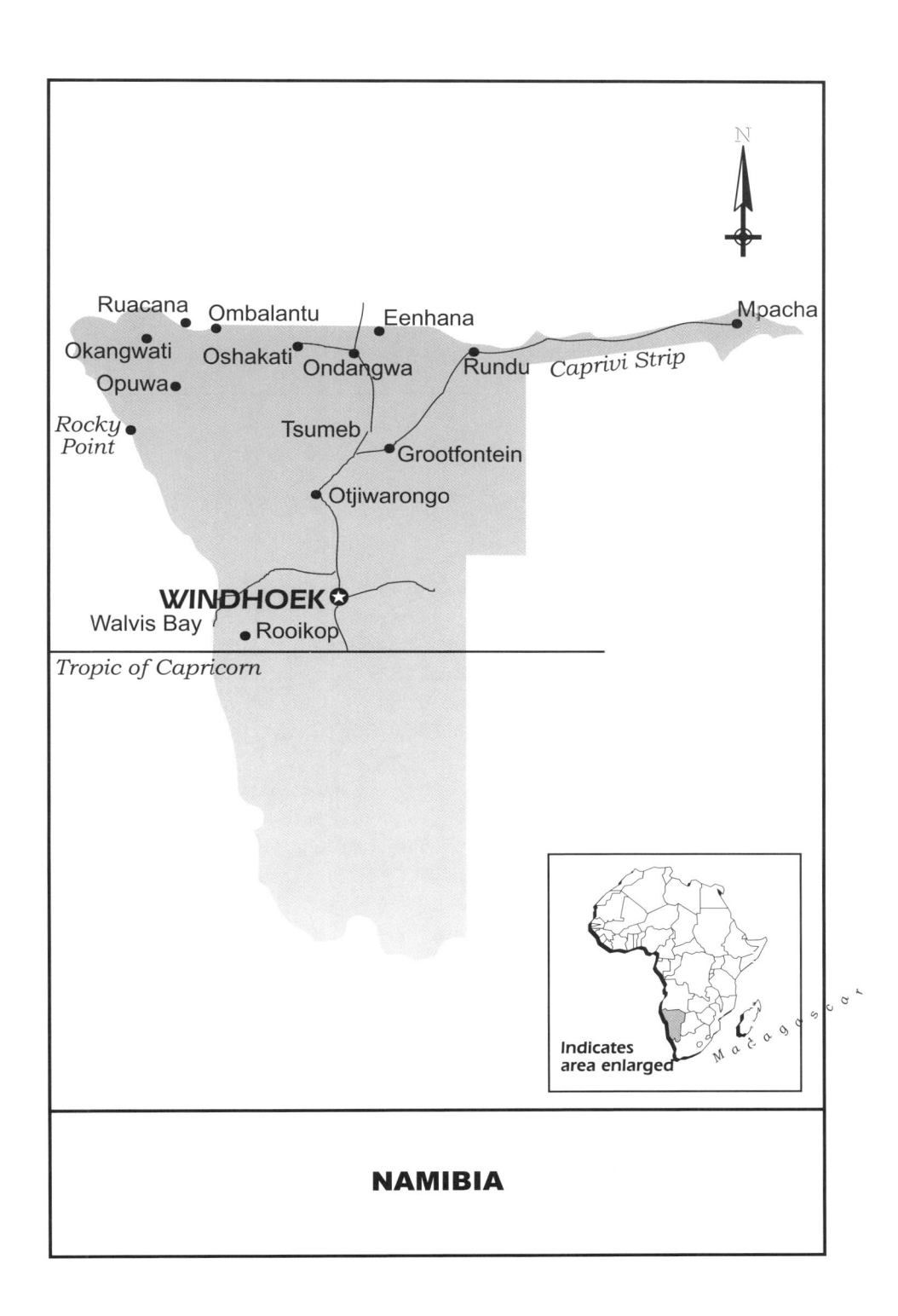

# Chapter 5

# 1978:
# Border war escalation

**Talk of war**

The New Year opened with 3 Squadron still playing host to the homeless 1 Squadron, which was awkward for both units. 3 Squadron's flight line and hangar were bursting at the seams trying to cope with 48 Mirage F1 aircraft, in place of their planned complement of 16 F1CZs. However, it was to be 12 months before 1 Squadron would get premises of its own. Only when AFB Hoedspruit was ready to receive 2 Squadron, could 1 Squadron take over the vacated facilities at AFB Waterkloof.

However, developments in the border war situation had instilled a new sense of urgency into the preparations to prepare both squadrons for combat. During December, a decision taken at President John Vorster's holiday home had a galvanizing effect on the Defence Force. Purely defensive tactics could not stop terrorist incursions into South West Africa from Angola. There were not sufficient men available to patrol the extensive border between South West Africa and Angola effectively. Pre-emptive attacks against SWAPO concentrations were deemed to be a more cost-effective method of protecting sovereignty. Cross-border raids implied protective air cover—a step further up the escalation ladder.

During non-flying days, the pilots held in-depth discussions on all aspects of operations. One of these concerned academic and operational weapon assessment criteria, for both pilots and aircraft. Results obtained on a known weapons range are always better than those achieved using operational tactics on unknown targets.

At this early stage of development, 1 Squadron averages were as follows:

- Air-to-air              29 per cent hits on the flag
- Air-to-ground           40 per cent hits on an effective 4m x 4m target
- 68mm RP (rockets)       18.5 metres miss-distance from the 'coke'
- Bombs (pilot-released)  38 metres miss-distance
- Bombs (computer released) results unplottable

The results for air-to-air and air-to-ground were reasonable, when one hit from a 30mm cannon shell can be sufficient to down an aircraft or destroy a soft-skinned vehicle. However, the RP score was not particularly good. A direct hit is required to put an armoured vehicle out of action. The pilot-released bomb results were fair, indicating that pilots had reached an average level of skill. However, to estimate operational results, a factor of 1.5 of the academic scores can be added to the academic result. The 38-metre bombing result, plus 57 metres (1.5 x 38) translates into an operational miss-distance of 95 metres—which was totally unacceptable.

Therefore, the big disappointment was the automatic release results. The function of the bombing computer was to predict accurately the moment of automatic bomb release, to place the centre of the stick of bombs directly over the target. These figures emphasized for 1 Squadron the necessary focus area of attention.

Early in February, Captain Wasserman lifted off from short runway 33 at Jan Smuts airport, to ferry an F1AZ to Waterkloof. As he raised the undercarriage the fire-warning system illuminated—it turned out to be a spurious warning, although he did not know this at the time. Declaring the emergency to the tower, he entered a tight right-hand turn to land immediately on runway 21, wanting to get his burning aircraft onto the ground as quickly as possible.

The air traffic controller gave landing permission, while watching the steeply banked F1 turn. In the moist air close to the ground vortices were streaming off the wingtips. The controller informed Wasserman that he could see 'smoke' trailing behind the Mirage, which increased Wasserman's desire to land his aircraft. Looking backwards, Wasserman could see the whole wing covered in vortices and found it difficult to convince himself that this was not smoke. However, he landed the aircraft and stopped safely, but only came down from his adrenaline high much, much later.

## Grounding frustrations

On 10 February 1978, the entire Mirage fleet of the SAAF was grounded, until the locking bolts on the starter generators had been checked—a small inspection but one which could affect the safety of the aircraft and, therefore, very necessary. Although pilots are quickly bored when forced to stay on the ground, they always appreciated the vigilance of the maintenance crews, who detected such loose locking bolts and other such small but potentially lethal issues.

Lieutenant Thys Muller being congratulated by Commandant Freddie du Toit after achieving a perfect 50/50 score when firing air-to-air on a towed target.

The first of the twice-yearly pilgrimages to AFB Langebaan for air-to-air firing took place in March. Pilots practised firing using 'pegged' ranges in the event of radar failure. They would set the sight for the expected range at which they hoped to fire, usually about 300 metres. Scores of 0, 2, 3 and 7 out of 50 bullets were common—an indication of how difficult shooting is from a moving platform.

Scores improved dramatically when the Aida ranging radar in the F1AZ was used. Lieutenant Thys Muller achieved an unbelievable 50/50. To avoid inter-squadron banter, Major Chris Brits and Captain Carlo Gagiano from 3 Squadron verified this incredible score. A finely tuned Mirage F1 in the hands of a skilled pilot was to prove a deadly weapon of war.

For three days early in April, the F1s were grounded again, this time for modification of the fuel control units (FCUs). At the end of June, over a six-day period, the process was repeated when faults were again detected in the control units.

After un-grounding, the F1AZs departed to AFB Bloemspruit for an air-to-ground weapons camp. Once again results were disappointing, with many unplottable bombs—the bombing computer still proving unreliable. Bomb hang-ups (bombs that would not release from the aircraft) indicated the engineers had a further problem to solve before the aircraft were released for real operations.

AZ pilots carried out V3 air-to-air missile trials over the telemetry range at

St Lucia in Zululand. Under range conditions the results were tremendously successful, though in later years, when the F1 entered the South West African–Angolan conflict, unforeseen problems with the missiles did arise.

In May, Major Roelf Beukes dropped 250kg bombs armed with the new variable-time (VT) fuses at the Potchefstroom weapons range. These fuses allowed bombs to detonate at preset heights above the ground. A contact fused bomb, dropped into the Angolan sands, exploded underground. The resulting crater was hugely impressive but, unless the bomb was a direct hit, little damage occurred to targets in the near vicinity. However, the effect of an air-burst bomb was totally different. Unhindered by the dampening effect of the sand the blast and shrapnel flew outwards and downwards in a fan pattern. Greater coverage from each dropped bomb assured better results.

## Cassinga

While the Mirage F1s were still being prepared for combat the war against SWAPO escalated. On 5 May 1978, more than 250 paratroopers were air-dropped onto the village of Cassinga, from C-130 and C-160 transport aircraft, minutes after Buccaneers and Canberra bombers had struck SWAPO targets in the village.

After hours of fighting the Parabats were extracted by a large force of helicopters. The paratroopers suffered three dead and eleven wounded. SWAPO lost over 1,000 members. To this day the success of the attack is disputed, with SWAPO claiming the people killed were refugees. Afterwards, at the debrief, paratroopers told in detail how these 'refugees' used 23mm anti-aircraft cannons in the ground role against them, how hundreds of AK-47s were found next to bodies and how the 'refugees' offered stiff resistance from the extensive fortifications surrounding the village.

Soldiers who fought at Cassinga say it was a heavily defended SWAPO target. Propagandists, not present at the fight, offered the 'refugee' story. The only indisputable result of Cassinga was the escalation of the bush war. The introduction of fighter aircraft into what had been a helicopter-supported counter-insurgency struggle raised the tempo and sophistication of the war.

## War by default

The Mirage F1 entered the war almost by default. On 6 July 1978, Captain Steve Ferreira flew a 2 Squadron Mirage III R2Z on a reconnaissance mission from AFB Mpacha, at the eastern end of the Caprivi Strip in South West Africa. Captain André van der Heever, flying an F1AZ, accompanied him on the mission into Zambia, flying the first operational sortie performed by the F1.

André van der Heever was responsible for compiling performance data of the aircraft when configured with two 1,200-litre underwing tanks. The long photographic sortie was ideal for extracting data on fuel consumption, acceleration times and on the handling of the aircraft in that configuration. The sortie was unopposed.

Meanwhile, the remaining AZ pilots continued with weapons carriage and release trials using the ESC-10 bomb pylon. Again bombs landed near Roodewaal, but not too many landed near the target. Captain Bill Einkamerer took the prize when the range officer reported his bomb as unnoticeable at 12 o'clock. By mid-August, problems had increased with unserviceabilities occurring with laser and radar range-finders. At the Upington weapons deployment, poor flight-line safety control during arming resulted in a 68mm rocket being launched across Upington's main runway. The civilian air traffic control officers were not amused. Fortunately, nobody was injured.

The weapons camp was curtailed on 25 August and the F1s flew back to Waterkloof, to take part in the funeral of ex-State President Diederichs the following day. As a mark of respect, Commandant Hechter led a 16-ship formation over Bloemfontein but not without great difficulty. The weather was appalling, forcing Hechter and his 15 associates to duck and dive between rainstorms. The heavy rain caused considerable delays at the graveside, requiring the 16-ship formation to orbit in and out of the rainsqualls. As a consequence, 12 aircraft landed at AFB Bloemspruit to refuel, while the remaining four flew directly back to Waterkloof.

During the return flight after refuelling, the 12 Mirage F1s flew in low-level battle formation. Approaching Potchefstroom, a Papa-Charlie ('Piss-Cat' light aircraft) was seen at a late stage, crossing the path of the oncoming high-speed jets. The sighting call produced a spectacular Red Arrow-type 'bomb-burst' as all the aircraft took avoiding action.

During late August, the military camp at Katima Mulilo at the eastern end of the Caprivi Strip was bombarded by SWAPO. A 122mm rocket demolished a bungalow, killing ten soldiers and wounding another ten. Within half an hour of the completion of the bombardment, South African forces launched a follow-up operation, using ground forces supported by Alouette helicopter gunships. Before the operation was halted, Buccaneer and Canberra bombers attacked known SWAPO targets in Zambia. Although only 16 SWAPO were accounted for, the cross-border follow-up achieved a far greater result. It crushed the insurgency campaign in the Caprivi Strip where SWAPO were never to regain a position of strength.

By September, although the manual release results had improved, the auto-bombing results were still poor. The October visit to AFB Langebaan produced excellent air-to-air results, with few system failures. The toil and sweat put into preparing the aircraft systems was beginning to pay dividends.

*****

1978: Border war escalation

Pilots who participated in the 50-ship Mirage F1 and III formation.

The inauguration ceremony of new State President, B. J. Vorster, took place on 10 October 1978. A highlight was the flypast of a 49-ship Mirage formation over the Union Buildings in Pretoria. Fifty Mirages took to the air, with the spare aircraft acting as the 'whipper-inner', responsible for talking all the other aircraft into proper position in the large formation.

## Foreign inputs

During 1978, the Israeli Air Force approached the SAAF, with a request that two experienced pilots be allowed to fly the Mirage III R2Z and F1CZ. Iran, one of Israel's belligerent neighbours, had been negotiating with Dassault over the possible purchase of both types of aircraft. The ever-vigilant Israelis, wanting to stay ahead of possible opposition, needed to study the performance of the aircraft.

In return, 3 Squadron requested the Israeli visit be extended so the flying hours could be traded for operational lessons, with the emphasis on air-combat manoeuvring. This valuable inset gave the SAAF a quantum leap ahead in this exacting art.

Late in October 1978, Major Theo Nell and lieutenants Norman Minne and Dirk de Villiers joined 1 Squadron. Commandant 'Spyker' Jacobs, an old Mirage III pilot serving on the staff of AFB Waterkloof, joined them for the F1 conversion course. On 16 November, Major Nell flew his first solo in an AZ. He found the aircraft similar to the Mirage III under normal flying conditions but far easier to handle in the circuit. Take-off performance in a clean F1 was appreciably better than that in a Mirage III with supersonic underwing tanks—the configuration

65

usually used by the fighter school to allow a reasonable sortie length. However, he landed with a feeling of relief. The reason was that he was still haunted by memories of his first flight in a dual-seat Mirage III. With Major Derek Kirkland as his instructor, Nell's landing in the delta-winged III had been almost perfect except for the speed which was too high. The aircraft ballooned after touchdown, which resulted in a harder than normal *second* landing which burst both tyres. Running on the wheel rims, the aircraft slewed to the right and ran off the runway. Not a good first arrival, hence the pleasure at flying the F1.

In November, both squadrons deployed to AFB Ondangwa in South West Africa, leaving Captain Wasserman behind to continue instruction to the newcomers.

After 13 years of low-intensity, counter-insurgency bush war, the time had come for the Mirage F1s to enter the fray.

The Mirage III of Derek Kirkland and Theo Nell lying off runway 05 at AFB Pietersburg. Landing the high-nosed, delta-winged III was none too easy!

# Chapter 6

# 1979:
# The rising storm

## First operational deployment
The first of many operational deployments began on 3 November 1978. Five F1CZs deployed to AFB Ondangwa, flown by Commandant Fred du Toit and captains Carlo Gagiano, Pierre du Plessis, Darryl Lee and Tinkie Jones. These aircraft were used to escort Mirage III R2Zs from 2 Squadron, who were flying extensive photo-reconnaissance missions over southern Angola.

On 11 November, one of the sorties flew close to the Angolan port of Namibe. On the return leg, du Plessis and Lee who were flying as escorts were called up by Commandant Tom Engela, the 'Dayton' radar controller. (Dayton was the call sign of the Marconi mobile radar system permanently deployed at AFB Ondangwa, to give much-needed cover to our aircraft). Engela warned the formation that two high-speed blips were approaching from the north. Regretfully, having minimum combat fuel available after the long flight, the F1s could not engage the enemy fighters. They accelerated towards Ondangwa. The interceptors gave up the chase, returning to the airfield at Lubango, 300 kilometres north of the border.

On 6 November 1978, five 1 Squadron AZs, flown by Major André van der Heever and captains I. C. du Plessis, Thys Muller, Piet Truter and Ed Deschamps, joined 3 Squadron at AFB Ondangwa. These ground-attack aircraft were needed on standby for the ground forces. Before returning to Waterkloof, on 20 November, they also flew armed recce sorties, a close air-support (CAS) mission, and escorts for 2 Squadron PR flights. By 12 December, all the Mirages were back at Waterkloof. The sparring had begun.

## Schism
At the end of that year, 1 Squadron finally abandoned its squatter status and

moved into the facilities vacated by 2 Squadron on their move to AFB Hoedspruit. As it turned out, this move was also temporary. Noise pollution and air traffic congestion in the Pretoria region played their part in 1 Squadron being moved to AFB Hoedspruit at the end of 1980.

The situation improved dramatically for both squadrons. 3 Squadron found the breathing space they needed, while 1 Squadron finally became an autonomous unit, the objective set by Commandant Hechter. However, the rebirth was not without pain. As happened to 3 Squadron when they recommissioned, 1 Squadron had to beg, borrow and steal carpets, curtains and furnishings to make their new home habitable. The air force budget is spent acquiring aircraft—everything else has to be purloined.

The threat of MiG intervention in the bush war had increased considerably with the attempted interception of 11 November 1978. In order to expand knowledge and experience in combat manoeuvring, 3 Squadron hosted an ACM clinic. Two selected pilots from each of 1, 2 and 3 Squadrons, plus two instructors from 85 ADFS participated. Apart from classroom instruction, a comprehensive flying programme consisting of one-vs-one, two-vs-one and two-vs-two sorties were flown. It was an exhausting programme during which the pilots were continually under high-G stress loads.

## Tragedy

At 09h00 on 15 February 1979, Major Chris Brits in an F1CZ and Captain Wassie Wasserman in an F1AZ, took off for a one-vs-one combat sortie. After 40 minutes of hard 'fighting' during which Brits achieved a 'kill' against Wasserman, the aircraft landed back at base. After a cup of coffee and a rebrief, the pair took off again at 11h00, with Wasserman determined to get his revenge.

Brits led the ten-second-stream take-off and turned out towards Cullinan, east of Pretoria. Wasserman, in AZ 246, was climbing through 3,000 feet AGL (above ground level) at 400 knots when his engine suddenly flamed out. An immediate hot relight was successful but, as he opened the throttle past 75 per cent, the engine again flamed out. An immediate relight succeeded but once more the engine flamed out. By this time Wasserman was anxiously steering his aircraft away from the suburbs surrounding the city. His speed had diminished during the loss of power and at 250 knots he had to push the nose down to keep the engine idling speed sufficiently high to attempt a cold relight. At this speed, both his generators cut out and it became necessary to rely on the aircraft's battery for electrical power.

His cold relight was unsuccessful. Wasserman tightened his seat straps, telling Brits he would make one more attempt. This also failed and, as he was now down to 1,000 feet above ground level, he pulled the nose upwards and ejected, using the bottom seat handle. He remained conscious during the entire ejection sequence and remembers the massive bang as he flew through the embrittled canopy. He was aware of a sudden blast of wind as he left the shelter of the cockpit, the tumbling of his seat and the relief of the jerk as the main parachute canopy opened.

As he stabilized under the open canopy he was amazed to find he was still pointing in the direction his aircraft had been flying. He watched as Mirage F1AZ 246 impacted the ground in a 15° right-hand bank, nose-down attitude.

Looking down from his parachute, Wasserman was alarmed to see additional dangers. What concerned him most of all was the sight of a yellow Mercedes-Benz speeding along a farm road where Wasserman judged he would land. However, parachute drift removed the imminent danger of being run over but brought another painful hazard into view. He was now headed directly for the top of an *Acacia tortillas*—the well-known bushveld Umbrella thorn tree. The tree is covered with long, six-centimetre white thorns and the wicked curved thorns that account for the very descriptive Afrikaans name of *Haak-en-steek*—literally hook and prick. By pulling on his parachute risers he started an oscillation that allowed him to miss the dangers of the thorns, but slammed him sideways into the ground.

Fortunately, the Mercedes driver had seen Wasserman descending and stopped close by to ascertain whether he was injured. However, it was Wasserman who had to pacify the excited driver. Wasserman then took a few minutes while he checked his arms, legs and joints for normal movement. Fortunately, everything was in working order.

Meanwhile, Chris Brits informed AFB Waterkloof over the radio of the ejection and proceeded to fly a low, slow flypast over the crash scene. Wasserman heard the Mirage approaching and waved both hands to indicate that he was fine. Then Brits flew a circuit around the crash site to make a second run past Wasserman. On the final turn, Wasserman noticed the aircraft descending rapidly. Moments before it disappeared from his view, he saw Brits roll the aircraft out of the turn. Seconds later it impacted the ground in a tail-down attitude, no more than 500 metres from where Wasserman was standing.

Accepting the offer of a lift from the Mercedes driver, Wasserman sped to the new crash site. Brits had crashed within 25 metres of the Cullinan–Groblersdal road. Three cars were already at the scene. Brits had ejected, but had not separated from his seat when it hit the ground. He was killed instantly. An onlooker had covered Brits's body with the parachute.

Within minutes a Puma helicopter, flown by Major Daantjie Beneke, landed at the sight of the second crash. Major André van der Heever alighted to look after Wasserman, while the doctor removed Brits's body in the helicopter. Later the helicopter returned to take Wasserman to 1 Military Hospital for a medical check-up. Wasserman was able to walk into the hospital but the doctor warned him that when the medical staff got hold of him it could be the most dangerous part of his day. In the event, Wasserman required nothing more than a sedative before being allowed home. However, the following morning he was as stiff and sore as if he had just completed the Comrades Marathon.

Farm workers had been busy in the field where Wasserman's aircraft crashed. The shock sent the labourers running directly away from the explosion. They had only travelled 400 metres when the second Mirage crashed just ahead of them. Avenues of escape were decreasing, so they turned 90° and, with added momentum, continued to flee. Colonel Paul Neser, the AFB Waterkloof commander, was airborne in an Impala jet when he was notified of the crashes. He flew directly to the scene and circled overhead. The labourers, expecting yet another crash, were now in complete disarray and did not know which way to run.

## The pot starts simmering

During January and February 1979, Foreign Minister Pik Botha was in contact with the United Nations. In a diplomatic note to the UN Secretary-General, Kurt Waldheim, he asked whether United Nations Transitional Agreement Group (UNTAG) troops would be arriving to commence the independence process for South West Africa. No significant reaction was received from UN headquarters.

However, SWAPO responded by stepping up attacks on Owambo civilians and launching a stand-off bombardment on the security force base at Elundu. All their 122mm Katusha rockets and mortars missed the base, but that did not stop them from claiming, outrageously, to have killed 300 South African soldiers in the previous three months, destroyed two military bases, 40 military vehicles and shot down two SAAF reconnaissance aircraft. This posturing by SWAPO brought a swift riposte from South Africa. Authority was granted to carry out two cross-border military operations during March 1979.

Early in March, ground forces crossed into southern Angola to destroy known SWAPO bases near Mongua, Oncocua and Henhombe in Operation *Rekstok I*. The SAAF supported these attacks using aerial bombardment from Canberra bombers of 12 Squadron and photo-reconnaissance flights by Mirage III RZs of 2 Squadron. As a safeguard for these vulnerable aircraft, 3 Squadron deployed to AFB Ondangwa until the end of March. Combat air patrols (CAPS), escort missions and low-level armed reconnaissance flights were flown, and many long hours were spent on cockpit standby.

## Canberra down

At 17h00 on 14 March, Captains Darryl Lee and Tinkie Jones had just completed a hot, two-hour sit at the end of the Ondangwa runway. As Major Dries Wehmeyer placed his foot on the cockpit ladder to take over the standby and Lee undid his ejection seat quick-release buckle, the radio came alive with the order to

Seven Canberra bombers of 12 Squadron formate for a final flypast after being sold to a country in South America.

'scramble' ... the call all fighter pilots wait for in a war.

Wehmeyer jumped off the ladder as Lee pushed the start button. Closing their canopies the pilots taxiied the 40 metres onto the runway threshold, opened full throttle and blasted into the air. Turning immediately onto the vector given by the air traffic controller, they set heading to the scene of the emergency Only then did Lee have time to rebuckle himself safely into the ejection seat.

In transit, Commandant Tom Engela, the Dayton radar controller, informed them that a Canberra had been shot down by ground fire in the Cahama area. The F1 pilots were to search for the wreckage and try to establish whether either of the crew had ejected successfully. This piece of information was particularly upsetting for Tinkie Jones, as he knew his brother Roly had been flying one of the Canberras in that formation. It took ten agonizing minutes before it was verified that Roly was safe. Unfortunately, after a long search no sign of the wreckage, the pilot Lieutenant Marais or navigator Second Lieutenant Doyle was found.

As the fuel states approached 'bingo', the minimum for a safe return to AFB Ondangwa, the pilots spotted a military lorry parked on the side of the road and received permission to destroy it. Jones fired his 30mm cannon, becoming the first 3 Squadron pilot since the end of World War II to fire in anger. His elation was short-lived when intelligence reported the truck had been abandoned, having previously been shot up by Impala aircraft. On a later sortie, Major Jack Gründling and Darryl Lee rolled in to attack a lorry driving on a road south of Ongiva. They did not fire because just before release they realized that it was a civilian vehicle.

On 28 March, before returning to Waterkloof, 3 Squadron flew their last mission. They carried out an attack on a SWAPO camp north of Beacon 10. Seven F1CZs, led by Commandant Fred du Toit, fired 68mm rockets and 30mm cannon into the base, moments before ground forces swept through the target area.

## Saffraan

Operation *Saffraan* was launched to seek and destroy SWAPO terrorists known to have moved into Zambia. 1 Squadron deployed to AFB Mpacha, at the eastern end of the Caprivi Strip on 24 March. Earlier in the month ground forces, supported by Canberra bombers, had attacked known SWAPO bush camps. The F1AZ pilots flew armed reconnaissance sorties without finding any worthwhile targets. Using standard dive-attacks, they also bombed and strafed a terrorist camp designated target No 52, five nautical miles east of Senanga in Zambia. All the air-strike results throughout *Saffraan* were disappointing, mainly because intelligence covering that theatre was sketchy at best.

Captain Norman Minne flew his first operational sortie on this deployment as wingman to Captain I. C. du Plessis on an armed recce flight. Understandably nervous, he recalled the briefing officer stating that provided their speed at low level remained above 450 knots, the shoulder-launched SA-7 Strela missiles were no threat. However, du Plessis, hungry for action, kept slowing down whenever his eye picked up a possible target. After an hour of a suspenseful but uneventful flight both aircraft landed safely. A visit to the pub that evening helped settle Minne's 'first-night' nerves.

*****

Returning from a weapons camp at Upington on 25 April 1979, Lieutenant Darryl Lee in F1CZ 203 found he had to use progressively more throttle to maintain his position in the formation. Eventually, he asked Commandant Fred du Toit, the formation leader, to check his power settings. He even selected afterburner to see if this would improve the situation. It did not help and he decided to return to Upington.

When he rolled out of his turn, the indicated airspeed dropped to 240 knots and even with full dry power he could not maintain height. Arriving over the little town of Kuruman, he began circling the local airfield. He informed Upington air traffic control of his predicament and they promptly warned the authorities at Kuruman, who reacted very quickly. Lee could see ambulances and other vehicles scurrying around the unmanned airfield. However, it was a short sand strip on which Lee was not too keen to land.

He then operated the F1's emergency throttle and increased engine revolutions to 109 per cent. This setting allowed him to maintain his height at 15,000 feet and speed of 240 knots. Because the extremely long runway at Upington was within the 20-minute limit, using this high-power setting, he opted to continue to Upington. Ten miles short of the field he converted his speed, which had now built up to 290 knots, to altitude. Reaching 19,000 feet he entered an emergency-landing pattern. Landing hot, off his 240-knot descending approach, he managed to bring the F1 to a halt on the runway.

That afternoon, a C-160 Transall of 28 Squadron arrived with a spare engine and a team of 3 Squadron maintenance personnel. These men worked through the night changing the engine, while Lee found a spot in the hangar where he managed a few hours' sleep. At first light the aircraft was ready to fly. Lee combined the obligatory test flight, after an engine change, with the transit back to AFB Waterkloof.

It was subsequently discovered the problem was a hairline crack in the thin P2 pressure pipe which controls the opening and closing of the engine nozzle flaps. Like a garden hose, if the opening is narrowed, the water jet becomes more powerful. Lee's engine flaps had moved to the wide-open position thus reducing the jet thrust of the engine. The crack was so small it could not be seen by the naked eye and was only discovered by a crack detector.

## *Dikvel*

Pilots who attended one of the ACM clinics hosted by 3 Squadron. Standing from left: Pierre du Plessis, Carlo Gagiano, John Orr, Jack Gründling, Jogai Eshkol, Mac van der Merwe, Graham Rochat, Norman Bruton. Kneeling from left: Tinkie Jones, Uzi Rozen, Mark Crooks (aka 'Spiderman').

In May 1979, another ACM clinic, known as Project *Dikvel*, was held under the auspices of 3 Squadron. The aim was to raise the standard of aerial combat within the fighter squadrons of the SAAF. Course members would take back the experience gained to their home units. Major Jack Gründling and captains Carlo Gagiano, Pierre du Plessis, Mark Crooks and Tinkie Jones represented 3 Squadron, majors Graham Rochat and Norman Bruton 85 ADFS, captains Wassie Wasserman and Thys Muller 1 Squadron and John Orr and Bart Hauptfleisch 2 Squadron. Once again, experienced combat pilots from the Israeli Air Force instructed and flew against the SAAF pilots and valuable lessons were learned.

Shortly before Commandant Hechter left 1 Squadron, he and logistician, Commandant Frikkie Bolton, started programming the F1AZs through the ESDAP tester. This machine had the capability for testing and fine-tuning all the electronic systems in the aircraft. This move resulted in the formation of an F1 Support Group (FSG) tasked with improving the reliability and efficiency of the integrated aircraft systems.

On 2 June 1979, Commandant Hechter left 1 Squadron and was replaced by Commandant D. J. ('Casey') Lewis. Lewis, a very experienced pilot-attack instructor, was the driving force behind the South African V3A air-to-air missile programme for the Mirage III. In 1974, he had visited France to assist with the integration of the V3B onto the South African F1s. During 1976, he had carried out the clearance trials of the missile on the F1CZ and by 1978 on the F1AZ. This flying was carried out from his post at headquarters as Staff Officer Fighters.

The South African-developed missiles were designed for integration with a helmet-mounted sight, also of South African design. Development of the helmets began in 1975 and the SAAF was the first air force to fly operationally with this type of system. One of these helmets was stolen during the Commodore Dieter Gerhard spy saga. It was passed on to the Soviets and was partly the reason the spy was eventually apprehended. On completion of the Cold War and when South Africa's relations with Russia had been established, it was interesting to note that the helmet sight used by the Soviet Air Force was basically the same as the helmet stolen from the SAAF. The latest version of the South African helmet is an integral part of the considerable weapons capability of the Rooivalk attack helicopter.

On 3 June, 3 Squadron returned to AFB Ondangwa to protect Impala crews on a strike against a SWAPO target near Humbe. The Impalas went through the target unimpeded and the F1CZs were not brought into action.

On 25 June, Major Frans Pretorius, Captain Frik Viljoen and Lieutenant Hennie Louw started the F1AZ conversion course on 1 Squadron.

## *Rekstok*

Cabinet approval was given for an air strike on SWAPO's Tobias Haneko Training

Camp, on 6 July 1979. This strike, originally part of Operation *Rekstok* carried out between 6 and 13 March, became known as *Rekstok II*. Two Buccaneers and seven F1AZs from 1 Squadron attacked the target situated ten nautical miles northeast of Lubango. Commandant Lewis flew in the formation, his second flight in the squadron.

'Gamblers', the Buccaneer formation took off from Grootfontein and the F1AZs from Ondangwa. Independent low-level navigational routes were flown by both formations. The AZs were to attack 40 seconds after the Buccaneers' time on target (TOT). The Buccaneers were to run in from the south and each aircraft was to long-toss a stick of eight 450kg bombs in to the target. Equipment aboard the Buccaneer, originally incorporated for the tossing of nuclear weapons, was modified to allow the aircraft to toss bombs. This they did by pitching-up from low level at 450 knots. At 45° nose-up, the bombs were released, to fly a parabolic curve, before impacting the ground nearly 4.5 nautical miles from the release point. By varying the sequential release of the bombs by a set number of milliseconds the bombs would land in a stick, through the target. The explosions would assist the pitching Mirages to acquire their targets as they entered their attack dives.

Except for a slight navigational error, both formations approached the target without incident. The Buccaneers missed the initial point (IP) for their bombing run. They circled, found the correct point, ran in and tossed their bombs into the target. Unfortunately, the time taken to circle meant that the bombs arrived, arcing through the air, at the same time as the seven F1s attacked from the north. The Mirages pulled off the target through the rain of bombs, luckily without mishap.

During August 1979, 1 Squadron carried out a live weapons camp from Upington, in the northern Cape. One Thursday evening in the pub, Casey Lewis discussed the flying with a local farmer, who was extremely keen to see a Mirage F1 perform. Lewis invited him out to the airfield to view the aircraft on Saturday morning. However, owing perhaps to several beers, the farmer misunderstood the invitation. On Friday evening, Lewis was horrified to hear an announcement over the local radio station that he was holding an airshow at Upington airfield the following day, to which all the townsfolk were invited.

Early next morning, Lewis was asked over the telephone by the Upington air traffic controller (ATCO) if he had authority to carry out an airshow. Lewis told him not to worry and that it was a mistake he would rectify by phoning the farmer. To this the ATCO replied by asking what he must do with the hordes of locals who were gathering at the airport gates.

Eventually, half the town gathered, to wander around a hastily arranged static display of Bosboks, Kudus, Canberras, Mirage IIIs and F1s. Major Theo Nell, who'd flown a bombing mission that morning came racing back to Upington with plenty of fuel. Calling Upington he 'conveniently' declared an emergency because of problems with the aircraft's undercarriage. He was granted permission to overfly the airfield so observers on the ground could check for abnormalities in the undercarriage. This, of course, required runs with the wheels down and up. It was extraordinary how many fast, slow, upside-down and rolling manoeuvres were flown, before Nell was fully satisfied that he could land safely. The townspeople went away happy and there were no repercussions from headquarters.

Later during the deployment, the squadron fired AS-30 air-to-ground missiles without much success. A number of missiles lost the steering signal, put on 20° nose-up and disappeared out of sight over the hills, but down range. However, Captain Norman Minne's missile turned 90° off track and entered the valley where the range-control team and Puma helicopter were situated. Fortunately, the errant missile did not cause any damage, (if nine pairs of lightly soiled underpants are discounted).

The quality of intelligence often determines the success or failure of operations. All forms of intelligence-gathering are used to build an overall picture of enemy dispositions and intentions. Photographic intelligence, while not always the best method, is certainly the most convincing. PR work requires tremendous planning and precise flying—it is an exacting task. On missions over enemy territory, the vulnerable PR aircraft are always given the protection of an accompanying escort. This allows the PR crew to concentrate solely on their task.

On 15 September 1979, 3 Squadron F1CZs escorted two Canberra reconnaissance missions over targets in Angola.

## Accidental discharge

With 3 Squadron up on the border, 1 Squadron had their aircraft in the hangar undergoing routine maintenance. Both sides of the hangar were full of F1AZs and two more were parked, one behind the other, in the centre. While checking bombing circuits, a mechanic in a cockpit pulled the cannon trigger. Four rounds of 30mm ball ammunition fired from each cannon. The noise in the enclosed hangar was unbelievably loud. After everyone had recovered from the shock, it was noticed that flames were licking around the damaged nozzle flaps of the lead aircraft, where the hydraulic and oil pipes had been destroyed. Fortunately, quick reactions by the ground crew allowed them to douse the fires almost immediately and no further damage ensued.

This unfortunate mishap occurred because in the effort to increase sortie rates and flying hours to cope with the growing threat of war, shortcuts were being taken in the servicing schedules. The guns had not been unloaded, the safety slide behind the trigger had been removed and the trigger pulled during the checking of the armament circuits. Safety was jeopardized but fortunately nobody suffered injury or worse. The damaged aircraft was repaired and flew again.

Towards the end of the year both F1 Squadrons departed again to AFB Langebaan for air-to-air firings. These deployments were eagerly awaited because the flying was good and the recreation facilities at the coast were certainly different from those available at the inland fighter bases. Diving for crayfish and perlemoen (abalone) was usually top of the list. Nightly visits to Langebaan town were also enjoyed, with seafood at Franel's and then drinks at the old Panoramic Hotel being the usual agenda.

On this visit, the 1 Squadron pilots were delighted to find that an attractive Rhodesian girl was entertaining at the Panoramic. This old establishment, known throughout the air force as the Roman Panic, had a colourful history before it was taken over by the Parks Board. The Rhodesian lass was a stripper by trade and her presence sent the bar sales soaring when the squadron pitched up in the evenings.

One thing led to another and she was adopted as the squadron's mascot. She was taken to the base to see and pose with the aircraft and pilots. She was also taken to watch air-to-ground weapons being fired at Tooth Rock range. Major Frans Pretorius's results were so good that the lady at once changed her allegiance from the Rhodesian Air Force to 1 Squadron. The photographs had pride of place in the 1 Squadron lines book until, unfortunately, a jealous wife ripped them out.

To keep themselves entertained over the mid-deployment weekend, the pilots departed on a tour of the Cape winelands. After many enjoyable samples, they decided unanimously that the tour should end with a squadron visit to Sandy Bay, the well-known nudist beach. By Sunday evening a number of pilots had sunburn on places that normally never saw the sun.

Weapons results for the camp showed that all the hard development work was starting to pay off. Major van der Heever had a best score of 45/60 on the flag, was also camp 'top gun' with an overall 57.5 per cent hits. At Tooth Rock, live 68mm rockets and 30mm cannon were fired and 250kg bombs and Mk 5 napalm tanks were dropped.

## Combat flap

Early in November 3 Squadron deployed to AFB Ondangwa for escort duties. While the war allowed, Canberra PR aircraft were photographing large areas of southern Angola to supplement the old and inadequate Portuguese maps of that territory. On 6 November, during this deployment, Captain Pierre du Plessis flew back to AFB Waterkloof in a Mirage F1CZ, taking off from Ondangwa at 06h55. On arrival at Waterkloof he was handed a technical manual, placed in a car and driven off to Atlas Aircraft Corporation with the instruction to study the documentation en route. He discovered that it covered the working and limitations of the combat flap modification to be fitted to the entire F1 fleet.

He took off from Atlas at 12h00 in F1CZ 205, onto which the prototype modification had been fitted. He carried out the service trials on the exciting modification, before returning to operations on the border. When 205, with combat flaps, finally arrived back on 3 Squadron, du Plessis as the 'test pilot' claimed it as his own. Not surprisingly, he quickly became the squadron's dog-fighting ace—until additional modified aircraft started arriving in numbers on the squadron.

The introduction of the combat flap drastically improved F1 performance in the middle-speed range. At around 300 knots, the aircraft could very nearly sustain the same turning rate as at Mach 0.9. Acceleration out of that speed range was also quicker and gave the F1 the edge over the Mirage III.

On 30 November, a mixed formation of 16 Mirage AZ and CZ aircraft performed a flypast in honour of General Bob Rogers, who was retiring as Chief of the Air Force.

On 17 December 1979, 3 Squadron deployed to AFB Ondangwa. The following day Commandant Fred du Toit flew his last operational sortie. With Captain Pierre du Plessis as his wingman, he flew escort to Captain Otto Schür in a Mirage III R2Z on a photographic reconnaissance deep into Angola, along the Lubango–Menonque railway line.

Warrant Officer Ken van Straaten, most decorated NCO during the border war, firing an MAG machine gun out of a Puma.

On rotation for take-off in F1CZ 201, his afterburner failed. After a quick mental calculation on runway length and temperature, he continued with the take-off and climbed away safely. Realizing the importance of the mission he elected to continue the flight, understanding the implications of flying a severely handicapped aircraft, if they were intercepted by Angolan MiG-21s. Fortunately, the sortie was completed without problems, but it indicates the confidence level that had been attained in the aircraft and its on-board systems.

At the end of the year, Commandant Fred du Toit handed over command of 3 Squadron to Commandant Jack Gründling. Du Toit's achievements can be measured by the results attained over succeeding years by his personnel. Warrant officers like Shane Beeton, 'Poen' Henning, 'Oosie' Oosthuizen and 'Tubby' de Wet became the core of technical experience on which the future of the F1 was built. Interestingly, a large number of du Toits's pilots like Jack Gründling, Carlo Gagiano, Willie Hartogh and Dolf Prinsloo became future officers commanding of F1 squadrons.

# Chapter 7

# 1980:
# Nearing boiling point

## New OC 3 Squadron

In January 1980, when Commandant Jack Gründling assumed command of 3 Squadron he had two objectives. Many years before, while flying Vampires at AFB Pietersburg, he had been inspired by the work done by Captain 'Ollie' Holmes regarding dogfighting. Using information from copies of USAF newsletters, Holmes had started introducing jet fighter tactics into the SAAF. From those early days, Gründling decided that if ever he became officer commanding of a fighter squadron, it would be the best aerial combat squadron in the air force. By 1980 the situation on the border had escalated and it was inevitable that aerial dogfights against MiGs would take place. Within his period of command Gründling's vision was to prove important.

Renowned for his managerial abilities, Gründling had a second goal—to extract maximum performance from his squadron. Being strongly task-orientated, he introduced measuring systems that allowed him to keep a watchful eye over all aspects of 3 Squadron's performance. When he discovered that one of his Mirage F1CZs had been standing at Atlas Aircraft Corporation for 232 working days he erupted. The improvements to the management control system ensured that this lapse never occurred again.

Shortly before taking command Gründling and Major Gerrie Radloff flew the Kfir in Israel. During their stay they discussed operating differences between the two air forces. The Israeli Air Force makes great use of part-time and reserve pilots to keep their squadrons up to strength. This prospect intrigued Gründling. He saw possibilities of utilizing the same idea in his newly acquired squadron. On their way back to South Africa, he asked Radloff if he would like to join 3 Squadron as a part-time pilot. Radloff, then staff officer electronic warfare at headquarters, jumped at the offer. He joined captains Vic Kaiser and Mark Clulow on the F1 technical course presented by 1 Squadron. While both units were stationed at AFB Waterkloof, they took turns presenting this course; the similarities in the CZ and AZ allowed this. When Kaiser and Clulow began learning the AZ navigation–weapon system, Radloff returned to 3 Squadron to study radar intercept theory.

Radloff remembers he was not overly impressed by the F1's performance when he went solo on 11 February 1980, having recently flown the Kfir at sea level. Compared to the Kfir and Mirage III, turn rates and accelerations were not markedly different but the F1 was definitely easier to fly and land. Ergonomically the cockpit was vastly superior to the other types and, being new, everything worked.

Between January 1980 and December 1982, he flew 144 hours with 3 Squadron. However, as a part-time pilot, he never really mastered the Cyrano IV radar and felt that the IV was just as difficult to operate as the Cyrano II fitted into the Mirage IIICZ. Disappointingly, the moving target indicator (MTI) never worked properly while he was on the squadron strength.

## Formation mishap

The annual celebration of Air Force Day was to be held on 31 January 1980 at AFB Ysterplaat, on the outskirts of Cape Town. Four F1AZs from 1 Squadron, led by Commandant Casey Lewis, were allocated for the airshow, but were not allowed to include low-level aerobatics in their display. This honour was reserved for the Silver Falcon Impala aerobatic team. Towards the end of January, Commandant Lewis led his four-ship formation in a number of practices in the general flying (GF) area east of Pretoria. Captains Dirk de Villiers No 2, Hennie Louw No 3 and Wassie Wasserman No 4, made up the box formation.

At 10h30 on 30 January, Lewis led the formation over AFB Waterkloof for the final practice. The display sequence was flown in front of onlookers from the base. Everything went as planned, except that the height was considerably lower than during previous practice runs. On the final run-in for a horizontal bomb-burst over the field, the aircraft were extremely close to the ground. Wasserman, sitting below and behind the leader in the box position, started feeling uncomfortable. This feeling changed to distinct unease, when somebody called out on the radio "Watch the hangar!"

Easing up from his position below the leader, Wasserman entered Lewis's slipstream. A slight collision between the nose cone of Wasserman's aircraft, and Lewis's nozzle flaps, pushed Wasserman's Mirage into a steep nose-down position. He countered this manoeuvre by pulling sharply backwards on the stick, preventing a collision with the ground and the rapidly approaching hangar. The readings on his G metre after landing, showed -2 and +7 Gs, all within 100 feet of the ground. The following day the same team flew to Cape Town to complete the planned display, this time at a more comfortable height.

## Temporary OC 1 Squadron

On 4 March 1980, Commandant Lewis was posted back to headquarters to concentrate on the air-to-air missile project, leaving Major Theo Nell as acting Officer Commanding 1 Squadron. Nell received a directive from Colonel Huyser containing two objectives. Firstly, he had to improve the morale of the squadron's personnel. Secondly, he had to plan the move of 1 Squadron to AFB Hoedspruit, which was to take place over December 1980.

The two objectives were closely interrelated. The proposed move to Hoedspruit was the root cause of low squadron morale. Twenty percent of officers and half the senior non-commissioned officers did not want to leave Waterkloof. The problem was not one of disloyalty to the air force—it was purely based on domestic implications. Hoedspruit was situated in the bush 70 kilometres from the nearest town. Many wives had jobs in Pretoria supplementing the family income. But, because of its relative isolation, very few jobs were available in the Hoedspruit area. Teenage children living in Hoedspruit had to attend boarding schools and hostel and transportation costs could not be claimed from the state.

Nell also set his own objective, which was to improve Mirage F1AZ serviceability by 50 per cent. Extremely long lead times were being experienced in obtaining spares from France. F1 brake assemblies were a major problem and the normal flow of spares could not cope with the demand. Nell spent many hours in discussion with Mr J. C. Buissoin, the Dassault representative in South Africa, trying to improve the situation.

Nell remembers returning home late one evening, soon after taking over command of the squadron. Replying to his wife's question as to why he looked worried, he told her he had just signed for the 1 Squadron inventory; taking responsibility for over R500m worth of aircraft and equipment. This amount exceeded, by far, the total assets of some of the leading insurance companies in the country and Nell was a young major, whose net pay was approximately R1,000 per month.

Shortly afterwards, Nell flew an unsuccessful practice rocket-firing sortie to Roodewal range. All his rockets hung up, despite repeated attempts to fire them. He returned to AFB Waterkloof and, almost immediately after requesting joining instructions from the control tower, he felt a bump on the left side of his aircraft. Glancing left he had the impression of something falling off the F1AZ. He told the tower about the incident and said he would leave the circuit area to carry out a precautionary stall check of his aeroplane.

Turning through 180° he carried out the handling check which was perfect. Once again, returning to land, he noticed a rapidly spreading veld fire on both the northern and southern sides of the freeway that approaches Pretoria from the east. This fire had not been there on his first approach.

After landing, he carried out his afterflight check of the Mirage and noticed damage to the left-hand rocket pod. Heat build-up during the flight had caused a detonation of a rocket motor. Nell must have seen the inert head of a practice rocket as it jettisoned forward out of the pod. Rocket propellant falling from the aircraft had ignited both veld fires.

On 11 May 1980, Commandant Gründling led a nine-ship Mirage F1 formation flypast over Bay's Hill at AFB Swartkops, for the annual Air Force memorial service. On the run-in, in poor visibility from the winter inversion, Gründling realized that a heading change was needed to get the formation overhead the monument. He called, "Come left" to the formation and eight of the aircraft responded in a quick bank to the left. However, Captain Norman Minne, flying in the No 5 position on the end of the port echelon, missed the radio call. Suddenly he saw eight F1s turning into him. After a hasty stirring of his controls he regained position with a fluttering heart.

Republic Day 1980 was celebrated in the various provincial capitals. 1 Squadron was tasked to participate in two events. Captain Wasserman with four F1AZs led the flypast in Durban, while Major Theo Nell led another four to operate out of Port Elizabeth for the flypast in East London.

Landing at Port Elizabeth, after the ferry flight from AFB Waterkloof, Nell's aircraft burst a tyre. Being unsure that his aircraft would be repaired in time for the flypast he gave the formation lead to Captain Norman Minne. The tyre burst had delayed the turnaround of all the Mirages and Minne took off with his depleted formation ten minutes late. He accelerated to nearly 500 knots to make the planned rendezvous with an Impala formation. Nell, who managed to take off after the others had left, used full afterburner and joined the formation on the run-in to the saluting base. At 600 knots the formation positioned behind the slower Impalas for the crucial few seconds over the dais.

In Durban, the situation was reversed with the formation extending dive brakes, undercarriage and flaps to avoid being too early. Ground observers at both parades, blissfully ignorant of the frantic airborne evolutions, reported both flypasts to be on time and in the right place.

## *Smokeshell* and *Sceptic*

The border war had become cyclical. Every summer, during the rainy season, the terrorists would carry out their annual incursion into South West Africa from Angola. Lush foliage in the bush provided the cover they needed and there was a plentiful supply of water to sustain them during the infiltration. By mid-year, water supplies dwindled, foliage became sparse and the terrorists, if they wanted to survive, had to be out of Owamboland. They returned to base camps deep in

Angola to carry out retraining for the following year's operations.

During the 1980 incursion, SWAPO had demonstrated their aggressive intent by attacking AFB Ondangwa with a stand-off bombardment of mortars. The long-distance attack was inaccurate and the facilities suffered only minor damage. By mid-May, 324 SWAPO terrorists and 30 South African personnel had been killed in numerous contacts. Intelligence pinpointed two large SWAPO concentrations inside Angola, where retraining was taking place. Cabinet approval was given to attack these bases.

It had long been suspected that informants, living in the exclusive Waterkloof Ridge suburb of Pretoria, notified certain unfriendly embassies whenever large formations of armed aircraft took off from Waterkloof Air Base. These departures often heralded the next series of operations into Angola. To avoid the usual telltale signs, a deception plan was implemented when both F1 squadrons departed for operations *Smokeshell* and *Sceptic* on 6 June 1980. Throughout the afternoon aircraft took off in pairs, at irregular intervals, without visible underwing stores.

At 12h45, a 28 Squadron C-160 Transall left Waterkloof for AFB Hoedspruit, loaded with underwing tanks and wing-tip missiles for 3 Squadron. Between 13h00 and 14h00, 1 Squadron took off and flew to Upington for an overnight stop, as if deploying for a routine weapons training camp. From 14h00 onwards 3 Squadron flew clean aircraft to AFB Hoedspruit. On landing, 3 Squadron maintenance personnel, flown down in the C-160, configured all the F1CZs with external fuel tanks and Matra 550 missiles for the long ferry flight to AFB Ondangwa the following morning.

The next day, 7 June, both squadrons set out very early.

At 05h00 1 Squadron F1AZs took off from Upington on a 75-minute night ferry flight to AFB Grootfontein, where each aircraft was refuelled and armed with four Mk 82 bombs.

At 05h15 3 Squadron took off from AFB Hoedspruit on a 2h05-minute ferry flight to AFB Ondangwa. As it was winter, 1h45 minutes of the route were flown in darkness. Formation leader, Jack Gründling, made a critical decision as his flight came abeam Grootfontein. Although their fuel states were on minimum, he elected to go on to Ondangwa. Had they landed at Grootfontein the element of surprise would have been lost; it was suspected that informers were also operating near that airfield. On landing at AFB Ondangwa the belly tanks were removed and replaced with four Mk 82 bombs.

At 10h00 1 Squadron took off from AFB Grootfontein to strike the SWAPO base QFL as part of operation *Smokeshell*. QFL was just north of the Angolan border and posed an immediate threat to Owamboland. SWAPO terrorists easily slipped into South West Africa from this camp on nefarious incursions to plant mines and intimidate the local population.

Norman Minne's AZ had starting problems so he took off after the formation had left. He flew the mission alone, just slotting into the No 5 position of the last four-ship formation as the aircraft pitched-up from their low-level approach. The target was spread out along either side of a dry riverbed. 14.5mm and 23mm anti-aircraft fire was drawn from the camp but no aircraft were hit. The formation reformed after the attack and landed safely at AFB Ondangwa. Ground crew re-armed and refuelled the aircraft while the pilots planned the following strike.

At 12h30 Captain Otto Schür, a 2 Squadron Mirage III R2Z reconnaissance pilot, took off from Ondangwa with Pierre du Plessis and Darryl Lee flying escort in F1CZs. His mission was to photograph the airfield southeast of Lubango in Angola, to confirm an intelligence report that SA-3 missile batteries had been deployed around the airfield.

This confirmation was required before SAAF aircraft could strike the nearby SWAPO Tobias Haneko Training Camp (THTC). SWAPO sheltered under the umbrella of safety provided by FAPLA anti-aircraft installations, positioning their camps and bases within range of these facilities. This ploy did not always help them, as SAAF aircraft attacked SWAPO wherever they were found. It did, however, escalate the war as their Angolan hosts were drawn into the fight by default.

The reconnaissance flight proceeded as planned, with the three aircraft passing directly overhead the airfield. In transit, through the critical zone, the three pilots heard their BF1 radar-warning receivers (RWR) pick up the ominous sounds of locked-on enemy radar. However, no fire was drawn and the aircraft landed safely back at Ondangwa. At the debriefing, Commandant Mossie Basson confirmed that the warning received on the RWR was the guidance radar of the SA-3 system.

This fact caused considerable debate among the crews who were busy planning the strike on THTC. Schür's photographs, which would have visually confirmed the situation, were not available by the time the attack decision had to be made. Major Theo Nell, the leader of the planned strike, was understandably deeply concerned about the situation and suggested that the strike be delayed until the following day, so the photography could be studied beforehand. Nell was also worried that visibility at low level would cause problems en route, particularly looking up-sun late in the afternoon. However, the planners decided that if missiles had been deployed, they would have been launched at the photographic reconnaissance formation. In this case, it would be better to fly the strike sortie before missiles were deployed. Unfortunate logic as events were to prove. The advice of the operations and intelligence officers, as well as pressure from senior 3 Squadron pilots, outweighed and outranked the suggestions put forward by 1 Squadron aircrew. The decision was made to fly the strike.

At 16h45 Major Frans Pretorius, deputy leader of the last four-ship, had to stop the armourers from loading the last four bombs onto his aircraft, so that he could taxi out with the formation. Loading 16 Mirages was a long, back-breaking job for the ground support personnel. The other 15 F1s were configured with two underwing drop tanks and six Mk 82 bombs: four under the belly and two under the wings. Buccaneers from 24 Squadron, flying a different route to the target, were to participate in the strike by dropping their bombs on completion of the Mirage attack.

At 17h00, led by Major Nell, the combined strike of 16 Mirage F1s lifted off from AFB Ondangwa. He flew a large, teardrop pattern to allow all 16 fighters to join into their allotted positions. Leaders and deputy leaders of each four-ship flight were ground-attack F1AZs, with the CZ pilots flying as wingmen. If Angolan MiGs threatened the formation, these wingmen would jettison their bombs and give air defence cover to the formation. The four flights were planned to fly in line-astern.

Abeam Ombalantu, a standard navigational check confirmed that Nell's navigation computer was giving 'duff gen', so he handed overall lead of the strike to his No 3, Captain Dirk de Villiers. As predicted, visibility, especially towards the fast-setting sun, was appalling. Trying to maintain station within the formation became increasingly difficult as time progressed. The concertina effect, usual in any large formation, assumed major proportions as the leaders jockeyed to keep position. As always, it was the tail-end-Charlies at the back of the gaggle who suffered the extreme effects. Afterburner to catch up, dive brakes and idle throttle to avoid overtaking aircraft ahead, followed by quick dog-legs to fall back into position. A most uncomfortable situation, which became progressively worse as the flight continued.

The planned route took the aircraft well west of the target to a pitch-up point that allowed the aircraft to attack from north to south. The advantage of this profile was that the element of surprise could be expected as the enemy had their defensive positions facing south. The other advantage was that the run-out from the target was south towards base. Because all the aircraft would be low on fuel, this was an important consideration.

The formation pitched early, leaving the aircraft exposed to anti-aircraft fire for longer than was planned. The first three flights of four aircraft were all in reasonable formation positions. The fourth flight, at the extended edge of the concertina effect, was left dangerously exposed. As the aircraft broke cover, the SA-3 search radar immediately illuminated them. RWRs started screeching and Les Bennett, No 4 in the first flight, was heard to say, over the radio, "They're looking at us."

The correct roll-in point was achieved and the F1s entered the attack dive. The first four aircraft had a trouble-free attack, without drawing any defensive fire. Captains Hennie Louw and Darryl Lee, in the second formation, realized their dive angle was shallow and made bold corrections to their sight pictures before dropping their bombs. At release, Lee could see the entire camp area filling his windscreen. On pull-out he looked back to check where his bombs had fallen. He was in time to see a Soviet-built Gaz truck, driving around the camp perimeter, disappear in a cloud of smoke from one of the bombs. Later at the debriefing Colonel Ollie Holmes confirmed that the truck had been destroyed. It was mentioned in damage assessment signals sent out by the SWAPO camp commander after the strike.

During the pitch to roll-in point Norman Minne, the No 3 of the third flight, could see his designated target through the haze as well as a number of smoke trails. As he rolled in, he spotted three flaming missiles coming from his right-hand side. All three flames appeared to be standing still—the optical effect of missiles that are guiding onto your aircraft. He managed to call "SAM-3s, right 3 o'clock ... *'n hele kakhuis vol!*" (a whole shithouse full) before selecting afterburner, bunting his aircraft and pickling his bombs, which he overtook on his way down to low level.

At treetop height and full power he proved that the aircraft's belly tank, which had only been cleared for flight up to M0.95, could exceed the speed of sound. Once out of missile range he climbed up to altitude, finding himself among the lead formation. He had taken off as No 11 but landed No 3! On engine shutdown he had 300 litres of fuel remaining, enough for three minutes' flying at full power.

As the second four-ship approached release point, Norman Minne's warning was heard on the operational radio frequency. Captain Pierre du Plessis, seconds before release altitude, ignored the call, dropped his bombs and only then looked out for the missiles.

Minne's missile call and the strident tones of the RWRs convinced most of the pilots to egress at low level from the target, instead of climbing to altitude as planned. This low-level, fast run-out from the target combat zone played havoc with the planned fuel-flow figures. Consequently, all pilots became dangerously low on fuel during the return to base.

Flying on time and heading, the fourth formation arrived at pitch-up point for the attack. As they climbed, someone called, "Smoke to the right!" while Frans Pretorius, the No 3, saw smoke to the left. Fortunately, I. C. du Plessis, the leader, chose to fly onto the right-hand smoke that happened to be the bomb explosions, on target, of the previous formations.

At the apex of the pitch, the SA-3 search radar audio signals changed to continuous lock-on mode. Pretorius saw smoke trails of the missiles fired at the third formation and it took him a second or two to realize what they were. Looking up-sun, he realized that the missiles were flying out of a dark black hole near the town of Lubango. As he pulled his aircraft's nose down into the dive he saw two more thick beige-brown trails in front of him, passing from right to left.

Concentrating on his sight picture he released his bombs, initiated the pull-out while selecting bomb jettison in case any of the bombs had hung up, then looked to his right again. He saw three smoke trails coming towards him, but they seemed to be miles away and travelling very slowly. He could see that the right- and left-hand missiles had gone ballistic and were not guiding, because their flight paths were straight. However, the centre missile had a curved smoke trail, indicating that it was tracking his aircraft. Waiting to turn sharply into the missile at the right moment seemed to take forever; suddenly the missile's speed appeared to treble. Breaking hard right, he had rolled on 90° of bank when he felt a jolt and heard a sound similar to that of a breaking guitar string. This was followed immediately by a cacophony as all the emergency warnings were activated and the warning panel illuminated

Ignoring the emergency warnings, Pretorius dived to very low level away from the area. He did not want to eject over the target he had just bombed. He then realized that his aircraft was still handling correctly. The audio from the locked-on enemy radar was still blaring in his ears so he did not dare gain height to sort out the emergencies. Approaching a ridge, he realized that if he could descend below the level of its top the enemy radar would lose lock. Inverting his aircraft he pulled down into a valley, narrowly avoiding the treetops as he rolled out. He started to think rationally again once he was safe, realizing that if he were to make it back to base he would have to climb.

He began a shallow climb, but immediately picked up the missile audio warning. He turned his head around to look for missiles and saw a thick smoke trail right behind him. He broke immediately to the left but to his horror saw the trail following him. He snapped the aircraft into a reverse break to the right; the trail still followed him. Only when he glanced in his rear-view mirror did he realize the smoke was the trail left by fuel leaking out of his aircraft. His glance at the fuel gauges confirmed his serious predicament.

Cruise-climbing back towards base, he was eventually joined by Captain John Inggs. As he passed 30,000 feet, he heard the voice of the fighter controller at Dayton air defence radar, situated at AFB Ondangwa. The controller was warning all the returning pilots about MiGs trying to intercept our aircraft. Pretorius realized that his leaking aircraft would attract interceptors like bees to the hive. However, it turned out that the controllers, expecting a neat formation, were reacting to the blips of the spread-out strike force appearing on their screens.

Captain Dirk de Villiers, in the first formation, checking to see what was happening behind him, immediately focused on the trail left by Pretorius's leaking aircraft. He assumed it was the MiG formation approaching from 6 o'clock. De Villiers decided to plunge to low level but then glanced at his fuel gauges. He had 800 litres remaining but was 80 nautical miles from base. At low level, flying at ten miles per minute, the F1 uses 100 litres per minute. Under those conditions he would have arrived overhead with zero fuel. Although the plunge call was given, none of the aircraft plunged—all the pilots had done the same calculations.

As Pretorius crossed the cut-line at 31,000 feet, still 28 nautical miles from Ondangwa, the engine flamed out. He set up a glide and then glimpsed the thin black strip of runway just left of his aircraft's nose. The aircraft, minus fuel and underwing tanks that he had jettisoned over Angola, was so light that he realized he would make the runway. In fact, in the forced landing pattern, he had to make a 360° turn to lose sufficient height. On the downwind leg he delayed lowering his undercarriage and was then alarmed at how long it took to lock into position, using emergency procedures. He lowered half flap, then full flap, realizing he was still too high. To lose height he employed the old Harvard sideslip, learned many years before at flying school, which worked too well On rolling wings level he judged that he was now too low.

At this critical time, after the sweat and trauma of trying to fly back, emergency warnings still ringing in his earphones and with all 16 Mirages calling low fuel states and asking for joining and landing instructions, Pretorius describes how a guiding hand lifted his Mirage and placed it on the concrete strip at the very beginning of the runway. The drag-'chute worked and slowed the light aircraft quickly. Not wanting to block the runway, Pretorius turned off into the veld and stopped. After putting in his ejection seat pins, he slid down the side of the fuselage onto the ground, where he kissed the Owamboland sand. He walked back to the line hut on extremely rubbery legs. Pretorius was awarded the Southern Cross medal for the airmanship he displayed in saving F1AZ 244

On hearing Pretorius's Mayday call, Major Errol Hart, the air traffic controller at AFB Ondangwa, instructed all the other approaching Mirages to clear the airfield while Pretorius carried out his forced landing. None of the pilots obeyed this call—they couldn't! Their fuel states were so low they were all in imminent danger of suffering the same fate.

Meanwhile, Captain I. C. du Plessis in F1AZ 237, the leader of Pretorius's four-ship formation, was experiencing severe troubles of his own. In the mayhem around the target, du Plessis had been hit by two missiles and had lost hydraulic pressure and the use of the engine nozzle flaps. Although he had called that he had been hit, none of the other pilots had sufficient fuel to go to his aid. The Buccaneer crews had aborted their attack, after hearing over the radio the misfortunes that had befallen the Mirages. Disconcertingly, they were heard on the radio talking about du Plessis in the past tense.

Fortunately, Captain 'Budgie' Burgers, flying an Impala as Telstar radio relay for the strike mission, answered du Plessis's call for help over the VHF radio.

As du Plessis struggled to keep his damaged F1 in the sky he realized that Ondangwa was out of reach and he needed to divert to the forward airstrip at Ruacana. Having lost his navigational computer, he was not sure of the headings and distances he had to fly. However, as the senior Impala pilot at Ondangwa, Burgers had built up a wealth of knowledge about the terrain and topography of the operational flying area. Using the visual references that du Plessis said he could see, Burgers worked out where the damaged Mirage was and gave du Plessis headings and distances for Ruacana.

Du Plessis found the airfield and carried out a flapless landing. Using the emergency undercarriage selection, he managed to lower the two main wheels, but not his nose wheel. As a result, his landing run was much shorter than normal, because the aircraft nose scraped along the Ruacana runway. Captain du Plessis was awarded the Honoris Crux for his airmanship and courage in saving an irreplaceable aircraft. Both damaged F1s were eventually repaired and returned to operations.

When all the aircraft and pilots had been accounted for, a long debriefing was held in an attempt to sort out the root causes of the catastrophe. The intelligence officer produced the Mirage III R2Z photography from the midday reconnaissance flight, which had become available. Exactly in the middle of an 8 x 8 photo was a picture of an SA-3 quad-launcher with four white missiles clearly visible. A hard lesson was learned that wartime sorties required that all intelligence inputs be available before embarking on a mission.

Fearing possible retaliation from the Angolan Air Force, the planners decided to have the entire strike force ferry back to the safety of AFB Grootfontein. After debriefing, the pilots manned their aircraft and took off in the dark. Most of them had been on the go since 03h00 that morning. They had ferried to the operational airfields before dawn, carried out two operational missions, the second of which had been an adrenaline-charged affair and now were required to complete their 'longest day' with another night ferry flight.

AFB Grootfontein had a long runway, but the runway lighting had not been completed. To solve the temporary problem, emergency lights were used to mark the runway edges. Unfortunately, one of the first Mirage F1s to arrive landed a little short and dragged out the emergency lighting cable. The result was that for the rest of the aircraft the runway had lights only down one side. This was the straw that broke the camel's back. Not all of the pilots landed on the correct side of the one set of lights. Captain Mark Clulow alerted aircraft still in the air to the problem when his plaintive voice was picked up on the radio saying "Hey, major, I think I've missed the runway." After a visual check of the aircraft the next morning, a number were found to have grass and sand stuck in the wheel rims. One aircraft had even flattened a runway marker but none of the Mirages suffered major damage.

Mirage F1AZ 237 on the runway after being hit by an SA-3 missile over Lubango, Angola. Captain I. C. du Plessis received the Honoris Crux decoration for recovering his aircraft.

At about the same time as the strike sortie took off, Major Gerrie Radloff taxiied out at AFB Waterkloof to ferry a spare F1CZ to Ondangwa. The ground crew had hung and filled three external fuel tanks under the aircraft for the long flight. Unfortunately, this exceeded the maximum all-up-weight of the aircraft. It was the middle of winter and temperatures were low, so Radloff decided to fly the aircraft in that configuration.

The willing F1 staggered into the air and climbed, albeit slowly. However, for the first 400 miles it would not cruise without using mini-afterburner. Every time Radloff came back into dry power, the speed would decay and the angle of incidence would increase. The problem was solved only after sufficient fuel had been burned off.

That evening, as the strike aircraft ferried to Grootfontein, air traffic control diverted Radloff to the same airfield to join his squadron. Upon arrival, he had to descend to low level to burn off excess fuel before he could get his aircraft down to a safe landing weight.

A further combined strike on 10 June saw captains Darryl Lee and Wassie Wasserman paired up in another 16-ship formation. This time each aircraft was armed with eight Mk 82 bombs as the range to the selected SWAPO camp was much less than that of the Lubango raid. After an early morning take-off a perfect attack was carried out. All pilots dropped their bombs on the designated targets.

After bomb release, Lee pulled off to the left and looked back to check the fall of shot. What he saw was the smoke trail of an SA-7 missile curving towards Wasserman and himself. He called, "Stand by for manoeuvring!" but the missile broke lock and dived towards the ground. The relief was short-lived because a second missile appeared from the same area. Calling "Stand by to break left!" Lee watched as the heat-seeking missile broke lock and headed for the sun. A third missile, curving in behind, forced both aircraft to break to port. The missile then disappeared and exploded safely behind the F1s. To this day, Wasserman recalls this story to a tune taken from the 1970s' *Rocky Horror Picture Show*—'It's just a jump to the left and then a jump to the right'.

## Permanent OC 1 Squadron

During 1980, I was serving as the operations co-ordinator at AFB Hoedspruit. I had requested the appointment on completion of my tour as Officer Commanding 85 Advanced Flying School, AFB Pietersburg, in December 1978. I was 42 years old and convinced I had completed my last flying tour, but wanted to stay close to operations. The magnificent fighter base at Hoedspruit was still under construction and it was an exciting time to be stationed there.

One of the many tasks that fall on the shoulders of the operations co-ordinator (Ops Co) at any base is that of 'meeter and greeter'. It is customary and polite for visitors to a base to be formally welcomed, whatever time they decide to arrive. On the first Sunday in August 1980, I was at home in the 'House of Lords' at Drakensig preparing to sit down for lunch, when the duty air traffic control officer phoned to tell me that a light aircraft had just requested landing instructions. The aircraft was en route from AFB Swartkops and had started its descent over the Drakensberg escarpment. Apologizing to my wife, June, I jumped into my car and sped off to the base. On entering the main gates, I called the ATCO on the car radio and asked him which dispersal the aircraft would taxi to. He said that the passenger was in a hurry and did not want to bother with the extremely long taxi tracks. He had requested that I meet the aircraft as it cleared the main runway onto the high-speed turn off. As it was Sunday and no other traffic expected, I agreed and arrived at the meeting place at the same time as the aircraft.

I was curious and surprised at the demands from the aircraft passenger, but when Colonel Bossie Huyser emerged from the cabin, the mystery was explained. A fighter pilot to the core, he always operated in this manner. I imagine we probably did say hello to each other, although I can only recall that he immediately got down to the reasons for his visit. Normal greetings start with mundane small talk such as "How are you? Hot for this time of year" etc, but not Huyser. Standing on the runway he opened with, "Dick, how would you like 1 Squadron?" After considering the proposition for all of five seconds, I answered that I would like it very much. With that he clambered back into the aircraft, shouting over his shoulder as they closed the door, "Good, you start tomorrow." The aircraft engines burst into life and moments later Huyser was winging his way back to Pretoria.

Lunch was hardly cold when I returned after the briefest of meetings, but it took the rest of the afternoon to explain to June how our life had changed in those few, wonderful moments on the runway. To be given, virtually out of the blue, the opportunity to command the premier squadron in the air force was beyond my wildest dreams. In retrospect, my time in 1 Squadron was the culmination of a flying career in fighters that I would happily repeat, if that were possible.

Because I had asked to go to Hoedspruit, I was very positive about the place. The development of the base was unbelievably exciting and the lowveld had a charm and an appeal that made family living a pleasure. Only later did I learn to qualify that statement by adding, "... except for January, February and March when the heat is appalling". It was this positive attitude towards Hoedspruit that probably had most to do with my being appointed Officer Commanding.

1 Squadron was firmly entrenched at AFB Waterkloof in Pretoria. This arrangement suited most married personnel, as jobs for wives were available in the metropolis to boost the family income and improve the standard of life. The Mirage F1 project was relatively new in the SAAF and senior maintenance personnel had been posted in to ensure the success of the aircraft's introduction into service. These senior people also had children of high-school age nearing the crucial matriculation stage where they had opportunities of becoming prefects and earning coveted school colours for sports or academics. Houses had been bought and mortgage agreements entered into, using the combined incomes of both parents. Unmarried youngsters had the attractions of both Johannesburg and Pretoria to occupy their spare time.

Hoedspruit had none of this. New military housing was available but plentiful game, birds and bushveld were no substitute for the lifestyle available at Waterkloof. Air force planners decided that 1 Squadron was to move home over the Christmas period of 1980 when the new accommodation at Hoedspruit became available. This bombshell caused a crisis in the ranks of the maintenance personnel. Pilots are conditioned to relocate every three years or so and, generally, they are happy to move on to their next flying appointment. However, the ground crew were in turmoil for all the reasons already mentioned Some just could not afford to move. Huyser, in his wisdom, had realized that my major role would be to influence the squadron personnel positively and then move them successfully to the lowveld.

From August to December 1980, I commuted weekly between Hoedspruit and the squadron at Waterkloof. Even today, if I close my eyes, I can picture every bend of the 492 kilometres, through the Strydom Tunnel, Abel Erasmus Pass, Ohrigstad, Lydenburg, Dullstroom, until one enters the freeway to Pretoria.

I talked to the whole squadron on the pros and cons of Hoedspruit. We took the personnel on visits to show them the wonderful housing that would be theirs. Most of the men enjoyed the prospect of working in the custom-built environment of the new fighter base, so it was the wives we had to convince. On these visits we flew them down in DC-4 Skymasters as we did not want them to drive and realize quite how far it was from anywhere.

We were only partly successful. Despite all our efforts, some people just could not adapt and in December were posted out of the squadron. Unfortunately, most of those that left were the men who had been to France on orientation courses and had most experience on F1s. On the other hand, what we did achieve was to take only personnel who wanted to go. Although we had lost a great deal of experience, the positive approach of those who remained welded them into a team that overcame all difficulties. In every aspect of life, enthusiasm is the key that distinguishes winners from losers, and the men who formed the backbone of 1 Squadron in the move to Hoedspruit were winners.

Any success I might have had throughout my entire military career has been based on two beliefs, both of which I learned during my 12 years as a pilot in the Fleet Air Arm of the Royal Navy. Life in the military, on board ship, during operations and existing on a government salary, is tough. Therefore, it is a fundamental task of anyone placed in a position of responsibility to ensure that work becomes a fun place to be. By this I do not mean that a slipshod, happy-go-lucky approach should prevail. On the contrary, the more professional the atmosphere the better the team likes it, provided all unnecessary bull is removed. I have always believed that discipline, the basis of all things military, can best be achieved by an adult approach as opposed to the more traditional autocratic army manner of stamping of feet and shouting. This is certainly true in a flying environment, and I believe we succeeded. During this period not one pilot left the squadron for the more lucrative civilian flying sector—a testament to the fact that they enjoyed working in 1 Squadron.

My other philosophy was based on the words 'can do'. This quality is ingrained in naval aviation operations. Being much smaller than their respective air forces, both the RN and the USN have had to carry out operations without the services of acknowledged experts. The air forces have bombers, fighters, reconnaissance aircraft and in-flight refuelling squadrons with which to complete tasks—which they do expertly. The navies, not having the luxury of all these assets, have to do the job with whatever aircraft they have on board. Jacks of all trades by necessity but they do it. If a call goes out for help to an aircraft carrier the answer is always, "Yes, can do".

The SAAF, being a small air force, has the same problems as those facing the captain of an aircraft carrier. We have to use whatever aircraft we have to carry out tasks, and in the early 1980s, 1 Squadron was a 'can do' squadron. It would have been quite easy to plead not ready for operations owing to the loss of experienced ground staff, or the massive disruption to our logistics lines through the move to Hoedspruit, but not once did 1 Squadron fail to answer the call to duty. More on this later.

The task to successfully move and establish the squadron in its new home was carried out using the two philosophies as guidelines. This consumed the major portion of my time and effort throughout my years in command; all the rest was pure enjoyment.

I remember well the F1 conversion course which started on the Monday morning after Huyser's visit to Hoedspruit. Ronnie Knott-Craig, Ed Every, Billy Collier and Frans Coetzee were fellow students, all 20 or so years younger than me, all highly intelligent and eager to demonstrate to their new boss how keen and efficient they were—and they were. My long hours on the road commuting, the task of taking over a new squadron, combined with (I hate to admit it) my age, made me definitely not the brightest student on course. However, after I had been coaxed through the ground-school theory, they discovered that the 'old man' could at least fly properly, so all was forgiven.

My initial impression of the aircraft was formed on my first take-off from Waterkloof in F1AZ 224. She was responsive, easy and a delight to fly. Unlike the Mirage III, one felt in complete command from brakes off. The cockpit was small and pilot-friendly, with good all-round visibility and the flying controls well balanced. The roller map made navigation simple, provided that the set-up procedures were correct. One of the better improvements over the Mirage III was in fuel specifics. Although one still had to keep a close eye on the fuel remaining, it was nowhere near as critical as in the older aeroplane. The landing was 'a piece of old takkie' compared to the high nose-angle, high-speed, poor-visibility approach in the old Mirage III. First impressions are lasting and today I think back with very fond memories of the Mirage F1.

One of the secrets to effective command is to realize the latent capability of all those in your team and then give them the responsibility to blossom in their respective fields. Ronnie Knott-Craig for instance, was a brilliant scholar as well as a good pilot, who became an acknowledged expert on the F1AZ systems. The combined contribution of Knott-Craig, Jan Henning and the statistical genius of Mac Macatamney eventually produced the *Vergooi* bomb-delivery profile that was so successfully applied during the later stages of the border war. Knott-Craig was a great loss to the air force when he eventually decided to enter the commercial field in the Eastern Cape.

Billy Collier was a different kettle of fish. Also intelligent but he was, in today's parlance, much more laid-back. Collier first came to my notice by his repeated, slightly late arrivals for the daily 08h00 briefing. When I asked him why, he told me that it was because he was so regular, which sounded a bit Irish to me. I then found out that the regularity he spoke of pertained to his bowel movement which occurred at that precise time each day. Who am I to confront nature, so throughout our time in the squadron regular Collier was always that little bit late.

We worked long and irregular hours and I was in the habit of varying our home-going time to compensate for long hours worked. My other reason was to try to avoid the squadron getting into a 'factory' mentality of eight to four regardless. When I felt that I had had enough for the day all I needed to do was shout, "Billy". He would then wander through the readiness shelter which we were using as our headquarters at the time, shouting, "Time gentlemen, please". With that we would close up the shop for the day, or night, and head off back to the living area.

To the wives' disgust we developed Monday night into the squadron pub night, where among other things, the sins committed during the previous week were accounted for. Poor formation flying, breaks of radio discipline and late or occasional non-arrival at rendezvous points were all brought before the kangaroo court, of which I was the sole arbiter. If found guilty the offenders were punished by having to down a 'Yellowy'. This mixture of beer and Galliano, a bright yellow liquor of Italian origin, was supposed to put people off from ever offending again. It was only much later that Paddy Carolan pointed out to me that Billy Collier offended every week. It seemed that he had developed a taste for the evil potion.

The characteristic I remember most about Billy Collier was that his aircraft never ever went unserviceable. To this day I am not sure if he was just plain lucky, didn't know enough about the aircraft to realize when it was not serviceable or didn't notice if this or that was not working. Whatever it was, it was one of two reasons I picked him to fly as my wingman for operations during the border war. I knew he would always be there. The other reason quite simply was that he was an excellent pilot. Whenever I looked back at the formation, Collier would be in exactly the right position. No one can ask for more than that.

By mid-September the ground theory course, the familiarization flights and Mach 2 runs had all been completed and all we 'new boys' were being absorbed into the normal squadron programme. On 18 September I started exerting my responsibility as officer commanding by flying down on my own to Mafeking (now Mafikeng). A parade was to be held there the next morning and 1 Squadron had been asked to perform the flypast. I went to seek out the landmarks, turning points and holding positions necessary to ensure a spot-on time and place flypast. Professionals never 'cuff' it!

The following morning, after a thorough briefing to the rest of the four-ship formation, we manned our aircraft at the required time for a 09h30 take-off. Everything went perfectly until after start-up, when the ground crew signalled to

Top left: Bosbok light reconnaissance aircraft over Owamboland during the border war. Experienced recce pilots, studying the terrain from the air, could detect telltale tracks left by the passage of guerrilla groups through the area.

Top right: A 2 Squadron Mirage III R2Z reconnaissance aircraft on the ground at AFB Waterkloof. Each aperture under the nose housed a camera, allowing the pilot to take vertical and oblique photographs.

Left: When the bush was too thick to allow the Oryx to land, the pilots would hover while quick-reaction troops abseiled to the ground.

B-707 tanker of 60 Squadron with Mirage F1AZs ready to plug, escorted by four Cheetahs from AFB Louis Trichardt.

Above left: B-707 tanker refuelling an F1AZ, a Buccaneer and a Cheetah, representing the entire in-flight refuelling capability of the SAAF.

Above right: Parabats jumping from a C-130 Hercules. Often used for such operations but perhaps better remembered by troops as the 'Flossie' which transported them to and from the war.

B-707 low level over Roodewal bombing range, leading a formation of six F1AZ and six Cheetah fighters.

Alouette III being held aloft by a member of the ground crew.

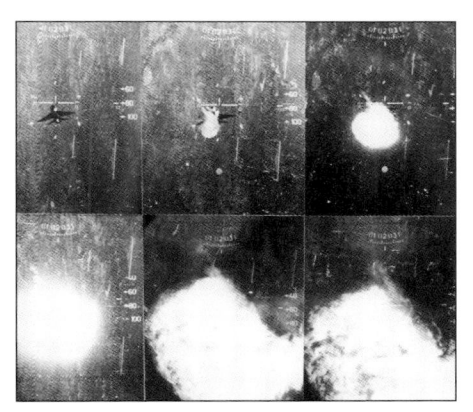

Above left: Camera-gun film of an Angolan Air Force MiG-21 being destroyed by Major Johan Rankin using 30mm cannon fire.

Above right: C-160 Transall of 28 Squadron landing at AFB Ondangwa during the bush war.

Left: A stick of Mk 82 250kg bombs exploding on the range at Riemvasmark in the Kalahari Desert.

Centre: South African 5.5 artillery pieces, captured by the Angolan Army, displayed in Luanda, along with other tropies of war.

Below: Seeker remotely piloted reconnaisance aircraft, used with success in the bush war.

The venerable DC-3 Dakota. This one survived a hit from an SA-7 Strela missile and landed safely back at AFB Ondangwa. The crew displayed outstanding airmanship.

1 Squadron in arrowhead formation with landing lights on and undercarriage down.

Below: Commandant Bossie Huyser leading three F1AZs escorted by two Mirage III aircraft prior to landing for the first F1 visit to AFB Pietersburg. High temperatures caused the tyres on all three F1s to deflate when they reached the hardstanding.

Pilots standing in position after flying a 16-ship Mirage F1 formation.
Front V from left: Pierre du Plessis, Jack Gründling, Wassie Wasserman, Willem Hechter (leader), André van der Heever, Fred du Toit, Carlo Gagiano.
Second V from left: Dieter Ortman, Dries Wehmeyer, Ed Deschamp, Darryl Lee, Les Bennett.
Third V from left: Thys Muller, Roelf Beukes, Bill Einkamerer. Tail-end Charlie: Piet Truter.

The first F1AZ 1 Squadron.
From left: Alan Norrie, Thys Muller, Gawie Winterbach, André van der Heever, Willem Hechter, Mossie Basson, Roelf Beukes, WO Wïid.

Above left: Remains of a civilian light delivery vehicle after detonating a SWAPO landmine in Owamboland.

Above right: A 3 Squadron F1CZ performing at an AFB Swartkop airshow, overhead a former 1 Squadron WWII Spitfire.

Left: F1AZ dropping four cluster bombs.

Below: A pair of Mirage F1s thread their way through mountainous terrain.

Above left: Alan Brand celebrates his 1,000th hour in the Mirage F1AZ with the traditional garland around his neck.

Above right: Retarded bombs exploding.

3 Squadron under Commandant Skillie Hartog.
Standing from left: Lt Tobie (T/O), Louis du Plessis, Frank Tonkin, Dave Klopper, Rudi Mes, Anton van Rensburg, Attie Niemann, Barnie Steyn.
Seated from left: Arthur Piercy, Steve Bothma (T/O), Mýk Lembisch (T/O), Martin Louw, Skillie Hartogh, Cobus Toerien, Jan Mienie, Peter Cooke.

Above left: Five F1AZs at the final flypast at the decommissioning ceremony of 1 Squadron AFB Hoedspruit, with everything hanging.

Above right: Mirage F1 diamond-nine formation.

Left: VC-10 tanker of the Royal Air Force topping up two 1 Squadron F1AZs.

Below: The author with his squadron at the revetments during the bush war.

F1AZ aircraft on the line at AFB Waterkloof.

Above: Dries Wehmeyer in 'Captain Caprivi' pose.

Centre right: Mac Macatamney, weapon system analyst, holding a Mk 82 pre-fragmented bomb on the weapons trial range.

Right: Mozambique Air Force MiG-17 escorted by two F1AZs of 1 Squadron. Lt Bomba defected to South Africa in this.

Above: 1 Squadron's operations room at AFB Ondangwa during Operation *Protea*. The artwork is courtesy of Paddy Carolan.

Left: Buddy-buddy in-flight refuelling from Buccaneer to Mirage.

Below: The tracks left by Mirage F1AZ 221 after Rickus de Beer force-landed 500 metres short of a runway threshold.

Heated ACM debrief in progress between Jeronkie Venter, Wayne Smal, Alan Brand and Rudi Mes.

Centre: The wreckage of Mirage F1AZ 228 near Lydenburg after Captain Digby Holdsworth ejected.

Left: A full-frontal exposure of an F1AZ configured with four rocket pods and air-to-air missiles at AFB Waterkloof.

1 Squadron under Johan Rankin.
Standing from left: Chris Skinner, John van Zyl, Dawid Kleynhans, Ivan Pentz, Johan Rankin, Trompie Nel, Norman Minne, Frans Coetzee, Nelis Genis.
Kneeling from left: Wayne Westoby, Lynch Jordaan (I/O), James Spies (T/O), Reg van Eeden.

Lear Jet target tug. Note the target winch under the wing.

Captured SA-8 surface-to-air missile system being recovered from a battlefield in Angola. Note the shrapnel holes from Mk 82 pre-fragmented bombs. This equipment is still used during SAAF ECM training exercises. Angola was a useful source of weaponry procurement during the arms embargo against South Africa.

Dolf Prinsloo dunked in a bath to celebrate his 1,000th Mirage F1 hour.

Above: The memorial stone to Major Ed Every who was shot down by an SA-13 missile in Angola. This stone stands in the Voortrekkerhoogte military cemetry outside Pretoria.

Centre: Fibreglass T-55 tanks used as targets to improve pilot skills. Project officer, Major Theo Nell, produced copies of a large variety of Soviet military equipment to enhance pilot recognition and weaponry training.

Left: Fibreglass SA-3 missile, another of Nell's creations.

```
>
                            = FREE TEXT MESSAGE =                    9106251216
FROM: HS001
TO: 40SD1

MESSAGE: TO COL LORD.,,,URGENT !!!!
         DEAR COLONEL, I THINK ALL THE F1CZ A/C ARE U/S DUE TO SQUARE
         TYRES FROM STANDING TOO LONG!!!!!AND THE FATTIES AND MOANIES
         ARE NOW FLATTIES AND MOANIES FROM FLYING TOO MUCH.
         KINDLY REQUEST URGENT RECTIFICATION TO SAVE THE BLUE FORCES!!!
         COBUS TOERIEN....F1CZ HUURSOLDAAT PILOT AND S/O FIGHTER/BOMB
```

Context of a free-text message to the author, complaining that the ability of the AZs to stay on task using IFR prevented 3 Squadron from getting their aircraft into the air during a force preparation exercise.

1 Squadron circa 1989.
Standing from left: James Spies (T/O), Alan Brand, Dawid Kleynhans, Ivan Pentz, Dieter Niehbur (FSG), Rehan van Tonder, Wayne Westoby, Nelis Genis, Lynch Jordaan (I/O). Seated from left: Trompie Nel, Paulus Truter, Frans Coetzee, Norman Minne, Dolf Prinsloo, Dirk de Villiers, John van Zyl.

Above left: Nine-ship Mirage F1 formation as seen through the HUD of the tail-end Charlie.

Above right: F1 formation with the snow-covered Drakensberg mountains as a backdrop.

Above left: Vic Kaiser wearing a big-headed East German helmet recovered from a battlefield in Angola.

Above right: A learner's plate drawn onto an F1 tail prior to a first solo flight.

Left: Commandant Dick Lord saying farewell to 1 Squadron while handing over command to Commandant Gerrie Radloff.

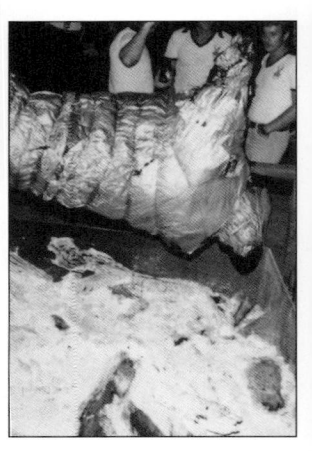

Life without a braai would be unthinkable.

me to cut my engine because of a hydraulic leak. Notice how cunningly 'Murphy' selected the only member of the formation that had been to Mafeking. After telling Frans Pretorius to take over as deputy leader, I shut down as fast as I could and ran for the spare aircraft. Pretorius and the other two took off and headed west. Time was critical as I rushed to get airborne, reflecting that a professional would have taken the deputy leader with him the previous morning—I had not. Pretorius would now have to cuff it if I couldn't get there on time.

ATC gave me a clearance to blast off immediately and after a high-speed drift onto the runway, I was into full afterburner and away on runway 01. Straight after take-off, a steep port turn onto the heading for the Western Transvaal. Unfortunately, the visibility was extremely poor as I came up for Hartebeespoort Dam at 500-plus knots. Suddenly, out of the gloom, at what seemed like the speed of light, appeared a Frelon helicopter. It was so quick that I did not have time to take any avoiding action, but thanks be to God, I passed directly underneath the helicopter with one or two feet to spare. Only 'Os' de Waal, the helicopter pilot, and I know how close we were to disaster that gloomy morning.

After a gulp, a deep breath and a quick "Sorry!" over the radio, I concentrated on getting to Mafeking quickly but safely. I arrived as the three-ship was on the run-in to the saluting dais. Frans and the others opened up formation for me to drop in as leader and we passed over on time and in position.

## 'Panty-ripping'

In November 1980 we managed to persuade 24 Squadron to configure their Buccaneers into the tanker role and the new course members carried out their first in-flight re-fuelling. My log book records that I had a success rate of 7/9 and 5/6 plugs on my first two sorties, emphasizing how controllable the aircraft is even under slow-speed handling conditions. Later on during my tour I seem to recall Billy Collier and I achieving a perfect 20/20 plugs between us—but memory might be a bit misty over the missed attempts. However, the aircraft is good in this role, once the tendency to over-control at the moment of entering the basket is overcome.

I remember briefing the squadron on re-fuelling techniques and emphasizing that you must look through the basket, not at it. Also you must approach with definite positive speed. Ed Every listened to my 'every' word and conscientiously applied this technique. Unfortunately, he missed the initial part of the briefing where I said you must stabilize your aircraft about three metres behind the basket before applying power to approach. Every stabilized about 30 metres astern, applied power positively, charged the basket, missed and went sliding up underneath the tanker, with the hose flailing down his starboard fuselage all the way to the tailplane—an exciting second or two, especially as it was accompanied by the basket rim beating a tattoo on the aircraft's skin.

Wassie Wasserman, one of 1 Squadron's well-known 'panty-rippers'.

We also had our fair share of 'panty-rippers' in the squadron. Surrounding the edge of the open basket is a canvas spreader whose aim is to stabilize the basket in flight. A desperate stab of the probe at the basket by a pilot who has made a poor approach sometimes resulted in the ripping of this canvas known in the squadron as the 'panty'. Not only did this curtail the remainder of the exercise but resulted, in our case, in the downing of a 'Yellowy' the following Monday night.

## A screw loose

While 1 Squadron were tanking, 3 Squadron were night flying. At 20h30 on the evening of 4 November, captains Johan ('Klein Dup') du Plessis and Les Bennett took off from AFB Waterkloof to practise night interceptions. It was a dark-moon period, the weather being overcast with a fresh westerly wind blowing at the surface.

On climb-out the pair checked with Major 'Dellies' Delport, their fighter controller at Devon radar centre. During the climb the fighters were separated with du Plessis turning north and Bennett, in Mirage F1CZ 208, going south. Once the required separation had been achieved the fighters were turned towards each other. Du Plessis acted as target, flying at 34,000 feet at Mach 1.3. Bennett, as fighter, was at 30,000 feet and Mach 1.2. The aim of the exercise was to practise a head-on Matra 530 guided-missile launch.

At about 15 nautical miles Bennett locked his radar onto du Plessis's aircraft and followed the head-up display flight orders to achieve the optimum launch position. Up until this point Bennett had been flying on autopilot but disengaged as the range rushed down to seven nautical miles in order to fly more accurately. As soon as the autopilot disengaged the aircraft started climbing quite slowly. Bennett checked forward on the stick but there was no response. The pitch rate was increasing while Bennett pushed the control column fully forward. He ran the pitch trimmer fully forward but the nose continued skywards. As 208 flashed through the target's height, fortunately without mishap, Bennett cancelled the exercise, realizing he had a serious problem.

As the nose reached 50° Bennett cut the afterburner and throttled back, hoping to reduce elevator efficiency. This did not help and as Bennett passed 42,000 feet he ruddered the aircraft nose down below the horizon. At this low speed, he moved the control column to the limits of its travel in a circular motion, without response. The aircraft was now in a 40° banked turn and descended rapidly to 8,000 feet. It took less than a 360° turn to get there. Bennett extended the take-off flap and lit the afterburner in an attempt to keep the nose attitude within reasonable limits while he tried to sort out the problem.

The aircraft 'stabilized' in a slow turn with the pitch attitude varying between 20° and 35°, speed oscillating around 120 knots and altitude changing between 8,000 and 6,000 feet. (Ground level over the highveld is nearly 5,000 feet.) The Mirage performed slow oscillations in altitude and airspeed, the period being about a minute. Buffet was severe and rudder control reversal occurred several times as the Mirage was almost completely stalled. The nose kept falling, first to one side and then to the other. It was like trying to ride a bicycle without handlebars over vicious corrugations.

Bennett was still in contact with Dellies Delport at Devon and the squadron's operations room whose personnel offered many suggestions to alleviate the problem. None of them worked. However, Bennett did manage to steer the aircraft closer to Waterkloof and away from built-up areas. His Tacan beacon gave a range of 62 nautical miles on a radial of 065° from the base.

While controlling the noseattitude, Bennett had kept the engine in mini-afterburner and consequently rapidly burned up his fuel. Thirty-five minutes after take-off and 20 minutes after declaring the emergency, the fuel low-level (400 litre) light illuminated, followed by the red fuel low-pressure warning light. The buffet at this stage was so severe that Bennett had to physically hold the instrument panel still in order to read the fuel quantity remaining. There were 60 litres left. (The consumption at this stage was about 200 litres per minute.)

With the nose now entering a downward cycle and a rate of descent approaching 2,000 feet per minute, Bennett tightened the seat straps, operated the canopy 'embrittlement' system, called on the radio that he was ejecting and pulled the lower ejection handle.

As the seat started moving upwards, his head sank onto his knees. He felt the drogue gun fire and the stabilizing parachute pulling him out of his seat. As he released the lower firing handle to allow the seat to fall away the main canopy opened with a jerk. Unfortunately, the cable whiplashed and broke Bennett's right arm.

He remembers seeing the aircraft's navigation lights rotating as Mirage 208 spun out of control. The engine flamed out about six seconds after the ejection and crashed about five seconds later. There was a very bright secondary explosion as the liquid oxygen ignited but remarkably little fire.

Bennett woke up on his back with the canopy dragging him over the ground in the brisk wind. He collapsed the 'chute and removed the harness and then discovered that he could not walk very well. His wrist was painful and when he looked at it he thought some of the canopy had lodged in his arm. There was a smooth grey thing just under the skin that turned out to be the bone. He had lost his helmet and there was a lot of blood down the front of his flying overall.

He tried to contact Dup du Plessis on the survival radio without success. Because walking was difficult he was pleased to see car lights bouncing across the veld towards him. Bennett fired a few flares to guide the driver in. A young man drove up in a Mazda 323 and gave Bennett a lift to the local clinic where he was cleaned up. A magistrate arrived and drove him to Groblersdal where he waited until a helicopter arrived to fly him to 1 Military Hospital in Pretoria. He spent four weeks in hospital with compression fractures of the spine and a spiral fracture of his right arm.

The board of inquiry found that a nut was missing from the bolt that connects the control column to the pitch pre-servo. When disconnected, the pitch pre-servo runs to the full pitch-up position and stays there. The SAAF discovered after the accident that the French Air Force had had an almost identical accident with a Mirage IV. (The Mirage F1 and the Mirage IV have similar control systems.) Bennett was returned to flying status six months after the ejection.

December 1980 was a traumatic period for all the personnel of 1 Squadron. Three pilots, I. C. du Plessis, Wassie Wasserman and Bill Einkamerer left on postings, while everyone else had the double task of packing up their homes and the squadron for the move to Hoedspruit. Before departing Wasserman took Dirk de Villiers aside and explained that there were very few people that fully understood the integrated F1AZ navigation and weapon system. He suggested that de Villiers should really study the system in detail to become the squadron expert in this field. That little input paid dividends to the squadron and the F1 for the remainder of its service life in the SAAF.

On 18 December 1980, in the middle of the move, the squadron was called on unexpectedly for another quick deployment to the operational area for Operation *Wishbone*. The aircraft flew two strikes against SWAPO targets at Oshiheng near

Ongiva and Palela near Xangongo in southern Angola. Four formations of five aircraft were flown with each Mirage F1 four-ship being led by a Canberra of 12 Squadron. Level bombing was carried out with all aircraft dropping their bombs on the orders of the Canberra bomb-aimers. Both sorties achieved poor results owing to bad weather, the inherent inaccuracy of medium-level deliveries and poor intelligence, which later showed that both camps were unoccupied. Both AZ and CZ aircraft were used.

Captain Norman Minne had arranged for the furniture removal company to move his belongings on 19 December, which his unhappy wife had to handle on her own. On the same day, she had to take delivery of the first brand-new car Minne had ever bought. Military duty expects a lot from the military wife and family.

# Chapter 8

# 1981:
# The pot boils over

### Arrival in Hoedspruit

Furniture removal companies worked overtime during the festive season moving families from Pretoria to Hoedspruit. Leaving one's home to settle into a new area is never an easy task and mid-summer temperatures in the lowveld made the move particularly trying.

On 14 January, the pilots drove back to Waterkloof by road to ferry the last seven aircraft to Hoedspruit. Major-General Ed Pienaar, a former 1 Squadron officer commanding, took the salute as we flew past in a figure 1 formation on our official departure from Waterkloof, after so many eventful years. On arrival at Hoedspruit, we were welcomed by Colonel Pierre Gouws, the base officer commanding, with ice-cold champagne.

When I study my flying logbook, I realize now how difficult the move really was. Instead of being concentrated in a hangar and on a flight line, the aircraft and personnel were now dispersed. Spread over a distance of three kilometres, each hardened revetment required servicing personnel and equipment. In the seven months from January to July I flew only 47 hours—hardly sufficient to keep a pilot current, never mind preparing him for the war which was getting ever closer. From August onwards, after what had been a long, hard struggle for the ground crew, serviceability started improving.

1 Squadron arrived at Hoedspruit without a technical officer because the previous CTO, Major E. P. Smith, had remained behind in Pretoria. In addition, the squadron had no sergeant-major, the traditional link between the aircrew and the ground crew. After a running battle with the personnel department at headquarters, I finally persuaded them to send Major Chris Venter from AFB Pietersburg to see me. Venter and his wife Rika arrived at Hoedspruit early in

January 1981 on one of those lowveld summer days that are best forgotten. The temperature of 42°C made conditions far from ideal in which to contemplate moving home. Fortunately, neither of them was deterred by the sweltering conditions and agreed to come to 1 Squadron. Venter arrived early in March as our only technical officer.

His first meeting with sectional heads gave Venter the shock of his life. The most sophisticated aircraft in the air force inventory were being maintained by technicians who had probably the least experience. Sergeant Chris de Lange was in charge of second-line airframe servicing and his wife, Annatjie, was serving in the stores department. Sergeant Willem Botha was chief armourer. Sergeants Gawie van Rheede van Outschoorn and 'Wessie' van de Westhuizen, the radio/radar section heads, were kept busy driving trucks between Waterkloof and Hoedspruit bringing down all the required squadron equipment. In charge of the instrument shop was a young corporal who had been qualified for only three months.

In view of the difficult conditions facing the squadron, I decided to ground all aircraft to give the ground crew time to work up into a team. It was a decision I never regretted. The one common factor prevailing among all the members was enthusiasm for the squadron, the aircraft and the air force. As Winston Churchill quoted during the crisis period early in the Second World War: "One volunteer is worth ten pressed men". We had enthusiastic volunteers who moved mountains to get the squadron flying and keep it thereafter in the air.

1 Squadron greeted on arrival at AFB Hoedspruit by Colonel Pierre Gouws, the base commander. From left: Mark Clulow, Ronnie Knott-Craig, Hennie Louw, Pierre Gouws, Dick Lord, Norman Minne, Frans Coetzee, Billy Collier, Theo Nell.

## FSG

A major step in the right direction was the formation of the F1 Support Group (FSG) in August 1980. The rush to get the aircraft into South Africa, before the arms embargo came into effect, resulted in the F1AZ not being fully developed by Dassault before delivery. Another serious implication was that information regarding the design parameters used by the French engineers in the equipment, like the navigation and bombing computers, was also withheld under the enforced embargo. Not being fully developed, the aircraft equipment had latent design errors, which would have been found and removed during testing if time had permitted. It became a matter of urgency to undertake this daunting task within the capability of the resources in the country.

Colonel Gert Nel and Mr Dawie Joubert, two very competent engineers, were presented with the headache. Gert Nel was the air force maintenance officer responsible for the F1 project. Joubert was manager of V Division at Atlas Aircraft Corporation. Together, they came to the conclusion that to resolve these problems successfully in an aircraft as sophisticated as the F1AZ, a top-down systems approach should be used. Instead of concentrating on individual aircraft components, the aircraft would be considered a system. Technical and logistical support was needed to be able to reach and maintain the required serviceability levels. Easier said than done, however.

It took six months to decide on the strategy to be followed. The SAAF did not have all the skills required within its own organization. Expertise from the aircraft industry would be necessary to cope with the expected problems. They decided to form a support group of highly skilled and motivated members of the Atlas Aircraft Corporation, who would be posted to 1 Squadron. These men would be under control of the officer commanding to obviate possible integration problems. This decision was a stroke of genius, as proved by problem-free acceptance of the FSG into the SAAF environment.

The Human Resources (HR) division of Atlas deserve an accolade for their composition of the group. Steve Blignaut of the avionics division was selected as the factory manager and co-ordinator, ably assisted by 'Onno' Sakkers and Richard Nichols. These three were notable for the resolving of in-depth engineering problems. The squadron group was led by Dawie Uys—once again an inspired selection. Competent, efficient and a brilliant team leader, he ensured that the FSG became an integral and indispensable part of 1 Squadron. His 14 colleagues included two married couples, Riaan and Rita Byleveldt and Hendrik and Sandra Terblanche, who were all members of the group. With housing a problem at Hoedspruit this coincidence was a bonus.

Between August and the end of 1980, the group studied the aircraft systems comprehensibly, to ensure that they understood the involved technical problems.

On arrival at Hoedspruit in January 1981, they commenced integration of the entire aircraft as a system. I can well remember Dawie Uys calling me to have a look at the first F1 the group had connected to the ESDAP testing rig. The aircraft looked for all the world like a patient in intensive care. There were pipes, tubes and wires connecting every orifice on the aircraft to oscilloscopes, cathode ray displays and even an instrument that appeared to measure the Mirage's heartbeat! From a painfully slow beginning the number of successful integrations mounted as the group's expertise increased. With each success, the enthusiasm of the pilots grew as they finally began to appreciate what a capability they had in their hands.

Enthusiasm is perhaps the greatest characteristic any person can have because it rubs off on others and is self-generating—the greater the success, the greater the enthusiasm. Job satisfaction for all the squadron personnel reached an all-time high during those early years at Hoedspruit. The FSG were solving complex engineering problems. The pilots were flying increasingly more accurate and reliable aircraft. SAAF maintenance personnel were increasing their skills by cross-pollination and all this, despite the long hours of hard work in the severe climatic conditions of an extremely hot lowveld. Team spirit within 1 Squadron was increasing all the time and was to pay dividends later in 1981 when the war escalated from counter-insurgency to a semi-conventional conflict.

The crucial 'heart' of the F1AZ is the linking of the navigation and bombing computers. Both these vital components had to be back-engineered to understand how the French-designed algorithms worked and how the sensitivity of transfer functions was affected. During these studies it was discovered that identical components lasted longer when installed in the CZ than in the AZ version. Identical air-conditioning systems were fitted to both aircraft but the substantially increased avionics in the AZ generated a heat increase that the air-conditioning system could not cope with.

Tacan (tactical air navigation system) failures were common, probably because of the heat factor, and at one stage reached critical proportions. An in-depth study revealed that the long logistic channel from Hoedspruit to 5 Air Depot in Pretoria was partly to blame. However, the main culprit turned out to be 3 Squadron! Being virtually next-door neighbours to the repair depot, their logistics personnel would appropriate repaired 1 Squadron Tacans, while 1 Squadron was kept under-supplied. Dire inter-squadron threats resolved the situation once the 'illegal' route was uncovered.

*****

Everyone was aware that the war was intensifying. The helicopter fraternity had been involved for many years and the signs of escalation were increasing steadily. At this time, one of the young security guards, who was supposed to be looking after the base, had taken a squadron *bakkie* (pick-up truck) for a joy ride around the revetments and had overturned it. There was precious little for a 19-year-old to do at Hoedspruit and the temptation had been too great to resist. Secretly, I sympathized with these youngsters who did an unrewarding, tedious job very well. However, with a deteriorating military situation, I felt that the guards needed to be made aware of the seriousness of the task they had to perform.

I contacted the base legal officer, a newly qualified university law graduate called up for his national service. I told him I wanted the case solved forthwith. The following morning I arrived at work to be met by this beaming law officer. He reported happily that the culprit had been found and would be dealt with.

At this point I interrupted, saying that I wanted an example made of the guard and that he should be charged with treason. Laughingly, the law officer said that would not be possible. I explained that we were in a war situation, with which he reluctantly agreed. I also pointed out that the culprit was damaging our war effort by destroying vital squadron transport. (This part was true because, without transport at Hoedspruit, nothing works.)

The law officer, with a perplexed frown, reluctantly agreed and said he would study the regulations to see if the young man could be charged as requested. I thanked him and then spoiled his whole day by adding that if the culprit was found guilty of treason I wanted the death penalty. With difficulty, I maintained my serious pose as the legal officer rushed off to check through his law books. At the summary trial the guard was fined a nominal amount, but cases of negligence and vandalism stopped immediately.

The lowveld, for all its charm, has no attraction for unmarried, red-blooded young men. The action was in the bright lights of the Witwatersrand. Consequently, on Friday afternoons a stream of cars left the base, heading at break-neck speed towards Pretoria. Late Sunday night, the weary warriors could be found wending their way back to Hoedspruit. It was expensive, exhausting and very dangerous.

After consultation with the squadron members I changed our work routine. Every day we started work 30 minutes before the rest of the SAAF. This extra half hour per day allowed me to close the Squadron at 1.45pm on a Friday afternoon, thus giving the young bloods more time to safely negotiate the perils of the weekend. They enjoyed it and so did the married members who lived at Drakensig. Friday afternoon developed into 1 Squadron's golf day, so we all benefited. However, there were some members of the SAAF who ignored all the beneficial reasons for the introduction of the new schedule. These people implied that if you wanted 1 Squadron, your best bet was to look on the golf course. Petty, but unfortunately some people are like that.

## 'The Snake Park'

Snakes were a way of life at Hoedspruit, although I can recall only two people being bitten. The first was the lady doctor who opened her garage door, disturbing the serpent lying along the bottom edge. The reptile took umbrage and sank its fangs into her foot. The other was Flight Sergeant Quintus Knobel from base workshops, who ran over a puff adder while driving back to the base. Instead of leaving well alone, he stopped and picked the flattened body up by the tail. The snake, with his last ounce of strength, struck out and grazed Quintus on his knee. Although only a graze, the venom was strong enough to lay Quintus low for a considerable period of time.

When the new residents started fashioning gardens out of the virgin bushveld, snakes were two a penny. Major Norman Bruton, who knew of my aversion to the creatures, used to refer to the place as 'The Snake Park'. Captain Paddy Carolan entered my office one day and invited me outside to look at his new pet. A large, thick puff adder had been seen slithering around the revetment and had disappeared behind a grey, filing cabinet. Innovative Carolan grabbed the nearest fire extinguisher and froze the creature. Taking the solid, stick-like body out into the sun, he had tied a cord round its neck and tethered it to a ring bolt in the concrete. He was most upset when I told him that he couldn't keep it.

John Orr, a 2 Squadron stalwart, caused a stir one Saturday by blowing off the roof tiles on his eaves with a double-barrelled shotgun, to kill a boomslang before it slithered into the roof. Oom Hennie Venter had to remove a baby python from a gutter near where children caught the bus for school. Oom Kerneels, a farmer who used to play tennis at the base club, capped them all by bringing a 14-foot python in the back of his bakkie to my house to show my wife. Kerneels thought it would be nice for June, who is from England, to get a close-up of things African.

The worst, by far, were the mambas. Second Lieutenant Les Carlisle, a national service security officer, rode over a two-metre black mamba on his 350cc Honda scrambler motorcycle while carrying out a security patrol. He watched as the obviously confused snake slithered away to enter a hole in a nearby tree. Carlisle, realizing that the snake could not see him as its face was buried in the tree, seized the reptile behind the head. He brought it back to the security camp where he kept it in his clothes locker. The 'kept' part was very short because as soon as we discovered what he had done, he was told in no uncertain terms to get rid of his pet.

The Mirage IIIs of 2 Squadron, the famous flying Cheetahs, shared the base with us. Great rivalry and camaraderie were the order of the day. Each squadron—quite correctly—thought that it was the best and went to great lengths to prove its superiority. Commandant Mac van der Merwe, the 2 Sqaudron OC, was an excellent all-round sportsman, so their sports results tended to overshadow ours.

The real truth has to be recorded— at flying 1 Squadron was always first, while

2 Squadron, by virtue of their name, always remained second. However, they did try manfully, especially Captain 'Jeronkie' Venter, a good, keen fighter pilot. The two squadrons would arrange 'Battle of Britain' type contests over the lowveld. Under GCI (ground control interception) radar control, we would be brought into ideal firing positions and proceed to simulate all sorts of missile 'kills' against 2 Squadron. At the debriefing Venter, who had just been shot to pieces, would open with his stock phrase: "Now this is where you made your mistake!" Fighter pilots the world over never lose their training fights. It is for this reason that I suspect, if Venter or van der Merwe were writing this, 2 Squadron might have emerged the winner.

## Border war escalation

Grim statistics at the end of 1980 showed that 1,447 terrorists had been killed at the cost of 100 South African and South West African soldiers—the heaviest yearly casualty figure of the war. Despite their grievous losses, SWAPO again embarked on an incursion into South West Africa during the rains of 1981. In an effort to expand the war, they sent infiltration units into Kavango as well as Owamboland. This SWAPO move achieved the desired result, effectively doubling the length of border that had to be defended.

Army, police and air force units in Sector 20, the military area centred on the town of Rundu, were reinforced to cope with the additional threat. By April 1981, 365 terrorists had been killed. The first week of July became the bloodiest of the year, when a further 93 SWAPO insurgents were killed.

The situation prevailing along the South West African–Angolan border had become intolerable. Escalation in an expanded area, and in the intensity of the war, could not be accepted. Defence Force capabilities and resources were being stretched unnecessarily. SWAPO, using the protection and often the logistics capability offered by the Angolan army, could approach close to the South West African border with impunity. From temporary bases they carried out quick forays into South West Africa to lay mines, intimidate local population, abduct schoolchildren and kill headmen, before slipping safely back into Angola.

With limited resources in equipment and particularly manpower, it made little economic or military sense to attempt an impossible task. Imagine a 1.2-metre-high, broken, four-strand wire fence stretching from Brussels to Milan. All the NATO forces in Europe would have extreme difficulty trying to stop determined people crossing from one side to the other. In South West Africa the problem was compounded by the dense bush, visibility often being reduced to 30 metres and less.

While politicians on both sides prevaricated, a military option to solve the problem was required. The answer decided upon was to prevent SWAPO using the 'shallow area' in Angola (up to 50 kilometres north of the border), from which to launch their raids.

**ANGOLA AND NAMIBIA**

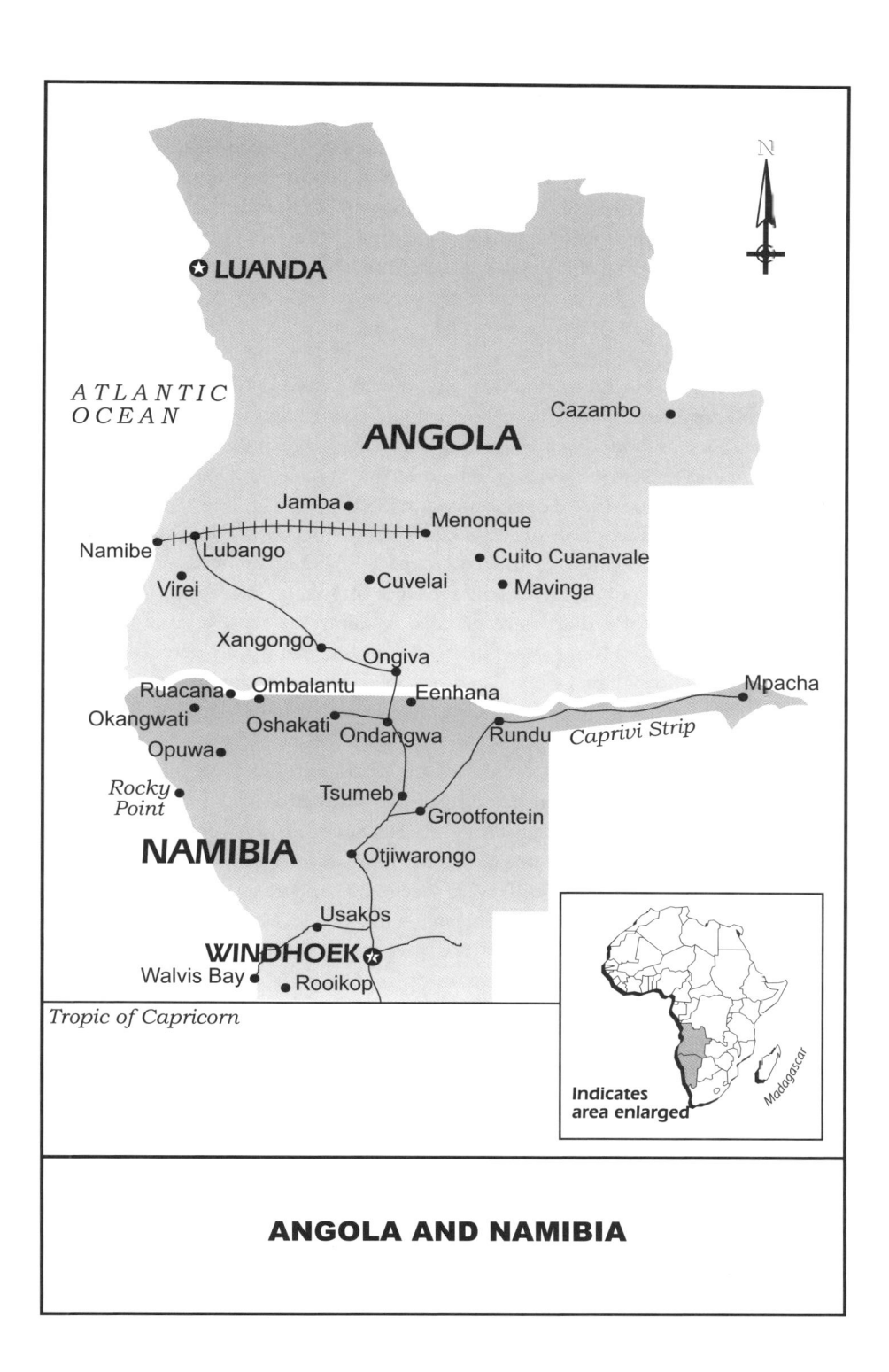

During mid-July Major Willie Meyer phoned 1 Squadron and asked to speak to me. I was flying at the time so the duty officer asked Meyer if he could take a message. Meyer declined, with the request for me to phone Headquarters as soon as possible. I returned from flying to find the aircrew gathered expectantly around my office. A call from Willie Meyer, an operations officer at Headquarters, meant one only thing—an operation was looming. When I spoke to him, he asked me to attend a meeting at Headquarters, nothing else. This snippet of news was all the pilots required to put two and two together.

## *Protea*

The meeting at Headquarters was attended by the planning staff and all squadron commanding officers. Approval had been received from the Cabinet for the launch of Operations *Protea* and *Konyn*, the air plan for *Protea*. All cross-border operational plans were presented to the Minister of Defence and only after Cabinet approval were operations launched.

The aim of *Protea* was to destroy SWAPO's military forces and logistical supply lines in the central theatre of southern Angola. SWAPO, and if necessary FAPLA, were to be cleared out of the Cunene Province of Angola, in order to safeguard our long border. Air strikes were planned to allow the army to take the key towns of Ongiva and Xangongo. Air attacks on the enemy's air-defence radars at Chibemba and Cahama were also sanctioned. The operation was planned to take place in the dry season—late August into September—to allow mechanized vehicles to be used.

Security was so tight that only after the operation had been planned and approved were the officers commanding of all participating squadrons informed. After a highly secretive meeting at Air Force Headquarters, we were told—almost under pain of death—that no one else in our units was to be informed. However, we had to ensure that all aircraft were serviceable and properly configured by mid-August. What a daft instruction, what naïveté!

On arrival back at Hoedspruit, I was greeted by the aircrew and technical officers who just happened to be near my office. Although I could not tell anyone what I knew, I still had to explain that squadron leave for August and September had been cancelled. But no one must know a thing!

I called Major Chris Venter, squadron technical officer, into my office. After ensuring that both doors were tightly shut, I told him I needed 12 F1AZs fully serviceable by mid-August. In addition, they must be equipped with live V3B missiles, drop tanks and rocket pods. Multi-ejection racks (MERs) and twin-ejection bomb racks (TERs) had to be ready at the same time for air transportation. When Venter asked me what all the preparations were required for, I looked at the ceiling, whistled a little, and told him I was not allowed to divulge any information. Live missiles could only mean border duty.

1981: The pot boils over

Miss South Africa, Michelle Bruce, who officially opened the 1 Squadron bomb shelter at AFB Ondangwa, with Commandant Dick Lord.

*Protea* was sub-divided into many smaller operations, all of which were designed to support the main objective. Mechanized ground forces were organized into two task forces, Alpha and Bravo. Both task forces included mobile air operations teams (MAOTs), made up of air force personnel. These small teams were to provide the army commander with necessary air support. Task Force Alpha, equipped with armoured cars, artillery, Ratel and Buffel armoured personnel carriers, was to bear the brunt of the operation, with the Angolan military establishments in Xangongo and Ongiva as the main targets. Task Force Bravo was to operate farther eastward to attack SWAPO logistical and transit bases in order to force them to positions north of Cassinga.

## *Konyn*

Operation *Konyn* was the comprehensive SAAF plan designed to achieve two main objectives. Firstly, the disruption and destruction of FAPLA and SWAPO's air defence system by means of air strikes against the radar installations at Chibembe and Cahama. These strikes, conducted independently of ground operations, were aimed at achieving air superiority giving freedom of movement to the ground forces. Secondly, air strikes were to be used against selected targets in support of the ground forces.

The helicopter, light aircraft and transport units had shouldered the burden of the war for many years. Now, as conventional operations were envisaged, they were complemented by Mirage IIIs, Canberra and Buccaneer bombers and the

Mirage F1s of both 1 and 3 Squadrons. *Protea* was the biggest SAAF operation since the Korean War—another step up the escalation ladder.

## Knife

Operation *Knife*, also a SAAF plan, provided electronic-warfare (EW) support to all forces during *Protea*. A ground communication–intelligence (Comint) team, based at Ruacana and ECM-equipped aircraft built up assessments of enemy radar and air defence dispositions.

On the morning of 21 August 1981, 12 F1AZs flew to AFB Grootfontein via Upington. Fuel and weather considerations dictated the route. Nevertheless, very heavy weather was still encountered en route. Three of the aircraft suffered hail and turbulence damage. Radar warning receiver (RWR) radomes, navigation lights and missile heads were broken or cracked. After aircraft repairs and lunch, the pilots flew on to AFB Ondangwa.

The rest of the afternoon and evening was spent in briefing and preparing for a strike the following morning. The target was the radar installation at Chibemba, codenamed Elephant. This revetment-protected site consisted of radar ramps housing Sidenet, Spoonrest and Flatface radars. The names are standard NATO codenames for the Soviet height-finding and early-warning radars supplied to Angola.

The combined attack was to begin with an AS-30 (air-to-surface guided missile) strike by low-flying Buccaneers against the radars. The Buccaneer pilots were to call if any SA-2, SA-3 or SA-6 missiles were launched and were to call off the next strike if any of these missiles were encountered. The F1s were to fly formation with Canberras to saturate the Elephant site with bombs. The F1 pilots were to release their bombs on command from the Canberra bomb-aimers.

At 10h30 the next morning, 12 fully loaded F1AZs took off from Ondangwa. The rendezvous with the Canberras over Ruacana was successful and the 'bomber-stream' then set off for the target. At 20,000 feet, the release altitude, the fully loaded F1 was difficult to handle at the slow speeds flown by the Canberras. Each Canberra had two Mirages in close formation on each wing. Navigation turns, particularly for the Mirage pilots positioned on the inside of the turn, were extremely demanding. Some pilots used dive brakes, flaps and afterburner in quick succession, trying to find a reasonable solution to the situation.

The target came up and passed directly under the nose. The formation flew on and on until finally the call was heard and the bombs dropped. Looking backwards, the crew could see that the bombs detonated in the bush, kilometres away from the target. Subsequently it was discovered that the Canberra leader had opened his bomb-bay doors too late, hence all the bombs were way over the target.

On landing, Bossie Huyser, now a brigadier in charge of Western Air Command, was hopping mad. The secret of survival in aerial combat is never to carry out a second run on a target that has just been attacked. Huyser had the decency to ask me as I stepped off the cockpit ladder if I would mind going back to repeat the strike. I agreed, but on condition that I took only Mirage F1s.

After the armourers had re-armed all the aircraft—a mammoth, backbreaking task, 1 Squadron re-flew the mission. This time the aircraft were easier to handle as the correct Mirage speeds were flown. The route was repeated, except that it was flown at low level to minimize radar warning, with a pitch-up to release altitude on the final navigation leg. This flight ranks in my memory as one of the best that I flew in an AZ. The reason was that I was flying F1AZ 232—an aircraft that had just come out of the rigorous ESDAP testing programme. Everything worked perfectly. Navigation computer, roller map, bombing computer and 'Sir Ponsonby', the automatic pilot.

The target was covered with a layer of solid, medium-height cloud, stretching east as far as the eye could see. Luckily, however, the edge of the cloud began directly over the radar installations. As we attacked out of the sun from the west, all the pilots had a perfect view of the target until after bombs were released. The pull-out was up and through the solid cloud into the clear air above.

Pilots reported that over 70 per cent of the bombs exploded within the target area. These results were confirmed by Operation *Knife* EW operators who reported that at strike time all enemy radars at Chibemba went off the air. Brigadier Huyser was all smiles in the pub that night.

On 1 September, a Flatface radar was picked up again, this time operating in the Cahama area. It too was subsequently eliminated by an air strike.

Major Gerrie Radloff, 3 Squadron's part-time pilot, was on an electronic warfare task overseas when the ops order had been issued. Sitting in the air-conditioned lounge of a five-star San Francisco hotel, he was called to the phone. Three days later, he found himself in the cockpit of an F1CZ at AFB Ondangwa, doing air defence standby duties in daytime temperatures approaching 40°C.

Meanwhile, Task Force Alpha had crossed into Angola, west of the Cunene River, and dug themselves into defensive positions near Humbe village, directly across the bridge from Xangongo. They prevented any FAPLA reinforcements from approaching the combat zone.

On 21 August, Xangongo was attacked from the air by Buccaneers and Mirage F1AZs and CZs. Each pilot had been allocated a target and received target photographs to make identification easier. Once again, the Buccaneers attacked, firing AS-30 missiles into the fort-like building at the northern end of the town. This building was the military headquarters of the area.

Each pair of Mirage F1s had been allocated to attack military targets, including transport-parking areas, defensive trench lines and anti-aircraft artillery sites, of which there were many. On completion of the air bombardment Task Force

Alpha fought their way into and then through the target zone.

Alpha then headed east to position for an assault on the airfield and military installations in Ongiva, formerly Pereira de Eca. Early on 27 August, four AZs, armed with four 155 rocket pods, each containing 18 x 68mm rockets, and 30mm cannon, launched the air assault on designated targets around the town. Moments later, another six F1s, each loaded with four Mk 82 (250kg) bombs attacked military installations around the airfield.

Being lieutenants, Johan du Plessis and Les Bennett found themselves flying as the 'tail-end Charlies' during this attack. By the time they rolled in, the Ongiva gunners had been fully alerted by the first eight Mirages. The two pilots found themselves diving through 57mm and 23mm flak layers on the way down and having to climb through them again on the way up.

Task Force Alpha fought their way through the airfield defensive positions and then regrouped, before continuing the assault on Ongiva. Jet aircraft of all types were used to pound FAPLA positions around the town before the ground assault began. Even then, close air support sorties were called in to attack pockets of stubborn enemy resistance. It was during one of these missions, that Captain Rynier Keet, flying a Mirage IIIC, was struck in the tail pipe by a heat-seeking, shoulder-launched, SA-7 Strela missile. Despite damage, he managed to land safely at AFB Ondangwa where the aircraft was repaired.

During the next few days the F1s were kept busy on close air support missions. Both Task Forces, Alpha and Bravo, intent on clearing remaining opposition from the designated combat zones, called for air support when faced with unexpected resistance.

## 'Citrus Board'

On 28 August, we were tasked to attack a SWAPO logistical base in the bush, northeast of Mupa. The briefing was excellent. Each pilot was given a photograph of the target. All ten AZs and four CZs were armed and ready to fly. Ground forces, under command of Commandant Deon Ferreira, were positioned just west of the target. They would attack immediately after the air strike, while the enemy was at his most vulnerable.

At 09h00, I led 14 Mirage F1s into the air. After impeccable low-level navigation, the formation rose as one to reach the perfect roll-in point. Photos made the target easily identifiable. A quick radio call to Ferreira ensured that the front line of own troops (FLOT) was faultlessly marked by the ignition of white phosphorus grenades. Pilots dropped all their bombs spot on the aiming points. The target was saturated. After release, while the aircraft returned to perfect battle formation, Ferreira called me on the radio to confirm a flawless strike. However, he added that during the entire attack, no enemy fire was seen. He later confirmed that his troops swept through the area without encountering any opposition. SWAPO had obviously received wind of the attack and had disappeared during the night. Ferreira and I were immediately elected as directors of the 'Citrus Board' for carrying out a combined attack that turned out to be the perfect 'lemon'.

## "Missile, 7 o'clock low"

Major Theo Nell taxiied out at AFB Grootfontein as a member of a large formation. The aircraft were heavily loaded with belly tanks, four Mk 82 (250kg) bombs and missiles on either wingtip. Leaving the security area, his aircraft bumped over the rail runner on which the security gate was mounted. The sharp bump caused the pitch-damper to pop, but it reset at the first attempt. Turning onto the runway threshold it popped again. Nell should have aborted the sortie at that stage. However, eager to fly the operational sortie, he reset the damper and started his take-off roll.

At rotation for lift-off, the most critical stage of take-off, the pitch-damper popped out again. As the heavy aircraft lifted into the air it started a pilot-induced oscillation (PIO). In a PIO the aircraft adopts a flight path similar to an undamped sine wave. The only way to stop the movement so close to the ground is to hold the stick rock steady, which Nell did. As the F1 accelerated, Nell reset the damper and continued the sortie without further problems.

Early on 1September, two formations of F1AZs took off from AFB Grootfontein to attack SWAPO installations south of Cahama town. Both strikes were met by heavy, but inaccurate anti-aircraft artillery (AAA) fire. Numerous SA-7 missiles streaked after the aircraft without scoring any hits.

At that stage of the war, mobile surface-to-air (SAM) systems had not been introduced by the enemy. The threat posed by Angolan SA-2 and SA-3 had been nullified. The positions of the static sites were known and avoided. If aircraft were tasked to strike targets close to these sites, low-level, high-speed profiles were used.

However, SWAPO cadres were equipped with SA-7 Strelas and these could be expected anywhere in the operational theatre. Light aircraft, transport planes and helicopters reduced the threat by flying very low, so the Strela operator usually had insufficient tracking time to achieve a successful launch.

The tactics employed by the Mirage fleet were to fly above 15,000 feet and 450 knots, the maximum height and speed of the missile. During strike sorties, targets were attacked using a 30° dive, releasing the stick of bombs at 10,000 feet above the target. The Mirages bottomed out of the ensuing pull-out at around 7,000 feet. Although this was within Strela range, if the aircraft speed was kept above 450 knots the missile could not, theoretically, overtake the aircraft. It was a good tactic that kept our aircraft safe, while raising the blood pressure of the pilots.

Heat-seeking missiles lock onto the hot jet-pipe exhaust plume given out by the aircraft's engine. The missile then follows a curve of pursuit profile, chasing the aircraft. All pilots in a formation strain their eyes watching for the telltale trail of smoke that signifies a missile launch. Immediate radio calls alert the rest of the formation. Time is critical as missiles travel at very high speeds. During training pilots are taught to call immediately a missile is sighted: "Missile, 7 o'clock low, three miles." At this warning all pilots swivel their heads around to the 7 o'clock position (12 o'clock indicates straight ahead and 6 o'clock straight astern). Pilots look below the horizon and focus their eyes at a three-mile focal length. On spotting the missile, pilots turn into the smoke trail. The reason is twofold. Firstly, the manoeuvre increases the tracking problem for the missile. Secondly, and more importantly, it allows the pilot to ascertain whether the missile is locked onto his aircraft or not. If the missile is locked on, the pilot will notice the distinct kink in the missile's smoke trail as it follows the turn of the aircraft.

During pull-out from the Cahama attack, this was the exact call that alerted me to the SA-7 locked onto my aircraft. As I turned, the missile turned, getting ever closer. At this stage, the flame from the rocket exhaust of the missile can be seen as an incandescent tip to the curving, approaching missile. I pulled the nose up into a steep climb, at the same time selecting full afterburner. Although this increased the exhaust plume being emitted from my engine, it helped keep the Mirage speed above 450 knots. During this hectic manoeuvring my eyes remained glued on the missile. It followed the aircraft's every move.

At what I judged to be 2,000 feet below me, the smoke trail and light suddenly disappeared—the missile had reached all-burnt range. However, the speed and energy of the missile allowed it to continue its flight. This was the most frightening moment of the encounter, not knowing where the missile was. Within a few seconds, which felt like a few minutes, I saw the missile detonate below and behind me. The theory had worked.

Late in the afternoon of 3 September, eight F1AZs and four F1CZs attacked the military vehicle park north of Cahama and the Flatface radar which had been detected nearby. Two F1CZs, configured for air-to-air combat, flew a combat air patrol as protection should Angolan MiG-21s venture into the arena.

On 4 September, *Protea* effectively ended with the withdrawal of Task Force Bravo to south of the cut-line. The only fighter mission of the day was a photo-recce sortie flown by two Mirage III RZs over the enemy fighter base, Menonque. The unarmed recce aircraft, escorted by four F1CZs, was unopposed.

Escort duty, particularly for the Mirage III R2Zs, proved to be extraordinarily difficult missions to fly because most of the sorties were being flown at extremely low level at 500 knots. Over the flat terrain of southern Angola, low flying is not too difficult. The major problem was keeping sight of the green and bright brown camouflaged PR aircraft.

Reconnaissance (recce) pilots like Major Otto Schür, captains Glen Warden (a really low flyer), Piet 'Pongo' van Zyl and at a later stage Keith Page and Leon Burger, were all extremely professional. They spent long hours planning the precise details of each sortie. Time of day, sun positions and length of shadow were meticulously planned to ensure maximum photographic coverage of each target. Rapid changes of heading and height to position their cameras made life difficult for the escort pilots protecting them. However, the effort was worthwhile and generally resulted in excellent photography.

Time is an imponderable of war. After five days a cricket test match is completed—not so a war. It is extremely difficult for operational planners to estimate the length of an operation. Enemy reaction, or the lack of it, often dictates how or when operations end.

On 30 August, I sent a signal to Commandant Willem Hechter, fighter planner at the Oshakati air force command post, requesting him to forecast how long the Mirage AZs would be required to stay in South West Africa. My concern was the continued efficiency of the onboard AZ systems. Constant flying caused deterioration in the accuracy of navigation and bombing computers. I needed to deploy the F1 Support Group (FSG) and their bulky ESDAP testing equipment to keep the AZs at peak performance. However, this was not required as on 6 September, all the F1s returned to their home bases as *Protea* was completed.

The aim of *Protea* was achieved. The Cunene Province of Angola had been cleared of both SWAPO and FAPLA. South African forces were firmly in control of Ongiva and Xangongo. UNITA forces were introduced into the area to help prevent SWAPO from re-establishing a presence. Short, sharp incursions by mine-laden terrorists became a thing of the past. Future insurgencies became physically more difficult for them. They had to trudge 200 kilometres carrying their weapons, before crossing the border. If they survived they had to return the same way. One has to admire their courage as every year they tried again.

During the elevn days of *Protea*, 1,112 individual sorties were flown from Grootfontein and Ondangwa, 333 tons of bombs were dropped and 1,774 x 8mm rockets and 18 x AS-30 missiles were fired. A Mirage III CZ was damaged by an SA-7 missile but landed safely. The air force lost an Alouette helicopter and the crew, Lieutenant Roos and Sergeant Stacey. They were shot down near the town of Mongua in Angola.

## Close shave in Durban

September and October were spent maintaining and retuning the F1 fleet. During this time Captain Darryl Lee was tasked to demonstrate the F1CZ at an airshow to be held at Louis Botha airport, Durban. He gave a low-level show in the morning and repeated it in the afternoon.

Before performing any aerobatics it is important to ensure that one is strapped very firmly into the ejection seat. When Lee took off for the afternoon's performance, he was unaware that his lap strap was entangled between the seat pan and his G-suit. Running in at 200 feet, he rotated his aircraft for an inverted pass down the runway. To maintain height while inverted requires negative G to be applied. As he pushed the stick forward he shot downwards, banging his head on the canopy as his straps pulled out from where they had been caught up. As his body moved downwards it automatically pulled the stick backwards, pulling the inverted nose of the aircraft down towards the runway. At 500 knots and only 200 feet above the ground, height is lost very quickly. Lee reacted by pushing forward on the control column and climbing away inverted. Only the experienced onlookers realized what had nearly occurred and why Lee took a long time before returning to complete the show!

Our experiences during *Protea* made me realize how fatigued all personnel became during sustained operations. The burden was particularly heavy on the aircrew. The operations co-ordinator at AFB Hoedspruit was Commandant Gawie Winterbach, who had been a founder member of the AZ community. He agreed with alacrity when I suggested that he should fly with us again. With his wealth of experience, he was soon a valued extra member of the squadron.

He realized that to become fully operational he needed to fly a number of night sorties, one of which occurred on a humid night when thunderstorms had been forecast. After take-off, he climbed out to the west only to enter a fast-approaching storm. Realizing the storm could cause problems, he turned around and returned to Hoedspruit to carry out circuits and landings.

The rapid descent from cold temperatures at height caused severe condensation in the cockpit, obscuring outside visibility, with moisture condensing on the inside of the canopy. Because of these problems, he decided to land off the first approach. The high nose-up angle on approach meant he had to look at the runway lights through the canopy where the front glass meets the nose. Unfortunately, being strapped in, his left hand could not reach the position to wipe the condensation away. His landing was probably the worst of his whole career. As it was night-time, nobody witnessed his undignified arrival, allowing him to preserve his pride.

## *Daisy*

By 2 November, both F1 squadrons were back in the bush, this time for Operation *Daisy*. Commandant Gawie Winterbach, on the staff of AFB Hoedspruit, was 'borrowed' by 1 Squadron to make up the required complement of 12 AZ pilots who were required. Winterbach had left 1 Squadron in July 1978, before they had entered operations in the border war. He was always very appreciative that he was given the chance to fly live missions.

When the pre-deployment activities were at their peak, our second technical officer arrived. Newly qualified Lieutenant Terry Crous had been appointed as the squadron electronic officer (EO). He was introduced to the ways of a front-line squadron when Major Chris Venter went to meet him as his furniture removal van arrived from Pretoria. Leaving Wilma, his eight-month-pregnant wife to unpack, Crous was taken to the base. After being shown round the squadron, he was told to pack his suitcase for operational deployment to AFB Grootfontein, together with the rest of the personnel.

On arrival at AFB Ondangwa, the ground crew began the laborious task of arming and hanging 250kg bombs. Meanwhile, the aircrew tried to persuade Commandant 'Div' de Villiers, Ondangwa's officer commanding, to give them better accommodation. The temporary nature of all operational bases in the bush meant that accommodation was always at a premium. During large operations, additional personnel were housed in traditional 16 x 16 army tents.

However, this was not the problem. It was the position where 1 Squadron's tents had been pitched, wedged between the noisy, continually running diesel generators that supplied electricity to the camp and, on the upwind side, the honey-sucker manhole. The quaintly named honey-sucker was a huge malodorous vehicle, used to empty the contents of latrines by means of a powerful suction system. It arrived at odd times during the day and night to fulfil its disgusting task, making life unbearable for those in the tents, especially during the mango season. We considered the tent quite suitable for the infantry or helicopter crews, but not for 'Vlammies'. We were unsuccessful.

Intelligence gathered from SWAPO prisoners captured during *Protea*, indicated the presence of a SWAPO headquarters in the Bambi area, southeast of Cassinga. It was suspected that the Angolans, with the assistance of Alpha and Bravo battalions, were contemplating retaking Xangongo and Ongiva.

A mechanized task force crossed the border on 1 November. After Ionde was found to be deserted, a tactical headquarters (Tac HQ) was established there, 120 kilometres inside Angola. The MAOT team at this headquarters was led by Commandant Dudley Foote, assisted by Major Mitz Maritz and Captain Ian Solomon. Air support officers (ASOs), majors Rod Penhall and 'Knoppies' Coetzer and Captain H. P. Cook, were attached to each of the ground force fighting teams assigned for the assault on SWAPO's Bambi headquarters, on D-Day, 4 November.

Radars knocked out during *Protea* were once again detected operating in the Cahama area. They posed a threat that severely compromised freedom of movement in the *Daisy* operational area. On 3 November, two Mirage III RZs, escorted by two 3 Squadron F1CZs, photographed the area to confirm the exact location of these radars. The high-speed pass over the target by the four Mirages proceeded without retaliation. On the developed films the radar installations showed up clearly.

On *Daisy* D-Day, 4 November, six C-130/C-160 transport aircraft took off from Grootfontein at 03h00 and dropped three companies of Parabats. Unfortunately, time constraints did not allow the recce team to illuminate the dropping zone (DZ), resulting in the main body of troops landing a few kilometres from the planned position.

The air strike began at 08h15 when three Buccaneers, using a low-level medium-toss manoeuvre, dropped 24 x 460kg bombs into the SWAPO Headquarters target. These bombs were fused with alternate Limbo (airburst) and contact fuses.

At 08h16 four Mirage F1AZs/CZs using a high-dive profile, attacked SWAPO's Bravo Battalion, each aircraft dropping eight Mk 82 (250kg) bombs that saturated the target. An SA-7 was launched but detonated harmlessly.

At 08h16:30 a further three F1AZs/CZs delivered 24 Mk 82s onto the same target. This formation drew AAA and SA-7 fire but no aircraft were hit.

Thirty seconds later, at 08h17, the next four-ship AZ/CZ combination attacked the same target. Dust from the previous bombs obscured the aiming point so the pilots released into the dust cloud. Certain of the bombs that did not release, owing to an electrical fault, were jettisoned over the target area.

The last AZ/CZ formation attacked at 08h17:30, drawing Strela and 23mm

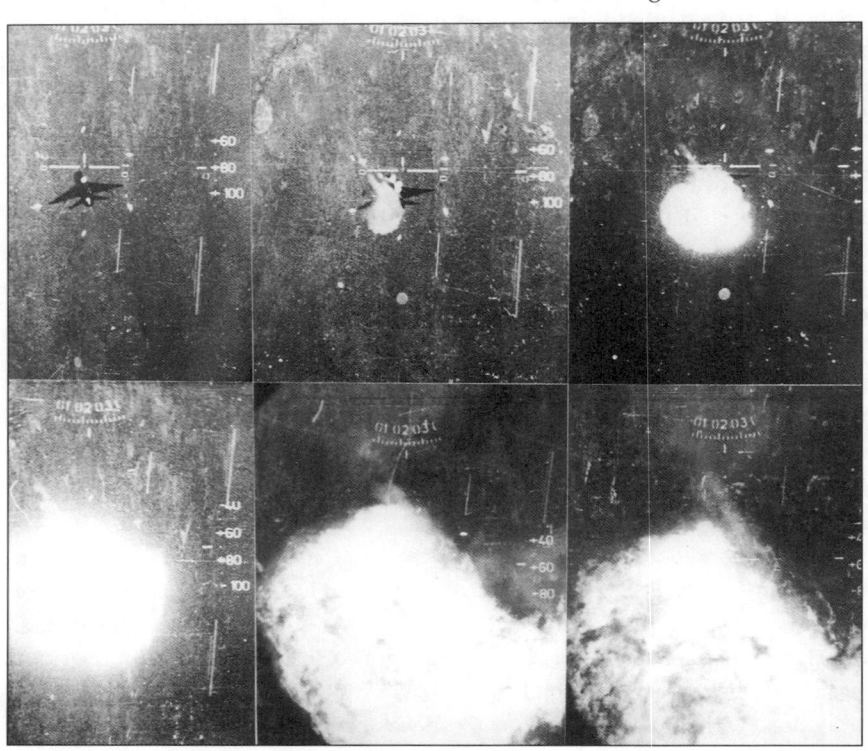

MiG-21 kill sequence as seen through the gun sight.

Johan Rankin being congratulated by Jack Gründling after shooting down a MiG-21.

anti-aircraft artillery fire which seen to air-burst at around 10,000 feet.

At 08h55 and 09h30 two pairs of rocket-firing F1CZs were called in by the ASO, Major Rod Penhall, to attack positions from where ground forces were receiving opposition.

Between 12h00 and 14h00, Mirage F1s and Impalas flew low-level armed recce flights to monitor the roads linking Bambi with Techamutete and Cassinga. No vehicle movement was reported.

An interesting feature of D-Day, which became more apparent as *Daisy* progressed, was the vast increase in MiG activity in southern Angola. Throughout the day reports of MiGs scrambling from Mocamedes (now Namibe), Lubango and Menonque were received. However, they appeared to be in a purely defensive role. The MiGs did nothing more than hold position around the Angolan airfields whenever SAAF jets were in the air.

At 07h00 on D+1, 5 November, 12 Mirage F1AZs/CZs attacked the Sidenet radar installation at Cahama that had been detected on the photographs taken on the recce flight. Each aircraft carried eight Mk 82 bombs with Limbo (airburst) fuses. Once again, pilots at the tail of the attack had difficulty determining the exact aiming point because of the dust and smoke thrown up by the earlier bomb detonations. F1CZ fighters, armed with missiles and cannon, flew protective combat air patrols during the attack.

During the fighting, Captain Paddy Carolan returned to base with the head of one V3 missile missing. Commandant Gawie Winterbach, who had carried out most of the initial test firings, assumed Carolan had done something wrong until, when pulling out of an attack on his next sortie, Winterbach lost the heads of both his missiles. A weak point, which broke under conditions of high G, was discovered. This led to a strengthened support being incorporated on all subsequent missiles.

In peacetime, the task of air combat manoeuvring (ACM—dogfighting in the old parlance) is probably the most exciting form of flying possible. However, during war fighter pilots spend vast numbers of hours on air-defence cockpit standby duty. Three or four one-hour shifts per day, strapped into an aircraft positioned in a readiness revetment, is a tedious duty in the extreme, although very necessary. This was 3 Squadron's lot throughout the day.

At 12h34 two F1CZs were scrambled to intercept a high-flying twin-engined aircraft reported by ground forces over the *Daisy* area. By the time the Mirages arrived over the area the unidentified aircraft had disappeared.

Major Gerrie Radloff was on the second-last standby duty of the afternoon, when the duty officer made him an offer he could not refuse. If he volunteered to stay in the cockpit for the last half shift before nightfall, he could sleep late the following morning instead of taking the early standby. Radloff accepted with alacrity. By doing so he missed the opportunity all fighter pilots dream of.

## First MiG kill

At 07h00 on 6 November Mission 269, the early morning shift, was scrambled by Major Marsh Facer, the Dayton radar fighter controller. He was tracking enemy aircraft moving south towards Quiteve. Previously during attempted interceptions the MiGs had always retired out of range whenever SAAF fighters were detected by their early-warning radar. On this occasion, the F1CZs used a low-level penetration up to the Cunene River to stay below enemy radar cover, while accelerating to combat speed.

Major Johan Rankin and Lieutenant Johan du Plessis pitched to 25,000 feet in fewer than 30 seconds and were undetected by the enemy radar controllers. Johan du Plessis sighted the enemy flying in the opposite direction as they passed between three and five nautical miles on the port beam. They identified the enemy as two MiG-21s flying in a fighting element formation at the same height as the Mirages.

Jettisoning their drop tanks, the F1s entered a hard left turn that brought them in behind the unsuspecting MiGs. The enemy were flying 1,000 to 1,500 metres apart, with the No 2 aircraft trailing 30° behind the leader's beam. The MiGs were flying directly into sun, precluding a shot with the Matra 550 infrared guided missile. Instead Rankin, closing from astern of enemy No 2, fired a burst of 30mm explosive shells from approximately 350 metres. Immediately, a puff of smoke appeared around the MiG and fuel started leaking from the fuselage.

The MiGs entered a tight, descending, left-hand turn and jettisoned their

**FIRST MiG KILL**

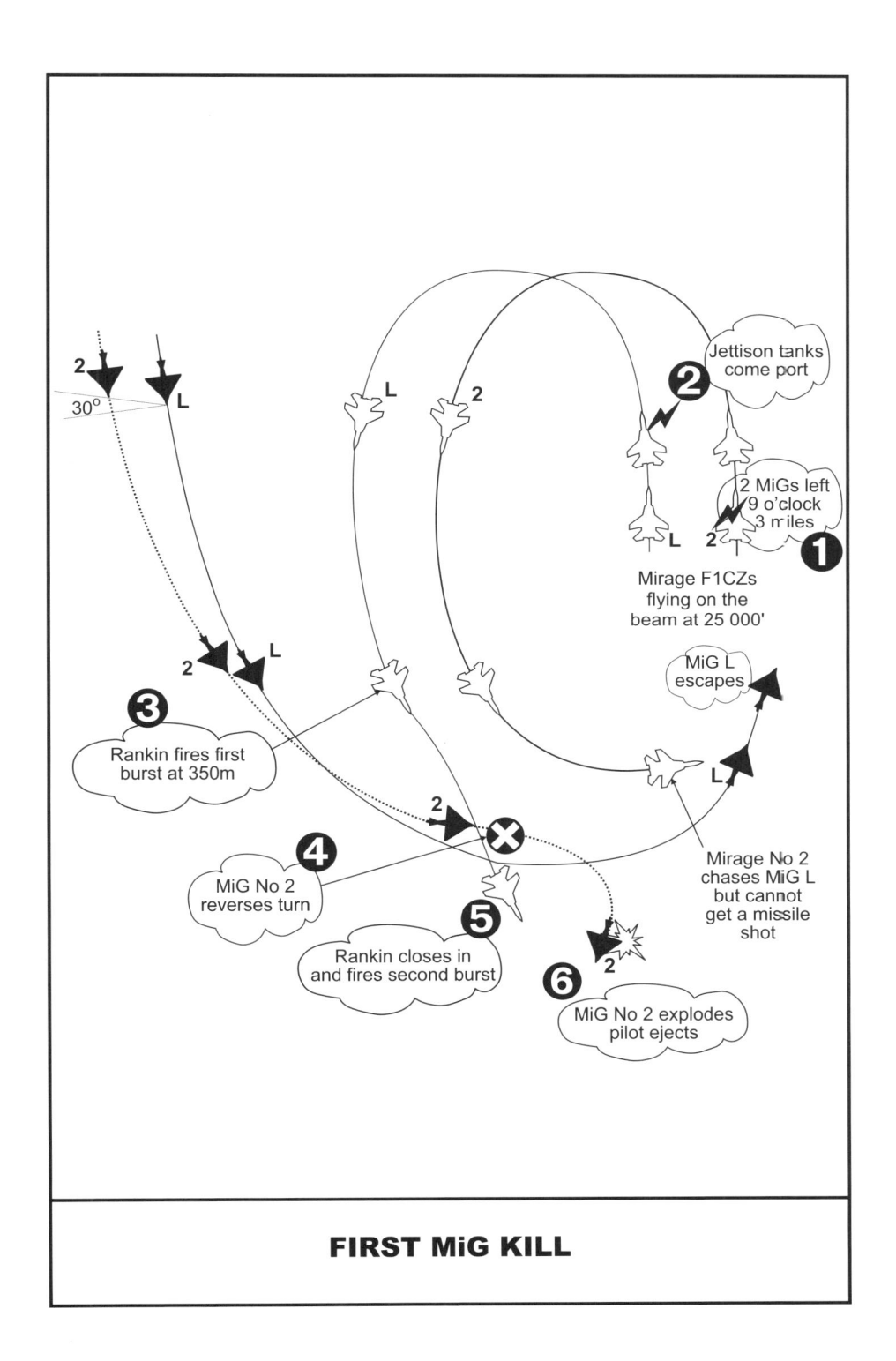

fuel tanks. Major Rankin, by now in missile range of the lead MiG, attempted to launch his own missile, which malfunctioned. Rankin re-entered a curve of pursuit on MiG No 2, telling Johan du Plessis to go after the MiG leader. MiG No 2 then committed a cardinal sin of aerial combat and reversed his turn, allowing Johan to close range rapidly and fire again with his cannons. The MiG exploded, immediately breaking in two behind the cockpit and forcing Johan to break away violently to avoid the debris. He watched as the stricken aircraft spiralled down in flames and saw the enemy pilot eject.

Meanwhile, Johan du Plessis followed the MiG leader who had entered a last-ditch spiral manoeuvre. Twice he entered the firing parameters for a missile launch but his missiles also failed to fire, the high-G descending turn possibly exceeding the Matra 550 launch limits.

Both Mirage pilots were fêted on their return to Ondangwa, the MiG-21 being the first aircraft shot down by the SAAF since Korea. The celebration was short-lived as all indications pointed to further encounters with MiGs with our air-to-air missiles shown to be below standard.

*****

Combat air patrols (CAPS) were flown over the ground forces' positions throughout the next few days, but enemy aircraft kept well away from the combat zone. Mirage F1AZs, escorted by CZs, flew a number of low-level armed recce sorties, looking for enemy vehicular reinforcements along roads leading towards our ground forces in the Bambi area, but nothing was sighted.

Major Gerrie Radloff and Captain John Inggs, tasked to fly an armed recce sortie, decided to fly at 15,000 feet above the Strela threat instead of at low level. They felt that at low level, the high speed of the Mirage made it difficult to pick up vehicles. The two aircraft, flying abeam of each other in a combat spread formation, flew either side of the roads they were scanning.

A truck was sighted leaving Tetchamutete heading south. Dust from moving vehicles on the sand roads of Angola is easily detected, provided that the flight takes place during the middle of the day. Long shadows early in the morning or late afternoon made visual sightings difficult. Radloff checked in with Captain Pierre du Plessis, the ASO with the ground forces, who assured him that it was definitely an enemy truck. Using a high-dive profile, the pilots attacked and destroyed the vehicle—their initiative had paid dividends.

It is never wise to climb back to altitude in an enemy-dominated area—the hot exhausts from climbing jets make excellent targets for heat-seeking missiles. Radloff and Inggs, therefore, stayed at low level as they returned to base. Coincidentally, Dayton radar had detected two MiGs vectoring in to attack the Mirages. Before Dayton could warn the F1 pilots, the Mirages disappeared off

**ARMED RECCE**

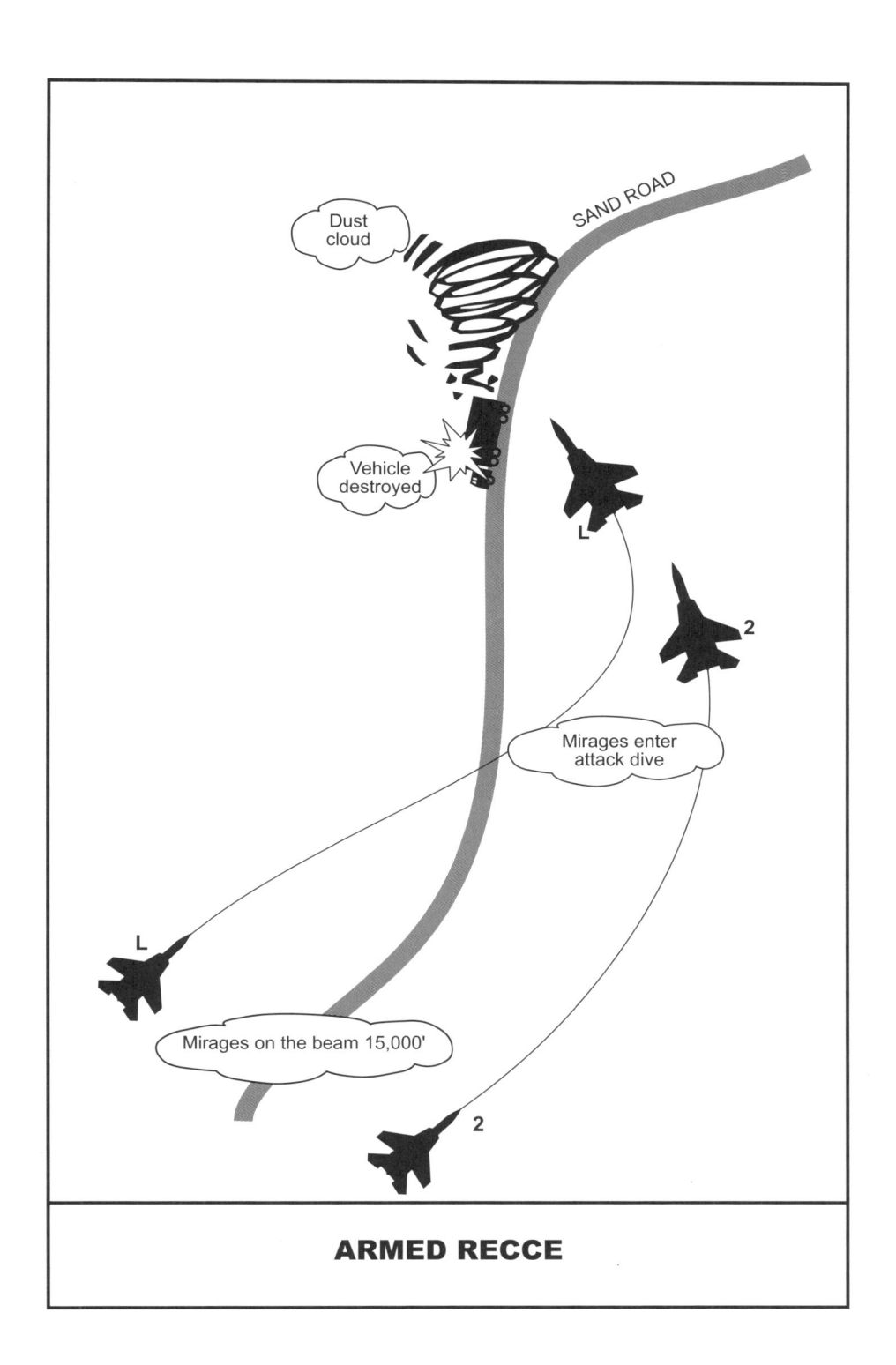

Dayton's radar screen. The Dayton controller did not realize it was because of the attacking high dive to low level. Dayton assumed that the MiGs had destroyed the two Mirages, causing great consternation. The problem was resolved only when the F1s landed safely at Ondangwa.

On the afternoon of 9 November, all Mirage F1s were placed on close air support (CAS) standby. Two Puma-loads of Parabats had engaged in a fire fight with SWAPO's Bravo Battalion. However, with the aid of four Alouette gunships, 24 out of a group of 40 SWAPO terrorists were killed and another five wounded. The jets were not needed.

Subsequently, *Daisy* petered out and by 17 November, the F1s of 1 and 3 Squadrons had returned to South Africa.

Alouette III 634 over Pretoria.

Oryx from 17 Squadron in a bank over Sutherland High School, Centurion.

# Chapter 9

# 1982:
# Stoking the fire

## Breathing space

As the New Year began and despite the debilitating effects of *Daisy*, the enemy still demonstrated aggressive intent. On 5 January 1982, a SAAF Puma helicopter was shot down and all three crew members, Captain Robinson, Lieutenant Earp and Sergeant Dalgleish, were killed. All signs indicated that the yearly incursion into South West Africa was about to begin and the bloodshed continue. This close-contact, seek-and-destroy warfare was fought by troops on the ground with helicopter and light-aircraft support. The fast fighters were not required, allowing much-needed time for aircraft maintenance and pilot training.

During the last week in January, in an attempt to improve operational weaponry results, I deployed 1 Squadron to Port Elizabeth. The army had a small shooting range near Grahamstown that none of us had ever used. We knew Roodewal range intimately and I felt that the good academic results being obtained by the pilots were as a result of their knowing exactly where to turn in for each attack. A change is as good as a holiday and the unknown surroundings in the Eastern Cape proved to be a challenge. I was delighted, therefore, when the pilots still maintained their high standard of shooting.

In order to raise the standard of technical proficiency of the maintenance personnel, Alf Claridge of the F1 Support Group, presented theoretical courses at AFB Hoedspruit. He was a brilliant instructor who was largely responsible for the high calibre of technicians who progressed through the squadron. Today, many of those young corporals and sergeants are serving in the SAAF as technical officers. The standard of technical competence improved in leaps and bounds. It was eventually possible for Dawie Uys of the FSG to hand over ESDAP responsibilities to Sergeant Dolf Bekker.

Eventually, the striving for technical excellence was to backfire on 1 Squadron. A large number of the most experienced personnel were removed to form the nucleus of the Cheetah maintenance and support team.

A very positive factor that greatly improved the availability of the F1AZ was the setting up of D-level test facilities at Hoedspruit. This facility, run by Deon Byleveldt of the FSG, catered for the servicing and testing of the roller map display, Aida radar, navigation and bombing computers of the aircraft. The long logistic channel to the servicing depots in Pretoria was thus eliminated. It was in this facility that modifications to the bombing computers were incorporated, to allow for the *Boomstomp* and *Vergooi* profiles that were to prove so effective in 1987/88.

## Armourers

A group that directly influenced the spirit of the squadron in those early years at Hoedspruit was the armourers. A more hard-working, enthusiastic and willing group of men would be hard to find. Always to the fore, whenever hard work was called for, were people like Daantjie Fourie, Willem Botha, Alan Dillon, 'Skippy' Scheepers and the rest of the team. So great was their contribution that Major Chris Venter informed Lieutenant Terry Crous on his first operation: "If you want to learn about the Mirage F1, work with the armourers."

Flight Sergeant Alan Dillon was in the habit of abbreviating ranks. He used to refer to a captain as 'capo' and a major as 'maj'. Once, on a deployment to AFB Ondangwa, all the armourers were taken directly to the bomb dump upon arrival. An early-morning strike the next day called for 180 x 250kg bombs to be prepared, fused and hung under the F1s, which meant an all-night slog for the armourers.

In the darkened surroundings of the bomb dump, Alan saw a 'capo' watching the activities. Being short-handed, he invited the capo to assist with the humping and the lugging of the bombs. He promised that in the morning he would personally show the officer around the best aircraft in the SAAF. Capo was set to work and ably assisted the armourers until well into the early hours of the next morning. As the sky lightened, capo was back on the scene. Only then did Alan see the capo's shoulder boards. He saluted at the same time as he stammered, "Oh shit, capo! You're a colonel!" 'Capo' was none other than Colonel Spyker Jacobs, the commanding officer of Ondangwa, who had willingly assisted with the night's hard labour while hugely enjoying the humour of the moment.

*****

Going up to the bush was always easier than getting back. Somehow, the planners at headquarters always supplied the correct number of transport aircraft at the right time to deploy the squadron. However, after an operation transport aircraft were never as freely available.

On one occasion, three C-130s were used to fly 1 Squadron to Ondangwa. On the return journey, only two were available. Fortunately, Major Peter Gardner, commanding one of the C-130s, realized how anxious everyone was to return to Hoedspruit. He divided the squadron equipment from three aircraft and somehow managed to get it all into the holds of two C-130s. There was no seating for the personnel except on the floor. The heavily loaded aircraft managed to creep into the air and only after they were well south of the Etosha Pan could they start the slow climb to cruising altitude. It was actions like this that welded all the air force components into a formidable team.

*****

Early in March, 1 Squadron deployed to AFB Bloemspruit, to carry out forward air controlling (FAC) training exercises with the army. Army officers were taught how to 'talk' pilots in to attack targets in close proximity to a land battle. Training is required to alter the mindset of soldiers, from the slow grind of an infantry assault to fighters moving at close to 14 kilometres per minute.

The army officer positions himself on a suitable vantage point overlooking the battlefield. When he has selected suitable targets that require immediate attention, he requests air support. Fighter bombers, armed with the correct weapons, fly to predetermined holding points within close proximity of the battle area. On arrival, the pilots check in with the ground FAC officer on radio. While the aircraft orbit the holding point, the FAC describes the target and its defences to the pilot. The FAC then passes a carefully worked-out heading and time for the pilot to fly from his holding position. Immediately after the pilot pitches-up, the FAC describes the target and surrounding area. The FAC tries to orientate the pilot to acquire the target visually and carry out the desired attack.

This training is vital for success in the heat of battle. However, on the training range these flights often result in extreme frustration for the pilots. Trainee FAC officers often suffer stage fright the first time they find themselves in charge of jet fighters. Instead of the fast, accurate commentary that is required by the pilot to find his target, the trainee frequently comes up with statements like: "As you pitch-up look for the tree in the big green field." Little does he realize that from 5,000 feet the pilot can see a thousand trees in hundreds of green fields. A good FAC can make a difference between life and death on a battlefield, hence the necessity for training.

After returning to Hoedspruit on 17 March, 1 Squadron had only a few days to prepare the aircraft for another operation.

## Super

Earlier in the month, a mobile Fireforce, consisting of 45 men of 32 Battalion, transported in Puma helicopters and supported by Alouette gunships, was involved in a highly successful operation north of Kaokoland. Operation *Super* resulted from an accurate intelligence report that SWAPO was attempting to open up infiltration routes in the far-western theatre. Their reason was twofold. Firstly, their casualty rate when trying to infiltrate through Owamboland was becoming prohibitive. Secondly, the opening up of routes through Kaokoland would stretch our resources and defensive capabilities.

Kaokoland is rugged in the extreme. It has a topography resembling the face of the moon. It is arid, with little vegetation or natural water and suffers the rigours of a desert climate—hot as Hades during the daytime and as cold as charity at night. The rocky, hilly terrain makes mobile, vehicular warfare almost impossible. This factor perhaps induced SWAPO to attempt an infiltration there.

Intelligence pinpointed the base camp, north of the Cunene River in Angola, from where the incursion would start. The Fireforce, led by Major Jan Hougaard, descended in a perfect surprise attack on the base. Fire from the gunships and soldiers accounted for 201 terrorists for the loss of three soldiers from 32 Battalion. After this setback, SWAPO withdrew permanently from the far-western theatre.

Close-up of an Alouette gunship 'office' during business hours. These helicopter crews performed excellent work during Operation *Super*.

## *Rekstok III*

However, this attempt by SWAPO to expand the area of the war worried the military planners, emphasizing the need for photographic reconnaissance throughout the operational theatre. Authority was granted for Mirage III and Canberra photographic aircraft to cross into Angola. Canberra coverage was required to update maps of southern Angola, while the Mirage III RZs gained tactical intelligence of specific pinpoint targets. Because 3 Squadron was unavailable, Mirage F1AZs of 1 Squadron were tasked to fly escort on these missions.

On 25 March, nine F1AZs arrived at AFB Ondangwa for Operation *Rekstok III*. Mission planners had scheduled the PR programme to be completed in two flying days. The climate on the western side of southern Africa is clearly divided into a predominantly long, dry season and four months of 'big rains'—when moist, tropical air produces huge, cumulo-nimbus thunderstorms. March is in the middle of the 'big rains'!

Twelve days later, after escorting a three-ship Canberra and a two-ship Mirage III RZ formation, 1 Squadron returned to Hoedspruit. Both escort missions were uneventful. The MiG pilots sensibly stayed on the ground, the threat posed by the weather probably being assessed as greater than that of the SAAF formations.

During the long Canberra sortie, escorts were provided in relays. As the first pair of fighters reached bingo (minimum to get home) fuel states, Captain 'Spook' Geraghty and I replaced them. Shortly afterwards, my radio failed and, waggling my wings, I indicated that Geraghty was to take over leadership of our pair of aircraft. This is standard procedure, except that our new boy, Geraghty, with only 20 hours' experience on the aircraft, was on his first operational mission in the theatre and hadn't a clue where we were. Blissfully unaware of his predicament, I maintained formation. Fortunately, the return route of the Canberras passed directly overhead AFB Ondangwa, the only place in Owamboland Geraghty recognized, and he led us down to a safe landing.

## Busy weekend

On 14 May 1982, after nearly six weeks at home, both 1 and 3 Squadrons flew into AFB Ondangwa. SWAPO's 1982 incursion into Owamboland and the Kavango had again been costly for their organization. Five hundred and twelve terrorists had been killed since the beginning of the year. Combined security forces had lost nearly 50 men in the same period. Despite operations *Protea* and *Daisy*, SWAPO was still operating hand-in-glove with FAPLA. The 'big rains' had ceased and targets identified from the March photographic flights were, therefore, to be attacked.

On the long flight north, Captain Geraghty was flying in a three-ship formation led by Major Paddy Carolan. Crossing Botswana, Geraghty realized that Carolan was drifting off course. Radio silence was a prerequisite to prevent enemy listeners from learning that the strike force was once more heading into their region. Therefore, Geraghty flew up alongside Carolan's aircraft and was perturbed to see Carolan's head slumped forward. Fearing anoxia, he moved into close formation for a closer inspection, which must have attracted Carolan's attention. Carolan looked up, raised the paperback book he was engrossed in, nudged the autopilot to bring the formation back on track and resumed his reading.

Two hours after landing two F1AZs took off to strike the railhead at Jamba, a mining town north of Cassinga. Both aircraft pitched-up from a low-level approach and delivered their bombs from a high-dive profile. Surprise was complete and no enemy retaliation fire was experienced.

At 07h55 the following morning, eight AZs and four CZs attacked a SWAPO logistics base northeast of Cassinga. Forty-eight Mk 82 bombs were released into the base, half armed with contact fuses and half with Limbo (airburst) fuses. Once again the enemy was caught off guard and no return fire was drawn. Two secondary explosions indicated that damage had been inflicted to SWAPO's logistics.

By 14h30, nine AZs lifted off to attack another logistics base in the bush, just south of Mulondo. The low-level approach caught the enemy napping and only limited AAA fire was drawn from the target area. Intelligence interceptions of the SWAPO communication system confirmed that substantial quantities of arms and ammunition had been destroyed.

By 07h17 the next morning, 16 May, eight AZs and four CZs departed at low level on track for Ruacana. Overhead Ruacana airfield 14 minutes 15 seconds later, the formation turned north across the border, accelerating to 540 knots. Abeam Techipa the pilots 'hacked' (reset the cockpit clocks) to accurately time the run-in to the PUP (pitch-up point) three minutes later. At the pitch point, pilots pulled their aircraft in to a high nose-up attitude to climb rapidly to 18,000 feet. A left-hand roll-in ensured that the high dive came out of the rising sun, blinding the enemy gunners waiting on the ground. The pilots used the few seconds at the top of the dive to orientate themselves by glancing at the area photographs carried in each cockpit. In the dive, each pilot concentrated on his individual aiming point to achieve a good bomb release.

Cahama was famous for its resistance whenever a SAAF aircraft was in the vicinity of the town. On this occasion they did not disappoint. Heavy 23mm and 57mm fire was seen exploding among the diving aircraft, but no aeroplane was hit.

By 08h07 all the Mirage F1s had landed safely back at Ondangwa.

The hard-working ground crew had only three hours to prepare all the aircraft for the next strike at 11h50, against a Cuban position south of Jamba airfield. The

**DIAGRAM ILLUSTRATING
A STRIKE OUT OF THE SUN**

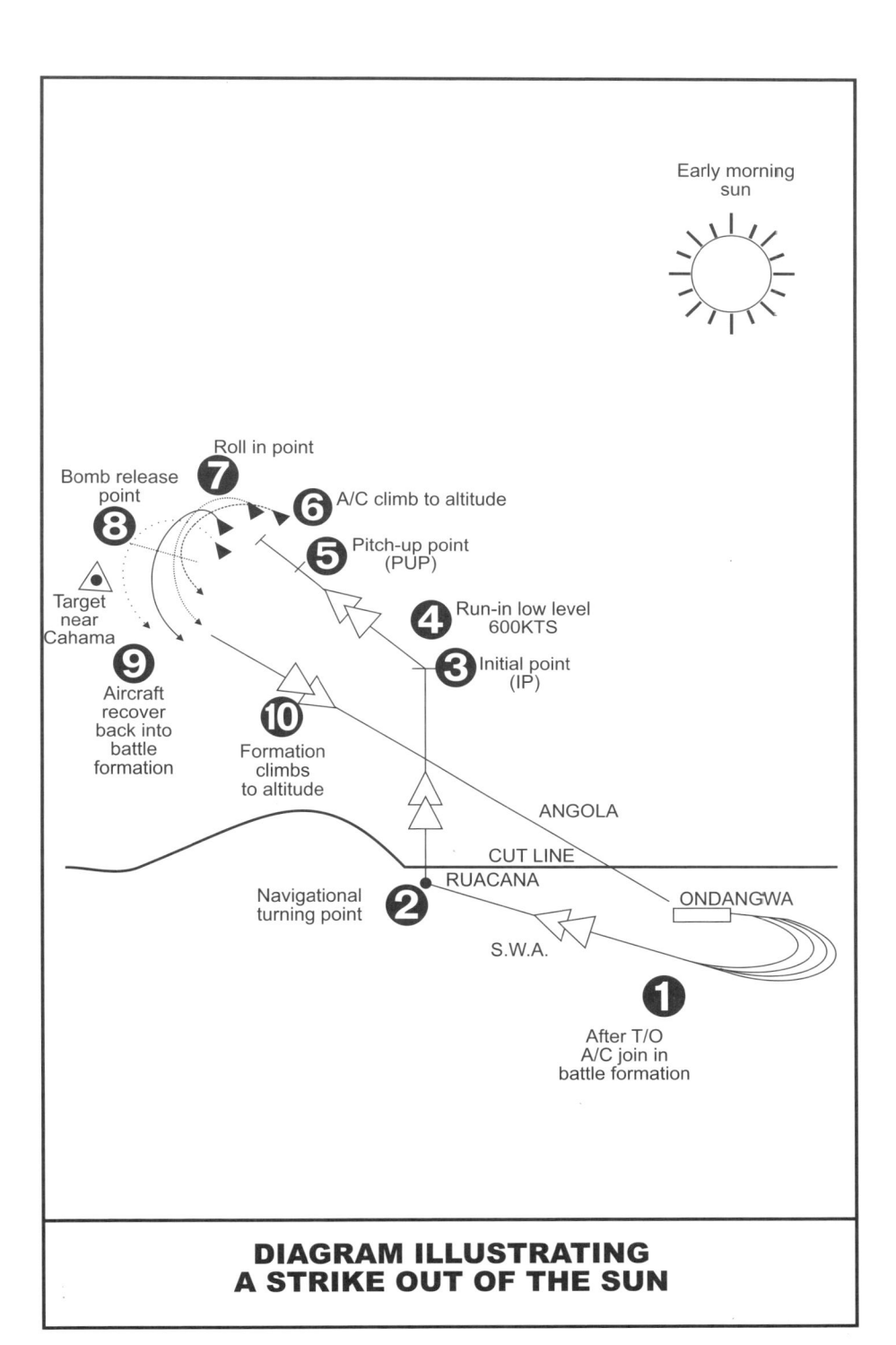

Graffiti on bombs bound for Sam Nujoma's guerrillas.

Cubans had been giving constant support to SWAPO and the aim of this strike was to persuade them that this was unhealthy.

Three four-ship F1 formations attacked the Cuban positions from the west. The usual 57mm AAA was drawn but on this occasion the Mirages were faced, for the first time, with heavy fire from mobile ZSU 23-4 Schilka batteries. These four-barrelled, rapid-firing cannons were off target, fortunately. However, their effect increases the pilot's adrenaline flow. As the shells explode, they form an immediate thick, white cloud bank. During the attack dive, an AN-26 Soviet-built, twin-engined, transport aircraft was observed on the airfield hardstanding, but was not attacked.

Later, the same afternoon, four AZs and four CZs returned to Cahama, this time to pound the active AAA sites that had been seen firing during the morning attack. This strike had fighter protection from Mirage F1CZs, so the procedure was altered. As the strike reached roll-in altitude, only the leader rolled in. The other pilots orbited, while watching the leader in his dive. When the expected AAA firing started, Mirage No 2 attacked that AAA site. This pattern repeated itself until all eight aircraft had dropped their bombs. No enemy MiGs attempted to gatecrash the party. The following day, all Mirages returned to their home bases after a most successful operation.

During operational deployment, ground crew often wrote derogatory anti-SWAPO messages on the aircrafts' bombs before they loaded them. If the target range allowed, underwing or belly fuel tanks were removed and stored in rows at the edge of the hardstanding. One morning rude, suggestive and lewd remarks were found painted and scratched onto these tanks. The culprits were passing soldiers who'd thought the tanks were extra-large bombs

## Rest and recreation

Squadron life is not all work and efforts are made to relax. 3 Squadron used to spend weekends at the Buffelspoort holiday resort in the Magaliesberg Mountains, west of Pretoria. During one of these visits the pilots, wives and girlfriends were standing around the communal braai, beers in hand, when a largish snake was spotted in a tree immediately above them. Everybody scattered, leaving the meat on the fire.

This unsatisfactory situation had to be resolved, so three junior lieutenants were tasked to remove the offending reptile. Grabbing a broom, Tinkie Jones, Darryl Lee and Les Bennett led the attack. After a few shakes of the branch, the snake fell onto the grass and was immediately seized behind the head by Bennett in a most professional manner. Unfortunately, he had already downed a 'Charles Glass' (Castle beer) or two and, although he grabbed the snake correctly between thumb and forefinger, his grip was too far from the creature's head. Upset by being so rudely disturbed, the snake turned around and bit Bennett on the hand.

Making a quick operational appreciation, the intrepid three loaded the snake into an empty container. With the snake bottle in one hand and a Castle in the other, Bennett was strapped into the passenger seat of a car by the two other lieutenants. They sped off to the Hartebeespoort Snake Park where, upon arrival, they rushed in to ask the curator to identify the snake.

Looking through the glass he remarked, "Man, what a beautiful boomslang!" at which Bennett nearly fainted with fright. The boomslang is one of Africa's most poisonous reptiles. They then informed the curator that Bennett had been bitten by it 45 minutes earlier. He shrugged and said, "If he's not dead yet, then he will be okay"—and walked off. Regaining their 'fighter-pilot' pose, three wiser young men hopped back into the car and returned to the slightly overdone meat on the braai.

## At Waterkloof

An interesting lesson was learned during training when, after a rapid descent from a long, high-level sortie flown by Commandant Jack Gründling, the aircraft's main-wheel tyres burst on landing. The micro-switches that allow the Spad braking system to operate had iced up. The rapid re-entry into the landing circuit did not allow sufficient time for the ice to thaw in the warmer temperatures at low level. When the foot brakes were applied, the wheels locked instead of gradually decelerating the aircraft.

The management system Gründling introduced at 3 Squadron helped them

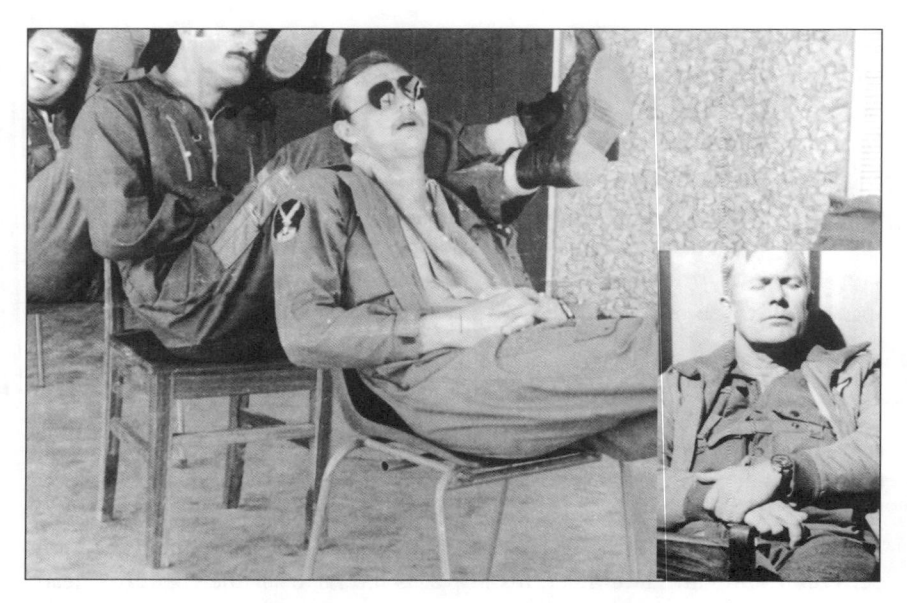

Your air force on alert! Crew-room standby could be a tedious business. Dick Lord (inset) set the example, which was followed by, from left: Jan Henning, Hennie Louw and Budgie Burgers during Operation *Meebos*.

win the SAAF Operational Award for 1982. The average daily serviceability figure jumped from 30.7 per cent in 1979 to 53.6 per cent in 1982. The average monthly sortie rate over the same period almost doubled from 125 to 231 and the pilot-to-aircraft ratio increased from 0.7 in 1979 to 1.2 in 1982.

In addition to the increase in performance the aircraft capability also improved. The undoubted success that the Atlas F1 Support Group (FSG) achieved in improving the capability of the F1AZ on 1 Squadron during 1980 was brought to 3 Squadron's attention. They formed a similar FSG, which implemented the ESDAP programme that had transformed the F1AZ at 1 Squadron. The integrated systems approach to weapon-system tuning raised the average air-to-air results from 45 to 57 per cent.

In 1970 the standard SAAF fighter camouflage had been adopted for both ground attack and interceptor aircraft. The results, while excellent for low-level missions or static dispersal on an airfield, were extremely poor against enemy aircraft at any other level. The ability of our aircraft to survive was thus threatened by the rapidly escalating war situation over Angola.

In 1981, 3 Squadron took the initiative and designed a prototype camouflage with unique features. Various shades of blue were used to disguise the visual geometry of the F1 silhouette. Aircraft pick-up and recognition became more difficult. Judgement of attitude in a dogfight, a critical element in combat, also became substantially more difficult to gauge. The success achieved by the prototype camouflage scheme resulted in approval being granted for the entire F1CZ fleet to adopt the new scheme in 1982.

During the first half of 1982 Israel Krieger, an Israeli Phantom squadron commander, completed a full six-month training cycle at 3 Squadron. He flew all the required sorties, suggesting areas of improvement where necessary. On completion of the cycle he pronounced that in terms of operational readiness, 3 Squadron was the equal of any Israeli squadron—high praise indeed.

Commandant Gründling left 3 Squadron to attend staff course in July 1982, He had accumulated 1,075 hours on the F1CZ. One of his personal highlights was obtaining a perfect score of 30/30 hits on the air-to-air flag.

## Honorary Colonel

During the bush war, sections of media were promoting the theory that the 'securocrats' were not only running the war but the country as well. At a press conference to brief the media on the progress of the war, General Magnus Malan, Chief of the Defence Force was supported by the other service chiefs. Foreign Minister Pik Botha was also present to state the government's views, if requested. It was a cold night and Botha, feeling chilly, borrowed an air force colonel's bush jacket to help ward off the cold. During question time a sharp-eyed reporter noted that the jacket obviously confirmed their suspicions. General Mike Muller, Chief of the Air Force, saved the day by replying that as an honorary colonel of the SAAF, Botha was entitled to wear his badge of rank.

Immediately after the conference ended, General Muller phoned Jack Gründling and instructed him to write a letter to Minister Botha. In the letter he was to thank the minister for graciously accepting the appointment of Honorary Colonel to 3 Squadron. As it turned out, this overnight appointment proved a mutually beneficial arrangement. Pik Botha became a very welcome member who honoured his commitment to the squadron until it was decommissioned.

### *Meebos*

Early in July 1982, intelligence sources discovered that SWAPO and the Angolans were planning to recapture Xangongo and Ongiva. Operation *Meebos* was launched to seek and destroy SWAPO's central area headquarters. Ground forces tracked this headquarters through Evale and Ionde and eventually established its position near Mupa. On 20 July, both F1 units were ordered to return to AFB Ondangwa for 'a few days', the usual headquarters' story. Six weeks later, the weary squadron members finally returned home.

To reassure ourselves that we had air superiority over the combat zone we needed periodically to devote attention to the enemy air-defence system.

This entailed the obligatory air strike on the radar systems operating in the vicinity of Cahama. Therefore at 13h40 on 21 July, eight AZs, escorted by two missile-armed CZs, took off from Ondangwa and 23 minutes later descended onto the radar site. For once, no retaliatory AAA fire or missiles were fired by the defenders. As it was a Sunday it was assumed that, like South Africans, the Angolans also enjoyed their Sunday afternoon nap.

Despite tracking SWAPO all over the combat zone, the ground forces had extreme difficulty establishing the exact position of the SWAPO headquarters. The F1 pilots spent many hours on CAS standby, but no really effective sorties were flown.

On 1 August, orders were received from 310 AFCP (air force command post) at Oshakati, for a strike the next day on a SWAPO base located 25 kilometres southeast of Tetchamutete. Eight AZs and four CZs, loaded with Mk 82 bombs, formed the strike formation. Two additional AZs, armed with 68mm rockets and 30mm cannon, accompanied the strike in a close air support (CAS) role. The strike went through the target unopposed. The pair of CAS F1s held above the target, while helicopters moved ground forces into the target area. Suddenly, the operational radio channel burst into life as the helicopters started drawing heavy fire from the target area.

AS-30 guided missile en route to the target seen through the HUD.

The helicopter pilots withdrew to safety, calling in the CAS F1s to attack the various AAA sites that had suddenly become active. Using all their rockets and cannon shells, the F1s were extremely successful, scoring many hits and destroying some of the AAA guns. The combined onslaught by all SAAF aircraft and ground forces accounted for 106 terrorists.

South African ground forces were now deep in Angola, one task force in an area northwest of Cuvelai, while another was operating just south of Tetchamutete. Both groups were constantly engaged with pockets of enemy resistance. While the Mirage F1s remained on CAS standby at AFB Ondangwa, Puma and Alouette helicopters were used in support on the battlefields.

On 9 August, Puma helicopters were used to leapfrog troops in a follow-up operation. While the helicopters were crossing a riverbed at very low level, the sky was suddenly filled with clouds of smoke from exploding AAA and small-arms fire. One of the Pumas, apparently struck by an RPG-7, crashed, killing the crew of three and all 12 Parabats on board.

The CAS standby F1s were scrambled to the scene, arriving 18 minutes later. 68mm rocket and cannon attacks were carried out on the fleeing enemy, who fired inaccurate AAA and launched SA-7s at the Mirages. Having exhausted their ammunition, the Mirages returned to Ondangwa. Pairs of fighters remained overhead the combat areas for the rest of the afternoon.

Early the next morning, Captain Norman Minne and I, on cockpit readiness for CAS duties, were scrambled. Alouette pilots, majors Neall Ellis and Harry Anderson, had found a SWAPO camp 30 kilometres north of Cuvelai, on the banks of the Calonga River. The enemy had opened fire aggressively with 14.5mm AAA, RPG-7s and SA-7 Strela missiles, hoping to repeat their success of the day before. It wasn't long before they realized that they had made a serious error. Instead of transport helicopters, the Alouettes were gunships, armed with 20mm cannons.

A serious fire fight began, with the gunship pilots preventing the enemy from escaping, keeping them trapped against the riverbank. On arriving overhead, the AZs were given targets by the circling Alouette pilots and, amid missile smoke trails, began decimating the enemy defenders. As on the previous afternoon, the next pair of Mirages was on hand to take over the attack as ammunition was expended. A hectic day ensued with jets and helicopters acting in harmony. As resistance crumbled, the fight petered out. When they cleared the target zone, ground forces counted 118 SWAPO dead.

After suffering these severe setbacks, SWAPO retreated from the combat area. It took the army a long while to realize that the battle was over. Finally, at the end of the month, ground forces returned to South West Africa and *Meebos* was completed. After nearly three weeks of CAS standby duty, with very little flying, the Mirages returned to Hoedspruit on 28 August.

## Second MiG

Between 3–8 October, it was 3 Squadron's turn to deploy to AFB Ondangwa. Canberras from 12 Squadron were required to carry out a photographic small-area-coverage (SAC) of Cahama. The F1CZs were tasked to escort the vulnerable medium bombers during this task.

At 11h20 on 5 October, Major Johan Rankin and Captain Cobus Toerien rendezvoused with a Canberra flown by Commandant Bertus Burger and his navigator Captain Frans Conradie. Under positive control from Dayton radar, the formation headed for Cahama. While monitoring the formation during the photographic runs, Captain Les Lomberg, Dayton radar fighter-controller, detected approaching enemy aircraft.

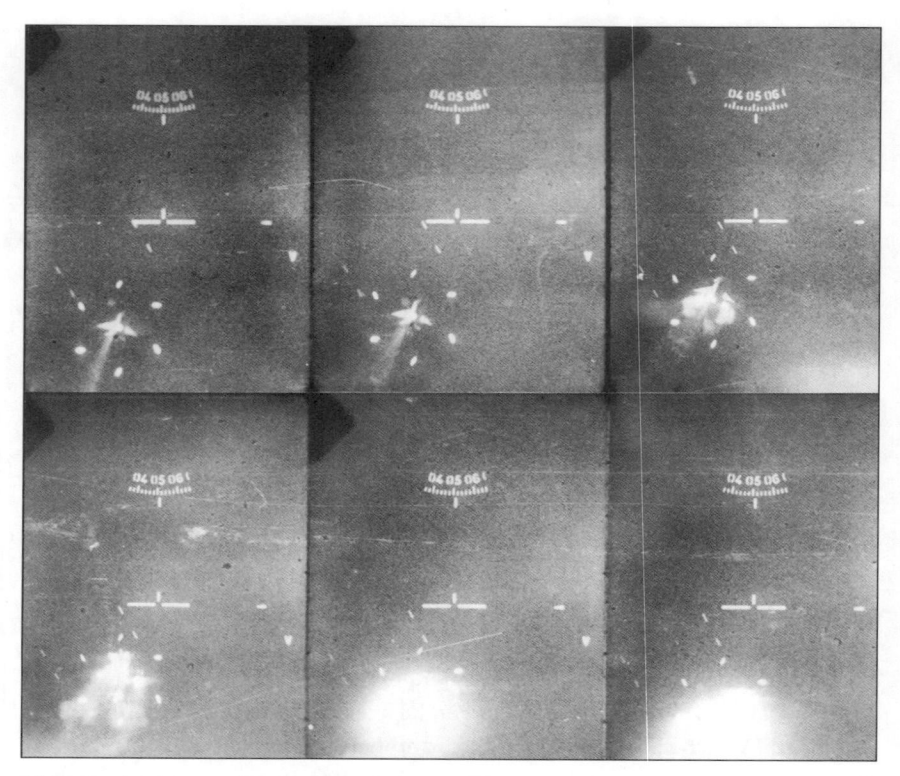

Major Rankin's second MiG-21 kill.

Detaching the Canberra to run south for safety, Lomberg turned the F1s north, instructing them to climb to 30,000 feet and accelerate to Mach 0.95, the limiting speed for external tanks. This turn placed the opposing formations nose to nose with each other, 12 nautical miles apart, approaching at twice the speed of sound.

Rankin picked up two MiG-21s at the same level, approximately five nautical miles away, as they flashed down the right-hand side. The F1 pilots jettisoned their drop tanks, went into afterburner and started a hard right-hand turn in pursuit. Shortly before the formations crossed, the enemy fired their missiles but they had no chance of guiding correctly. Perhaps the enemy pilots wanted to rid their aircraft of the extra drag before engaging in a dogfight at close quarters.

The F1s completed a 180° turn while the MiGs were turning only gently to the right, maintaining supersonic speed. Radar confirmed the MiGs were outdistancing the F1s. Unable to close to firing range, Johan switched his intercept radar onto transmit, hoping the MiGs' radar warning receiver would warn their pilots and force them to turn into the F1s. As was hoped, the MiGs did reverse their turn. Whether this resulted from the radar warning or whether they were

**SECOND MiG**

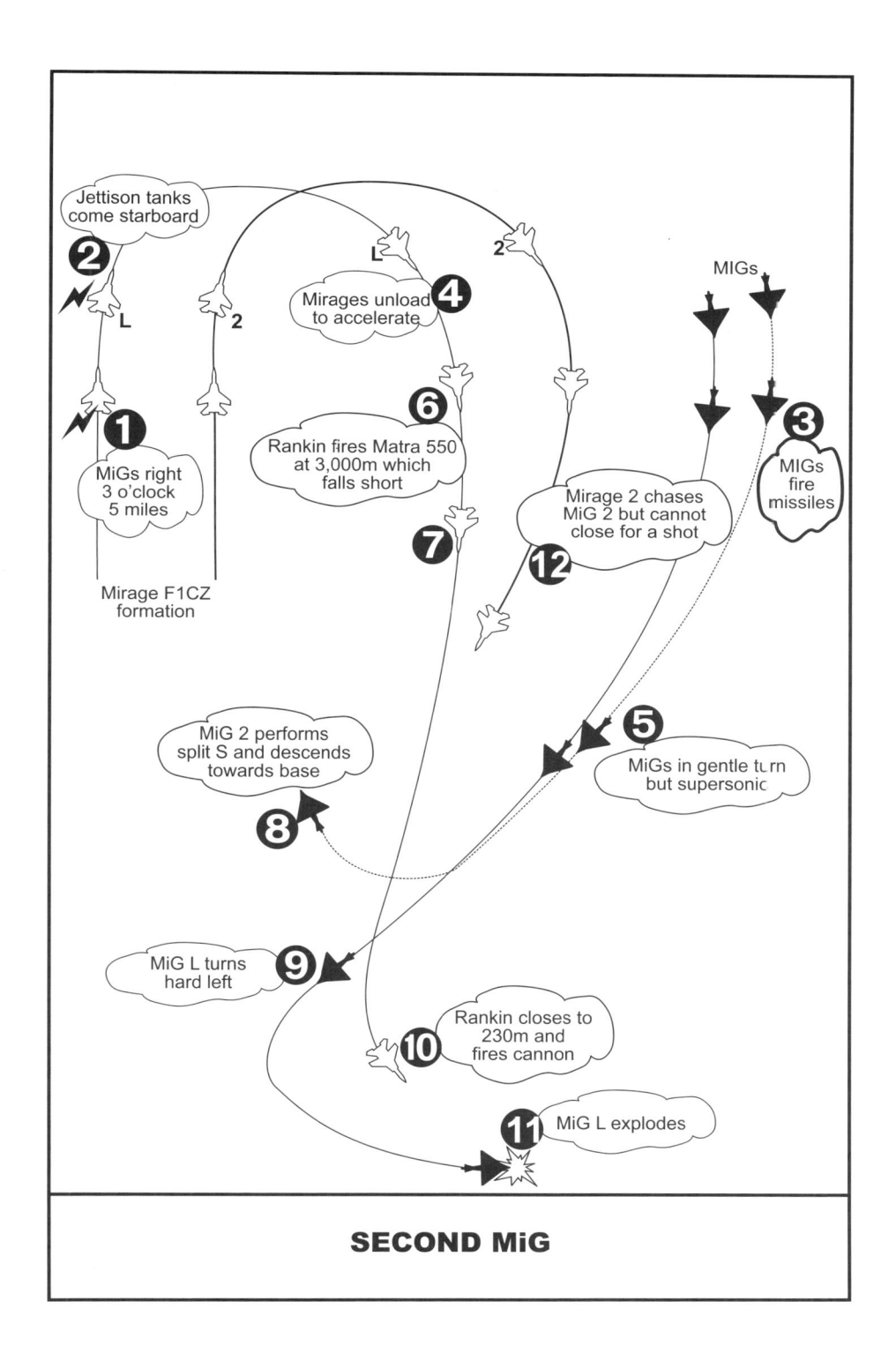

still intent on intercepting the Canberra was uncertain, but the manoeuvre did allow the F1s to cut the corner and close the range.

Unloading the G, the F1s performed an energy acceleration, reaching Mach 1.3. Entering a curve of pursuit and judging the range to be correct, although his radar had not locked onto the target, Rankin fired a Matra 550 infrared missile. The missile tracked the MiG until it reached all-burnt range, then dropped away. Subsequent examination of the gun-camera film showed that the missile had been fired at 3,000 metres, the extreme limit of its range at those speeds.

Closing range, Rankin fired his second missile from about 1,500 metres. This missile tracked the MiG, which had entered a descending split-S manoeuvre and exploded right behind it. The MiG was hit but still controllable and continued its left-hand roll before heading back to base, trailing smoke. According to information acquired later, the MiG-21, although damaged, made it back to base. There, however, the pilot was unable to lower the undercarriage and the ensuing forced landing caused additional serious damage.

With one enemy aircraft out of the fight, Rankin closed on the lead MiG, which entered a split-S to the left. Rankin followed, overtaking rapidly and at 230 metres started firing his 30mm Defa cannons. The MiG exploded directly in front of him and he could not avoid flying through the fireball of the explosion. The heat and smoke caused the F1's engine to develop a compressor stall. Only after cutting the engine and performing a hot-relight did his engine return to normal.

In contrast, Cobus Toerien found the sortie utterly depressing. He managed to get a MiG in his sights at 12 o'clock, but at 1,500 metres and 80° angle off, he could do nothing about it.

On this flight, Rankin was flying F1CZ 203. This aircraft was the first, and at that time the only aircraft painted in the SAAF air-superiority blue–grey colour scheme. The aircraft had been christened *Le Spectre* (French for ghost) by General Jan van Loggerrenberg because of the effectiveness of the colour scheme. The camouflage was still under evaluation but was soon applied to the other F1CZ aircraft.

## Déjà-vu

Captain Geraghty took off from AFB Hoedspruit as target for a session of dusk ground-controlled interceptions (GCIs). Flying on autopilot, he watched the beautiful sunset while I acted as the attacker.

Many years before, I was flying a Phantom over the sea off the Californian coast at sunset when I received the shock of my life. Heading eastward towards a dark sky I became the victim of a colleague's sense of humour.

Returning from a training sortie, Lieutenant Jake Jacanin, USN, spotted my aircraft cruising gently back towards base. At supersonic speed he came up astern and passed very closely underneath my aircraft. The shockwave buffeting my aircraft roused me instantly from my reveries. Then he pulled up directly in front of me, with long flames issuing from the exhausts of the two J-79 engines. The bump and the flames silhouetted against the night sky caused an adrenaline surge I remember vividly to this day.

So it was, that as I approached astern of Geraghty's aircraft, I had a distinct feeling of déjà-vu. In full afterburner I performed the same manoeuvre. Poor Geraghty had the impression of a missile explosion as I passed directly underneath his right wingtip.

## Ox braai and farewell

Val and Wendy Beretta, wonderful friends of the air force, presented 1 Squadron with a young ox bred on their farm near Klaserie. At an all-day, all-night, and for some an all-next-morning function, the ox was braaied whole on a spit. The entire squadron, men, women, children, plus friends of the squadron enjoyed the occasion. Major Paddy Carolan distinguished himself as the 'master braaier' and the meat, albeit a little late, was enjoyed by all.

My time in charge of 1 Squadron came to an end in December 1982. I felt the squadron had successfully moved to AFB Hoedspruit, had performed admirably in all the operations we had participated in and the pilots, ground crew and F1 Support Group had welded into a formidable and happy team. It was time to hand over to my successor, Commandant Gerrie Radloff. I admit with pride to shedding a tear when the band played 'Auld Lang Syne' at the change-of-command ceremony. Little did the men realize that in the immediate future 1 Squadron would be working for me again. I had been promoted and appointed as the air boss in Oshakati to run the air side of the bush war.

# Chapter 10

# 1983:
# Paradigm shift

## Phoenix

Although SWAPO had been militarily active since 1965, the results achieved by their insurgents were poor. In mid-1982, in an effort to improve the situation, Soviet, East German and Cuban advisors had begun training a SWAPO specialist unit. Called Volcano, this unit was created to produce in South West Africa the eruption and violence of its active namesake. The elite members, grandly referred to as Typhoon comrades, were probably better motivated than the normal terrorist, but in the operational theatre they proved to be of similar calibre.

Late in January 1983, 14 groups of up to 50 men per group infiltrated across the border into Kaokaland, Owamboland and the Kavango. The objective of 13 of these groups was to sow mayhem in the border regions. The 14th group was tasked to utilize expected reaction as a diversion. Their aim was to slip through the security force defences and enter the farming area of South West Africa around the towns of Tsumeb and Grootfontein.

Operation *Phoenix* was launched to counteract the incursion and by 15 February, 129 terrorists and two security force members had been killed. Two months later, on 15 April, the operation was completed. By that time, 309 insurgents and 27 security force personnel were dead. Only 12 of the original Volcano group tasked for the farming area reached their objective and the dozen had been killed.

## Saamwerk

When Commandant Dries Wehmeyer took over command of 3 Squadron, he was understandably worried by the escalation of the threat to our operations in southern Angola. During 1982, SA-8 and SA-9 surface-to-air missile systems were being deployed by the Angolans. Intelligence inputs also indicated that

SA-6 systems had arrived in the operational theatre. All these systems were mobile and could be deployed anywhere in the combat zone. The fixed SA-2 and SA-3 sites lost their effectiveness as soon as their launching sites were located. Therefore, the new enemy missile systems created a serious challenge to the SAAF's dominance of the battlefield.

The longer the war continued the more apparent it became that success would be more easily attainable if all our resources were used in concert. The early tendencies had been to use units or squadrons individually, instead of in a synchronized, joint manner. The habits of a peacetime force are hard to break. Wehmeyer, to his credit, realized that the benefit 3 Squadron had obtained through their liaison with the Israeli pilots should be shared with the rest of the air force.

He deployed 3 Squadron to AFB Durban and AFB Hoedspruit during 1983, where joint air combat training was carried out with 1, 2 and 5 Squadrons. These exercises provided the fighter fraternity with a quantum increase in this capability. Joint exercises were also flown with 4 (Impala), 12 (Canberra) and 24 (Buccaneer) Squadrons as well as with the instructors from 85 Advanced Fighter School. Operation *Saamwerk* concentrated on joint-mission training with eight SAAF squadrons. The results were so successful that Director Force Preparation (DFP) included the training on an annual basis.

Fighters are always in demand in a small air force. Training cycles had to cover the main role of the particular squadron, as well as a variety of secondary roles. 3 Squadron was often tasked to carry out ground-attack sorties when large strikes were planned. The air-to-air sight in the F1CZ had only rudimentary capabilities for traditional dive attacks. Accuracy, particularly in dive-bombing, left a great deal to be desired. 3 Squadron technicians modified the gun sight to include an artificial horizon. This modification allowed the pilot to select his rolling-in point, dive angle and aiming pipper position with much greater accuracy. Forty-degree, high-release dive-bombing results improved by an astonishing 80 per cent. This improvement assisted the weapon effort planners considerably. The greater accuracy of bomb deliveries allowed fewer aircraft to be tasked to destroy targets.

During 1983 rust created havoc with the serviceability of the Mirage F1s. Many weeks' flying were lost while the entire fleet was grounded. Once repair schemes had been set up, many aircraft were taken out of operations to be overhauled. In 1982, 3 Squadron flew 1,784 hours with a daily serviceability averaging 7.6 aircraft out of their unit strength of eleven. During 1983, they flew almost the same total: 1,750 hours with only 4.9 aircraft being available daily. This effort testifies to the dedication of the ground crew who, despite their enormous problems, allowed squadron training and operations to be unaffected.

Great attention was paid to the onboard Cyrano IV radar equipment. Mean time between failures (MTBF) had never exceeded 12.2 hours since the aircraft had been in service. Pilot confidence in the radar was on the wane and morale was not as high as it should always be in a fighter squadron. Major Pete Vivier, a pilot and electronics engineering graduate, was tasked to carry out an in-depth investigation into the poor performance of the equipment.

This investigation discovered shortcomings in the methods used to recognize defects, plus problems in both the maintenance and servicing procedures used on the radar. The incorporation of the findings of the investigation raised the MTBF to 16.3 hours. This may seem insignificant, but the 33.7 per cent increase in MTBF had additional benefits—lock-on ranges increased, the air-to-air sighting system improved and the pilots developed the confidence necessary to utilize the system fully during aerial combat.

The psychological effects of all these improvements in 3 Squadron's performance rubbed off on other air force units. When 1, 12 or 24 Squadrons were flying ground-attack sorties, their pilots always felt more confident, knowing that well-prepared 3 Squadron F1CZs were around to protect their heavily loaded strike aircraft.

## *Skerwe*

On 20 May 1983, members of the ANC, using tactics and techniques similar to those used against the US embassies in Nairobi and Dar es Salaam in August 1998, detonated a large car bomb outside SAAF Headquarters in Church Street, Pretoria. The time chosen for the detonation was as employees left the building to go home in the afternoon, thereby ensuring maximum casualties. This typical terrorist tactic could not go unanswered and on 23 May the SAAF replied by launching Operation *Skerwe*.

Twelve Impala jets attacked known ANC houses in the Matolo suburb of Maputo, Mozambique. In an effort to keep collateral damage to a minimum, weaponry was restricted to accurate 68mm rockets and 30mm cannon fire. Maputo was defended by SA-3 missile batteries that posed a threat to the safety of the Impalas. Two F1AZs from 1 Squadron attacked the Low Blow radar-guidance system used by the SA-3 batteries to protect the slower jets. A further pair of AZs was airborne during the strike as top cover in the case of an aircraft being shot down. They were not required.

*****

The annual supersonic ACM camp was held out of AFB Durban during the first two weeks of June 1983. 1 Squadron flew 118 sorties during the ten flying days. The only crisis occurred when the equipment-bay panel of Captain Giep Vermeulen's F1AZ came off during supersonic flight. The effect was so great that Vermeulen thought he had been in a mid-air collision. However, after reducing

Scene of carnage outside SAAF Headquarters in Pretoria after the ANC's MK detonated a massive car bomb during rush hour. This deed led to the SAAF reprisal raid in Maputo three days later, when only legitimate ANC targets were attacked.

speed, he managed to land the aircraft safely.

Captain Spook Geraghty engaged in a one-versus-one fight with Captain Giep Vermeulen under radar control off the Durban coast. The skies were clear of clouds but the conditions were hazy. As they were 70 nautical miles out to sea the coast was out of sight. Both sky and sea were blue with no clear horizon. Passing head-on at supersonic speed, Geraghty entered a high-G turn while looking backwards over his shoulder to keep Vermeulen's aircraft in sight. The big sin in air fighting is to lose sight of one's opponent.

Within seconds Geraghty experienced a severe attack of vertigo, the spatial disorientation so feared by airmen. Looking down at his instrument panel, he rolled his wings level on the attitude indicator and punched in the autopilot. 'Sir Ponsonby', the F1's answer to the traditional 'George', immediately saved the situation by bringing the aircraft back under control, allowing Geraghty to regain his bearings.

Late in June 1 Squadron achieved some excellent air-to-ground firing results, indicating that the hard work put in by the ground crew was paying off and the weapons system was improving. Captains Ronnie Knott-Craig scored 38/60, Trevor Bernberg 45/60 and Billy Collier a superb 52/60.

Early in July 1 Squadron received three new pilots: captains Jan Mienie, Chris Skinner and Rikus de Beer joined for the F1 conversion course.

## Spoof raids

On 5 August, six F1AZs landed at AFB Ondangwa after a two-and-a-quarter-hour ferry flight from AFB Hoedspruit. The aircraft were configured with one 1,200-litre belly tank, two V3B missiles and 30mm cannon.

MiG-21s, configured for ground attack, were operating against our ground forces and UNITA out of the Angolan base Menonque in the southeastern region of Angola. The F1AZs were used to threaten the MiGs and make them reconfigure to the air-to-air role, thus reducing their effectiveness against ground troops.

Three sorties were flown, with the AZs penetrating at low level, then pitching rapidly to 30,000 feet inside Angolan radar cover towards and even north of Menonque. A SAAF electronic counter-measure (ECM) DC-4 was airborne to monitor the enemy reaction. After the first sortie, the MiGs ceased their ground-attack sorties. The Angolan Air Defence Headquarters at Lubango placed their forces at Alert Condition 1, not knowing what to expect next. By late afternoon of 7 August the F1AZs were back in Hoedspruit, having achieved the desired results.

1 Squadron continued the weapons programme at Roodewal range, which had been interrupted by the border deployment, with improving results. Top guns were Captain Trevor Bernberg's 27/30 in air-to-ground firing and Commandant Gerrie Radloff's rocket centre error probability (CEP) of 8.75 metres.

During September, 24 Squadron supplied Buccaneer tankers for 1 Squadron to practise in-flight refuelling. The programme started well but was interrupted when Captain 'Moolies' Moolman ripped off the panty. Next day the Buccaneer reappeared with the basket repaired, but the plug-in rate was abysmal. After the experience of the day before, the Buccaneer seemed to have turned frigid.

In October, 1 Squadron deployed to AFB Bloemspruit for a *Vergooi* bombing programme. Results achieved by the weapons system were extremely good. The exception was a smoke-and-flash practice bomb that landed 50 metres from the range officer's hut and another that fell 19 nautical miles short of the range.

By November, both F1 Squadrons were busy with air-to-air training at AFB Langebaan. Initial flags returned in almost virgin condition, but results improved as the pilots' handling improved. Captain 'Floors' Visser annoyed everybody, including the target tug pilot, by shooting off a couple of flags.

The return home—always the best flight of any deployment—proved to be quite exciting. Captain Ronnie Knott-Craig led a three-ship formation with Ed Every as No 2 and Spook Geraghty as No 3. Taking off from AFB Langebaanweg at last light, the formation climbed to flight level 330 (33,000 feet). Abeam Kimberley they entered a layer of stratus cloud, effectively obscuring the horizon. Formation flying through cloud is never easy and Every was the first to experience the onset of vertigo. He descended to FL 290 on instruments and, once below cloud, regained orientation.

Meanwhile, Knott-Craig and Geraghty entered a severe squall line. They were granted authority to climb to FL 390, but their aircraft remained in the cloud. In the turbulence and lightning associated with a summer highveld thunderstorm, Geraghty was the next to suffer disorientation as he lost sight of his leader. Switching to instrument flight he noticed that his air speed indication was falling rapidly, although his attitude was correct. The autopilot, his saviour off the Durban coast earlier in the year, would not engage. Icing, which had caused his instrument problems, disappeared as he descended below cloud over Witbank and he regained full control of his aircraft.

All three aircraft landed safely at Hoedspruit. Only the controllers at Johannesburg ATC centre were peeved at the rapidly changing altitudes of the three jets. Perhaps it is a little easier sitting in a control tower than dicing with thunderstorms at night in single seat aircraft.

## *Askari*

By 1983 the war in South West Africa–Angola had developed a predictable cyclical pattern. Seasonal variations allowed SWAPO to take up the offensive during the summer passage of the inter-tropical convergence zone (ITCZ) across northern South West Africa. The ITCZ is that low pressure belt of unstable, moist air that traverses southward to the latitude of Rehoboth during late October and returns northward across Owamboland in late January through to April. The passage of this belt gives rise to the phenomenon of the 'small rains' before Christmas and the 'big rains' from February to April.

The rainy season gave mobility to the SWAPO insurgents. It supplied the water they required for their trek south. Foliage on the trees and bushes provided concealment from the security forces. Torrential rains washed out the tracks they had left, making follow-up difficult and they could crisscross standing water in the *shonas* (pans) to add to the difficulties of the trackers. Therefore, the SWAPO insurgency usually commenced in late January of every new year and continued until the end of April or early May when the water started to dry up.

The onset of the dry season brought about a change in the tactical situation. SWAPO withdrew its forces to bases in Angola for so-called 'rehearsals'—the regrouping and retraining of their members prior to the next year's incursion. With SWAPO concentrated in bases, it became cost-effective for the security forces to launch offensive operations into Angolan territory during the dry winter months. Mobility of vehicles in the mud of summer was always considered a restricting factor.

Until the spring of 1983 this had been the pattern of conduct of the war. A summer incursion by SWAPO and a semi-conventional/conventional offensive by security forces into Angola during the winter. The military results of these activities were overwhelmingly in favour of the security forces. However

SWAPO, like the migrating swallow, returned every year.

In an attempt to surprise the enemy and to alter the pattern of predictability, Operation *Askari* was planned. Bearing in mind the difficulties of mobile operations in the wet season, it was decided that *Askari* would be a semi-conventional operation, using conventional arms against SWAPO while they were still massed in their training bases. Therefore, the timing of the operation was set to commence just after the 'little rains' in November 1983.

Preparing for the expected operational deployment, some of the 1 Squadron men sent their wives and families to spend Christmas with their parents, instead of waiting alone at Hoedspruit. On 7 December, Captain Ed Every was late for work—not an uncommon occurrence as Every was a great sleeper. He explained that, following his wife's departure to Pretoria at 05h00, he had fallen asleep in their lounge and had not heard his alarm clock ring because it was in the bedroom.

On 10 December, ten F1AZs and six F1CZs flew into AFB Ondangwa to support the Impala jets already there. Canberra and Buccaneer bombers operated out of AFB Grootfontein. Although treacherous summer cumulo-nimbus rainstorms restricted flying, numerous air strikes were flown, concentrating on the defences at Caiundo. CZs of 3 Squadron were on constant cockpit standby to ward off enemy aircraft interfering with the ground forces. They also escorted Mirage III and Canberra photographic flights.

As in all the major operations during the bush war, results were heavily against SWAPO. By 14 January 1984 when *Askari* was completed, 361 SWAPO insurgents had been killed as opposed to 13 ground force troops—a ratio of nearly 24 to one. SWAPO logistical channels and their command-and-control networks had been severely damaged, but in the 'big rains' of 1984 they ventured south again.

# Chapter 11

# 1984:
# An uneasy peace

## *Askari* winds down

Angolan complaints about *Askari* resulted in condemnation of South Africa by the United Nations. Intense political pressure forced the government to order the withdrawal of South African troops from Angola before the objectives of *Askari* had been attained. The last major action was an aerial bombardment of the defences around Cuvelai by Canberra and Impala jets, followed by an attack by ground troops. After a serious fire fight on 3 January 1984, Cuvelai was captured along with large quantities of Soviet-supplied weaponry.

On 5 January, eight Mirage F1AZs redeployed to Ondangwa, but too late to take part in the battle. By 14 January, they had all returned to Hoedspruit.

## Joint Monitoring Commission

A flurry of diplomatic activity accompanied the ending of *Askari*. Under conditions agreed to by both sides, a joint monitoring committee (JMC), composed of members from both sides would control the 'area in dispute' (basically from the border to Cuvelai). South Africa would withdraw in stages from Angola, the Cuban forces would remain north of the 'area in dispute', the Angolans would ensure that the 'area in dispute' would be kept free of SWAPO terrorists and a joint monitoring force composed of South African and Angolan troops would patrol the 'area in dispute' to verify that both sides kept to the terms of the agreement.

South Africa adhered to all conditions laid down and by the end of the year had withdrawn from Angola. The Angolans, manipulated by their communist masters in Russia and Cuba, failed to honour any of their agreements. SWAPO passed without hindrance through the 'area in dispute'—it was even suspected

Angolan Air Force (FAPA) Mi-8 helicopters arriving for a Joint Monitoring Committee meeting in the bush near Cuvelai in southern Angola, 1984.

that they were once again aided logistically by the Angolan defence force. The annual incursion into South West Africa cost the lives of another 584 SWAPO and 39 security force members.

However, the intensity of the conventional war decreased significantly, removing the need to constantly deploy the Mirage F1, Buccaneer and Canberra squadrons. The introduction of SA-8 mobile ground-to-air missile batteries and the suspected presence of SA-6 systems changed the combat scenario. SAAF flying tactics and attack profiles were seriously affected. The lull in the air war allowed the squadrons valuable training time to counter the new threat.

On 18 January 1984, Captain Digby Holdsworth and Commandant Lavi joined 1 Squadron, while captains Arthur Piercy and Mike Weingartz joined 3 Squadron.

## Loss of Mirage F1AZ 228

Traditionally, number 13 is considered unlucky—so it was for Digby Holdsworth. On 13 March, he ejected from Mirage F1AZ 228, which crashed five kilometres outside Lydenburg. At that stage he had accumulated only 17 hours on the Mirage F1.

He climbed to 20,000 feet into the training sector southeast of Hoedspruit. On the ascent he passed through a solid cloud layer between 5,000 and 9,000 feet. These clouds effectively covered the tops of the mountains of the Drakensberg escarpment, 20 nautical miles to the west of the airfield. Once established in the sector, he initiated the planned performance investigation exercises that consisted mainly of maximum-rate turns and looping manoeuvres at various speeds. Nothing unusual occurred during the exercises and when he reached bingo fuel he set heading for base using the indications displayed on the roller map and radioed for airfield joining instructions. He turned on his Tacan (tactical air navigation) system to confirm direction to base and waited patiently to give the next call at 30 miles out.

He called as the roller map indicated 30 nautical miles but noticed that his Tacan indicated 50 nautical miles with the range increasing instead of decreasing. Air traffic control told him to make his next call overhead the base. Shortly thereafter the autopilot disconnected itself with the necessary warnings coming up on the panel. At about the same time he received air traffic instructions from the tower in a broken transmission. He incorrectly perceived these indications as an imminent electrical failure and requested an early descent.

The tower cleared him down to 6,000 feet as "you are coming up overhead the airfield now". Holdsworth initiated a slow descent into the cloud. Passing 8,000 feet, the aircraft entered a gap in the cloud through which the pilot was alarmed to see mountains right below the Mirage. He immediately pulled up and requested the tower to identify his position. He was then told that the radar was on maintenance but according to RDF (radio direction finding) he was still south of the airfield.

Holdsworth received this information through increasingly broken radio transmissions. Then, realizing that he was in a serious predicament he radioed the Mayday distress call. He received no response from the tower but was answered by Major Frans Coetzee who was also in the air, although in another training sector. Coetzee relayed the Mayday to the tower. Holdsworth then realized that his entire navigation system had done an about-turn through 180 degrees. He had flown away from base after reaching bingo fuel, not towards it. He was then about 150 nautical miles from base somewhere over Mbabane in Swaziland. He had very little fuel remaining, poor communications because of the distance and was unsure of his position.

At this point Holdsworth selected emergency heading and saw all the navigation needles rotate through 180 degrees. Only then did he start to understand all the symptoms he had experienced. He then flew northward in a futile attempt to rendezvous with Frans Coetzee. The next sighting Holdsworth had of the ground confirmed that he was over Chrissiesmeer, near Carolina in the Eastern Transvaal. He had 300 litres of fuel remaining and started looking desperately for somewhere to land. Devon radar came on the air giving him a heading and range for the nearest airfield at Nelspruit but fuel levels did not allow Holdsworth to take this option, particularly as by this juncture all his flying instruments had toppled, making a descent through cloud extremely hazardous. He continued heading towards Hoedspruit and at about 60 nautical miles from base a gap in the cloud allowed him to descend visually below the clouds.

Once below, still with little idea of where he was, he found himself in a valley with enough air space to allow him to turn the aircraft around but with no gaps to get out of. He was completely ringed by mountains whose tops were embedded in the clouds. The valley turned out to be the Lydenburg–Ohrigstad valley. At this point, he had 100 litres remaining on the fuel detote with no idea how accurate this fuel-flow measuring instrument was. He expected a flame-out at any second. He found a long stretch of road with what appeared to be a good surface and decided to attempt a landing.

With his Dunlops dangling, flaps down and landing light on, he tried to communicate his intentions to the motorists sparsely scattered along the stretch on which he wanted to land. However, the motorists saw this as being a good old-fashioned shoot-up and proceeded to hang their children out of the windows to get a better view. They flashed their headlights but would not get off the road.

He then found a deserted stretch, better and wider than the previous one but on initiating final approach noticed high-tension power cables crossing the road at an acute angle that spanned nearly the entire useful length of road.

Feeling very desperate, with the detote now reading zero litres, he noticed a grass landing strip on the far side of a small town so decided to land wheels-up. By so doing he thought he could minimize damage to the Mirage.

Just then Holdsworth made radio contact with Jan Mienie and Ed Every who had been scrambled from Hoedspruit to assist. Mariepskop radar controller also came on the air, while Jan Mienie called up from the AFB Hoedspruit tower. At that moment the engine flamed out. Curiously, Holdsworth noticed that the detote read 60 litres, the amount of fuel stored in the inverted flight accumulator, which confirmed the accuracy of the instrument. He also noticed the flame-out sequence of LP lights on, fuel pump lights on, drop in RPM and then DC and electrical lights on. He relayed these events over the radio with the thought that someone might learn from the situation.

He then broadcast his intentions to land without power to which Nic Oosthuysen screamed "Get out, NOW!" Needing no further encouragement, Holdsworth straightened his back and pulled the seat panhandle. As he had been anticipating the ejection, he had already removed his pens and kneepad and had tightened his seat straps. He clearly remembers the long wait (0.75 seconds to be exact), then a tremendous explosion and kick up the backside. He did not black out and clearly recalls noticing his head between his knees while watching the rapidly alternating blue then green background as his seat tumbled.

It was later established that the ejection sequence did not function perfectly. Two cordite rods, situated at the base of the perspex canopy, failed to detonate at the

50-millisecond interval that they were supposed to. This timed explosion creates a resonant frequency designed to shatter the canopy like a car's windscreen, through which the ejection seat punches. Holdsworth was fortunate that he did not incur greater damage than the four compression fractures to his back that he suffered during his exit.

After the parachute had fully deployed Holdsworth looked for the Mirage. The well-trimmed aircraft was descending slowly towards a large green cornfield and he noticed a brief orange flame and black smoke as it crashed into the field. As there was no fuel left, the fire lasted very briefly.

He then looked down and saw to his horror that having survived the ejection, he was now going to drown in the only dam in sight. Tugging the various parachute cords and strops only seemed to aggravate the situation. Finally, by pulling as hard as he could on the two rear strops, he reached a configuration which allowed his parachute to traverse across-wind. Although this manoeuvring allowed him to reach dry land, the spilling of air from the canopy increased his rate of descent and he hit the ground with a fearful thump. A farmer, who had watched the ejection, was soon on the scene with a bakkie and he kindly drove Holdsworth to the Lydenburg hospital. There, a Puma helicopter piloted by Major Carl Volker transferred him to the Hoedspruit hospital. After being X-rayed he was put to bed, given a few *tranquillizers* and told to rest. Shortly thereafter, the remaining pilots arrived for a chat and tried to sneak Holdsworth out to the officers' club for a pint. The planned exodus was interrupted by the hospital matron as Holdsworth was being wheeled out into the parking area. She intercepted the cortège and yelling blue murder, forced the pilots to return Holdsworth to the safety of the ward.

The sequel to this episode brought to light a number of interesting facts. Major Ed Every, as president of the board of inquiry, was ably assisted by Captain Chris Skinner. Both men were commended for the professional and comprehensive manner in which they completed the inquiry.

The board found that during Holdsworth's flight, the gyro centre had experienced a partial failure. No failure warnings were indicated but the centre operated 180° out of true. Months earlier, Major Frans Coetzee had experienced an uncannily similar incident where he too found himself above cloud with a huge direction error with the first glimpse of the ground the same as Holdsworth's— Chrissiesmeer. Fortunately, Coetzee's Mirage was carrying a belly fuel tank and he had a vast amount of experience on F1s that prevented a similar result.

The board found too many similarities between the two incidents and, on further investigation, discovered that the serial number of the gyro centre was the same in each case. It was then realized that this gyro centre had been bounced back and forth between Atlas and the squadron numerous times but always with the same result: ground-tested and found serviceable. The paper trail of F700 snags involving this gyro centre was extensive but each time it came back with the error apparently 'fixed'. The result was the loss of a valuable aircraft.

## Frustration

At the end of June Commandant Lavi was posted from 1 to 3 Squadron, where he literally arrived with a bang. On his first landing in F1CZ 209, he was caught out by the increase in density altitude between Hoedspruit in the lowveld and AFB Waterkloof on the highveld. The very heavy landing resulted in damage to the undercarriage, tail cone and pilot's ego.

In mid-July captains Dawid Kleynhans, Johan Botha and Lyle Dodds joined 1 Squadron. After completing the conversion course, Lyle Dodds was posted to the Test Flight and Development Centre (TFDC). At this time the entire Mirage F1 fleet suffered from poor aircraft serviceability. At 1 Squadron the situation had deteriorated to the stage that Commandant Radloff contemplated grounding the entire unit.

On 11 and 12 August, 3 Squadron returned to AFB Ondangwa where they escorted a Canberra carrying out a photographic-reconnaissance mission over southern Angola.

August 1984 was noticeable for two events, the first being the grounding of the Mirage fleet again, this time for rust which was found in the aircraft's bell-cranks. This utter frustration brought about the second notable event that pleased the pilots at 1 Squadron. Out of sheer desperation, Commandant Gerry Radloff played golf. In Radloff's's eyes, golf had always been a waste of working time but now he resorted to the therapeutic power of the game.

By late November the aircraft were still grounded so 1 Squadron laid on a survival exercise in the Klaserie Game Reserve. The course was presented by Irwin Liebnitz, a vastly experienced conservationist ably assisted by Warrant Officer Dewald de Beer from the survival school.

On 29 November, Major Nic Oosthuysen returned from an operational tour in Windhoek vividly illustrating the words of the old music hall song: 'Two lovely black eyes'. While socializing in a Windhoek tavern, Oosthuysen had received a head butt from André Stoop, South West Africa's rugby full back.

The frustrating year came to an end with two Mirages serviceable at each of the front-line squadrons. Fortunately, the lull in the conventional side of the bush war coincided with this drastic reduction in capability.

Alouette III with troops wearing camouflage cream.

# Chapter 12

# 1985:
# Internationalization of the conflict

## Squadron training

Within 3 Squadron, aircraft serviceability problems seriously curtailed the number of hours available to fly. A major fault had developed with the bellcranks that drive the spoilers and ailerons. The Teflon-coated bushes had to be removed, re-coated and replaced.

With the border war intensifying, Commandant Dries Wehmeyer made a decision to reduce pilot strength. He felt it would be better to keep fewer fully qualified pilots in the squadron. The decision was understandably unpopular with the newer pilots and the tours of captains Mike Edwards, Ian Jones, Jaco de Beer, Hennie Louw and Arthur Piercy were curtailed in July 1985. Captain Edwards had flown only 51 hours in the first six months of 1985. Commandant Wehmeyer based his decision on this type of statistic. Ironically, within months the aircraft situation had improved and, as the war was placing high demands on the squadron, pilots recently posted out were recalled.

3 Squadron set extremely high requirements before their pilots were pronounced operationally qualified. Their training cycle, covering all aspects of flying, lasted six months. New pilots were required to complete two full cycles before being allowed to participate in the bush war. This stringent requirement precluded Mike Edwards from taking part in border operations in Mirage F1CZs, although he had flown Impalas many times in battle.

After dark on 22 February, Mike Edwards was leading Mark Raymond on a ferry flight from AFB Langebaanweg to Waterkloof. They climbed to FL 350 and proceeded in a loose formation. Approaching Kimberley, they saw lightning flashes, indicating the presence of a huge squall line stretching across their planned track. Mike Weingartz, leading the pair ahead of Mike Edwards, told them that he had diverted off track to the north to clear the squall line. Mike Edwards heeded the advice but perhaps did not fly far enough north. As the two Mirages approached the storm clouds, they obtained clearance to climb to FL 420. Edwards told Raymond to drop into a two-mile trail in case they entered cloud.

Scraping over the top of one cloud, with the head of another cumulo-nimbus towering above them on the left hand side, Edwards noticed that his indicated airspeed (IAS) was dropping. To compensate for the massive downdraught that was causing the situation, Edwards increased power all the way into afterburner. He eventually had to descend in full PC (post combustion, the French abbreviation for the more commonly used afterburner) to maintain 220 knots IAS. Fortunately, he managed to avoid the cloud below him. When he broke clear of the downdraught, the situation returned to normal and he climbed back to his cruising altitude.

Mark Raymond, flying two miles astern, was not so lucky. Firmly in the grip of the vicious downdraught, he had to descend into the very heart of the thunderstorm. Within 20 seconds of entering the cloud, he shouted over the radio that his aircraft had entered a spin. Edwards relayed the spin recovery actions over the radio and then, to his relief, heard Raymond reply that he had recovered at FL260. Before Edwards had time to enjoy the good news, Raymond shouted once again that his aeroplane had flipped into a spin in the opposite direction, still inside the cloud. After a long period of silence, Raymond contacted Edwards to say that he had recovered to stable flight clear of the cloud at FL160. He then began the climb back to the given cruising altitude.

Edwards, as leader, informed Bloemfontein ATC that they were returning to altitude—only to receive a bollocking from the controller who was not in the least amused that both aircraft had violated his regulations. The pair eventually landed at AFB Waterkloof, undoubtedely much wiser than before they had taken off.

## *Valknes*

Mozambican government officials perpetually lodged complaints about unlawful aircraft from South Africa violating their air space. As a result the SAAF launched Operation *Valknes* where radars and fighters were placed on immediate standby to intercept these illegal flights.

On 31 March, Major Jan Henning and Captain Moolies Moolman intercepted a Zimbabwean Air Force Casa 212 and forced it to land at Hoedspruit. It was found to be carrying supporters of their national soccer team on their way to a football match in Swaziland. The pilots had lost their way in bad weather and had strayed over the international border. Remarkable how, despite Mozambique's protestations, the only problem came from South Africa's neighbours. After half an hour the Zimbabweans were released, pointed in the right direction and allowed to continue their flight. One wonders if South Africans would have received the same sort of treatment.

## Loss of Mirage F1AZ 'Cripple 2'

The day of 4 April was a beautiful autumn day in the lowveld. Major Jan Henning, the squadron operations officer, had just presented the daily flying programme at the morning briefing and had returned to his office. Captain Ronnie Knott-Craig entered and asked Henning if he could get someone else to fly the scheduled test flight on Mirage F1AZ 222, because he had urgent paperwork to complete. Henning, being one of the squadron 'flying hogs', seized the opportunity; he would do Knott-Craig a favour and fly the sortie, little realizing what the outcome would be.

Half an hour later he was ready to fly. Henning is extremely tall and, despite a continual search, never found an anti-G suit long enough to accommodate his exceptionally lanky legs. He wore the G-suit like a gunslinger's chaps—tight and low on the hips—earning him the nickname of 'Kalahari Kid'.

Pre-flight inspections, start up and taxi tests all went well and Henning reached the threshold of runway 36 in good order. Here he was slightly delayed, while Commandant 'Polla' Kruger in a Puma helicopter from 31 Squadron performed a rolling take-off. After air traffic clearance, Henning lit the afterburner and accelerated down the tarmac strip, but on lift-off all hell broke loose. Red lights started flashing and warning horns assaulted his eardrums. The emergency panel illuminated with the warning: 'Fire in the afterburner section'.

Henning's instincts and training took over. Drills that he had practised hundreds of times were carried out automatically. He cut the afterburner, reduced power, turned right to zoom up to circuit height and called Mayday on the radio, saying that he wanted to land as soon as possible. He was cleared for landing and all emergency vehicles were alerted.

Unfortunately, F1AZ 222, fondly known as 'Cripple 2', decided otherwise. Halfway down the downwind leg, the nose started to drop. Despite Henning's pulling the stick fully backwards and applying full power, it continued to drop. At 40° below the horizon, precious height was being lost very rapidly. As visions of safety reports of pilots 'leaving it too late' to eject flashed through his brain, he grabbed the seat panhandle and yanked violently. He saw the canopy embrittle, before experiencing the terrible wind noise as he shot out of the Mirage. The feeling of complete freedom, courtesy of Martin Baker, was rudely interrupted by a violent jerk as the parachute deployed. An instant later, just ahead of him, 222 hit the ground with a massive explosion. The heat of the fireball singed Henning's face and he feared that he would fall directly into the furnace. Moments later, having fallen through a thorn tree, he hit the ground with his chin, which was between his ankles.

Alouette III at sunset.

Above left: Vlamgat! F1AZ 218 in full afterburner as the pilot releases the brakes for take-off. This aircraft is painted in the final approved camouflage scheme.

Above right: Close-up of a Mirage F1AZ 'in the basket' while carrying bombs.

Below: An Oryx formation in transit over the Angolan bush. Although ideal for really low flying, the flat terrain offered very few navigational features to assist the crew during flying.

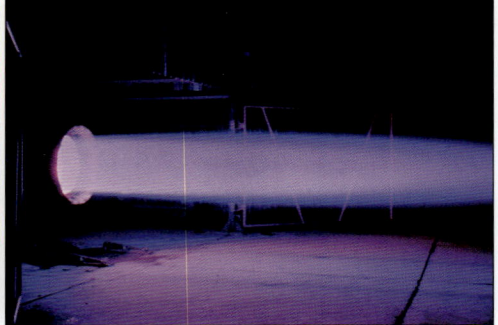

Above left: A line of F1s ready to taxi out at sunset.

Above right: The business end of an Atar engine on the test bed.

Left: Two F1AZ fighters silhouetted against an African sunset.

Below: F1AZ climbing away with heat from the afterburner causing distortion.

Top: F1AZ at low level, leaving a heat haze over the bush.

Centre left: An F1AZ rolling into an attack dive, carrying long-range tanks, missiles and four Mk 82 bombs under the belly.

Centre right: AS-11 wire-guided air-to-surface missile leaves the wing of an Impala. For pilot training purposes these missiles and aircraft were used prior to the pilot firing the larger, more expensive AS-30.

Left: F1AZ firing a surface-to-ground AS-30 missile.

Top: AFB Grootfontein in SWA was an extremely busy airfield during the bush war. Here a Mirage F1AZ taxiies out while a C-130 Hercules, the famous 'Flossie', taxiies into dispersal.

Centre: F1AZ taking off with belly tank and four rocket pods. An unpopular configuration with pilots because of the extremely high drag index. Frangible covers were used to reduce drag en route to the target.

Below: Black Widow, the display Mirage III, landing behind an F1AZ and the pilot's 'toys'.

Top: A clean F1AZ leaving a readiness revetment. 'Clean' aircraft, without the weight and drag from underwing stores, were a delight to fly.

Centre: Lt-Col Jan Mienie, the last 1 Squadron commanding officer, saying a fond farewell to the beloved F1AZ.

Below: F1AZ close up.

Bottom: Time exposure of F1 take-off at night using afterburner.

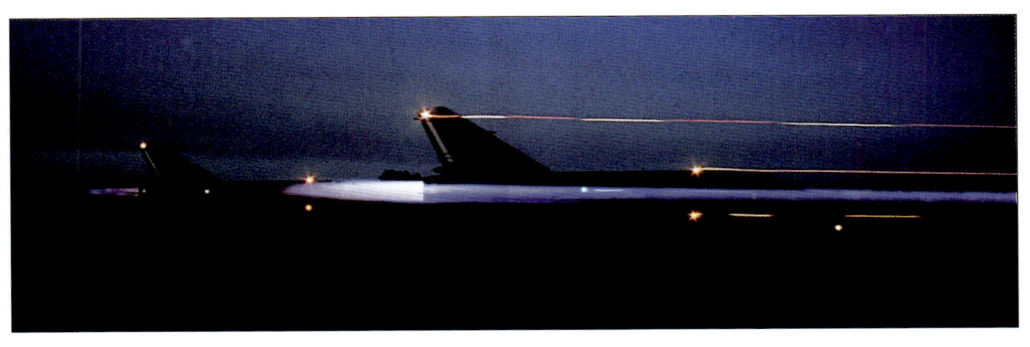

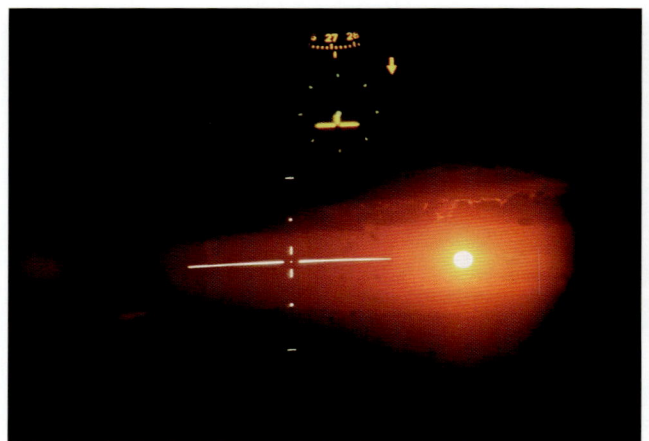

Top: F1AZ head-up display (HUD) sight picture against a sunset background.

Centre: Napalm dropped by a low-flying F1AZ on target at Roodewal bombing range. Napalm, although spectaular, was considered ineffective against targets hidden in the thick bush terrain of southern Angola.

Below: F1AZ taxiing out for an operational strike at AFB Grootfontein. The F1CZ, although primarily an interceptor, was often utilized in its secondary strike role during the bush war.

Left: The needle-nosed F1AZ between revetments.

Below left: Preparing for night operations, three F1AZ aircraft in readiness shelters, illuminated by white light. These lights are doused during flying, leaving only the red lights for illumination.

Below right: MiG-17 escorted by F1AZs over the runway at AFB Hoedspruit. Note how the shadows of the aircraft are more readily discernible than the camouflaged aircraft.

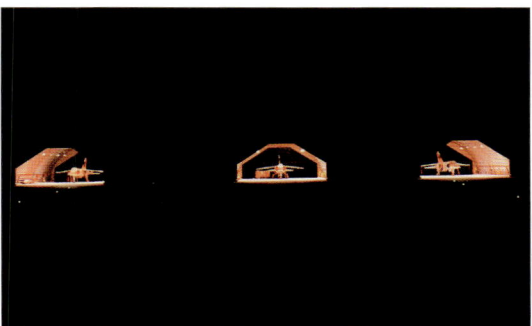

Avove: Two Mirage F1s on the runway with afterburners lit for take-off.

Below: Mirage IIIs of 85 Advanced Flying School make an impressive picture at AFB Pietersburg.

Left: Illustrating the need for camouflage. The silver drop tank acts as an attention seeker.

Left: Interesting study in camouflage of a MiG-17 and two F1AZs over Drakensig.

Above: Manning up in the shade of a revetment was always better than climbing into a red-hot cockpit out on the line.

Left: Cockpit standby under tropical conditions was extremely trying. Makeshift covers were adapted to shield the pilot from the sun.

Left: 1 Squadron F1AZ at sunset with landing lights on, wheels down, probe extended and trailing a wingtip vortex.

Between flight turnaround inspection in a revetment at AFB Hoedspruit. Constant attention to detail by the ground crew ensured the excellent safety record achieved by the Mirage F1.

Top: Aircraft lined up at AFB Durban during the annual supersonic ACM camp. A number of aircraft were painted with distinctive white noses for orientation purposes during multi-aircraft combat training.

Centre left: The approach to the in-flight refuelling basket trailed by a 24 Squadron Buccaneer, as seen through the front windscreen of a Mirage F1AZ.

Centre right: Cockpit of an F1AZ, showing the height at 36,000 feet and speed Mach 1.9. The roller-map display can be seen at the bottom of the photograph.

Above left: Drag-'chute deployed during landing run.

Above right: Night landing with drag-'chute deployed.

Above left: F1AZ trailing wingtip vortices over Bredasdorp.

Above right: B-707 refuelling a Mirage F1AZ fighter during a turn.

Left: F1AZ with long-range drop tanks rolls into an attack.

Above: 1 Squadron at the steakhouse in Oshakati during Operation *Askari*. From left: Trevor Bernberg, Nic Oosthuysen, Michael Lord, Dick Lord, June Lord, Jan Henning.

Above: 'Spectre', the first F1CZ to be painted in air-superiority blue camouflage.

Centre: SAA 727 escorted by Mirage F1s.

Below: There was an engine in here somewhere ...

Left: Mirage III CZ 800, the 'Black Widow', in display livery. Photo: Sgt Johnny Snodgrass.

Centre: 'Panty ripper' Wassie Wasserman with the canvas ring of a damaged refuelling basket around his neck.

Below left: F1AZ, full frontal.

Below right: Vlamgat!

Above: Mobile radar deployed in the bush.

Inset: A fighter controller at his consol concentrating on an interception.

F1AZ 233 trailing wingtip vortices over the Test Flight and Development Centre at Bredasdorp in the Cape.

Above left: 3 Squadron F1CZ in revetment at AFB Ondangwa during the bush war.

Above right: The dust cloud that formed behind the F1CZs before the ceremonial shut-down at AFB Waterkloof.

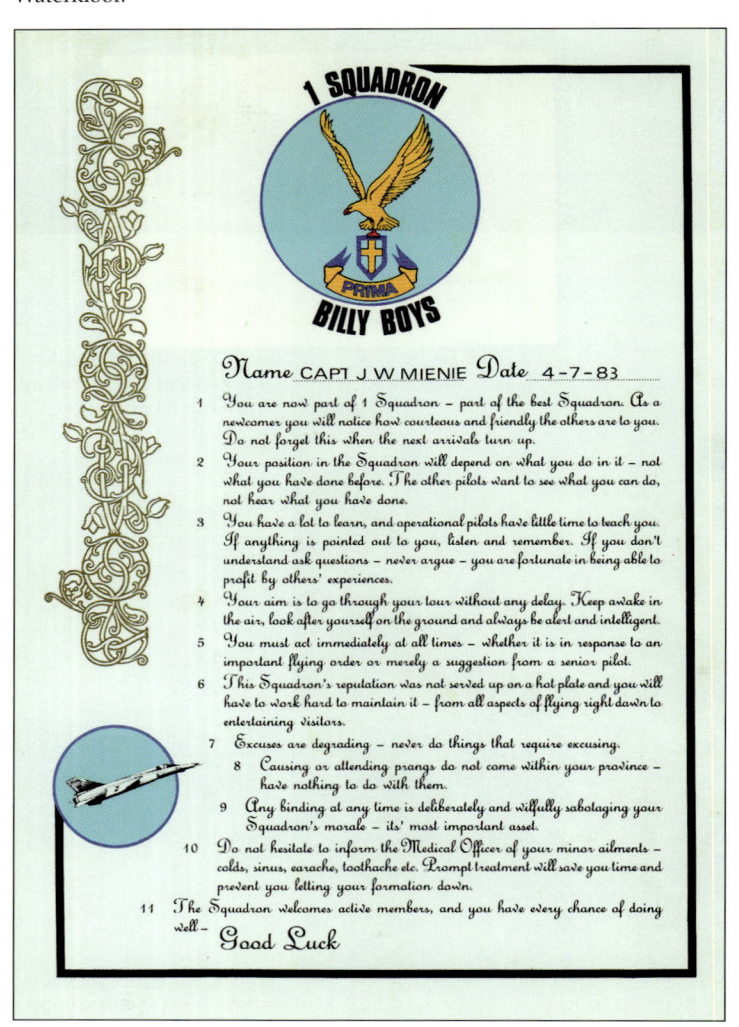

## 1 SQUADRON
### BILLY BOYS
**PRIMA**

Name: CAPT J W MIENIE   Date: 4-7-83

1. You are now part of 1 Squadron – part of the best Squadron. As a newcomer you will notice how courteous and friendly the others are to you. Do not forget this when the next arrivals turn up.

2. Your position in the Squadron will depend on what you do in it – not what you have done before. The other pilots want to see what you can do, not hear what you have done.

3. You have a lot to learn, and operational pilots have little time to teach you. If anything is pointed out to you, listen and remember. If you don't understand ask questions – never argue – you are fortunate in being able to profit by others' experiences.

4. Your aim is to go through your tour without any delay. Keep awake in the air, look after yourself on the ground and always be alert and intelligent.

5. You must act immediately at all times – whether it is in response to an important flying order or merely a suggestion from a senior pilot.

6. This Squadron's reputation was not served up on a hot plate and you will have to work hard to maintain it – from all aspects of flying right down to entertaining visitors.

7. Excuses are degrading – never do things that require excusing.

8. Causing or attending prangs do not come within your province – have nothing to do with them.

9. Any binding at any time is deliberately and wilfully sabotaging your Squadron's morale – its' most important asset.

10. Do not hesitate to inform the Medical Officer of your minor ailments – colds, sinus, earache, toothache etc. Prompt treatment will save you time and prevent you letting your formation down.

11. The Squadron welcomes active members, and you have every chance of doing well – Good Luck

Left: 'Billy Boy' certificate. This certificate, first issued in the desert during World War II, is presented to every new pilot joining 1 Squadron. This message is as pertinent today as it was 50 years ago.

# 1985: Internationalization of the conflict

He stumbled to his feet and discarded the canopy that had just saved his life. Fifty metres away, tinder dry bushveld was crackling fiercely from the huge fire. As he began to run from the blaze, he was delighted to hear the clapping sounds of helicopter blades as Major Polla Kruger brought his Puma into the hover for a rescue.

On hearing Henning's Mayday call on the radio, Kruger had turned the Puma back to the airfield, where he witnessed the complete drama. Having years of bush war experience, Kruger reacted instinctively, knowing also that as a witness to an accident he could not be appointed to the board of inquiry. Fewer than five minutes from releasing brakes to beginning the take-off roll, Henning was hoisted aboard the rescue helicopter.

Once Kruger had ascertained that Henning was alright, he immediately turned his attention to the fire; Henning could hear him giving orders and instructions to air traffic control. He recommended routes for the fire tenders to reach the fire, told ATC to inform Colonel Lombard, the base commanding officer, that Henning was okay, and instructed them to contact Drakensig hospital to have a doctor on standby as he was heading straight there.

As the hospital helipad had not been completed, Kruger landed on the sports field. He told Henning that an arrangement had been made for an ambulance to fetch him. Commandant Kruger immediately flew back to the airfield to pick up firefighters to ferry them to the scene of the crash.

As Henning waited under the shade of a tree, he realized that his arms and face were covered in blood from his sudden passage through the *haak-en-steek* thorn tree. He also became aware of a numbing pain in his lower back, not realizing at the time that this pain would remind him of his ordeal for the rest of his life.

After a long wait that seemed like an hour but was no more than ten minutes, it dawned on Henning that in all probability the ambulance was not going to arrive. Decision time—the hospital was one and a half kilometres away and Henning's home half that distance. Out of consideration for his wife, he decided not to go home. If she saw him walk in covered in blood, she would either have suffered a heart attack or sense-of-humour failure, either of which would have been catastrophic.

With his 'bone dome' in one hand and his G-suit over his shoulder, he started walking towards the hospital. After a few hundred metres, Henning saw a SAAF police van driving towards him. He jumped into the road to stop it and requested the shocked policeman to drive him to the hospital.

On arrival, he noticed an ambulance with its engine running, standing at the entrance and could not resist the temptation of speaking to the driver. Henning was immediately made to understand that he, the driver, must not be disturbed because he was waiting for a helicopter to bring in casualties from a terrible accident. Inside the hospital, Henning had better luck in persuading the sister and doctor that he was the patient they had indeed been waiting for.

Commandant Graham Rochat was president of the board of inquiry. Among the wreckage he found a spanner with chaff marks on it. This could have lodged in the flight controls, causing the loss of control. Another possibility was a 30cm piece of the elevator control rod that was missing from a position alongside the afterburner section. The afterburner fire could have destroyed this section of the control rod, which would definitely have resulted in a serious loss of pitch control.

## Mirage F1AZ cabriolet

On 5 June, during a one-versus-one ACM sortie against Major Nic Oosthuysen, Captain Digby Holdsworth was alerted as the 'cabin-unlocked' warning light illuminated. He was flying at FL 180 and Mach 0.98. He stopped fighting, rolled wings level, checked all the switches and the problem disappeared. He then checked his emergency procedures in his emergency book to confirm that he had performed all the correct actions. Over the radio he repeated the actions a third time with Major Oosthuysen. As everything was normal and all the warnings lights had gone out, the fight was continued.

Oosthuysen disengaged from the fight while Holdsworth was trying to get into missile range. With full afterburner, he accelerated once again to Mach 0.98. He had raised his seat to the maximum safe height to improve his lookout. Approaching missile-firing range, he leaned forward to check in the head-up display for the wingspan against fixed cross ratio. Just then there was an enormous explosion followed by rushing air booming in his ears.

His initial diagnosis was that the canopy had shattered owing to over-pressure. The F1 did have a history of over-pressure at high speeds, even though this normally occurred above 30,000 feet and Mach 1.6 plus. He also had a fleeting glimpse of what looked like white smoke all around him. It appeared that this was condensation vapour caused by the difference in outside and inside pressure at the time of the explosion. Holdsworth decided to get to low level as soon as possible, so he rolled onto his back and screamed downwards, while selecting 100 per cent oxygen.

At this point, the radar controller who had been monitoring the fight lost Holdsworth's blip from his screen. He called up the formation to ask why one aircraft had descended below the exercise minimum altitude. Oosthuysen immediately answered the controller and called Holdsworth, but with no response. At this time Holdsworth could hear nothing except the screaming of the wind and other cockpit noises as he headed for the ground.

With no radar image, no visual sighting and no radio response, Oosthuysen assumed the worst and started searching for a plume of smoke to indicate the crash site. Holdsworth, now down at 200 feet above the ground and with his speed below 200 knots was "riding my F1 like a Chevy with the top down". At this reduced speed the wind noise had subsided considerably, so he could call Major Oosthuysen and inform him of the emergency. Holdsworth then surveyed the damage, to discover that the entire canopy had disappeared but the canopy jettison lever was still in the fully forward position. It has to be pulled to jettison the canopy.

Not too many F1 pilots had the opportunity of flying with the 'top down' and Holdsworth made the most of the memorable experience. At 150 knots he found he could fly with his elbow out the side of the cockpit and look over the cockpit sill. It was beautifully open and very different. He landed off a straight-in approach and taxiied back to the aircraft revetment. Even today, Holdsworth chuckles as he remembers the look on the mechanic's face as he turned his cabriolet in to the parking area.

The board of inquiry could not find any conclusive reason for the loss of the canopy. The canopy was never found so any clues that it could have provided were also lost. Signs of filing were found on the aircraft around the canopy-locking points. Ground crew stated that this had to be done on a number of the aircraft because some canopies "just didn't fit". It was presumed, after this information, that the loss may have resulted from a high-frequency vibration caused by a badly fitting canopy. The high pressures during transonic speed would have exacerbated this condition, causing the canopy-locking horns to sever.

## Mirage F1AZ 221 into the barrier

On 23 July, captains 'Vissie' Visser and Rikus de Beer were practising *Gatup* attacks against selected dummy targets 30 nautical miles southeast of Hoedspruit. At pitch-up on the second attack, de Beer, flying Mirage F1AZ 221, experienced a problem. The pair of fighters had been running at 200 feet and 600 knots. As de Beer applied full afterburner for the pitch he felt a definite deceleration of his aircraft. Looking at his engine instruments he could see that although the engine RPM was constant, the jet pipe temperature (JPT) had dropped from the normal 730° to 435 degrees.

He converted his excess speed to height while turning back towards Hoedspruit. At the same time he called Visser and asked him to initiate the Mayday call. His aircraft configured with belly tank, pylons and missile rails, managed to climb to 5,000 feet before his speed had dropped to 250 knots, which de Beer then maintained. Over the radio, the two pilots went through the emergency checklist, to ensure de Beer had carried out the correct procedures.

While in transit, de Beer tried using the emergency throttle but it had no effect. Visser, now in close formation, told de Beer that a heavy stream of fuel was venting out of the fuselage of 221. At five nautical miles and 5,000 feet from the threshold of runway 36, de Beer confirmed with Visser that a forced landing was possible. The speed was now 245 knots and as de Beer lowered the aircraft's nose, his engine flamed out. He tried a hot relight without success. However, he felt that he could still achieve a touchdown in the normal position on the runway.

He attempted a cold relight of his engine, but again the engine failed to respond. During this procedure he lowered the undercarriage but it took a long time to complete the cycle using emergency pressure. He had to lower the nose to maintain 220 knots, but this changed his projected touchdown point to a position approximately 500 metres short of the threshold. During these actions he descended below 1,500 feet, the minimum height recommended for an ideal ejection. He was committed to a dead-stick landing.

At 400 feet above the ground, de Beer raised the nose to flare the aircraft and reduce the rapid rate of descent; his speed decreased to 180 knots. In the flare, he noticed for the first time a sand wall about 500 metres short of the threshold. He raised the nose to 18° incidence to clear the wall, although from the cockpit, de Beer thought that a collision was inevitable. The aircraft touched down shortly after clearing the wall, slightly right wing low and with the tail cone striking the ground before the wheels.

Almost immediately the right hand oleo broke off and the right wing touched the ground. Dust and smoke surrounded the skidding aircraft as its nose turned to the right. Shortly thereafter a tremendous jolt broke the nose wheel and brought the aircraft's nose thumping onto the ground. The severe bang caused canopy embrittlement cartridges to fire and the perspex canopy to disintegrate into a thousand pieces. De Beer was now driving his Mirage across country best suited to a 4x4 offroad vehicle. The drag caused by the right wing continued to turn the Mirage as it slid along the ground. Inertia, however, kept the jet moving towards the runway. De Beer finally crossed the threshold but by now he was going backwards. As the aircraft crossed the safety barrier, which was in the down position, the wingtip and pylon hooked the net which succeeded in bringing the aircraft to a halt.

Ensuring all switches were selected off, de Beer unstrapped and abandoned the aircraft. He had no need to open the canopy; he just stepped through it onto the ground. Sounds and smells of burning set de Beer running for safety. After 150 metres he saw the base fire brigade hurtling towards the wrecked Mirage. De Beer ran back to ensure that the eager firemen only doused the flames, not the entire aircraft. Two fires were doused, one underneath the fuselage and the other burning fuel that had pooled under the aircraft's tail. Looking at the wreckage de Beer realized that the belly tank, which had been flattened, had probably saved the aircraft from major damage. Very little fuselage damage had occurred. The undercarriage and right wingtip had absorbed most of the impact. Immediately behind the cockpit the fuselage had rippled, probably when the nose slammed down on the ground. De Beer was unhurt. His most painful experience was the injection administered by the doctor for the treatment of shock.

The accident occurred at 09h20. By 22h00, the engine had been removed and flown to Atlas Aircraft Corporation in the back of a C-130 Hercules. It was run on a test bed and the fault was been found. A circlip, joining fuel pipes attached to the engine casing, had come off. On application of G the pipes had separated and fuel was pumped overboard instead of passing through the engine. While the RPM had remained stable, the reduction in fuel flow had lowered the JPT and the thrust.

The rear portion of 221 was eventually mated with the cockpit of F1CZ 205 and the hybrid returned to the fleet. De Beer, who had saved the aircraft, was severely reprimanded by the board of inquiry for not ejecting. He gambled his life to save the aircraft and, thanks to the highest authority, he won.

## *Golden Eagle*

During the annual *Golden Eagle* force preparation exercise, Captain Spook Geraghty flew a bombing sortie to Roodewal range, which he remembers as a highlight of his period on F1s. On the run-in to attack, his aircraft was subjected to wide-band frequency jamming. Five different audio signals began ringing in his headphones and his bombing computer failed prior to pitch-up for a *Gatup* attack profile. This profile was designed to destroy the tracking solution of enemy radar-guided anti-aircraft artillery, while allowing the pilot to watch for threatening surface-to-air missiles.

Running in low-level at 550 knots, Geraghty decided to release the bombs manually—not an easy task. He pitched-up into a 4G manoeuvre until the aircraft's nose was 70° above the horizon. Then he rolled through 90° to focus his eyes onto the target, while inverted. Quickly pulling the nose down onto the target, he rolled out and fired a laser shot. The laser fires a burst of energy that marks the target in the computer system. This action takes a fraction of a second, after which Geraghty initiated the pullout of the dive. Under normal circumstances, the bombing computer releases the bombs at the correct instant. Geraghty had to judge when to release his bomb, then press the release button. The instant the bomb was clear of the aircraft Geraghty broke off the attack, turning through 120° before reversing to check his tail for missile smoke trails as he descended rapidly to the comparative safety of low level. His practice bomb, released manually during this hectic manoeuvring, landed 30 metres from the target, an outstanding result.

## Out-negotiated by the communists

By 17 April, under conditions imposed by the joint monitoring commission, the last South African troops withdrew from Angola. While honouring the agreement and obtaining the moral high ground, South Africa had been out-negotiated by the communist-backed Angolans. SWAPO was back in the shallow area of Angola. Mine-planting incidents increased and the annual incursion took place. The situation had, therefore, reverted to that prevailing in 1981, which had then provoked Operation *Protea*.

On the diplomatic front, lie was followed by counter-lie, claim by counter-claim. However, the character of the war had changed. SWAPO's struggle became little more than a sideshow, while the Angolan civil war assumed prominence. It became internationalized, with the Americans strongly divided over support to UNITA, Soviet and Cuban advisors dominating Angolan military strategy and South Africa appealing to the United Nations to find a suitable settlement. Emphasis shifted eastward from Owamboland to Kavango and the Caprivi.

## Second Congress

Communist Bloc advisors convinced the Angolans (FAPLA) that Mavinga with its airstrip was the key to solving the military situation inside Angola. By occupying that strategic hamlet FAPLA would have a stepping stone into UNITA's heartland. Therefore, in July, FAPLA launched a pincer movement. One arm headed east to clear UNITA forces out of the Cazombo enclave before turning south. The right hook headed south from Cuito Cuanavale before turning east to close the pincer on Mavinga. Both task forces were heavily supported by armour, against which the guerrilla forces of UNITA were no match.

Although the FAPLA advance was slow, it soon became obvious that UNITA could not fight successfully on both fronts. Jonas Savimbi, UNITA's leader, requested South African help to move his troops from the Cazombo enclave to reinforce his defences around Mavinga. Operations *Magneto* and *Wallpaper* were launched to shuttle these soldiers by SAAF transport aircraft from one front to the other.

By mid-September, despite receiving reinforcements, Mavinga was in imminent danger of falling to FAPLA. The Lomba River, the last obstacle on the approach to the town, had been negotiated and FAPLA was poised to attack. Savimbi spent many nights shuttling to and fro between his headquarters in the bush at Jamba and Pretoria, explaining to the politicians that his forces needed assistance as they could not stop the Angolan armoured advance. UNITA territory in Angola effectively sealed nearly 1,000 kilometres of South West Africa's border against penetration by SWAPO insurgents, therefore UNITA's continued presence was vital to South Africa.

Cabinet approval was given for Operation *Weldmesh* to be launched on 16 September. The aim was to provide UNITA with ground and air support to stop the FAPLA advance on Mavinga. Ground- and air-reconnaissance missions

1985: Internationalization of the conflict

An Impala Mk II, the workhorse of the bush war, firing a full salvo of rockets.

finally pinpointed the location of enemy brigades south of the Lomba River. Mobile brigades, traversing thick bush terrain, are often widely dispersed. However, when the attack order was given, the leading brigade was concentrated in an area roughly two kilometres square, providing a viable target for artillery and air bombardment. In an effort to protect themselves from UNITA ambushes, FAPLA used the Lomba River to protect its northern flank. In the forthcoming attack this precaution ensured their annihilation.

Orders had been sent by SAAF headquarters to all squadrons warning them to be prepared for operations while the government was deciding if and when help would be given to UNITA. On 16 September, like migrating birds, SAAF aircraft, including ten F1AZs and seven F1CZs, arrived at AFB Grootfontein and AFB Rundu. The bell rang the following day, heralding the beginning of the next round of the ding-dong battle.

A ferocious combined air strike by Canberras, Buccaneers, Impalas and Mirage F1AZs and CZs fell upon the luckless FAPLA brigades. The minute the last aircraft cleared the target the army, using artillery and multiple rocket launchers, continued the bombardment. The FAPLA vehicles were hampered by thick sand as they tried to escape. Soldiers abandoned stranded vehicles and fled on foot across the Lomba River, becoming easy prey for the revitalized UNITA forces. Air strikes continued until all signs of resistance had ceased. As usual, Mirage CZs were flying combat patrols to protect the battle zone and the pilots spent many hours on cockpit standby.

The initial co-ordinated air strike on 17 September created consternation in the control tower at AFB Grootfontein because for a year and a half Grootfontein had seen little action. Newly qualified air traffic control officers were appointed to the quiet backwater to gain experience before moving on to busier bases. The young woman on duty in the control tower who handled occasional Dakota and

Bosbok flights was suddenly faced with 18 Canberras, Buccaneers and Mirage F1AZs all returning to land at Grootfontein simultaneously. To her credit she brought them all down safely.

## Introduction of pre-frag bombs

The enemy lost one complete brigade south of the Lomba. The remaining brigade slowly retreated towards Cuito Cuanavale, harassed all the way by UNITA ambushes and South African attacks.

During the JMC period, the lull in the air war had been used beneficially by the air force. Pre-fragmented Mk 81 120kg bombs were designed, keeping the same shape and weight distribution as the original American weapons, thus obviating the requirement for further clearance flights or flutter tests. The bombs were fitted with airbursting Limbo fuses, to ensure a burst above ground level. The casing of the bomb was constructed to contain 17,000 small ball-bearings. At burst, these fragments would scatter at high speed in all directions, the effective lethal range of each ball-bearing being nearly 100 metres.

On 30 September, eight Mirage F1AZs dropped these new bombs on the fleeing enemy. The effect on enemy personnel was immediately obvious, as intercepted enemy signal traffic indicated a huge upsurge in casualties among their forces. This development prompted the enemy to alter their priorities. It was of the utmost urgency for them to extricate the Soviet advisors serving with the retreating brigade—they were always eager to let their surrogates do their fighting.

## Turkey shoot

It soon became apparent in the air force command post at AFB Rundu that enemy Mi-8, Mi-17 and Mi-25 helicopter gunships were being used to airlift Soviet personnel with a higher priority than their wounded comrades. Navigation was extremely difficult in the featureless expanse of southern Angola. Enemy pilots, unlike SAAF low fliers, would fly reasonably high to be able to follow river lines, these being the only reliable visible features.

A plan was devised to hamper the removal of the Soviets. Puma helicopters were tasked to fly these enemy profiles along river lines and *shonas* south of Rundu. Small, manoeuvrable Impala Mk II fighter jets were then despatched in pairs to fly at extremely low level along these routes to attempt to visually sight the Pumas and carry out simulated cannon-firing attacks on them. Mirage F1s were available but not used, because the Impala had a better turning performance at low level.

The profile proved viable and Impalas joined the F1CZs on cockpit standby. An army ground recce team, situated in the bush outside the enemy airfield at Menonque, passed on valuable information regarding the take-off movements

1985: Internationalization of the conflict

of enemy helicopters. Co-ordinating scramble times to ensure that the Impalas reached the target zone at the same time as the enemy helicopters caused initial problems. However, on 27 September, two Mi-25 Hind helicopters were destroyed by the Impalas. The action was so swift that the enemy never knew the fate of the two helicopters. Two days later, on the morning of 29 September, all four helicopters in a balanced formation consisting of two Mi-8/17 Hips and two Mi-25 Hinds were destroyed. Helicopter evacuation during operation *Second Congress* ceased immediately.

### *Vergooi* goes operational

As it moved north the mauled retreating brigade, spread over a large area, did not offer pinpoint targets for attack. The spread-out formation and the availability of the new pre-frag bombs allowed 1 Squadron to test the *Vergooi* bombing profile operationally for the first time. The AZs, which had returned home to Hoedspruit on 4 October, redeployed to Grootfontein on 13–15 October. Commandant Gerrie Radloff led eight F1AZs on the first *Vergooi* flight which proved very successful. The eight sticks of pre-frags running through the spread-out brigade caused severe problems for the enemy. On 17 October, another equally successful *Vergooi* mission proved the concept that allowed 1 Squadron to continue operating throughout the remainder of the war. The foresight of the early visionaries, the hard work of captains Ronnie Knott-Craig and Jan Henning among others, and

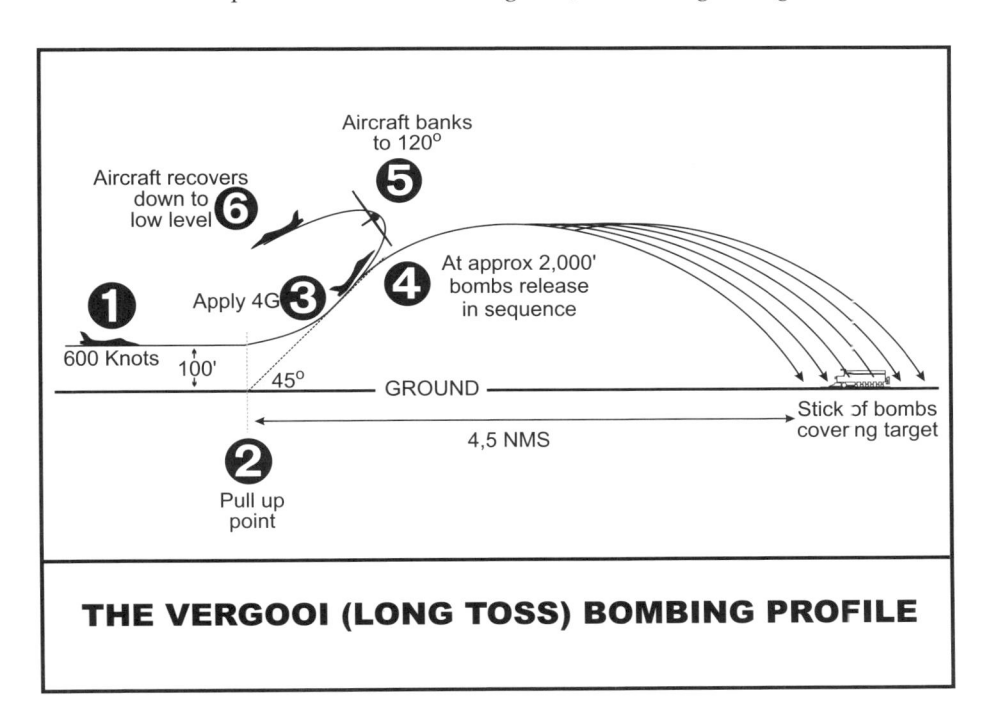

**THE VERGOOI (LONG TOSS) BOMBING PROFILE**

the mathematical genius of Mac Macatamney, finally paid off. By 18 October, the Mirages had returned to their bases in South Africa. During *Weldmesh*, the F1CZs flew 132 hours and 1 Squadron's AZs 171 hours.

Timing of operation *Weldmesh* was quite opportune. For most of December the entire F1 fleet, in the SAAF and the French Air Force, was grounded because of engine problems. It was necessary to remove the engine from each fuselage and check all the hydraulic pipes and clamps.

# Chapter 13

# 1986:
# The lull before the storm

## New OC 3 Squadron

Commandant Carlo Gagiano was appointed Officer Commanding 3 Squadron from January 1986. Captain Les Bennett, who had just completed his degree, also returned to the squadron. Although both men were experienced F1 pilots, they elected to complete the aircraft conversion course again in company with lieutenants Rudi Mes and John Sinclair who had arrived straight from 85 ADFS.

Gagiano set three objectives for himself when assuming command of the squadron, all based on his previous experience. Firstly, instead of operating in isolation, he recognized the need for 3 Squadron to co-operate closely with 1, 2, 12 and 24 Squadrons. On every border deployment that the squadrons operated together, Gagiano wanted them to train together. Secondly, he appreciated the importance of maintaining operational standards of efficiency of the aircraft and pilots in all roles. This included the Matra 530 missile, whose electromagnetic fuse was a constant problem area. Finally, he aimed to rid the squadron of all unnecessary paperwork.

By the end of his tenure he was satisfied that he had achieved his major aims, except for the Matra 530 missile. Despite much hard work, the missile failed to reach an acceptable operational standard. It would function satisfactorily in the Waterkloof test environment but did not retain the required standards in the rough and tumble of border conditions. The Matra 530 was never used operationally. The infrared fused Matra 550, while more reliable, failed to achieve hits when fired in operations, the fuse detonating the missile ineffectively as it entered the exhaust plume of the enemy aircraft.

Commandant Gagiano detached Captain Anton van Rensburg to 1 Squadron for a month to obtain, and then introduce to 3 Squadron, all the up-to-date trends in ground attack. While van Rensburg attended 1 Squadron's ground-attack weapons camps, pilots from 1 and 2 Squadrons and the fighter school attended 3 Squadron's ACM clinics. Cross-pollination raised the standard of all the squadrons.

The paperwork problem decreased to acceptable levels. On investigation, Gagiano discovered that headquarters' staff often failed to extract data from the squadron's monthly reports. It was far easier for the staff officers to order the squadrons to supply the answers they required. As a result, reams of reports were being generated by front-line personnel while it was imagined that the staff were playing golf. Gagiano's intervention brought a halt to this tendency.

On 4 May, Commandant Gagiano led a six-ship F1CZ flypast for Air Force Memorial Day. The formation flypast involved a few minutes of high stress for Gagiano. With the formation orbiting eight miles south of the monument in a holding pattern, Gagiano was in radio contact with the ground liaison officer situated at the monument. Traditionally the flypast is timed for 10 o'clock but the liaison officer may adjust the time if the VIP guests and foreign dignitaries are late in being seated.

At two minutes to ten, with his formation nicely tucked into position, Gagiano's radio failed. With insufficient time to change leadership, Gagiano decided to maintain the planned timing. The formation flew overhead the monument precisely on the hour to the approval of all the onlookers who had fortunately been seated on time.

On 19 May, 3 Squadron deployed to AFB Mpacha at the eastern end of the Caprivi Strip, to escort a 12 Squadron Canberra on a photographic sortie north of the cutline. The mission was uneventful and all the aircraft returned to Waterkloof the same day.

There had been a certain amount of consternation among the course members at 85 ADFS when trying to decide which squadron to transfer to: 1, 2 or 3. During his ACM training, Rudi Mes was so impressed with the FIs that he chose 3 Squadron. This decision, reinforced by a motivational talk by Major Clive Turner, convinced him that air defence would be his chosen role. Flying the simulator he gained his first impression of the aircraft. Although this was a non-moving trainer, the simulation was excellent and it made flying the aircraft easy, a pleasant surprise after the delta-winged Mirage III. He believes his greatest accomplishment was flying solo in that aircraft. On his first solo flight in the F1, he was impressed with the control harmony and responsiveness of the aeroplane. In his career he flew 921 hours in the F1CZ, and rues the fact of missing out on achieving the magical 1,000 hours on type. During that time he encountered very few technical problems with the airframe or the 9K50 engine.

3 Squadron used a six-month training cycle to keep the pilots operationally capable. This cycle culminated in combined mission training with the

Canberras of 12 Squadron and Buccaneers of 24 Squadron. Radio silent join-ups at rendezvous points, formation escort as well as combined strikes, were all flown in an area simulating southern Angola. A chart of the border-war area containing all the known FAPLA installations was superimposed over a section of the northeastern Transvaal. By laying the east–west Angola cut-line in a north–south direction, it was found that the distance between AFB Waterkloof and AFB Hoedspruit was almost identical to the distance of AFB Ondangwa to Menonque, one of the Angolan air bases.

Simulated PR missions were flown with Canberras or Buccaneers taking photos of 'Menonque'. Devon and Mariepskop radar controllers were used and 2 Squadron Mirage IIIs from Hoedspruit simulated MiG-21s and -23s. Solid templates were placed over the 'enemy' radarscopes to duplicate the exact amount of radar warning the Angolans would have during real missions. Time gates were studied to devise the most suitable profiles to use in the operational arena. Major Anton van Rensburg became the 'scenario king' and, thanks to his diligence, deployment to the actual war simply became an extension of the training cycle.

## Loss of Mirage F1CZ 215

Operations inside Angola called for low-level entries and exits from hostile target areas. A premium was, therefore, placed on low-flying and accurate navigation. Periodically, 3 Squadron pilots would plan and fly low-level training sorties through the mountainous areas of the Eastern Transvaal. On one of these sorties, three pilots taking off at ten-minute intervals behind one another flew the same routes

Only the first and third aircraft returned to AFB Waterkloof. On investigation it was found that F1CZ 215, flown by Captain John Sinclair was missing. A search and rescue operation was launched and information was soon gathered that the pilot was safe.

Flying down a valley, Sinclair had glanced inside the cockpit to check his position on the map. Looking up again, he was shocked to see a mountain ridge directly in front of him. In an attempt to avoid a collision, he pulled the aircraft's nose up. Unfortunately, the underneath of the fuselage struck the top of the ridge. The aircraft broke to pieces and Sinclair was forcibly ejected from the wreckage. Inertia of the flight threw his ejection seat over the ridge before the parachute deployed, allowing Sinclair to descend safely to the hillside below.

## New OC 1 Squadron

At Hoedspruit, 1986 began with the arrival of a new intake of pilots, which included the new officer commanding, Commandant Johan Rankin, Major J. P. Gouws and Captain Paulus Truter. Majors Peter Cooke and Des Barker joined them for the conversion onto the F1AZ.

Barker, a test pilot, would be responsible for clearance-testing the Mirage F1 under varying configuration patterns at the Test Flight Development Centre (TFDC) near Bredasdorp in the Cape. Pete Cooke was the project officer developing the night capability of the F1, which included refurbishing the entire cockpit lighting system. During night-attack missions, the pilot must be able to see the complete cockpit, but these lights must not reflect in the canopy or the head-up display (HUD).

By a fortunate coincidence, Johan Rankin had reached the same conclusion as Carlo Gagiano, that cross-pollination between both F1 squadrons was vital. The two of them brought their squadrons together during work and play. Camaraderie, a key element in the functioning of a team, was noticeably improved.

Having flown both versions of the F1, Commandant Rankin was in a position to compare the qualities of each aircraft. The most noticeable difference was the extra 200 litres of fuel in the AZ. Having been schooled on the Mirage III, all SAAF fighter pilots were aware of fuel or the lack thereof. Because of additional avionics the nose of the AZ was heavier than that of the CZ, which became most evident during ACM. The AZ navigation and roller-map system was excellent when finely tuned and a comfort deep inside enemy territory. On the other hand, he missed the capability of the CZ Cyrano VI radar, especially when MiGs were nearby.

The first quarter of 1986 produced numerous aircraft incidents. On 10 January, Captain Rikus de Beer lost his port drop tank and pylon. Six days later, perhaps in divine retribution for his application of excessive rolling G, he had a bird strike on the front windscreen. His forward vision was so impaired that he had to land in formation.

On 11 February, during pull-up for an auto-toss bomb profile at Roodewal range, Captain Holdsworth suffered a compressor stall. He tried numerous hot-relights but these did not clear the stall conditions. Only after cutting the engine did the stall clear, which allowed a successful relight.

Early in April, 1 Squadron achieved mixed results while practising in-flight refuelling exercises behind Buccaneer tankers. Captain Chris Skinner dented the nose of his AZ with the basket, while Paulus Truter broke the entire head off his probe.

At this stage, the B-707 tankers of 60 Squadron were becoming operational and Commandant Rankin decided to concentrate the training on utilizing these aircraft. The increased tanker capacity of the Boeing and the additional refuelling points added impetus to extended range operations practised by 1 Squadron.

The advice of doctors at the Institute of Aviation Medicine enabled operational ranges and airborne times to be greatly increased. Authorities recommend that motorists stop every two hours for a rest and to stretch their cramped limbs. Flying safety experts had voiced concern over aircrew remaining firmly strapped into ejection seats for long periods. While fatigue was an area of concern, the

## GATUP (DAY) OR NAGUP (NIGHT)

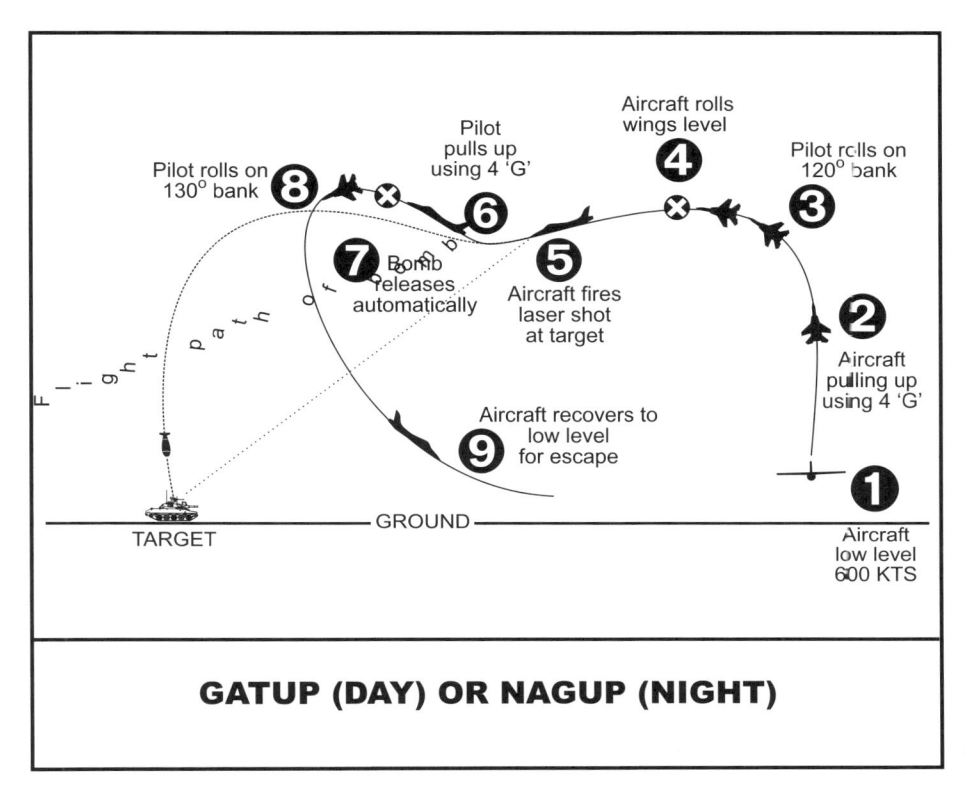

Diagram annotations:
- ① Aircraft low level 600 KTS
- ② Aircraft pulling up using 4 'G'
- ③ Pilot rolls on 120° bank
- ④ Aircraft rolls wings level
- ⑤ Aircraft fires laser shot at target
- ⑥ Pilot pulls up using 4 'G'
- ⑦ Bomb releases automatically
- ⑧ Pilot rolls on 130° bank
- ⑨ Aircraft recovers to low level for escape

most pressing issue, literally, was bladder control.

Bombing sorties, using the Jacob's Reef target off the Western Cape coast were flown, with Mirage F1AZs taking off and returning to AFB Hoedspruit. The rendezvous and top-up from tankers became second nature. These were involved, satisfying sorties, although trying on the bladder.

While Commandant Rankin concentrated on extended-range operations, Major Nic Oosthuysen and Captain Rikus de Beer continued developing the night-attack capability of the squadron. The combination of these efforts culminated in the squadron flying four-ship night sorties, including in-flight refuelling from B-707 tankers in radio silence. A typical night strike mission flown out of AFB Hoedspruit followed this pattern. Four F1AZs, each loaded with six bombs and two fuel tanks, would fly a tactical navigation to Roodewal to deliver four of their bombs. Then they would rendezvous with the tanker, top up with fuel and, before heading back to base, return to drop the last two bombs.

In May, history was made as the first night *Vergooi* attacks were carried out with very reasonable results. Daytime *Gatup* attacks were producing miss-distances of between four and eleven metres—excellent results when the effect of a 500kg high-explosive bomb is considered. The *Gatup* profile was developed by 1

Squadron specifically to be used against heavily defended targets. The approach was flown at very low level and high speeds. Both elements are crucial to aircraft survival in a hostile environment. A high-G pitch-up and roll-in onto the target is used. A laser shot is fired the moment the sight is pointed at the target. The pilot pulls up, the bombs release automatically at the optimum instant as calculated by the computer, before the pilot is cleared to escape from the combat zone.

Late in June, during the annual *Golden Eagle* force preparation exercise, 3 Squadron deployed to Punda Milia in the northern extremity of the Kruger National Park. Operating successfully out of this remote bush strip emphasized the adaptability of the Dassault Mirage fighter.

In July the fighter squadrons and mobile radar units deployed to Natal for the supersonic ACM camp, flying out of Durban. The situation in the holiday city was exceptionally tense as a terrorist bomb had exploded in Magoo's bar shortly before the squadrons arrived.

Aircraft incidents continued into the second half of the year. On 12 August, Captain Moolies Moolman took to the bush at Hoedspruit when, after landing, the nose-wheel steering deflected fully during rollout. Fortunately, his speed was down to 50 knots and he managed to stop before any damage was done. In September, a missile fell off Major Nic Oosthuysen's aircraft

In October 1 Squadron deployed to AFB Bloemspruit for weaponry training. Because aircraft serviceability was extremely good, the weapons programme was completed quickly, allowing the pilots to fly night strikes and low-level tactical navigation exercises. By the second week, the local farmers were incensed by the aircraft noise. In a conciliatory gesture, the base invited them to a braai to meet the pilots, which in the Orange Free State is akin to pouring oil on troubled waters. However, all ended well.

On 12 November, SAAF aircraft and radars were put on alert for an intercept, which occurred the following day. Commandant Rankin and Captain Reg van Eeden forced down a civilian aircraft at Hoedspruit.

1 Squadron graded their aircraft according to strict operational criteria. The aircraft were fine-tuned by the ESDAP team to ensure that all the on-board systems were kept continually at peak performance.

1986 was the lull before the storm.

## The state of the war

During 1986, the Angolans licked their wounds after the pounding they had received the previous year. This period of respite was used by both sides to catch up with training and much-needed maintenance. Operational planners on both sides of the border analyzed the battles of 1985 and began planning for the inevitable next round.

*Weldmesh* had been extremely successful and the FAPLA advance to Mavinga repulsed with the enemy suffering huge losses. The effectiveness of SAAF ground-attack strikes increased owing to the availability of the new pre-fragmented bombs and the low-level *Vergooi* bombing profile that had proved operationally sound. However, concern existed over the lack of radar cover for our own aircraft and the limited facilities for operating fighter aircraft at AFB Rundu.

The Angolans, with their Soviet and Cuban mentors, investigated the reasons for their defeat, of which there were many. The main problem was their lack of suitable air-defence systems, allowing the SAAF freedom of movement over the brigades. Another simple omission, which caused their ground troops dreadful hardships, was water. They began their operation in the dry season with insufficient water reserves. Morale among their soldiers suffered accordingly. The passive air-defence measures taken by the brigades against attacks by the SAAF were almost non-existent. Vehicles were exposed to shrapnel because they were not dug in.

Winning a battle, but not ending the war, is a two-edged sword. Victory brings euphoria and confidence, tinged with the certain knowledge that the next battle is going to be more difficult and dangerous. This was a pattern of the war. Every time we beat the opposition and captured tons of equipment, they came back for more, better equipped and better trained.

With this knowledge, the SAAF initiated corrective actions over a large spectrum, ranging from an updated command post to the deployment of mobile radar at AFB Rundu. Extensions and improvements to Rundu airfield were started but, unfortunately, these were not completed before the next offensive began in 1987.

An F1AZ between the strengthened revetments at AFB Hoedspruit.

# Chapter 14

# 1987:
# All hell breaks loose

### Tying up the loose ends

Major Norman Minne rejoined 1 Squadron in January 1987 and, together with Captain 'Trompie' Nel, completed the conversion course. By this stage the squadron had perfected a number of the projects that had been in their infancy during Minne's first tour on the AZ in the early 1980s. *Vergooi* had been operationally proven: the *Gatup* profile with automatic release of weapons was working; *Moonshine* and *Darkmoon* night tactical sorties were being flown and the Boeing 707 in-flight refuelling tanker had come on line.

From late February into early March a *Golden Eagle* force preparation exercise was held. 2 Squadron was deployed to AFB Langebaanweg to defend the base against attacks from 1, 3 and 24 Squadrons flying out of Upington. Using the facilities of 60 Squadron's B-707 tanker, a continuous combat air patrol (CAP) was maintained over Langebaanweg, the 'enemy' airfield, for over three hours. This action successfully closed down the base and precluded any air movement, much to the annoyance of the 'enemy' commanders.

Angolan MiGs were making their presence felt in the operational theatre and the probable reason for this unusual bravado was the presence of Cuban pilots. Over all the years, Angolan-piloted aircraft had remained in the area of the Namibe–Lubango–Matala railway line, 200 kilometres north of the border. On each of the two occasions, when they had dared to venture south, Major Johan Rankin had shot down a MiG-21, so they were probably wise to stay so far north.

However, the tendency was changing. A MiG base had been built at Cahama and one of their pilots even crossed the cut-line in the Ruacana area. It was never established whether this was by design or accident, but it certainly gained our attention.

## *Bellombra*

Operation *Bellombra* was planned in an attempt to curb this newfound aggression. The idea was to scramble pairs of Mirages to designated low-level holding points whenever the MiGs were in the air. Our radar controllers would watch the MiGs and, if they came into the area of one of the holding points, they would give the Mirages a radar vector and a time to pitch-up. Our aircraft would accelerate to 600 knots-plus before pitching-up. The idea was to climb to 4,000 feet below the targets. Airborne radar was only switched on during the pitch to give the enemy minimum warning before missile launch was achieved. When our aircraft were detected by Dayton radar they would be vectored onto the bogeys.

3 Squadron and the Devon controllers developed this profile in the Eastern Transvaal general flying area, using 2 Squadron as the enemy. Loskop Dam wall, Piet Gouws Dam wall and Pietersburg were the chosen holding points, closely simulating the distances between AFB Ondangwa, Oshikango and Ongiva in southern Angola. Initially, they named this attack method UNCIP, (unconventional intercept profile). Later the name changed to LIP (low-level intercept profile). Success in training was surprisingly high, until the 'MiG' ground-attackers were supported by 'MiG' escorts and combat air patrols (CAPs). On pitching-up, our pilots were never too sure which formation they were attacking. There was always the real danger of ending up sandwiched between enemy aircraft.

At Hoedspruit, the fighter controllers and 2 Squadron practised the profile using Hippo Pools, Phalaborwa, Thoyandou and Madimbo as low-level holding points. A Telstar relay aircraft was used to pass radio messages between the fighters and the controllers. The profile was also practised at AFB Langebaanweg using Buccaneers as the 'enemy'.

On 24 June, 3 Squadron and the dedicated team of Devon radar controllers deployed to AFB Ondangwa to operationally employ the profiles. By first light the following day, the pilots were on cockpit standby and controllers were positioned at the consoles of 140 Radar Squadron on the edge of the airfield. The waiting began. By mid-morning, MiG activity was detected and shortly thereafter the Mirage F1CZs were scrambled. An important aspect of this plan was to ensure its security. Our aircraft were not to pitch-up into enemy radar unless a kill was guaranteed. In retrospect, this was a harsh limiting factor and numerous unsuccessful scrambles were performed.

Another unsuccessful scramble to the Ongiva area occurred on 28 June, where our controllers wisely did not allow our aircraft to pitch-up. The reason was that, instead of the usual one or two MiG formations, radar controller, Commandant Delport, had picked up a total of 22 blips operating in the same area. On analysis, after landing, it appeared that the Angolans were aware of our plan and had created their own trap. In the event neither side gained success.

Meanwhile on 23 June, back in South Africa, General Jannie Geldenhuys was invited to fly in the Boeing 707 to experience the capability-enhancement in-flight refuelling provided. Four F1AZs from AFB Hoedspruit rendezvoused with the 60 Squadron B-707 that had taken off from AFB Waterkloof. After refuelling from the tanker, the Mirage formation flew to Hopefield bombing range north of Cape Town where a bombing attack was carried out. On the return flight, another refuelling rendezvous with the tanker allowed the formation to land back at Hoedspruit four hours after take-off.

On 24 June, 3 Squadron pilots at AFB Ondangwa were tasked to escort a Canberra photographic- reconnaissance mission over southern Angola that proved uneventful. After the sortie, the Mirage F1CZs were refuelled for the return flight to AFB Waterkloof. Commandant Gagiano noticed that, instead of refuelling from the customary bowser, the underground fuelling installation was used. This change of procedure made Gagiano uncomfortable and he asked for the condition of the fuel to be checked before allowing his F1s to take off.

His hunch proved to be correct as the fuel was badly contaminated. All the F1s had to be checked, have their fuel drained, engine fuel filters changed and the pilots returned home in the back of a C-130 transport aircraft The Air Force Safety Board awarded Gagiano a 'Well Done' certificate for professionalism that probably prevented a serious accident.

Between 28 and 30 June, 1 Squadron's Johan Rankin, Chris Skinner, Rikus de Beer and Willie van Coppenhagen deployed to AFB Grootfontein for electronic-intelligence gathering (elint) flights. On one of these flights, Skinner and de Beer flew low-level to a position northeast of Cuito Cuanavale. Turning onto a southwesterly heading they pitched to 2,000 feet as they passed just south of the enemy positions around the town. Before the enemy missiles could react, both aircraft plunged to very low level for the return to base. Recordings from the radar-warning receiver (RWS) equipment in both aircraft verified the presence of SA-3s and SA-8s.

3 Squadron deployed to AFB Ondangwa from 15 to 22 July but not a single operational sortie was flown. Both sides were flexing their muscles and nerves were becoming strained. In the fog of war, the commencement of hostilities is often difficult to predict.

## *Moduler*

In mid-1987, FAPLA, encouraged by their Cuban allies, crossed the bridge at Cuito Cuanavale and headed off towards Mavinga in the southeast. The strategy and approach routes were almost identical to the ones utilized in 1985, when they were repulsed and which ended disastrously for them. As the next serious conflict drew inexorably closer, however, they were better prepared logistically and in terms of air defence weaponry.

# 1987: All hell breaks loose

Low level over the Cuito River from the cockpit of an F1AZ during a sortie in the bush war.

This operation, almost a carbon copy of Weldmesh in 1985, developed into an unexpectedly long, seven-month deployment to support the subsequent operations *Hooper* and *Packer*.

Once again, FAPLA decided on a pincer movement, using basically the same advance routes as before. The South African Defence Force was asked to stop the enemy right-hook—two FAPLA brigades—against the key town Mavinga. As in 1985, UNITA did not have the capability of stopping the advancing armour and requested assistance from South Africa. Cabinet approval was only granted at a later stage, when the enemy 47th Brigade was south of the Lomba River. This is where the similarity to operation *Weldmesh* ended.

The communist brains trust had corrected their 1985 errors. They brought water- and air-defence missile systems with them. MiG-21s, -23s and SU-22s were deployed at Menonque and they stationed their helicopter force, consisting of Mi-8, Mi-17, Mi-25 and Mi-35s, at Cuito Cuanavale. Protecting Menonque were static SA-3 missile batteries. Within the advancing brigades they included mobile SA-6, SA-7, SA-8, SA-9, SA-13, SA-14 and SA-16 batteries as integral units. Their armoured fighting force was made up of 40 T-54 and T-55 tanks, BM21 multiple rocket launchers (the famous Stalin Organ), BRDM, BMP and BTR fighting vehicles. Their artillery support came from D-30 and M-46 cannons with firing ranges up to 30 kilometres.

On 4 September, 3 Squadron was deployed to AFB Rundu for air defence duties,

181

together with a Rodent mobile radar unit. The base itself was in chaos as the runway was being extended and a large building programme was in progress. Facilities were at a premium. This led 3 Squadron to christen their readiness tent at the end of the runway 'Little Siberia'. An arrestor barrier had been installed at the end of the runway but at that stage there was no available power to raise it.

Hygiene left a lot to be desired and, within a week of arrival, everybody was suffering from diarrhoea. Squadron strength was often down to four fit pilots, which caused an extremely stressful situation. Air defence required pilots to be strapped into their aircraft throughout the day, seven days a week. Under glass canopies, with temperatures soaring over 40°C, the pilots endured gruelling conditions. The hardship was amplified by the perennial problem of war—the impossibility to forecast when it would all end.

Because of substantial MiG activity over the advancing enemy brigades, the pilots of 3 Squadron and the radar controllers decided to modify the LIP profiles to suit the area north of Rundu. The AR3D radar was sited on a ridge ten nautical miles north of AFB Rundu and used the call sign Sunset Radar.

Holding points were worked out and cockpit standbys became the order of the day. The distances involved were so vast that, although a number of scrambles were made, our aircraft arrived in the area only after the MiGs had left. It must be pointed out that Rundu radar could only see aircraft in the combat area above 24,000 feet because of the limits of the radar horizon. However, the enemy, with radar at Cuito Cuanavale and Menonque, had coverage from the ground upwards. As most of the air activity took place below our radar horizon, our pilots were going in blind—like taking a knife to a gunfight.

Because of the realistic training programme they had undergone, pilots of 3 Squadron were full of confidence. They were tasked to escort the Mirage III RZs of Leon Burger and Keith Page during the many PR missions that were flown prior to the real outbreak of hostilities. At the back of their minds was the opportunity of a dogfight. Everybody wanted a MiG. Carlo Gagiano and Anton van Rensburg always seemed to fly together, while Pierre du Plessis, Frank Tonkin, Mark Raymond, John Sinclair, Jaco de Beer, Rudi Mes and Arthur Piercy used to rotate.

On 10 September, the *Bellombra* training paid off. Commandant Thinus du Toit, at 320 Forward Air Force Command Post, authorized the scramble of three pairs of F1CZs. Shortly after arriving at their holding point, Commandant Carlo Gagiano and Captain Anton van Rensburg were told to pitch-up into an intercept. It sounded as calm and as cool as a training exercise. Gagiano asked for a height check on the bogeys and climbed above them. As the range decreased he called, "Tanks" and both aircraft jettisoned their empty drop tanks.

Moments before the cross, on the head-on intercept profile, van Rensburg screamed that he had visual on one of the two MiG-23s. The MiG pilot had turned to the left, exposing his aircraft's tailpipe and van Rensburg immediately spiralled down behind him. Within seconds he achieved firing parameters and launched a Matra 550 missile. It guided, but exploded in the heat plume behind the MiG-23. He launched his other missile that also tracked the descending MiG. Not knowing where the second MiG was, van Rensburg broke off before seeing his second missile detonate.

Gagiano, who had missed the frantic action, joined van Rensburg as the MiGs fled back to Menonque. The second Matra 550 also failed to bring down the MiG, a failing of that generation of missiles. After the engagement, both Mirages returned 163 nautical miles to AFB Rundu. Following this incident, the pilots were even more confident and everyone volunteered to be on the next cockpit standby

Meanwhile, 1 Squadron had ferried to AFB Grootfontein. The opening sortie of the operation was scheduled for 16 September. Major Minne, being the new boy on the block, was allocated the only unserviceable aircraft. Persuading the ever-willing ground crew to pull out all the stops, he was finally airborne on 15 September at 22h30, for a night test flight (illegal in peacetime). After an engine change, the test schedule required an acceleration past Mach 1.4 to check the operation of the engine overspeed system. Minne carried out a full afterburner climb, levelled out, achieved the M1.4, then cut the afterburner and returned to land. He reported the aircraft serviceable.

Next morning, after an extensive briefing regarding the possibility of encountering SA-6s and SA-8s, the formation, including Minne, was airborne at 05h45. After his last experience over Lubango when 1 Squadron had two aircraft damaged by missiles, Minne flew the sortie with a certain amount of trepidation. As it turned out, this first sortie was a non-event as no enemy fire was experienced.

Initial South African artillery fire accounted for some tanks and over 200 enemy but their advance continued. On 16 September, the SAAF opened the air offensive with a combined air strike against 47 Brigade, delivering 100 x Mk 82 250kg pre-frag bombs.

The success of the Mk 81 (120kg) during 1985 had prompted the designers to modify the original American Mk 82 (250kg) bomb. The casing was constructed to contain larger diameter ball-bearings. The greater inertia of these heavier balls allowed them to penetrate the light armoured covering of the enemy's fighting vehicles.

During the early strikes against the enemy brigades deployed near the Lomba River, Commandant Johan Rankin led an attack that nearly proved to be his last. As planned, his formation pitched-up for a *Vergooi* delivery. After bomb release, the profile calls for a rapid application of 130° of bank to return to the comparative safety of low level as quickly as possible. As Rankin rolled into this turn a 'missile-launch' call was heard on the radio.

Swivelling his head to the rear, he soon picked up numerous smoke trails coming towards his aircraft. Distracted by the approaching missiles, he retained too much bank while pulling the nose down to avoid the missiles. As the danger receded he looked forward to see treetops filling his windscreen. Rolling wings level and pulling maximum G, he entered an open *shona*. The absence of trees provided the extra 50 feet he needed to recover. Leaving a plume of dust, he flashed below the spreading tops of a clump of makelani palms, before returning to more normal conditions for the return flight to AFB Grootfontein.

At the debrief when the situation was analyzed, it was discovered that Captain Reg van Eeden had ended up in a similar predicament. All subsequent strike briefings included a reminder of priorities during an attack sequence: first, accurate bomb release; second, avoidance of missiles and third, a safe recovery.

*****

Despite the intensity of the war, visiting groups from South Africa continued to make their almost daily appearance in the operational theatre. Time had to be set aside to brief each group—a tedious, but necessary part of the war. However, a welcome sight at AFB Rundu was the arrival of the members attending the senior joint staff course who were to be updated on the progress of the war.

During the army briefing, Brigadier Thackwray, a renowned practical joker, quietly whispered instructions into my ear. Slipping out of the side door, I hurried across to 3 Squadron's operations room. The guests broke off for tea, which was served under the trees outside the briefing room at 10h00 where Thackwray wanted to give them a surprise.

I had briefed Captain Arthur Piercy to take off shortly before teatime. At precisely 10h10 he was to make a high-speed, low-level pass over 32 Battalion headquarters where the briefing was being held. On the second, just as tea had been poured, Piercy's F1 arrived. When an aircraft travels faster than the speed of sound no warning sound indicates its approach. Piercy's was unheralded, although he claimed his aircraft was flying below Mach 1. Cups, saucers and people fell to the ground as if poleaxed. Minutes later some semblance of order was restored outside. However, inside the headquarters consternation reigned.

General Georg Meiring, General Officer Commanding the entire theatre, instead of going outside for tea, had been called to Colonel Eddie Viljoen's office to take an urgent phone call. He was deep in conversation when the shock wave from the Mirage F1 struck the building. Neon-lighting tubes and ceiling panels fell down. The accumulated dust of many years swirled through the building like advection fog on the Skeleton Coast. A shaken general appeared out of the gloom looking like a figure from Cape Town's famous Coon Carnival, with only his eyes not covered with dust. Being the man he is, he took the prank in the spirit it was intended—fortunately for Piercy.

# 1987: All hell breaks loose

## MiG surprise

During the morning of 27 September, 3 Squadron escorted a photographic-reconnaissance sortie over the Lomba River area without incident. At 15h30 that afternoon, three pairs of Mirage F1CZs, Carlo Gagiano and Arthur Piercy, Pierre du Plessis and Frank Tonkin and Rudi Mes and Jaco de Beer, were scrambled. The first two pairs set off in trail to a holding point. Mes and de Beer, the last pair, were vectored 40° off to the left to act as a cut-off in case other MiGs entered the area while the first pairs were occupied with the main intercept.

Gagiano and Piercy were given the order to pitch-up and once again the

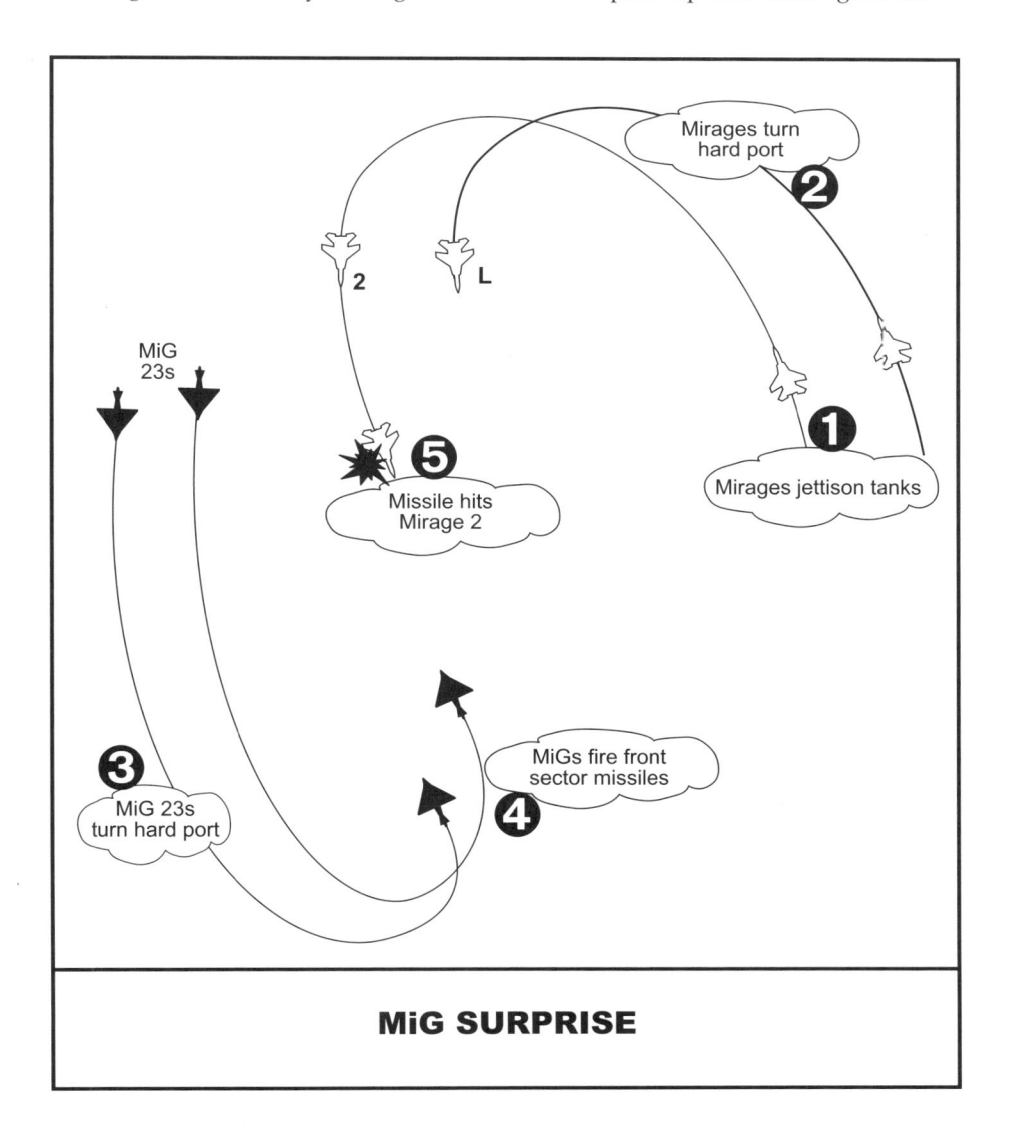

**MiG SURPRISE**

intercept happened as if in training. The range closed in a head-on profile, drop tanks were jettisoned and at the cross Gagiano saw an aircraft and called, "Su-22, correction Mig-23." Both pairs then entered left-hand turns to approach again in a head-on posture. At the extreme range of the turning circles, it was with difficulty that the pilots maintained visual contact with the MiGs.

As they were nearing the head-on position Piercy shouted, "Missiles!" as three front-sector missiles, probably AAM-8s, were launched from the MiGs. One missile, which could be seen in Gagiano's camera-gun film, passed directly over Gagiano's canopy. The other two guided onto Piercy, one of which exploded on the left-hand side of his aircraft alongside his tailpipe.

Gagiano shouted, "Arthur, you've been hit! Go down! Go down! Go down!" At this, Piercy disappeared from view.

Gagiano then asked, "Where are you?"

"Among the trees, going like the clappers!" replied Piercy. The MiGs had disappeared and Gagiano joined up with Piercy to help assess the damage.

Meanwhile Piercy had his hands full coping with all sorts of emergencies, hydraulics and fuel being the cause of greatest concern. When Gagiano drew alongside his first comment was possibly the understatement of the war: "Arthur, you've had your tail feathers ruffled." After that, as they flew back to Rundu, he nursed Piercy through all the emergency procedures. The drag-'chute had been shot off, fuel was leaking from holes on the right-hand side of the aircraft, hydraulics had failed and Piercy was using the emergency throttle to control engine power.

The deficiencies at AFB Rundu airfield now assumed major proportions. After a fine exhibition of piloting skills, Piercy managed to land the aircraft safely. Unfortunately, the lack of hydraulic pressure used to work the aircraft braking system, coupled with the loss of the braking drag-'chute, made the aircraft unstoppable. Because of the lack of an arrestor barrier, the aircraft shot off the end of the runway at high speed. A heavy impact on the rough surface caused the ejection seat to fire, throwing Piercy out of the cockpit. Unfortunately, because of insufficient time, the parachute did not deploy. When he was found, he was still strapped into his seat and had sustained major damage to his lower back, an unjust reward after a superb display of airmanship.

## A step into the third generation

This incident brought home the fact that the technology advantage now lay in the hands of our enemies. While the facts were being analyzed, 3 Squadron was restricted to base defence and escort duties; *Bellombra* sorties were cancelled.

Commandant Mossie Basson, a former 1 Squadron pilot, played a very important role in altering the entire air combat manoeuvring programme with regard to fighting against front-sector missiles. He gathered information relating to performance of the AAM-7 and AAM-8 missiles. He brought in tactical changes to our fighting doctrine, explaining why and when to cut afterburner to reduce the infrared signature of our aircraft. Training started at AFB Rundu, but without practice missiles it was a difficult and inexact science. Initially we were hopeful of acquiring the Matra Magic missile, but the weapons boycott eliminated that possibility.

On 4 October, Commandant Rankin led a four-ship F1AZ *Vergooi* strike against the Angolan 59th Brigade situated in the bush near the Lomba River, northeast of Mavinga. Digby Holdsworth, Norman Minne and Paulus Truter were the other pilots. Critical fuel factors limited the attack directions for these strikes from the south and shortage of navigable features further reduced the attack options open to the pilots. On this strike, because of these factors, they planned to use a pitch-up point previously used. This disregard for the principle of surprise almost resulted in drastic consequences.

The attack plan required two pairs of Mirage F1AZs, 15 seconds apart, to use the same pitch-up point (PUP). As Norman Minne, leading the second pair, released his bombs he thought he saw a smoke trail passing over his cockpit. Breaking down for the recovery, he saw a second SA-7 pass over the aircraft. Digby Holdsworth was called into a break as a third SAM guided onto his exhaust plume and exploded in the trees behind his F1. At the mission debrief, Minne asked Paulus Truter if he had seen the missiles. Truter replied in the affirmative, but as it was his first missile sighting, he had been too tense to call. The enemy's clever deployment to the previously used pitch-up point nearly paid dividends and a sobering lesson was re-learned.

After the first heavy strike, the enemy did not begin their retreat as expected so further bombardment by aircraft and artillery was continued until October when the remaining enemy soldiers fled on foot. When the battlefield was later cleared, it was discovered that their vehicles had been decimated by the larger ball-bearings in the new Mk 82 pre-fragmented bombs. Engines, radiators and tyres had been punctured and the vehicles were immovable.

*Moduler* was a complete success. The enemy advance on Mavinga had been stopped and all their brigades were retreating towards Cuito Cuanavale. It was at this juncture that adrenaline replaced reason. The aim of the operation changed and orders were issued, contrary to advice from the SAAF planners, to harass the enemy in their retreat.

## *Hooper*

Escalation in the numbers and sophistication of enemy aircraft seriously concerned SAAF planners. Mavinga was virtually equidistant between the Angolan fighter base of Menonque and the SAAF strike base at AFB Grootfontein. Radars sited at Cuito Cuanavale and AFB Rundu gave similar coverage to both sides operating over the battlefield. Survival odds for fighter aircraft were an evenly balanced 50/50.

As the chase continued, the battlefield moved farther and farther north, every kilometre increasing the aerial battle odds firmly in favour of the enemy. Eventually the pursuit reached a stalemate position around the Chambinga high ground, east of Cuito Cuanavale.

*Moduler* officially ended on 26 November and was replaced firstly by Operation *Hooper* and then *Packer* The aims of these operations were to destroy FAPLA forces east of the Cuito River and drive them off the east bank by 13 March in *Hooper*'s case, and 12 May in *Packer*'s. Neither objective was achieved, although the defending FAPLA forces were rendered impotent and unable to mount any further offensives.

During this long, drawn-out period the SAAF operated under the most trying conditions. Flight time for the Mirage F1AZ strike aircraft operating out of AFB Grootfontein was 43 minutes to the target area. Both entry and departure from the target area had to be flown at very low altitudes to avoid enemy radar warning. Fuel was critical, leaving the pilots only two minutes combat time if Angolan fighters intercepted them. The severe fuel limitations did not allow attacks to be made from different directions, thus making attack profiles predictable and, therefore, easier for the enemy to defend.

The most serious problem was that of radar cover. Radar coverage is restricted to line of sight. At low level the radar beam is restricted by the horizon to about 20 nautical miles. The curvature of the earth produces a blind area which the radar cannot penetrate (known in the SAAF as a red radar area). The battlefield was now so far north that the lower limit of radar from Rundu was 24,000 feet. Therefore, SAAF radar could only detect aircraft operating above that height. As the aerial support was predominantly for ground-attack sorties, the flying took place well below the horizon line. SAAF pilots received no assistance from radar whatsoever.

Angolan aircraft, operating out of Menonque, were within nine minutes' flying time of the combat zone. They could stay for over an hour above the ground battle before having to return to base to refuel. This situation led to justifiable complaints from ground forces embroiled in the battle that enemy MiGs were overhead all day but the SAAF never appeared.

Enemy pilots, both Angolan and Cuban, were delighted with the situation. For the first and only time in the entire war, they controlled the air. Their confidence was gained from the knowledge that they flew with positive radar cover from ground level up. Radar at Cuito Cuanavale, two minutes from the battlefield, ensured this advantage. The analogy can be compared to two boxers in the ring, one of whom is blindfolded. It is a dangerous situation when closing speeds of 2,000 kilometres per hour occur and guided missiles are the favoured weapons.

That the enemy still lost the battles was testimony to the excellent training the pilots received, the care and meticulous work that went into the planning and, not least, to the skill and enthusiasm of the pilots themselves. During seven months, virtually all flying was carried out between 500 and 600 knots at extremely low level. In the 1970s, Commandant (now Lieutenant-General) Hechter had concentrated on not gaining height during steep turns close to the ground. In the missile environment prevailing in southern Angola this was excellent farsightedness.

Visionaries had foreseen the need to develop a low-level toss-bomb (*Vergooi*) profile. Low-level navigation, while travelling at speeds approaching 16 kilometres per minute, was perfected with the assistance of finely tuned on-board computer systems. To ensure maximum effect, correct weapons were designed for the prevailing situation and brought into service.

On 24 October, 3 Squadron detached aircraft from AFB Rundu to AFB Ondangwa to escort a Mirage III R2Z photographic-reconnaissance mission. The same evening they returned to AFB Rundu to continue the war in that theatre.

On 11 November, Captain Chris Skinner was the leader of two three-ship F1AZ formations from AFB Grootfontein, on a strike sortie to a target east of Cuito Cuanavale. Because of the great distance and limited fuel availability, our strikes were becoming predictable. On this occasion, a Boeing 707 refuelling tanker was used to refuel our aircraft before the strike. This allowed the pilots to vary their ingress routes and attack the enemy from the north. Previously, tankers had been used to allow aircraft to refuel after strike sorties and avoid diverting to alternate airfields. At that stage the B-707 had only a centre station and the F1 pilots were not practised in refuelling with such heavily loaded aircraft. Mini-afterburner had to be used by the fighter pilots just to stay in the basket. The attempt was only partially successful.

The plan was for all Mirages to top up before passing over AFB Rundu. Turbulence and very heavily loaded Mirages forced refuelling to take place at a higher altitude than anticipated. The delay in taking on fuel, for all six aircraft, resulted in the second three-ship formation having to abort the sortie and return to Grootfontein. It was necessary for Chris and his two wingmen to plug a second time before they detached and carried out a successful attack.

On 25 November, four F1CZs were tasked to escort three Buccaneers on an H2 guided bomb mission to cut the runway at Menonque. A planning session had been held at AFB Grootfontein where co-ordination among formations was finalized. After a delay the Mirages were airborne from Rundu at 08h20. A radio-silent rendezvous was made with the Grootfontein Buccaneers. Previous combined training paid dividends. To avoid warning the enemy radar and SAM-3 missile systems defending the base, the entry was at low level

At the pitch, one pair of the F1s dropped chaff, carried in their dive brakes. The dispensers were not yet ready for operational use. Only the lead F1 was equipped with the CRWS ECM radar-warning receiver. However, it was installed in all the Buccaneers. Levelling off at altitude, all aircraft headed towards Menonque. Although they were inside SAM-3 range, the time gate was such that it was necessary to launch the guided bombs before any defensive missile could be fired at the formation. Unfortunately, a technical hitch prevented both bombs from launching and the formation homed to almost overhead Menonque before Commandant 'Lappies' Labuschagne, leader of the Buccaneers, called the abort, turned for home and plunged to low level. The second pair of F1s dropped chaff at the top of descent before screaming down to treetop level. Our GCI radar detected a MiG scramble and interception of the chaff blips when all our aircraft were safely out of range.

## The bridge over the River Cuito

On 8, 12 and 13 December, Mirage F1AZs were used to escort a 24 Squadron Buccaneer on H2 guided-bomb strikes on the bridge at Cuito Cuanavale. Major 'Pikkie' Siebrits and Captain Neil Napier were the crew of the Buccaneer. After repeated attempts success was achieved, although the bridge was never totally destroyed.

By late December, the enemy was trying to reinforce his position around Cuito Cuanavale. Huge logistical convoys were operating from Menonque and it was decided that attacks against the resupply route would hamper this build-up. At great risk, ground force reconnaissance teams infiltrated the area and, by radio, passed back information about the position and composition of these convoys and where they stopped for the night.

## The lion's testicles

This valuable intelligence was used to plan air attacks that were usually flown either at last light or early dawn. These extreme times were selected to reduce the threats faced by our pilots. FAPA, the Angolan Air Force did not operate well in the dark and was seldom seen. The poor visibility at dawn or nightfall was the only advantage our pilots had in their favour. As one Mirage pilot explained, "It was rather like playing with a lion's testicles."

After incoming intelligence had been assessed at Sector 20 Forward Air Command Post, plans were made and aircraft tasked to carry out the required strikes. Invariably, these orders only reached 1 Squadron pilots during the evening. Then the crews designated for the sortie would carry out the pre-strike planning before going to bed. A wake-up call at 03h00 the next day ensured that crews were tired as well as tense. Grootfontein had no meteorological station to provide updated weather information and very few navigational aids were available in this remote area of South West Africa. After briefing, the pilots would go out to the aircraft and, in complete radio silence, start up and taxi out. After line-up on the runway, the pilots were cleared for take-off by a green light from the tower.

It was planned that the formation set heading overhead a distinctive old mine dump northeast of Grootfontein town. The heavily loaded aircraft started their take-off roll using ten-second intervals between one aircraft and the next. On a number of these pre-dawn strikes, the aircraft lifted off and disappeared into cloud before the undercarriage was locked away. Each pilot was allocated a height difference of 300 feet. Nevertheless, it was an uncomfortable feeling knowing that there were another six or eight aircraft, all in the same piece of cloud, within 300 feet of one another. No pilot wanted to break radio silence or climb above the cloud because these actions would warn the enemy of the approaching formation. Often it was only after they had crossed into Angola that it was light enough to see the rest of the aircraft and settle into the briefed attack formation.

Then, the anxiety of the take-off and join-up was replaced by the excitement of really low flying. Five minutes before strike time this thrill altered to an adrenaline rush. At this juncture the formation would accelerate to 540 knots. Armament switches were checked and re-checked and electronic warfare (EW) equipment turned on. Approaching the initial point (IP) the speed was stabilized at 600 knots. Pilots held their aircraft level at 50 feet on the radio altimeter. Navigation was by reference to maps giving the maximum feature references.

Directly overhead the IP the formation leader 'hacked'. This procedure begins

F1AZs battened down during a tropical storm in South West Africa.

the final precise flying to the release point, using heading and ground speed gained from the roller map and the navigation computer. At the pitch-up point, usually around 5.2 nautical miles from the centre of the target, the pilots applied 4G to their aircraft within two seconds. Keeping the wings level, they pulled the aircraft's nose skyward, monitoring the fly-up light in the head-up display (HUD). At 2,000 feet the horizontal green light in the HUD illuminated and the pilots manually pressed the bomb-release button. The bombs were released in sequence according to the pre-set intervalometer settings to give the required bomb stick length.

A standard practice among the pilots was to press the bomb-jettison button immediately after the manual release to rid their aircraft of any bombs that may have hung up. The extra drag on the return flight often made the fuel situation extremely critical. Therefore, it was advisable to ensure that all bombs had left the aircraft.

After release, it was necessary from a safety point of view to return to low level as soon as possible. Each aircraft banked away from the target and the pilot pulled the nose down as quickly as possible. Each pilot had a different escape heading to ensure safety among aircraft and to make it difficult for the enemy defences to track the formation. Going down, the pilots looked backwards to watch for anti-aircraft fire (AAA) or the telltale smoke trails from surface-to-air missiles.

As mentioned, summer in Angola brings weather conditions known locally as the 'big rains'. Enormous tropical thunderstorms create extreme flying conditions with heavy rain, strong wind gusts and severe turbulence. Not knowing the positions of these storms often meant that pilots, running in low-level, pitched-up for the attack right into these enormous clouds. Bomb release would be done on instruments as well as the recovery to a normal flight attitude. The aircraft were safe from the enemy while inside the cloud, but in mortal danger from the elements.

One of the unfortunate characteristics of attacking under poor daylight conditions was the fact that enemy anti-aircraft fire and the flame emitted from the ground-to-air missiles were very easily seen. The impression etched on the pilot's brain was that targets then always appeared more dangerous.

3 Squadron 1987. Standing from left: Carel Wessels, Anton van Rensburg, Mark Raymond, Arthur Piercy, Rudi Mes, John Sinclair, Pierre Joubert. Seated from left: Johan Lubbe, Jako de Beer, Seun van Heerden, Carlo Gagiano, Pierre du Plessis, Frank Tonkin, André Schoeman.

Oryx helicopters would land in the spectacular Drakensberg Mountains during mountain-flying training.

# Chapter 15

# 1988: Stalemate

## *Hooper* continues

Operation *Moduler* ended in November 1987 and the forces were now engaged with Operation *Hooper*. The end of every year created problems for the army, because it was based on the national-service system. Soldiers, at the end of their two-year-service period had to be withdrawn from operations and replaced with a new intake. This changeover caused a hiccup in operations, much enjoyed by the primarily permanent force members of the SAAF. Over the festive season, while the army completed its reshuffle, 1 Squadron left five pilots and aircraft at AFB Grootfontein in a caretaker role. The remainder of 1 Squadron enjoyed the comforts of home.

By early February 1988, the battle resumed in earnest and air strikes were flown against the Angolan 21st, 25th and 59th Brigades. On 6 February, 24 Squadron Buccaneers escorted by F1AZs, again attacked the bridge over the Cuito River using the H2 guided bomb.

At 18h17 on 18 February, 12 F1AZs took off from AFB Grootfontein for the third strike of the day. After the attack, the aircraft had to divert to AFB Rundu as bad weather had closed the runway at Grootfontein. Three four-ship formations, low on fuel, arrived at Rundu in the dark. Rundu airfield had not been built for this amount of traffic. Like most remote airfields, no taxi strips had been constructed. Dumbbells at the end of the runway allowed landing aircraft to turn off, and then backtrack up the runway. The arrival of 1 Squadron certainly tested that theory.

As the aircraft were short of fuel, there was no time to individually clear the runway, as planned during the airfield's construction. The Mirages landed from west to east and had to stack themselves one behind the other down the side of the runway. Major Willie van Coppenhagen, landing behind Norman Minne, had a drag-'chute failure, but nevertheless managed to stop.

When all 12 Mirages had landed safely, they had to wait for an Impala Telstar aircraft that was also desperate to land. The Impala pilot, in the illumination of his landing light, saw aircraft blocking one side of the runway for close to half the runway length. This alarming sight made him very heavy-footed on the brakes and his attempt to stop burst the main-wheel tyres. After an uncomfortable night in makeshift accommodation, the pilots returned to Grootfontein the following morning.

## Lubango again

On 20 February, Colonel John Church, in charge of 310 AFCP at Oshakati, reported a SWAPO-initiated bomb blast in Oshakati town. A reprisal raid on two targets within the SWAPO Tobias Haneko Training Centre, close to Lubango, was planned. Mission planning at Grootfontein went on late into the night. The next morning a very early ferry to AFB Ondangwa was required to reduce the range to the target, thereby increasing the fuel safety margins.

Eventually retiring to bed, the tired crews were kept awake by the noise of a wedding party in full flow at Grootfontein. Before 06h00 the next morning Johan Rankin, in a fit of pique, led his eight aircraft at low level in full afterburner over the town. Presumably the wedding party woke up with a bang, perhaps a little earlier than anticipated.

Landing at AFB Ondangwa was a pleasant surprise. Colonel Koos Botha, the

Soviet-built SA-8 launch vehicle being loaded for recovery from the battlefield.

commanding officer, had laid on transport, breakfast and briefing facilities, in a show of organization that the squadron had not previously experienced when arriving at a base in the bush.

After refuelling, the aircraft took off from Ondangwa at 08h00. Major Norman Minne led the combined strike, flying F1AZ 218. This aircraft's excellent navigation system was giving errors of less than one mile at all the waypoints. Approaching Lubango from the southeast, the compact radar-warning receiver (CRWS) started picking up indications of Soviet-built Barlock and search radars on the air. He took his formation lower and lower. Because his navigation system was proving so accurate, Minne tucked away his standby map and prepared for the attack.

A famous quotation from the Second World War states: 'Battles always take place at the joins on the maps', indicating that there is always a 'buggerance' factor in the fog of war. This strike was no exception. The two targets were either side of the join in the maps. Unbeknown to Minne, this join gave ten minutes of a degree error in the measured target co-ordinates. With the aid of his perfect navigation system, he led Trompie Nel and Johan Rankin straight over the edge of Lubango airfield before initiating the *Vergooi* attack. Their bombs landed ten miles away in the bush. Each minute of a degree equates to one mile on the ground.

Fortunately, the co-ordinates of the target for the second formation were correct and a successful *Gatup* attack was carried out. In this attack three aircraft dropped their bombs. Major Willie van Coppenhagen, who realized that his sight conditions were not correct for an accurate release, performed a second attack on his own, with his bombs landing as planned. Probably the most dangerous act in warfare is to carry out a repeat attack on a target, but luckily van Coppenhagen got away with it. Most aircraft flew directly back to Grootfontein while the others, for safety reasons, refuelled at Ondangwa.

Around midday Major Minne led a four-ship strike on a target near Baixo Longa. Later that afternoon, Commandant Rankin and Captain Reg van Eeden, returning from another mission, also flew close to the small town. Their flight was rudely disturbed when a large, smoke-trailing missile, probably an SA-9, flashed between the two aircraft. The residents of Baixo Longa were obviously a little touchy after Major Minne's midday visit.

## Mirage F1AZ shoot-down

During the early afternoon, a message from a 32 Battalion reconnaissance detachment in the bush reported a large convoy movement on the Menonque–Cuito Cuanavale road. Planning was carried out and at 16h30 Norman Minne, Ed Every, Frans Coetzee and Trompie Nel took off to attack the convoy, using a *Vergooi* profile and dropping sticks of pre-fragmented air-burst bombs. Over the previous five or six days a number of sorties had been flown in the same area.

After releasing their bombs, Minne and Every broke out to the left while the other pair went right. Minne heard Every shout, "Break left!" and promptly obeyed. Seconds later he heard Nel shouting, "Eject! Eject!" Reaching the safety of low level, Minne could see the plume of smoke where Major Ed Every's aircraft had crashed. Flying over the crash site, he could see that the aircraft was totally broken up. No emergency calls were picked up on the emergency Pelba beacon so it was presumed that Every had been killed. It was his second tour. He was aged thirty-one.

During the seven-month deployment, squadron personnel were continually rotated to allow for rest and recreation back at Hoedspruit. Preference was given to married members so bachelors did not visit home quite so frequently. At this particular time, bachelor Captain Chris Skinner wanted to return to South Africa for a special occasion. Major Every, a married man, had volunteered to stay behind at Grootfontein in Skinner's place. Every was shot down that weekend.

At that stage, because of the static nature of the war, it is presumed that the enemy had studied our tactics. An air-defence battery had been moved close to the pitch-up point, allowing the missile system to attain a lock-on on the aircraft's exhaust plume, as Every broke off after bomb release. The missile successfully tracked and struck the aircraft as it reached low level.

An immense search and rescue (SAR) operation was launched. Captain Dave Stock flew a Telstar mission, listening for possible emergency radio transmissions. A C-160 Transall scoured the region with a team of Parabats who, if any sign of Every were found, were ready to jump into the hostile area. However, it was clear from Nel's description that Every had not survived. That night the air- and ground crew joined in what could only be described as a passionate farewell.

The continuous presence of enemy MiG fighters over the battlefield had become a genuine source of concern. Ground troops could move their vehicles only at night and the artillery were not able to give supporting fire during the day, the blast from each salvo being a perfect aiming point for patrolling enemy aircraft.

1 Squadron was tasked to show presence over our own troops as a confidence builder. Unfortunately, the F1AZs were configured for ground-attack sorties, with big fuel tanks and bomb pylons giving a high-drag index. This made the Mirages inferior to the MiG-23s that carried forward sector air-to-air missiles.

## Two quick dogfights

On 25 February, two of these sorties were intercepted by MiG-23s. In the first engagement, Major Willie van Coppenhagen and captains Dawid Kleynhans and Reg van Eeden turned to fight. The MiGs immediately broke away.

On the second sortie, Commandant Johan Rankin, Major Frans Coetzee and

Camera-gun film of a MiG-23. Fortunately for the MiG pilot the shot missed as his clean aircraft was able to out-accelerate the chasing F1AZs.

Captain Trompie Nel received a warning they were being stalked by a Cuban MiG-23 formation. Major I. C. du Plessis, an ex-F1AZ pilot, was monitoring enemy radio frequencies at the electronic warfare control centre. Positioned with him were two Chilean pilots interpreting the Cuban Spanish of the MiG pilots. They passed on the information by radio that the MiGs, flying at medium altitude, had spotted Rankin's three F1s flying at low level.

They were accurately describing the yellow/green camouflage of the F1s and descending, positioning themselves behind the Mirage formation. Rankin called the F1 pilots to jettison their fuel tanks and, at precisely the correct range, they broke into the fast-approaching enemy. In the turn Rankin saw two MiG-23s flash overhead and he manoeuvred to position the Mirage formation behind the MiGs.

Rolling out astern, but out of firing range was frustrating. The high-drag-configured Mirages could not close into firing range behind the fleeing MiGs. In a vain attempt to force the MiGs to turn, Rankin fired his missiles and cannons, but to no effect. He also watched as Nel's missile was outdistanced by the MiGs.

At the debrief when the intercepts were analyzed, it was obvious that the MiG pilots were picking up our aircraft visually by looking down on them. The yellow in the F1AZ camouflage scheme was probably too light. Rankin decided to modify the yellow to a darker brown. It was altered overnight in the hangar, without authority and with the pilots assisting the ground crew. Lieutenant Jimmy Spies, the squadron's technical officer, nearly had a heart attack. He was convinced General Frikkie Bolton, the logistics head of the air force, would court-martial Rankin. Whatever the repercussions were at headquarters, the matter was resolved when Chief of the Air Force, General Dennis Earp, backed Rankin's decision.

A project was then registered to develop a camouflage scheme that would best accommodate the Mirage F1AZ in its various roles. Aircraft 243 was painted dark blue underneath. This colour was later applied to either side of the vertical fin and the sides of the fuselage. The aircraft's upper surfaces became dark brown and green.

Early on the morning of 26 February, 1 Squadron was released from the operational area to attend Major Ed Every's memorial service, to be held in the community hall at AFB Hoedspruit. A C-160 Transall transported squadron members to AFB Hoedspruit, returning them to the conflict the following day.

The squadron presented Every's ceremonial dagger to his wife, Helga. Major Frans Coetzee was given the task of updating Every's logbook. Normally this would be a quick job as logbooks are summarized every month. In Every's case this involved nearly two years' flying.

On 2 March, the squadron was stood down from operations. All the aircraft were flown back to AFB Hoedspruit, where, as an interim measure they were officially modified to a dark earth and matt green colour scheme.

During this period, Commandant Rankin and Major Coetzee visited the Kentron missile factory to discuss the performance of V3B in dogfights with MiGs.

## Loss of Mirage F1AZ in Angola

On 19 March, six F1AZs returned to AFB Grootfontein from Hoedspruit. At 22h00 that evening, Commandant Rankin and Major Willie van Coppenhagen took off for a *Darkmoon* diversionary strike on an area target near the town of Longa. The aim was to draw enemy attention away from the Cuito Cuanavale battlefield. The flight was the first complete *Nagup* sortie to be flown—the night variation of the *Gatup* profile.

As they crossed the cut-line into Angola, the weather became marginal but, as the raid was only diversionary, the pilots continued. Van Coppenhagen flew on his own, trailing Rankin by three nautical miles. He maintained this distance by using readings from the Tacan beacon switched to the air-to-air mode.

Commandant Rankin returned from the flight at low level. For security reasons these flights were flown in radio silence. Shortly before he crossed back into South West Africa, he saw a momentary flash of fire that he thought was a bomb exploding. On landing, he found that van Coppenhagen was missing.

Commandant Thinus du Toit, commanding officer of the Rundu Forward Air Force Command Post, organized a massive search and rescue operation. He utilized all the aircraft available to him, including Impalas and the C-160 Transall, in a search pattern that lasted three days without any success. The dense bush obscured all traces of the missing aircraft.

On the fourth day, 24 March, realizing that visual reconnaissance was proving futile, du Toit adopted a new plan. He briefed the crews of two Alouettes to fly to the point where Rankin had crossed the river. There they were to separate, one aircraft working west and the other east. Each aircraft was to take a black soldier to act as an interpreter. The helicopters were to land at each kraal or settlement to inquire whether an explosion or loud bang had been heard during that fateful night.

Almost immediately, this change in tactics met with success. Captain Rob Sproul and Sergeant Major Bachus Rautenbach, the crew of the eastern helicopter, Alouette 61, came across a family that had heard the crash and indicated the direction from which the noise had come. Following this information the helicopter flew from kraal to kraal until eventually they found the impact point of the Mirage F1. Unfortunately a rescue was unnecessary, as van Coppenhagen had been killed in the crash.

The fighter had descended at a very shallow angle until it struck the treetops. Then it continued through the trees before impacting with the ground. The shallow angle embedded the wreckage underneath the leafy canopy of the trees over a distance of one and a half kilometers, removing the possibility of its ever being found directly from an air search. The subsequent board of inquiry offered a number of possibilities as to the cause of the crash. One of these was that fuel pipe corrosion could have caused the engine to flame-out. At low level, disaster would have been almost immediate.

On 21 and 22 March, while the search continued, a 600-foot cloud base and 7/8ths cumulo-nimbus cloud in the battle area prevented offensive operations. However, during the enforced lull, Captain Dawid Kleynhans arrived from AFB Hoedspruit in F1AZ 220 sporting the latest colour scheme, with the upper surfaces green and brown and the underneath and sides dark blue/grey.

On 23 March, after a 06h03 take-off in poor weather conditions, Major Norman Minne led Captain Chris Skinner and Major Frans Coetzee on a *Vergooi* attack at 100 feet. Between the initial point (IP) and the pitch the weather deteriorated so quickly that Minne decided to abort the attack. Remaining at low level, the aircraft turned through 180° and returned to AFB Grootfontein. This was the last sortie flown by the Mirages in the bush war. On 25 March, the squadron was stood down and returned to AFB Hoedspruit.

On 28 March, a memorial service for Major Willie van Coppenhagen was held at AFB Hoedspruit. On 31 March, many squadron members and their wives were flown to AFB Ysterplaat outside Cape Town to attend van Coppenhagen's funeral and burial in the Heroes' Acre of Strand cemetery. On that day the following entry was made in the squadron lines book:

> The Squadron has been deployed for nearly seven months. It has been a time of glory as the Billy Boys have performed excellently in extremely hostile conditions (enemy and weather). It has also been a time of sorrow, as we lost two great members of our Squadron. Everybody made

sacrifices, but none as much as the wives, children and girlfriends. They probably suffered most of all. We thank and salute them.

## Training, training, training

Despite political rumblings concerning a possible negotiated settlement, it was necessary for the front-line fighters to stay prepared. In the uncertainty of war, personnel took advantage of every opportunity for rest and recreation, for aircraft maintenance and more training, training and training.

As a young tank commander, General Jack Dutton of the South African Army had been seconded to a British tank regiment serving in the Korean War. He noted that the reason the British remained so efficient was their penchant for training. Every time his regiment came out of the line, they immediately embarked on a training programme. This lesson was well learned by the SAAF.

Early in April, Captain Wayne Westoby commenced his technical conversion onto the F1AZ while the rest of the pilots began an in-flight refuelling refresher course. Unfortunately, the culmination of the exercise turned sour when Major Minne nearly broke his probe while trying to plug. The B-707 was unable to retract the hose and had to land with 'it all hanging out'. General Dennis Earp, who was aboard the tanker at the time, witnessed the entire episode.

Later in the month, the Mirage pilots who had fired missiles during operations were flown by Dakota to Pretoria for serious discussions with engineers at Kentron, where the V3B was manufactured.

During May, Major Frans Coetzee and Captain Dawid Kleynhans were detached to Upington, to carry out integration trials of the H2 guided bomb onto the Mirage F1AZ. The remainder of the squadron embarked on a programme of two-versus-two ACM, where it was found that a great deal of homework was required. The advent of forward-sector missiles transformed conventional dogfighting. Firing shots could now be taken from all angles, instead of just from the conventional pursuit curve.

On the border the stalemate at Cuito Cuanavale continued. Opposing ground forces faced each other in an uneasy peace over the Chambinga high ground. By the middle of the year more serious developments were detected farther westward.

The Cuban 50th Division, which had been deployed in southern Angola, started posturing south of the Namibe–Lubango railway line, making moves southeast towards Oncocua. Simultaneously, their aircraft began appearing on our radar during the day and night. Some of their flights approached within 30 kilometres of the border north of Kaokoland.

Therefore, it was decided to hold the SAAF's annual *Golden Eagle* training exercise in Owamboland, to discourage any further displays of bravado from north of the border. 1 Squadron deployed to AFB Grootfontein while 2 and 3

Squadrons, as the 'enemy', operated from AFB Ondangwa. The resultant battle took place over the pans north of the Etosha Game Reserve. The situation was defused—the border war, for so long part of our lives, had virtually fizzled out.

On 28th June, at a change-of-command parade held in Pretoria, a flypast of nine F1s heralded the handing over of the air force from General Earp to General Jan van Loggerrenberg.

In July, captains John van Zyl, Nelis Genis and Ivan Pentz joined 1 Squadron. Captain Barrie Steyn, destined for 3 Squadron, participated in the technical phase of the conversion course.

During 1988, modifications so desperately needed during the bush war finally reached the F1 fleet. All the aircraft were fitted with compact radar-warning receivers (CRWS), plus chaff and flare dispensers, which would have relieved the pilot load during the battles over the Lomba River and Cuito Cuanavale. Matra 550 missiles, with fuses modified to prevent ineffective detonations in exhaust plumes, became available from Kentron.

During September, an air-to-ground weapons camp was held at AFB Bloemspruit. In October the venue had changed to AFB Langebaanweg for air-to-air, where Captain Chris Skinner ended up as top gun, scoring an impressive 28 hits out of 30 shells fired at the flag.

In October, the SAAF received 50 third-generation Snake missiles with genuine head-on capability. This was a direct result of Arthur Piercy's incident the previous year. Only then could the squadron pilots really master the problems of fighting in a new dimension.

Between 8 and 14 November, Mirage AZs were used in a series of weapons trials. Potentially dangerous profiles were flown from which Condib bombs were dropped. The bomb is dropped from level flight, 300 feet above a runway. When released, a rocket motor ignites driving the bomb through the hardened runway surface. A delayed-action fuse detonates the bomb after it has buried itself, causing an enormous crater that renders the runway unusable. The downside of the weapon is the delivery profile. No one in his right senses would, by choice, fly straight and level above an enemy's runway, airfields usually being the most heavily defended installations. During the Gulf War, Royal Air Force Tornado bombers were lost using similar tactics.

Cluster bombs were delivered from both *Vergooi* and *Gatup* profiles. As the name suggests, the bomb consists of numerous bomblets that are strewn along the flight path of the mother bomb. These can cause widespread damage to personnel and lightly armoured vehicles.

By November, it was apparent that the border war had ended. However, the peace was fragile and forces had to be kept in readiness. To this end, a *Golden Eagle* force preparation exercise was held at Upington. During the live-weapons programme the need for constant training was emphasized time and again following a 1 Squadron *Vergooi* attack. Captain Nelis Genis set his bomb-release altitude at 220 feet instead of 2,200 feet. After the low-level run-in the pair of F1AZs pitched-up for the attack. At 220 feet Genis's bombs left his aircraft to explode almost underneath Captain Paulus Truter's aircraft but fortunately without causing shrapnel damage. Truter remained on an adrenaline high for the remainder of the camp.

The year ended with both 1 and 3 Squadrons working hard to master the intricacies of third-generation ACM. The all-aspect capability of the new Snake missile called for immense co-ordination and practice. Air fighting became a succession of into afterburner, out of afterburner, firing self-defence flares, rolling the aircraft, pulling G while maintaining a constant lookout and commentary among aircraft. It was all a bit of a handful.

Three Super Frelon helicopters, magnificent over the sea but a handful high up in the mountains.

Cobus Toerien, wingman to Johan Rankin during the MiG shoot, with Div de Villiers, OC AFB Ondangwa.

Massive quantities of Soviet weaponry captured from FAPLA during Operation *Protea*.

# Chapter 16

# 1989–1992:
# Beginning of the end—3 Squadron

## New OC

Commandant Willie Hartogh—better known by his nickname 'Skilly'—was a fighter pilot throughout his career in the air force. He had flown Vampires and Sabres and during two tours on 2 Squadron had accumulated 1,100 hours on Mirage IIIs. In 1987–88 he served as the operations co-ordinator at AFB Hoedspruit where 2 Squadron was based. On completion of his tour in December 1988, it was planned that he would become Officer Commanding 2 Squadron. He had the necessary experience, was comfortably settled with his family on the base and fully understood the needs of the squadron. However, the air force planners, displaying that streak of originality for which they have become famous over the years, published the annual posting list appointing Hartogh as Officer Commanding 3 Squadron.

As they no doubt explained, it was for the good of the air force, but this sort of surprise certainly places a heavy burden on family life. Hartogh was surprised but pleased. He had flown 20 hours in the F1AZ, before the squadron deployed to AFB Grootfontein for Operation *Moduler* in 1987, and was excited about the aircraft. On the other hand, he and his family had to move into the Waterkloof officers' mess while they had a house built in Pretoria. Brigadier Gerrie Coetzee, the officer commanding at Waterkloof, having also experienced many surprise appointments during his long career, was very accommodating during this period of family upheaval.

Commandant Hartogh assumed command of 3 Squadron during the F1CZ conversion course with new pilots Major Jeronkie Venter and Captain Attie Niemann. This split in focus is never easy, but he had experienced personnel to run the squadron while he concentrated on the course. Major Martin Louw was his second-in-command and his officer team included majors Cobus Toerien, Jan Mienie, Rudi Mes and Citizen Force pilot Peter Cooke. Mes was later exchanged for Captain Wen-Soo , a pilot from the Taiwanese Air Force.

Wen-Soo, who was christened André by the squadron, joined the squadron for a year. He was a good pilot who excelled in weaponry and fitted into the squadron very well. His presence had a lasting effect on the personnel of the squadron. Both sides benefited from the many cultural differences that existed and learned the importance of acceptance. It was a maturing experience for everyone.

On taking command, Commandant Hartogh set himself one main and four secondary objectives. His main objective was to ensure that 3 Squadron would remain as a viable unit in the service of South Africa. Unfortunately, because of outside pressures over which he had no control, he failed and the squadron was closed down during his tenure as officer commanding. However, he succeeded with his secondary objectives.

Firstly, he felt the squadron had reached superb standards in all forms of aerial combat up to two-versus-two, but this horizon needed to be broadened to include multi-aircraft ACM. The scene had changed dramatically with the introduction of third-generation ACM. He had to start from scratch, learning the techniques and tactics applicable to all-sector missiles. A great deal of time was spent developing suitable tactics and, after long discussions, a three-versus-two exercise was developed.

To eliminate identification problems, half the aircraft had their noses and tails painted white. The fights were set up as for a two-versus-two, but during engagements the radar controllers would introduce the extra fighter to add realism and extra pressure to the exercise. Eventually, the controllers reached the stage where they could introduce fighters to the combat and take others out. The pilots learned to handle the situation by improving both their lookout and their commentary and control.

Secondly, he wanted to change the emphasis placed on 'kills' in the assessment of ACM. He felt the importance of survival in training engagements was often neglected in favour of achieving 'kills'. Captain Mike Edwards worked out a computer-based ACM survivability programme that balanced 'kills for' with 'kills against'. This system was introduced into the entire fighter line as it produced a better overall assessment of a pilot's capability.

Thirdly, he realized that technological advance had overtaken our attitude towards ACM. The SAAF concentrated on the close-in fight, whereas the rest of the technically advanced nations were concentrating on the beyond-visual-range (BVR) scenarios. This approach required a fundamental rethink of our ACM tactics, if we were to be equipped to hold our own in fights against aircraft with all-sector weapons. A new look had to be given to the setting up of training scenarios, how to fight, what actions to take on picking up radar warnings, when to use chaff, how to fly against semi-active missiles and what tactics the leader and number two should apply.

Finally, he felt a refinement was required for the assessing of air-to-air claims. Earlier, Major Peter Cooke had developed a manual method of prediction by studying the last frame of the camera-gun film. Measuring lead angles and sight movement, he could then predict hit possibility.

Captain Mike Edwards was tasked to develop this work, using a computer prediction programme. Utilizing the first, centre and last frame of film from each firing burst, he could accurately predict the pattern for the complete burst. This form of assessment was quicker and more accurate, because the computer did the calculations at a press of a button.

During actual firings on the flag at AFB Langebaan, camera film was assessed using this prediction programme before the hits on the flag were counted. At the last 3 Squadron camp, there was an average 1.85 bullet difference between the actual and assessed burst. This constant striving to improve led to high scores, for example 28/30 became commonplace when live firings were carried out.

This development work led to further improvements in aircraft sighting systems. A revised computer programme was introduced to the F1AZ, improving the symbology displayed in that aircraft's head-up display (HUD). Symbology in the Impala sight was altered to allow for the fact that, in that aircraft, firing was done without radar.

During an air-to-air camp at AFB Langebaanweg in May 1990, 3 Squadron made use of the opportunity to fly supersonic ACM sorties out to sea. Captain Rudi Mes, involved in a three-versus-two sortie, pulled up into a vertical loop. Rolling out at the top of the loop, he moved the throttle from full afterburner to half power. Immediately the engine compressor stalled, accompanied by classic engine burbling. He called, "Rabbit!"—the break-off safety call—headed for the coast 25 nautical miles away, set the aircraft into a 210-knot glide and explained his emergency over the radio.

Major Martin Louw, sitting in 3 Squadron's operations room at Langebaanweg, assisted Mes by calling out all the required emergency drills. After repeated attempts, Mes still could not clear the engine and Louw suggested that he cut the engine. Being far out to sea, Mes was loath to do this and turned towards the emergency landing strip at Tooth Rock, near Saldanha. Descending through 15,000 feet he crossed the coastline and, as he put his hand on the throttle to cut the motor, the burbling disappeared, the revs started to increase and the engine reverted to normal. Opening power, he returned to base and performed a precautionary landing.

Although the exact conditions were simulated repeatedly, no fault was found in the engine. The only difference was that these simulations were carried out over land, not 25 miles out to sea.

Mes's other major problem occurred during a weaponry exercise at the Roodewal bombing range. Flying a heavy, high-drag sortie with two drop tanks, four Mk 82 practice bombs and 100 rounds of 30mm cannon shells per side, the aircraft was on the edge of its hot and high performance curve. The bombs were dropped first to lighten the load, and the underwing tanks were empty before Mes started his air-to-ground cannon firing passes.

On pull-out from his first gun-firing run, he felt a thud as he rolled to the left, 200 feet above the target. He thought he had picked up some shrapnel from the cannon firing, but the range officer called him to say that his aircraft had just lost a drop tank. Looking under his right wing, Mes saw that both the jettisonable tank and the fixed pylon were missing. He could also see that his leading-edge slat had been damaged and torn away from the wing.

Reducing power and rolling out straight and level, he discovered that despite the asymmetric configuration of his aircraft, it still flew and handled well. He routed back to AFB Waterkloof carrying out slow-speed handling checks. He burned off fuel reserves and then approached the main runway for a flapless landing. He chose this option because of the condition of the slats on the right wing and in the event only one side worked. The landing was achieved without difficulty.

On investigation, it appeared from marks under the wing that the pylon had been incorrectly torqued. The pylon had shifted slightly on each of the four bombing runs, and finally ripped off in the thicker air at low level. Flight Sergeant Deon Griesel, as leader of the armourers responsible for attaching underwing stores, was the first person to apologize to Mes after he landed. The rarity of this incident highlights the extremely professional standard achieved by the maintenance personnel, who kept the F1s flying through all the years in service.

Shortly before the squadron closed down, Commandant Hartogh led Captain Charl Durandt in a two-versus-two combat sortie. The two pairs of F1s approached head-on with Durandt flying out on his leader's beam. As the formations flashed passed each other, Hartogh ordered a cross-manoeuvre. Both aircraft rolled in towards each other to perform a high-G 180° turn, during which Hartogh was watching over his shoulder to keep the opposing aircraft in sight. In this manoeuvre the wingman is responsible for avoiding the flight path of his leader.

With the Mirages flying at over 500 knots, the closing speed was very rapid indeed. At the last instant, realizing Durandt had not seen him, Hartogh reacted by pushing negative G. His aircraft slid underneath Durandt's F1 with only a metre or two to spare and entered its slipstream with a bang like a cannon shot. Calling "Rabbit" over the radio to stop the fight Hartogh, who had suddenly lost interest in the sortie, returned to Waterkloof to analyze the dangerous situation.

While flying Sabres, Hartogh had experienced a similar situation during an air-to-air deployment at AFB Langebaanweg. He was in a pattern of four Sabres, all firing on a towed target. He had just rolled in for a firing pass from the perch position as Major Jan Marais rolled off the flag. As Hartogh reversed his turn into the firing run, he was horrified to see Marais's aircraft filling his windscreen glass. They missed each other but the experience taught Hartogh that in this profession it is wiser to land and analyze what caused the near-accident than to continue flying.

## Personalities and projects

For sheer verve, Major Johan ('Jeronkie') Venter took a lot of beating. At a Durban airshow he performed a solo display in a Mirage F1CZ. He took off at 13h50 and entered straight into his display in humid conditions. Diving down onto the display line in front of the huge crowd, he selected auto-combat flap. To avoid overflying the display line he tightened his turn, but the aircraft did not respond. Only the leading-edge slats lowered—not the vital trailing-edge flaps.

Years of experience allowed Jeronkie Venter to apply full afterburner and maximum G and recover, breathtakingly low, over the main runway. With a quick adjustment to his planned routine he completed the show. The crowd went home thrilled and excited, unaware how close to disaster Venter had been.

On another occasion, Venter was the ferry pilot who flew an F1CZ to AFB Pietersburg for static display, during an airshow. On completion of the flying display, all visiting aircraft were cleared to return to their home bases. Venter, bored by spending the day in the static park, used the opportunity to give a little show of his own. Taking off on runway 23, he immediately performed a rapid left-hand turn out in full afterburner with his flaps down. His flight path took him directly over the VIP entertainment area, between two hangars, before setting heading for Pretoria. Onlookers, seated on the top of the specially erected four-metre-high stand, had a good view into the F1 cockpit as Venter shot past. Terrified children burst into tears while VIPs flattened themselves on the deck. Before landing back at AFB Waterkloof, Venter was officially grounded for six months.

After flying a low-level night *Moonshine* sortie Major Peter Cooke, the long-serving Citizen Force officer and airways 747 pilot, returned to the crewroom, depressed. He had experienced extreme difficulty in visually spotting the target and thought that age had finally caught up with him. Only after one of the younger pilots suggested that it would be easier if he flew with his helmet's sun visor up, did he discover the cause of his temporary night blindness.

Sergeant-Major Tubby de Wet, responsible for squadron discipline, kept a tight rein at all times and was not averse to keeping some of the younger officers in check. The excellent engine serviceability record can be ascribed largely to the dedication of Sergeant-Major 'Oosie' Oosthuizen and his staff. John O'Regan, an Irishman from Atlas Aircraft Corporation, was another star performer. As technical recorder, he supervised the management of aircraft logbooks, Form 700s and technical publications.

Throughout many years, Mariette du Preez served as the secretary of the officer commanding. Hers was the shoulder that people cried on. As squadron social secretary, she was magnificent in the way she looked after its interests. In February 1992, when the decision was made to close the unit that September, the tea club's finances were a little over R3,000. Under Mariette's orchestration, this amount rose to six figures, enabling the squadron to afford suitable functions during its closing-down ceremonies.

As a result of many deployments over the years, 3 Squadron had developed its own welfare organization to look after the families while the men were away. Sergeant-Major 'Skippy' Scheepers handled all electrical problems while Lieutenant Braam Hechter, son of the chief of the air force, looked after mechanical emergencies. Until the closing-down ceremony, morale within the squadron remained high, mainly owing to the family spirit that existed. People knew that under any circumstances they had friends to count on.

In an effort to assist the SAAF Museum preserve our aviation history, 3 Squadron adopted the *Sabre* project. Using technicians, many of whom had honed their considerable skills on Sabres, a Sabre was gradually restored. Unfortunately, before the grand old aircraft was ready to fly, budget cuts—the scourge of the military system—brought this worthwhile project to halt.

During their entire existence, 3 Squadron had occupied two hangars at AFB Waterkloof. In an attempt to improve productivity, a think-tank was held where personnel were tasked to solve existing problems within the two hangars. Aircraft under servicing were continually towed from one hangar to the other. Innovative suggestions led to a complete reorganization of the servicing arrangement. Because of the considerable improvement, aircraft availability increased and the squadron received a silver certificate in the annual productivity awards.

## Inadvertent discharge

In October 1991, during 3 Squadron's last weapons camp at AFB Langebaanweg, Captain Attie Niemann flew an air-to-air firing sortie on the banner. While returning to the perch position, he inadvertently fired a short burst from his cannon, having neglected to switch off his armament master switch. On landing, he consulted with Rudi Mes, his flight commander, and explained exactly what had happened. Mes then reported the incident to the base safety officer.

The following day the manager of Sea Harvest, a fish-processing plant at Saldanha, phoned to say that they had just extracted a red-tipped 30mm shell from one of their compressors, which had suddenly stopped working. Fortunately, as the company appreciated the problems of air-to-air sorties and the work being done for the country by the SAAF, the incident was amicably settled.

## Running down

In January 1992, Major Peter Cooke flew his final flight in a Mirage F1CZ. As a B-747 captain with South African Airways, he had been contracted to Singapore Airlines. His move brought to an end a colourful 22-year career with the SAAF. He ended his fighter-flying with an aerobatic display over the runway at AFB Waterkloof. Brigadier Ollie Holmes, the base officer commanding, in his farewell address made mention of the remarkable record held by Peter Cooke. At the age of 43, he was the only grandfather to fly the F1CZ.

The end of the bush war in South West Africa and the return towards political normality in South Africa put the defence force under great pressure to reduce both its size and budget. This phenomenon occurs, understandably, after every major conflict all over the world. Wars—especially long wars of attrition—cause escalation that has to be brought under control once all threats to the country's sovereignty have disappeared

Not so easily understandable to the fighting man, is the apparent change of heart of the population. The feeling of appreciation for a job well done evaporates amidst a rising clamour to reduce the burden on the taxpayer. In a frenzy of rationalization, it was decided that 3 Squadron would have to close.

Commandant Hartogh had the unenviable task of telling members of his superb team that they were to be retrenched—perhaps the most onerous duty he had to carry out in all his years of service. However, on the final day, the squadron personnel still ensured that all 12 F1CZs remaining in the inventory were fully serviceable. This personal display of loyalty was in stark contrast to that of the politicians who had so readily used them in times of crisis.

The wealth of ACM experience built up and developed by 3 Squadron could not be lost to the SAAF. An ACM clinic, attended by all F1AZ and Cheetah pilots, was held at AFB Hoedspruit from 8 to 26 June 1992. Using their beloved F1CZs to good effect, the pilots of 3 Squadron passed on their expertise to the 'mud-movers'.

During this late stage in the squadron's history, serviceability states of the aircraft attained new heights. CZ pilots were flying an average of 30 to 35 hours per month and there were more aircraft serviceable than pilots. The sad twist to this achievement was that by now all the aircraft were fully modified and fully serviceable. The day the squadron closed, every aircraft in the inventory was fully serviceable and ready to face any emergency situation.

## *Semper pugnans*—the end

An emotional closing down parade was held at AFB Waterkloof on 30 September 1992. The squadron flew an immaculate nine-ship flypast as a gesture of farewell to the base that had been their home for 17 momentous years. After the parade, majors Rudi Mes and Jeronkie Venter and captains Leon Meech-Noyes and Pietie le Roux took off for a four-ship flypast that broke into a two-versus-two dogfight display over the base. This was a special tribute to all the maintenance crews of 3 Squadron who, in all those years of preparing the aircraft for flight, had never witnessed their pilots in action.

Significantly, among the audience, were people with special reasons for attending. 'André' Wen-Soo Chang made the long journey from Taiwan to be present and Brian Cohen, who had entertained the squadron so often on their deployments to the Cape, came all the way from Cape Town.

After landing, the four aircraft taxiied back to the readiness platform, from where all the aircraft had operated that day. Waiting in the cockpits with engines turning, were the other four pilots. All the aircraft taxiied slowly back to the 3 Squadron hardstanding. When they were lined up and dressed by the right by the proud ground crew, they increased power. With a deafening roar the Mirage F1CZs blew up a storm of dust that turned the background brown. On a radio call all the aircraft shut down together. Instantaneously, the crescendo ceased to be replaced by an eerie silence, broken only by the ticking noise of the cooling metal.

Commandant Willie Hartogh then exploded onto the scene for a dramatic low-level aerobatic performance. Fittingly, he carried out the last official F1CZ landing before taxiing back to stop directly in front of the spectators who had gathered to pay homage to a great squadron. There was not a dry eye in the audience, amongs the ground crew or in the cockpits. Even that hardened politician and Honorary Colonel of 3 Squadron, Pik Botha, had tears streaming down his cheeks as he walked forward to present Skilly Hartogh with an olive branch to acknowledge, for the last time, the men of 3 Squadron.

3 Squadron pilots at the closing-down ceremony with their Honorary Colonel Pik Botha. Standing from left: Skilly Hartogh, Martin Louw, Pik Botha, Jeronkie Venter, Cobus Toerien, Leon Meech-Noyes, Ivan Pentz, Rudi Mes. Kneeling from left: Braam Hechter (T/O), Pietie le Roux, Mike Edwards, Charl du Rand.

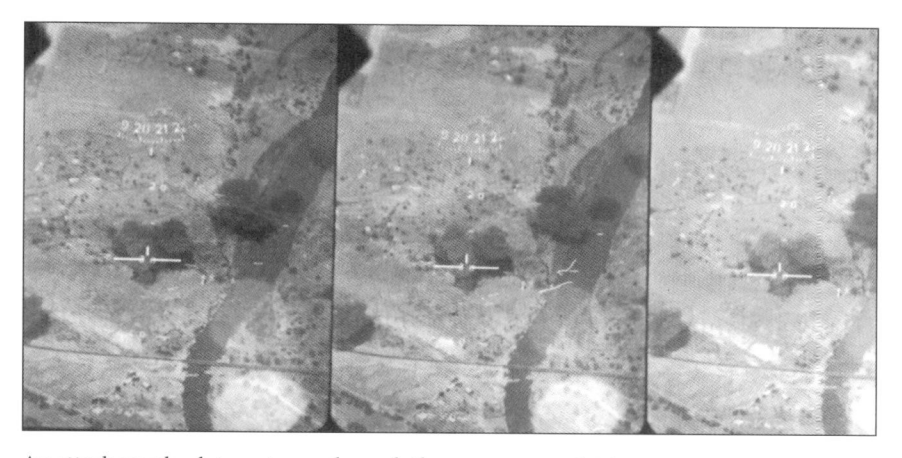

An attack on a bush target seen through the camera-gun sight.

# Chapter 17

# 1989–1991:
# Return to peace

## Temporary OC

Commandant Dick Warnke, an experienced Buccaneer ground-attack pilot, had been appointed to take over from Johan Rankin in January 1989, as Officer Commanding 1 Squadron. However, the fates were truly unkind, because Warnke was confirmed as having diabetes, before he could take command. During the ensuing disruption, Major Norman Minne was appointed acting officer commanding until May, when the appointment became permanent.

Captains Alan Brand and Riaan van Tonder joined 1 Squadron in January 1989, straight from a Cheetah conversion course held at 89 Advanced Flying School. Major Dirk de Villiers, returning for his second tour, joined them on the F1AZ conversion course. Alan Brand's impression of the aircraft, gained on his first solo flight, never altered throughout his 1,014 hours in the aircraft. Superb, compact and powerful, with impressive flight performance combining with ease of handling—particularly apparent after flying the delta-winged Cheetah. The aircraft was so easy to handle that after only 13 sorties they flew off to AFB Langebaanweg for air-to-air firing.

Two years earlier during operation *Moduler*, Mirage F1AZ 237 had become a 'hangar queen'. Against regulations, the airframe and engine had been stripped to supply spares for aircraft deployed on the border. Through much hard work, the ground crew, led by Captain Jimmy Spies, Chris de Lange and Nick van Zyl had reassembled it and, on 10 March 1989, Major Frans Coetzee took it for a test flight. Apart from a few minor snags it was fit to rejoin the fleet.

## April Fools' Day

Traditionally the 1st April each year is known as April Fools' Day, when elaborate hoaxes are expected, and allowed, until noon. 1 April 1989 was no different, except that the 'hoax' played out in South West Africa/Namibia lasted nine days with deadly consequences.

Legally, 1 April was the first day of official peace in the territory, after the acceptance by all sides of United Nations resolution 435. SWAPO forces were supposed to be north of latitude 16º south in Angola. South African troops were restricted to bases inside South West Africa/Namibia. Two hundred and eighty-six train-loads of heavy equipment and fighting vehicles had been transported back to South Africa. UNTAG, the UN task force was positioning to supervise the peaceful implementation of the negotiated settlement.

Sam Nujoma, in a blatant disregard for the negotiated settlement, ordered SWAPO terrorists to infiltrate into South West Africa on this first day of peace. His forces, instead of staying north of the defined latitude had moved south, with the connivance of FAPLA, to the international border. Before dawn on 1 April, nearly 1,600 terrorists crossed into Owamboland and Kaokoland—the largest infiltration of the entire war.

Hastily, Operation *Merlyn* was planned and implemented to stop the aggression. South African Police Koevoet units, supported by what remained of the South African Army and the SAAF entered the fray, resulting in nine days of vicious bloodshed.

The evening of 1 April, Colonel Steyn Venter, Officer Commanding AFB Hoedspruit, told Commandant Minne to prepare eight aircraft for deployment to AFB Ondangwa the following morning. In the event, 1 Squadron was not deployed, although by dawn on 2 April they were ready and raring to go.

The SAAF flew Alouette gunships back to AFB Grootfontein in C-130 transport aircraft. After reassembly they were flown directly into the battle to support the hard-pressed Koevoet teams. When the fighting stopped, 750 terrorists and 22 security force personnel were dead. Alouette crew members, Major McCarthy, captains Slade, Eksteen and Vergottini, Flight Sergeant Steyn and sergeants Fredriksen, de Rouxbaix and Fourie, were awarded Honoris Crux decorations for their invaluable contribution during the fighting.

Fortunately British Prime Minister Margaret Thatcher was in Windhoek to celebrate the onset of peace when the incursion occurred. For perhaps the only time during the entire 23-year conflict, South Africa was not held responsible for the incident.

## Training

In May 1989, 1 Squadron flew to Roodewal bombing range to carry out live Condib firing. These bombs are designed to penetrate through concrete or tarmac runway surfaces and are dropped from a low-level profile. The bombs are retarded after release to allow the carrying aircraft to clear the area before detonation. This retardation also places the bomb in a near vertical position to prevent it skipping off the hard surface.

The F1AZ has a laser that measures distance accurately. On the run-in, the pilot triggers the laser at about 3,000 metres before the target. When the precise range falls to 300 metres the pilot releases the bombs by manually pressing the 'pickle' button. Captain Nelis Genis was just short of the range hut when he attempted to 'update' his range reading. Using live weapons, he targeted the Charlie coke, positioned three kilometres down-range. Unfortunately, instead of pressing the laser button he hit the pickle button by mistake. The bomb released and buried itself in the range carpark, before exploding. Fortunately, the explosion was well contained, taking place underground as advertised. The only damage was to an ambulance, whose windscreen was cracked, and to the nerves of the range staff.

During the year, in-flight refuelling became second nature to the pilots of 1 Squadron. After Colonel Gawie Winterbach became Officer Commanding 60 Squadron and Commandant Jan Henning one of the B-707 pilots, the availability of tanker aircraft increased markedly. Both ex- Mirage F1AZ pilots enjoyed operating their huge aircraft out of AFB Hoedspruit, while exercising with 1 Squadron. During the tanker deployment in June 1989, 1 Squadron achieved 215 plugs out of 233 attempts—a success rate of 92.27 per cent.

On 6 June 1989, Commandant Norman Minne became the first F1AZ pilot to fly 1,000 hours in the aircraft. This remarkable feat included flying 96 operational sorties, 75 during *Moduler*, *Hooper* and *Packer* and 21 during 1980/81.

On 28 June, after a weapons camp at Upington, Alan Brand took off in 217 with full internal and external fuel (6,700 litres) for the return flight to AFB Hoedspruit. After take-off he selected 'undercarriage up' but the nose leg stuck in the half-up position and would not budge. He contacted Commandant Sandy Roy at Upington and reported the problem. He asked him to contact Air Force Headquarters so that they could decide where he should land, in the event that the 'emergency down' selection also failed. He had sufficient fuel to circle Upington or fly at reduced speed to AFB Waterkloof but with his wheel down he could not make Hoedspruit.

After 60 long minutes of circling, during which he reported to Sandy Roy that Waterkloof was now no longer an option, he finally received this belated, unhelpful message from headquarters: "The decision rests solely with the pilot."

As the aircraft was a Mirage, the emergency system worked perfectly and Brand landed safely back at Upington. The maintenance crew worked overnight on the aircraft and the following morning he flew it back safely to Hoedspruit.

In November, AS-30 air-to-surface missiles were fired at Riemvasmark weapons range, providing excitement for the pilots. The large missiles made a tremendous noise as they left the F1. The noise was followed immediately by thick smoke from the burning missile, momentarily obscuring it and the target. Once the smoke cleared, it was necessary to steer the missile electronically into the selected target. This was done by using a tiny joystick mounted in the cockpit. Optical problems were minimized by flying the Mirage as smoothly as possible. Because the F1 provided a good launching platform, this was relatively easy. However, in actual operations the required profile was most unpopular with the pilots—steady, predictable flight allows anti-aircraft artillery every possibility of scoring a hit.

## New Year

In January 1990, Major Giep Vermeulen rejoined the squadron for his second tour and alongwith newcomers Major Leon Bath and Captain Anthony Mathers completed the technical phase at 3 Squadron.

After the Cheetah, Leon Bath was surprised at the number of procedures necessary to fly the F1. However, the electrical and airframe systems were better than those in the Cheetah. The two-week simulator phase allowed them to become very familiar with the cockpit so their first flight in the aircraft did not seem strange. The performance of the F1 was markedly superior to that of the Cheetah. This feature was possibly accentuated by the lower-density altitude at AFB Hoedspruit compared to the Cheetah school at AFB Pietersburg.

During May 1990, a weapons demonstration was laid on for the parliamentary sub-committee on defence at the Tooth Rock range near Saldanha. The army used the practice day to fire all their weapons to ensure that at the display everything was on target. In order to save money, the Air force had to practise with one bomb and 30 rounds cannon fire per aircraft, so by comparison their display looked pretty feeble. However at the actual display, Commandant Norman Minne's Mirage F1AZs, Commandant Renier Keet's four Cheetah Es and Commandant Pikkie Siebrits's two Buccaneers released full loads, stealing the show with a spectacular display of mobile firepower. A dramatic flypast completed the air force display. Commandant Piet van Schalkwyk, in a Boeing 707 tanker, flew over with one aircraft of each aircraft type plugged into the extended refuelling hoses.

In October 1990, two F1AZs joined 3 Squadron at AFB Langebaanweg on an air-to-air camp. Commandant Dolf Prinsloo test-fired the first Snake missile at a target drone, towed 4,000 metres behind a Lear Jet.

In January 1991, the entire squadron flew back to Langebaan for the biannual firing practice. The flight from Hoedspruit involved a rendezvous and refuelling from a 60 Squadron B-707. Inter-squadron co-operation allowed new pilots, captains John Stipp, Nic Scheltema and Glen Watson, to complete the F1 technical course at 3 Squadron while 1 Squadron was away.

## Hydraulic problems

On 8 February 1991, Major Leon Bath was engaged in a one-versus-one dogfight with Captain Alan Brand when his warning panel sounded off. A ruptured pipe had caused a Hydraulic 1 failure, affecting normal undercarriage cycling, all flap and slat operation, use of dive brakes, loss of control dampers and a reduction of flying control response by 60 per cent.

Heading straight back to AFB Hoedspruit, he was assisted by Commandant Norman Minne, who verified all the emergency actions over the radio. On final approach, Bath used the angle of attack indicator to give a nose-up attitude of 10° at an approach speed of close to 230 knots. Without dampers the aircraft was extremely sensitive in the pitching plane, accentuated by the reduced control response and the hands of the understandably nervous pilot.

The landing was successful and the drag-'chute deployed correctly. The pilot was able to stop the aircraft by pulling the emergency brake handle. Although the nose-wheel steering was inoperative, the aircraft came to a halt at the end of the long runway.

At this stage in the aircraft's service life, hydraulic problems became more frequent. A number of sorties were aborted because of undercarriage cycling problems. A total of 16 micro-switches controlled the cycling of the wheels and doors. Wear and tear on these micro-switches interfered with the normal functioning, often preventing the landing gear from being lowered. Fortunately, in every case the emergency lowering system worked.

The hydraulic shuttle in the nose-wheel steering system also became sensitive to variations in hydraulic pressure. Captain Bath experienced two instances where the nose wheel deflected on touchdown. The first episode occurred when he had a total of five hours on the AZ. After lowering the nose, severe snaking led him to believe that the drag-'chute had deployed asymmetrically. He jettisoned the 'chute and used emergency brakes to halt the aircraft on the runway.

On the second occasion, as he lowered the nose the aircraft veered violently to the right. He applied differential braking, but could not stop the swing before running off the runway. The aircraft was undamaged despite dirt-tracking for a few hundred metres. An exhaust port in the sensitive steering mechanism was blocked, causing the wheel to be fully deflected on landing.

Towards the end of the aircraft's service life, the micron filters fitted throughout the hydraulic system deteriorated. Hydraulic fluid was replaced, filters were replaced, hydraulic support rigs were extensively checked—but still the problem persisted. A few pilots experienced moments of terror while raising undercarriage and flaps after take-off. Partially blocked filters could not cope with the sudden large demands on the hydraulic accumulators, causing the control stick momentarily to freeze. At any stage of flight this phenomenon is alarming, but particularly so on take-off, close to the ground.

Towards the end of February, Major Leon Bath was seconded to a board of inquiry into a fatal flying accident. Major Richard Miller had crashed while practising a low-level flying display over the airfield at AFB Pietersburg. Ironically, soon after this incident, 1 Squadron needed a new display pilot. Despite his in-depth study of the accident, Bath volunteered and was accepted for the post. Over the next two years he carried out low-level aerobatic displays in Potchefstroom, Pretoria, Rustenburg and Hoedspruit.

During March, the new pilots were introduced to in-flight refuelling behind the B-707. Captain John Stipp produced an excellent result, succeeding with 20 plugs out of 21 attempts.

The annual *Golden Eagle* training exercise in June 1991 began on a bad note. Commandant Ian Jones, soon after take-off from AFB Louis Trichardt, ejected from a Cheetah C. After this slight hiccup, the exercise continued.

The considerable advantages of in-flight refuelling were demonstrated by a tongue-in-cheek signal of complaint from 3 Squadron's Major Cobus Toerien. He reproached 1 Squadron F1AZs for hogging all the refuelling from the tankers during combat air patrol sorties, leaving 3 Squadron fighter pilots in their cockpits, waiting forlornly to be scrambled.

An interesting development in the overall capability of the SAAF occurred during the exercise. A new integrated radar-display and radio-relay system had been installed at the Air force command post in Pretoria. From the console in front of my position in the command cell, I could watch and listen to interceptions taking place at low level in the lee of the Drakensberg escarpment. Over the radio, I requested Commandant Norman Minne, flying a Mirage F1AZ, to intercept a C-206 Caravan light transport aircraft approaching AFB Hoedspruit. My voice was so clear Minne assumed I was flying in the Caravan.

Towards the end of July, majors Giep Vermeulen and Alan Brand deployed to Upington to carry out H2 guided-bomb trials. Early in the trial one of their aircraft went unserviceable and they requested a replacement from Hoedspruit. Commandant Minne decided to fly the replacement aircraft to see for himself how his team was progressing. He took off at 18h50, long after the winter sunset, and ferried happily westwards, eventually leaving the bright lights of Johannesburg and Potchefstroom behind. He was finally handed over by Bloemfontein ATC with the words: "You are clear to continue to Upington. Use unmanned procedures. Out."

Because Upington was used only occasionally at night, it became non-cost effective to maintain air traffic control staff on duty. Fortunately, Major Vermeulen had arranged for Upington's runway lights to be switched on. Nevertheless, it was an eerie and unpleasant sensation to land a high-speed jet knowing there were no emergency services available.

During August, brake assemblies—for a long time a major Mirage problem—

started arriving from France. Fortunately, aircraft availability began increasing to cope with the arrival of new pilots, captains Piet Ackerman and Marcel von Gunten.

In September, eleven F1AZs deployed to AFB Langebaanweg for air-to-air and V3B missile firings. 1 Squadron was definitely not looking its best when it arrived in the Cape because final decisions had still not been made regarding the correct camouflage scheme. The eleven aircraft were sporting four different paint schemes.

### 'Panty-rippers'

October became famous for the wrong reasons. A programme of in-flight refuelling had been arranged, which proceeded like a switchback railway with ups and downs. The first 'down' occurred when Captain Glen Watson joined the elite band of 'panty-rippers'. Fortunately, the 'up' occurred when State President F. W. de Klerk flew aboard the B-707 tanker and watched 1 Squadron perform immaculately. No sooner had he left the aircraft than the next 'down' happened. While a practice was taking place at low level—always extremely difficult in turbulent conditions—another panty was removed and the front windscreen glass of a Mirage F1AZ damaged.

On 28 November, Commandant Minne flew to Roodewal on the first mission using the new 14-bomb configuration. This configuration, planned during the original purchase phase of the F1AZ, had taken many years of development. Structural changes to strengthen the aircraft, particularly the undercarriage, had been completed to cater for the extra weight of bombs. His aircraft carried 14 x Mk 81 120kg bombs. To his dismay, after dropping a pair of bombs as a sighting check, the others hung up, making for a heavy landing back at Hoedspruit.

Norman Minne left the squadron at the end of 1991. His term in command had been a particularly difficult one, his goal being one of consolidation. Aircrew changeovers were frequent, as personnel planners tried to sort out careers interrupted by demands of the bush war. Pilots were sent on staff and test-pilot courses, instructional appointments and to the Cheetah squadrons to add operational experience. Training and retraining became top priorities. Minne wanted to ensure that all the young pilots were exposed to the skills and standards set during the war.

Finally, the long deployments in South West Africa began to take their toll on the stock of spares available for the aircraft, and unserviceabilities became common. Brake assemblies became critical. In order to save money it was decided that these units would be manufactured in South Africa and overseas orders were cancelled. It was then discovered that the local manufacturer could not produce the assemblies to the required specification. Because of the shortage, aircraft spent many months standing on jacks. At one stage, the situation became so serious that the squadron was running out of jacks. A maximum of three aircraft per day was available out of the 29 on inventory.

During this recuperation period, as many as possible overdue modifications were installed on the aircraft. The Station Zero modification saw the installation of the chaff and flare dispensers so desperately needed during the war. The ball-and-carrot modification included reinforcing the undercarriage system to handle the 16.2-ton all-up-weight of the 14-bomb configuration. The aircraft camouflage scheme, so hastily applied during the war, was standardized and the aircraft repainted. On recommendation by Colonel Gerry Radloff, the cockpit illumination system was upgraded under the direction of Dirk de Villiers, increasing the safety of night operations.

A mission-planning system was introduced to the squadron under the guidance of Major Giep Vermeulen. The facility was adapted to programme the navigation systems, station selector units (SSUs)—a laborious task that previously had to be carried out manually. V3S missiles were integrated on the aircraft. The squadron began flying weaponry profiles, releasing 120 and 250kg retarded Traan bombs.

Mirage F1AZ 221 was repaired at the Atlas Aircraft Corporation and returned to the squadron. It was this aircraft that Captain Rikus de Beer had forced landed on the runway at Hoedspruit. It had received all outstanding modifications while being repaired and became the most modern AZ in the fleet. Unfortunately, this pride of place was short-lived. The aircraft was destroyed when, after a bird strike over Drakensig, Major Leon Bath ejected.

Frantic activity during the war had seriously affected the squadron's bookkeeping. Commandant Minne used this time to update all the squadron procedures, manuals, syllabi and training handbooks into the standard LMU 3 format.

During a briefing to the visiting Air Force Staff Council, Colonel Steyn Venter mentioned that Commandant Minne was the only pilot left in 1 Squadron with operational experience. However, this statement upset the young pilots who were on the squadron. They responded magnificently by proving that they had not only acquired bush skills, but had improved in both tactics and techniques.

When flying the F1 for the first time after the Mirage III, perhaps the most difficult aspect to adapt to was managing the nose-wheel steering. It was a good system once you were familiar with it, but slightly tricky at first. For this reason, aircraft used for first solos were parked in the readiness shelters at Hoedspruit. After starting up, the pilots could taxi straight out onto the runway. Turning back into the revetment after landing was much easier when the aircraft was lighter. Pilots had the opportunity to practise on the long taxiways before negotiating the required sharp turn back into the revetment.

Unfortunately for Captain John Stipp, his aircraft was found to be unserviceable after start-up for his solo flight. He was allocated another aircraft that was standing in revetment L8. As its name implies, this is an L-shaped revetment, requiring a 90° turn immediately on leaving the entrance. Commandant Minne briefed the young man on how best to negotiate this turn, emphasizing the need to use sufficient power to allow the heavy aircraft to gain the momentum necessary to turn. Stipp must have been impressed when Minne, who is a big man, emphasized the need for power. After releasing the brakes his aircraft shot out of the revetment like a Saturn rocket. Realizing that at that speed the turning circle would be too great Minne and the aircraft fitter ran out, indicating to the pilot to stop. Fortunately, Stipp managed to bring the Mirage to a halt before its wingtip struck the revetment wall. By means of a tractor, the aircraft was towed onto the taxiway before Stipp finally set off on his first flight.

## Bagpipes

To the annoyance of Colonel Martin Rutsch, Officer Commanding AFB Langebaanweg, 1 Squadron had developed a tradition that they reserved for their air-to-air deployments. On the night of arrival, Captain Alan Brand playing his bagpipes would lead a parade of AZ pilots. Carrying suitable liquid rations, the procession would solemnly mount the outside spiral staircase and proceed all the way up to the water tower platform on top of the officers' mess. From there they would proceed to sing, loudly and melodiously, all the verses of the Billy Boys' song.

During *Golden Eagle* 1/91, captains Ivan Pentz and Glen Watson were flying a combat air patrol under the direction of the radar controllers at Lass. A Boeing 707 tanker was airborne, so instead of the Mirages returning to Hoedspruit for refuelling, they were directed to the tanker. After quickly refuelling, they returned to their patrol position.

On landing, both pilots were summoned to the office of the officer commanding where a furious Norman Minne confronted them. Because Watson had not previously done any in-flight refuelling in the AZ he was not qualified to plug under operational conditions. Ivan Pentz was lambasted because he had allowed Watson to plug. Fortunately no problem had arisen, illustrating how well the F1AZ and the pilots performed in this role.

Colonel Des Barker, for many years a SAAF test pilot, arrived at 1 Squadron to qualify in in-flight refuelling. Commandant Norman Minne briefed and led him on his first sortie, where they approached the tanker head-on. A tight 180° turn put them in a good position just astern of the Boeing. Minne watched Barker make his initial approach with considerable difficulty. On closer inspection, he noticed that Barker had his dive brakes extended. He plugged successfully after they were retracted. After landing, he explained that during the tight turn his G-suit had expanded and—unbeknown to him—pressed the dive brake switch, hence his initial difficulty.

# 1989–1991: Return to peace

Commandant Norman Minne's most embarrassing moment on the squadron was when he led a demonstration formation take-off. His wingmen were Frans Coetzee and Schalk van Heerden—all three experienced pilot attack instructors (PAIs). With the junior pilots looking on expectantly, Minne gave the twirling hand signal for the pilots to wind up the power. At full dry power Minne chopped his hand forward indicating the release of brakes and the start of the take-off roll. The two aircraft either side of the leader surged forward, leaving the leader firmly in place on the runway. While waiting for take-off clearance, Minne had applied the parking brake and promptly forgotten that he had done so. After a concertina performance Nico Carsten would have been proud of, the three aircraft finally lifted into the air.

Line-up of Mirage III EZ and twin-seat D2Z aircraft at AFB Pietersburg.

Anti-missile flares being ejected from an F1AZ.

# Chapter 18

# 1992–1994:
# Hanging on a thread

## New OC
1992 started with the arrival of Commandant Dolf Prinsloo who took over command of the squadron from Commandant Minne. On the conversion course with him were new pilots, captains Smal, Coetzer, Marais, du Plessis, Serfontein and Brand.

Commandant Prinsloo was appointed as the last Officer Commanding 1 Squadron, with the directive from SAAF Headquarters to prepare the squadron for closing down. He accepted the appointment but, for the first and only time in his career, decided to wilfully disobey orders. At his first meeting with his pilots, he told them what he had been ordered to do. In his next statement he told them that he had no intention of carrying out the directive. His objective was to make the squadron indispensable to the SAAF, so that it would become impossible to withdraw it from the SAAF's inventory. To his credit—and that of the personnel of the entire squadron—he achieved his goal with flying colours. The squadron stayed in service for a further five years.

## Loss of F1AZ 221
On 5 February 1992, in celebration of the SAAF's birthday, a parade was held at the Drakensig Sports Stadium, Hoedspruit. The highlight of the festivities was to be a low-level aerobatics display by Major Leon Bath flying Mirage F1AZ 221. He had developed an unusual display that commenced with a low-speed entry into the display area. After take-off, he entered a holding pattern west of the stadium waiting for Major Alan Brand, the safety officer, to call him in to begin the display.

While orbiting at 1,500 feet, he was given clearance to enter for the show.

Left: Ex-Mirage F1AZ pilot, Maj-Gen Roelf Beukes, addressing the audience at 1 Squadron's closing-down parade.

Below: 3 Squadron in the early 1980s.
Back row from left: Clive Turner, Kenny Williams, Johan Ackerman, Ed van Ravenstein, Dolf Prinsloo, Johan du Plessis, John Inggs, Cobus Toerien, Les Bennett.
Front row from left: Pete Vivier, Johan Rankin, Israel Krieger, Dries Wehmeyer, Jack Gründling, Eddie Dert (T/O), Gerrie Randloff, Tristan la Grange, Martin Louw.

Bottom: Jan Mienie's 1 Squadron in 'jet-jock' pose. From left: Drago Deviseljevic, Jaco Smit, Chris Pretorius, Phillip Potgieter, Jan Mienie, Marcel von Gruten, Patrick Flynn.

Top: Lear Jet target tug being escorted by a 3 Squadron F1CZ and a 1 Squadron F1AZ.

Centre: The man standing with his arm raised illustrates the depth and size on a Mk 82 bomb crater. During the bush war air-burst bombs were more efficient.

Below: 1 Squadron golf day at AFB Hoedspruit. This foursome was made up of 1 Squadron commanding officers. From left: Dick Lord, Johan Rankin, Norman Minne, Dolf Prinsloo. Unfortunately their wealth of experience on the Mirage F1AZ did not count on the golf course.

Above: The tail of Otto Schur's Mirage III RZ on display in Luanda.

Right: Smoke and dust blowing off a target in Angola immediately after an air strike.

Below: 1 Squadron with the the Mozambique Air Force MiG-17 flown by defector Lt Bomba. Standing from left: Frans Coetzee, Paddy Carolan, Frans Pretorius, Ronnie Knott-Craig, Dick Lord, Hennie Louw, Frik Viljoen, Jan Henning, Billy Collier, Norman Minne, Chris Venter, Dirk de Villiers and Budgie Burger. Front: Theo Nell.

Retarded bombs dropping from an F1AZ.

Above left: Close-up of the Dakota DC-3 tail after landing.

Above right: Alan Brand in mess uniform not long after ejecting from Mirage F1AZ 224.

Two Mirage F1s approach at low speed, low level up a valley.

Right: Diamond 16 from below.

Below: Pilots of the diamond-16 formation.
Front V from left: Mossie Basson, Casey Lewis, Les Bennett, Fred du Toit (leader), Tinkie Jones, Wassie Wasserman, Norman Minne.
Second V from left: Bill Einkamerer, André van der Heever, Darryl Lee, Frik Viljoen, Dirk de Villiers.
Third V from left: Dolf Prinsloo, Pierre du Plessis, Martin Louw.
Tail-end Charlie: John Inggs.

Top: Crash site of F1AZ 221 after Leon Bath ejected.

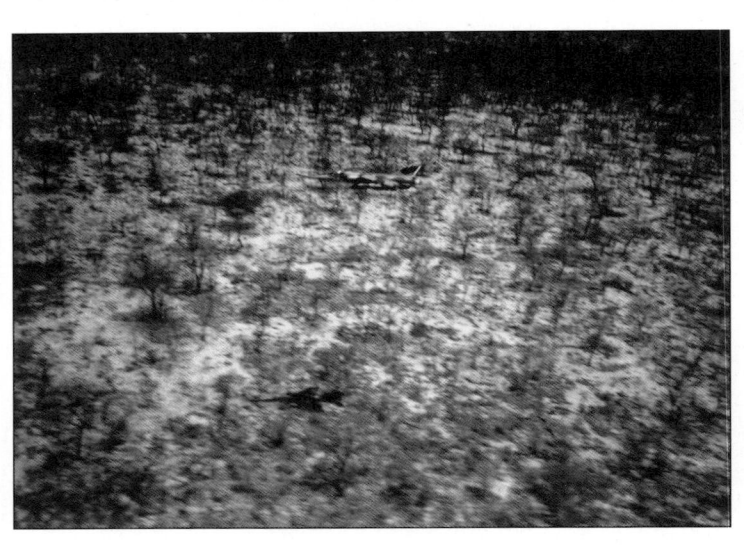

Centre: Camouflaged F1AZ over Angola. The aircraft's shadow was often easier to pick up than the aircraft.

Below: Free-text message sent by the author to all operational units on the day he retired from the SAAF.

```
>
                        = FREE TEXT MESSAGE =                    9406301115
FROM: 40NWM
TO: ALL

MESSAGE: " AND SO IT CAME TO PASS THAT ON THE THIRTIETH DAY OF JUNE 1994
          DICK LORD SHOULD BE TAKEN OUT OF THE PLACE OF COMMAND, AND BE
          PUT OUT TO PASTURE.

          HERE ENDETH THE LAST LESSON."

          I WANT TO THANK ALL OF YOU FOR YOUR SUPPORT AND FRIENDSHIP
          DURING MY YEARS IN THE AIR FORCE AND PARTICULARY IN THE
          COMMAND POST.

          I LEAVE WITH THE KNOWLEDGE THAT THE AIR FORCE AND THE COUNTRY
          ARE IN YOUR VERY GOOD AND CAPABLE HANDS.

          WITH ALL MY THANKS.

          BRIG DICK LORD
```

Above: Mitterand meets Madiba. An Air France B-747 is escorted into Cape Town, appropriately by French-built Mirage fighters.

Centre: F1AZ dropping four cluster bombs.

Below: Ground crew bombing-up an F1, a laborious, back-breaking task.

Commandant Fred du Toit, OC 3 Squadron, with his men in the 'lapa' outside the pub at AFB Ondangwa during the bush war.

An unusual photograph showing an F1CZ undercarriage cycling.

Below: A stick of bombs exploding on target.

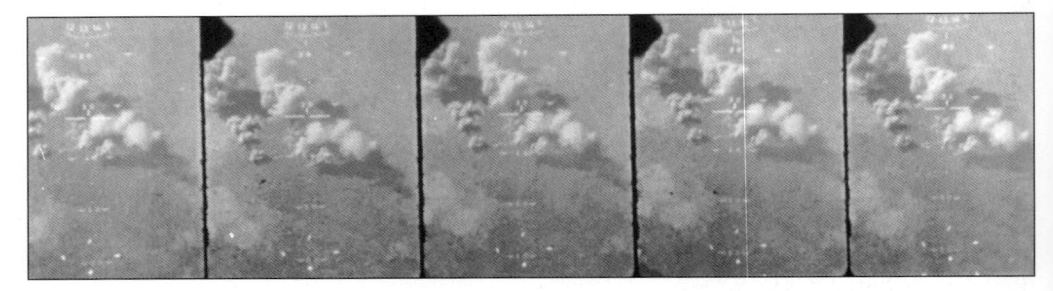

Letter addressed to Les Bennett.

```
                    JOHANNESBURG GENERAL HOSPITAL
                    SMIT STREET,
                    JOHANNESBURG,
                    2001

NAME   L.M. BENNETT
ADDRESS   3 SQN
          AFB WATERKLOOF
          ATA


Dear Sir,

Please be advised that your OPTRECTOMY OPERATION is scheduled for:

FRIDAY 10TH AUGUST AT 13.00 HOURS


The purpose of this delicate operation is to sever the cord that
connects your eyes to your rectum and hopefully get rid of your
shitty outlook on life.


Yours faithfully,


DR HANS GRABBER
```

Below: The railway terminal in Jamba, Angola, target of an F1 strike.

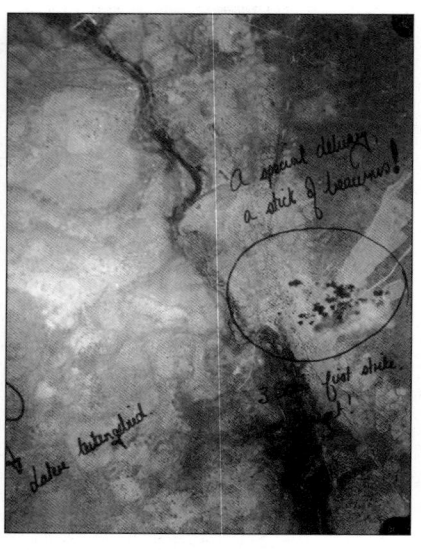

Above: A stick of bombs explodes through a target.

Left: When Chief of the SA Defence Force, Admiral Biermann, retired, Mirage F1s and IIIs performed an appropriate flypast.

Colonel Attie Bosch (centre), OC AFB Pietersburg, supervises the return of the famous 1 Squadron ostrich egg to its rightful owner. OC '13' Squadron, Fred du Toit (right), passes the egg to a youthful Commandant Willem Hechter (looking askance).

Above: Arrival of F1AZs at AFB Waterkloof. From left: Gawie Winterbach, Brigadier Mike Muller, General Bob Rogers CAF, General Ed Pienaar, Bossie Huyser and André van der Heever.

Centre: When General Bob Rogers handed over command of the South African Air Force to General Mike Muller, 16 Mirage F1s flew over as a mark of respect.

Below: A diamond-nine F1 formation over the SAAF memorial on Bays Hill, Pretoria.

Above: 3 Squadron at Buffelsfontein shortly before Les Bennett was bitten by a boomslang from the tree above him. From left: Dieter Ortmann, Darryl Lee and Les Bennett.

Above: MiG-17 lifting off.

Right: Mk 82 bombs ready for loading.

Left: Moolies Moolman wearing the panty.

Below: Target in the bush. Note the roads, tracks and two AAA sites.

Below: Pilots being hoisted by an Alouette III during wet-dinghy drill.

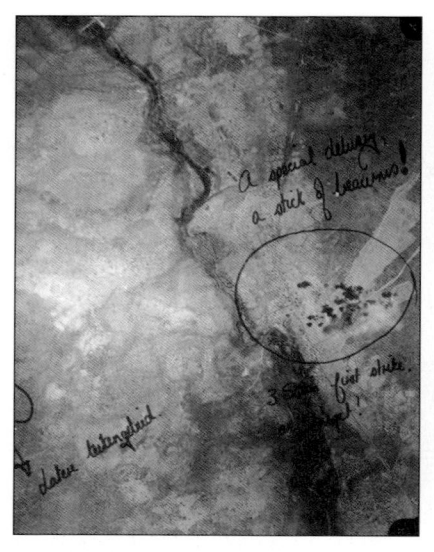

Above: Bomb craters evident in post-strike damage-assessment photography.

Above: Burnt our lorry with AAA gun mounted on the back and a Cuban helmet lying in the foreground.

Below: Ongiva under attack.

Above: South African infantry, debused from mine-protected Buffel troop carriers, wait for completion of the air strike on Xangongo before advancing.

Right: Chibemba radar site in Angola, target for the initial strike in Operation *Protea*.

Right: Triple-barrelled 20mm AAA gun captured from SWAPO.

Below: End result of an air strike.

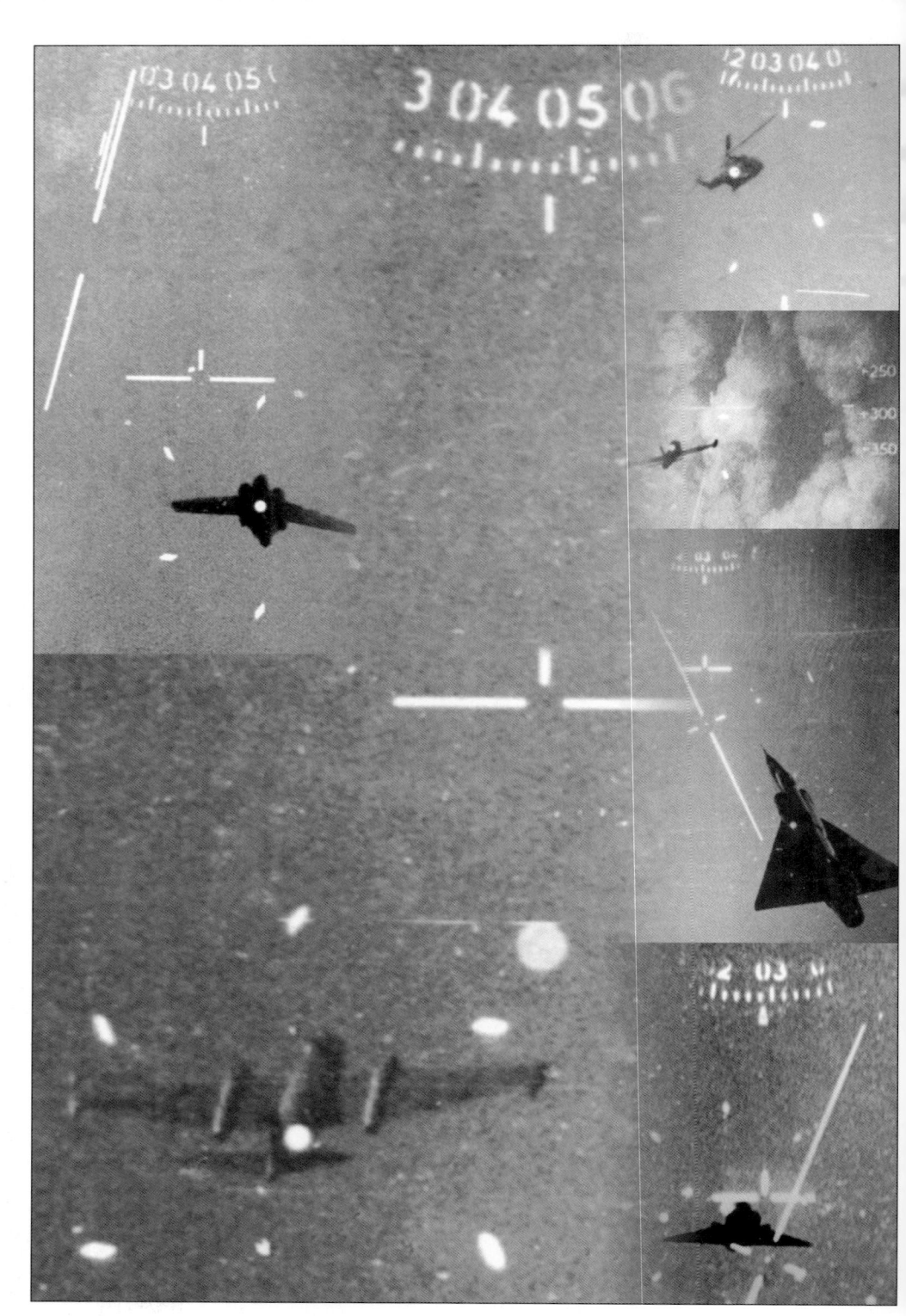

To a fighter pilot all aircraft are targets.

Heading for the stadium, he made a final cockpit inspection prior to starting the display. While his eyes were scanning the instruments, he heard an awesome bang and his aircraft began vibrating. His impression was that he had collided with a light aircraft or a microlight. His glance into the rear-view mirrors gave him no clue as to the problem.

Mirage 221 was still intact—no emergency lights had illuminated on the warning panel—but the aircraft was vibrating significantly. He reported the problem to Alan while heading directly back to Hoedspruit, 15 kilometres away. He retracted the IFR probe to eliminate the possibility of its causing the vibrating. Engine indications appeared normal at 7,900rpm with a jet-pipe temperature of 600 degrees. Apart from the thud and the vibrations, he felt he could recover safely onto runway eighteen.

However, on opening the throttle, the engine speed increased by only 100rpm before the throttle became ineffective. Alarmingly, the revs now began gradually decreasing no matter how hard he pushed the lever forward. With the revs winding down through 7,600rpm, he still felt he could make the runway—but the rev loss continued. While checking his aircraft after the thud, Bath had selected autopilot to ease the cockpit workload. As conditions were rapidly becoming critical, he deselected the autopilot to fly the aircraft as smoothly as possible. At slow speed, the autopilot tended to apply jerky control movements.

Wreckage of Mirage F1AZ 221 from which Leon Bath ejected after the engine ingested a large bird near AFB Hoedspruit in 1992. This aircraft had been rebuilt after Rikus de Beer's short landing in 1985.

He declared a full emergency as his speed decayed through 230 knots with his height at around 1,000 feet above the ground. He eliminated the possibility of an engine compressor stall and decided against cutting the engine and attempting a relight as the critical conditions did not allow this procedure.

He elected to use emergency throttle regulation in an attempt to regain engine revs. Alan Brand, assisting via the radio, agreed with the action, but to no avail. With his engine now down to 5,500rpm, the speed 200 knots and at a height he judged to be 200 feet above the ground, he radioed that he was ejecting. Pulling the aircraft nose up, he pulled the bottom seat-panhandle of his ejector seat and immediately felt the rocket seat accelerating smoothly through the shattered canopy.

Once out in the airstream, the seat began to tumble. He remained conscious throughout the ejection and was alarmed to see how close to the treetops he was as he went through the inverted position. His main parachute opened smoothly, allowing him to glimpse Mirage 221 as it plunged, wings level, into the ground. Looking down, he was appalled at how fast he seemed to be descending. He had time to assume the briefed landing posture before striking the ground very hard. Fortunately, his flying helmet absorbed most of the impact and apart from feeling dazed he ascertained that no bones had been broken. He discovered that he still had the seat panhandle firmly gripped in his right hand. Unstrapping, he removed his Pelba radio beacon and switched it on. Within a minute he could hear Major Billy Port, an Oryx helicopter pilot, talking to the tower. Billy Port and his co-pilot, Guy Waller, had been waiting to drop parachutists as part of the display, but were now speeding to the scene of the crash.

While waiting for the helicopter to arrive, Bath could hear the Mirage burning fiercely and loud detonations as oxygen bottles exploded. The subsequent board of inquiry found that Leon Bath and his ejector seat were only 160 metres from the wrecked Mirage.

Amidst thick dust clouds the helicopter landed. Much to Bath's annoyance the parachutists congratulated him on his first jump. The helicopter whisked him off to the Drakensig hospital, where Dr Vic Emslie was anxiously waiting. The X-rays showed a possible spinal deviation but, apart from some aches and pains, no other injuries were found. Bath was sedated and kept in the hospital under observation for the rest of the afternoon.

By 19h00, the Air Force Day function was gaining momentum. The squadron personnel decided that the party would be an anticlimax if the star of the show did not attend. The pilots, using their combined creative initiative, extracted Bath from the hospital to join the happy throng. Once again his attendance was short-lived because the hospital staff, led by the irate nurses, recovered their patient and placed him—for the second time—back in bed. Fortunately for Bath, neither the ejection nor the party had any adverse effects.

Lieutenant-Colonel Hans Zimmer presided over the board of inquiry. He ordered the engine to be removed and sent to Atlas Aircraft Corporation for evaluation. There the technicians removed pieces of a 'vulture'-sized bird from the compressor stage of the engine—the cause of the accident. Mirage F1AZ 221 crashed one mile short of the beginning of the runway—18 seconds from touchdown.

## The Russian connection

Confidential negotiations between the SAAF and the Russian aircraft industry had been going on for many months, when an article appeared in *Flight International* magazine in January 1992. The article stated that a joint programme was underway to re-engine the South African Mirage F1s with MiG-29 engines.

The announcement caused quite a stir in defence circles, as the international arms embargo on South Africa was still firmly in place. However, it was true and resulted from French unwillingness to supply the Snecma M88 engine. The Russians delivered two RD-33 Klimov engines to South Africa for mounting into a Mirage F1CZ and AZ. During April 1992, a Mirage F1 fuselage was transported to Moscow. In November, Rick Culpan went solo in an F1AZ. As a test pilot at Atlas Aircraft Corporation, he was later to test fly the Russian-engined F1. An accomplished guitarist, he was also composer of the 1 Squadron song, 'The Billy Boys' (*see* appendices).

Major Viktor Parkhomento of the Russian Air Force being congratulated by Alan Brand after his solo flight in a F1AZ.

## Projects

During 1992, the telemetry range at Hammanskraal north of Pretoria assumed a position of prominence. In March, EW systems fitted to the Mirage were tested against ground-based radars. A large variety of captured Soviet surface-to-air missiles and air-defence radars deployed at the range, added realism to the trials.

During April, V3C missile trials were conducted against parachute flare targets. During August, Mirage F1 and Cheetah aircraft carried out an EW camp over the range. Data gathered from all these sorties were continually assessed to improve the capability of the equipment developed for the aircraft.

During July, an ACM clinic was held at Hoedspruit, where 3 Squadron passed on the expertise they had accumulated over all the years as the top fighter squadron in the SAAF. The other participants were F1AZs from 1 Squadron and Cheetahs from 2 and 5 Squadrons. Sadly, this programme was the last joint exercise in which 3 Squadron took part.

Budget cuts and downsizing of the defence force suddenly became apparent to the SAAF. On 30 September, the superb 3 Squadron was disbanded. On 12 October, it was announced that AFB Pietersburg, the alma mater of the fighter fraternity of the SAAF, was also to close.

In October, the annual *Golden Eagle* force preparation exercise was held in conjunction with the army's exercise *Excalibur*. The withdrawal from service of the Canberra, Buccaneer and Mirage F1CZ squadrons seriously reduced the scope, but not necessarily the professionalism of the exercises. 1 Squadron performed excellent attacks dropping Condibs and retarded Traan bombs. However, it is worthy of note that the bombing computers—the F1AZ's Achilles heel—were still giving problems.

Late in October, the last air-to-air camp of the year once again produced some excellent results. Major Leon Bath shot a 26/30, to be pipped as 'top gun' by Captain Nic Scheltema who scored 27 hits out of 30 rounds fired. Nic Scheltema also took over as solo aerobatic display pilot when Leon Bath left 1 Squadron at the end of 1992.

## 1993

1993 started with AFB Hoedspruit changing hands from one Mirage III pilot to another, when Brigadier Mac van der Merwe took over as base officer commanding from Colonel Steyn Venter.

On 26 February, Commandant Dolf Prinsloo created excitement on the squadron when Mirage F1AZ 224 caught fire during start-up. Damage resulted to both fuselage and engine.

On 18 March, four Mirage F1AZs took off from AFB Hoedspruit on an extended-range, around-South Africa flight. Heading westward they rendezvoused with a 60 Squadron B-707 tanker for in-flight refuelling. Turning south they passed over Cape Town before heading towards East London. A second top-up from the tanker allowed them to continue overhead Durban, before returning to Hoedspruit. All four aircraft were airborne for over five hours, with Captain Francois Brand logging the bladder-bursting record of 5.4 hours.

Annually, the joint staff course was entertained by the air force at Roodewal bombing range. The demonstration on 7 April was highlighted by an attack by 1 Squadron during which two F1AZs each dropped six Traan retarded bombs, followed by four more, each releasing 14 x 120kg pre-frag bombs.

Commandant Prinsloo's secret objective to keep the squadron operational appeared to be succeeding as new pilots, captains Chris Pretorius and Louis Joubert, were appointed to the squadron in June.

During August 1993, 13 F1AZs deployed to Durban for the annual ACM camp. During an engagement a panel detached from the top of the fuselage of F1AZ 219, which was initially undetected by pilot Captain Piet Coetzer. However, the loss of streamlining severely disrupted the airflow around the engine, resulting in heat damage around the engine casing. Captain Coetzer only became aware of the problem on the illumination of the fire-warning light. He throttled back and returned safely to AFB Durban, where temporary repairs were carried out. On 20 August, Major Alan Brand flew the aircraft to the Atlas Aircraft Corporation at Jan Smuts airport for permanent repair.

Major Brand returned to Atlas on 31 August to collect the repaired aircraft. He decided to combine the obligatory test flight with the ferry flight back to the base at Hoedspruit. The test-flight schedule calls for an acceleration through Mach 1.4 at 36,000 feet. Just above this speed the afterburner fire-warning light came on. Applying the correct emergency procedure, he cut the afterburner to get the speed below Mach 1.4 before returning to dry power. During these few seconds he performed a turn to check for visible signs of smoke, but this did not reveal anything. Once sub-sonic, he brought the power back to idle. After a further 60 seconds the fire warning light was still burning. He therefore cut the fuel cock and, after a further 30 seconds, the warning light went out.

During this feverish activity he had given *out a Mayday* call and was considering ejection. When the warning light finally extinguished he was at 28,000 feet overhead the little mining community of Penge, 70 nautical miles from AFB Hoedspruit. His biggest concern was that the entire lowveld was covered by 8/8ths low cloud. In his haste, he tried a couple of relights that were unsuccessful. Then, allowing the F1 to enter the published relight envelope, the engine relit. Carrying out a precautionary approach, he landed safely.

On 3 October, squadron personnel were shocked by the horrific crash of an Impala aircraft that killed Major Charlie Rudnick. It appeared that a wing had broken as the aircraft was recovering from a steep dive during a display by the Silver Falcon aerobatic team at the Lanseria airshow.

## The Great Air Race

The eagerly awaited day finally arrived on 3 November. Early in 1993, in a rash moment, 19 Squadron threw down the gauntlet at the feet of 1 Squadron. On receipt of the high-powered Oryx helicopter, the helicopter pilots had convinced themselves that they now had the capability to humble the jet jocks. They challenged the F1 to a race from AFB Waterkloof at 5,000 feet above sea level up to 10,000 feet. The challenge was accompanied by the customary unsubtle, helicopter-inspired bluster—the excellent helicopter pilots are notoriously good at bluster but poor at reading basic performance graphs.

Vast sums of money changed hands as betting reached a frenzy. The final judge and arbiter was to be Chief of the Air Force, General James Kriel. The fact that he was an ex-helicopter man did not go unnoticed in the Mirage camp amidst suspicions of match-fixing. The judge was taken aloft to hover at the winning-post height of 10,000 feet in another Oryx. This bias was also commented on by the Mirage team, although they had to admit that it was difficult for a Mirage F1 to hover at that height.

To avoid nit-picking over pilot weights, it was decided that both officers commanding would fly their respective aircraft: Commandant Dolf Prinsloo the F1AZ 230 and Commandant Martin Kruger the Oryx. When the judge indicated that his helicopter was at the correct altitude, the competitors started their engines. Both aircraft positioned on the threshold of the main runway and ran up their engines to take-off power. At a signal from the tower the race began.

While the F1 sped down the long runway horizontally, the Oryx started ascending like a lift, accompanied by the raucous cheering of the helicopter crews watching the race. To the uninitiated, helicopter crews can be raucous! Martin Kruger's Oryx diminished in size as its altitude increased and seemed a certain winner. Just when all appeared lost, Dolf Prinsloo pulled back on his stick and the F1 climbed like a rocket. Within seconds the race was over. Even a biased ex-helicopter judge had to admit that, when the F1 flashed past 10,000 feet, the Oryx still had another 1,000 feet to go.

For months thereafter, pub nights became remarkably civilized, as the usual noise emanating from Chopper Corner was kept to a subdued muttering. Helicopter pilots are irrepressible and eventually started returning to normal. However, when their noise levels began intruding, a quick retelling of the Hare and the Tortoise fable restored decorum to the pub.

During November the annual air-to-air camp was held at AFB Langebaanweg. In addition to the usual firing on the flag, all the pilots shot V3B air-to-air missiles with a high success rate. The exception was the missile fired by Captain Louis Joubert, which exploded 100 metres ahead of his launching F1.

During the deployment, Major Alan Brand and Captain Wynand Serfontein formed up with the SAAF Harvard aerobatics team for a highly successful photographic sortie that produced some brilliant air-to-air shots. To achieve these pictures required a great deal of planning and some skilful flying on the part of the Harvard and the Mirage pilots. The Harvard team started a full-power descent taking their aircraft to 200 knots, very close to their VNE (velocity never exceed speed) of 206 knots. The F1 pilots joined the diving formation with their flaps, slats and wheels down, to keep them from sliding forward out of position.

## Operation *Reeftan*

As a contribution towards increasing SAAF competency, the navy offered the air force an obsolete trawler as a target and kindly offered to tow the hulk into the designated position, 50 miles south of Cape Point. To take full advantage of this opportunity the SAAF decided to test the effect of Traan bombs, before sinking the old ship. These high-drag, parachute-retarded, pre-fragmented bombs would be dropped, spraying the old vessel with shrapnel. By accurate and detailed post-strike photography the results of this strike could be determined for future strike-planning sorties. On completion of this sequence, the ship would be sunk by the following formation. The planned operation was given the designation of Operation *Reeftan*.

On 23 November 1993, a three-aircraft Mirage F1AZ formation, led by Major Alan Brand, was tasked to fly from AFB Langebaanweg to carry out the Traan attack. Flying as No 2 was Captain Wynand Serfontein while Captain Louis Joubert, flying Mirage F1AZ 234, filled the third spot. The Mirages were cleared in for the live attack, accelerating at low level to 500 knots. Dropping Traan requires the aircraft to be virtually line-abreast to avoid trailing aircraft being caught up in the blast from the leading aircraft. Louis Joubert, on the outside of the left-hand turn-in, possibly used his dive brakes to reduce slight excess speed. Without a radio call, his fast-travelling aircraft was seen to bank to the right and dive into the ocean. The cause could possibly have resulted from asymmetric rate of roll induced by faulty deployment of the dive brakes, or inadvertent deployment of the retardation parachute of one of the Traan bombs. The cause has never been conclusively established.

A helicopter flown by Major Mac McCarthy, already airborne with photographic observers, sped quickly to the scene. Joubert had ejected and was in the water, but despite a valiant rescue attempt by one of the observers, Mac Macatamney, Joubert disappeared. Presumably, his sinking parachute dragged him under water. The two remaining Mirages routed back to Langebaanweg, having to explain to the air traffic control centres in Cape Town and Langebaan why there were now just two aircraft. It was a tragic loss of an excellent pilot and officer.

## 1994 elections

During April 1994, South Africa reached a crucial stage in its transformation process. Democratic elections were planned to take place on 27 April.

Infrastructure, particularly in the rural areas, was minimal and huge problems were foreseen. Understandably perhaps, the Independent Electoral Commission (IEC) officials charged with overseeing the elections were loath to ask for help from the defence force. However the SAAF, through its countrywide command and control network, was ideally positioned to assist.

As election day approached it became increasingly obvious that without large-scale assistance, the election process would fail. Eventually, the SAAF shouldered the responsibility and allocated every available transport aircraft and helicopter to assist the process where required. The only aircraft not allocated were the fighters, but the pool of experienced personnel on the fighter squadrons was available to help. 1 Squadron closed down all flying operations to open a temporary forward air force command post (FACP) in Potchefstroom. The Cheetah squadron from AFB Louis Trichardt did likewise and opened a temporary FACP in Kimberley.

As predicted, election day proved chaotic in some areas. However, owing to the resourcefulness and dedication of all the SAAF personnel, most of the problems were resolved. Voting boxes, electoral papers, IEC officials, police and army troops were flown to troublespots. The speed of reaction of the air force to crisis areas proved vital in keeping voters' tempers from reaching boiling point.

The success of the elections was highlighted on 10 May at the inauguration of President Mandela. It was fitting that many of the air force personnel, who helped save the electoral process, flew in the magnificent flypast to honour the new State President.

However, after 48 years of National Party rule, the change of regime resurrected an age-old problem for the air force, which had only recently been solved. Flypasts are intricate manoeuvres to fly and control. Formation flying is inherently hazardous and, therefore, requires immense concentration. While one aircraft can easily tighten or relax a turn, a formation is considerably less manoeuvrable. Planning is critical to position a large formation in the right place, on the right heading at the correct time.

It took the air force 48 years to teach the politicians that flypasts are timed to the second and, therefore, must take place before they start on their customary speeches. During the planning session for a flypast a politician can promise to speak for exactly five minutes, but politicians don't always keep their promises. Over the years many flypasts have been compromised as a speech went on and on. Aircraft, especially fighters, are prone to run out of fuel during these political orations.

The inauguration of President Mandela proved to be no different. Speeches, hugs and embraces all added to the problem of guiding the new President onto the podium. A delay of almost an hour occurred, which resulted in frenetic reorganization. Fighters broke out of formation to refuel from tankers, already in formation for their part in the flypast. From AFB Swartkop, helicopters bobbed up and down like yo-yos to refuel and rejoin their formation. Despite an anxious 50 minutes, the flypast took place at the re-re-re-re-appointed time. All aircraft were in position, on heading and on time in a fitting climax to the historic day.

## Potchefstroom punch-out

On 9 June, a six-ship formation, led by Captain Wynand Serfontein, flew from AFB Hoedspruit to the bombing range, just north of Potchefstroom. The plan was for the first four aircraft to attack, using Traan bombs, followed by a pair dropping conventional bombs.

A pinpoint target was selected for *the Traan* attack, which required the four Mirages to fly in almost close formation during the drop. Because parachutes retard the bombs, the aircraft are clear of the explosion. The aircraft ran in a finger-four formation at 520 knots and 150 feet above the ground over the target; the four pilots released their bombs simultaneously.

Unfortunately, the retard parachute on one of the bombs failed to open and detonated underneath the formation. Major Alan Brand felt severe buffeting and had to dive under the rest of the formation to avoid a collision. Audio warnings prompted him to scan the emergency panel which had lit up like a Christmas tree. The right-hand alternator, hydraulic pump and fuel pump were malfunctioning and the flight augmentation had been disconnected, giving him yaw and roll problems.

Brand handled all the problems in the correct sequence, but then noticed that the right-hand fuel tank was empty. He declared an emergency and asked one of the other aircraft to formate and carry out an external inspection of his aircraft. Nic Scheltema advised Brand to plan for a forced landing at Potchefstroom airfield. He converted speed to height, climbing to 14,000 feet using 95 per cent revs, the maximum the damaged engine could achieve.

Captain Charl Marais drew alongside and reported smoke trailing astern. He confirmed that the aircraft was on fire and called for Brand to eject. While his seat was tumbling he remembers seeing Potchefstroom town over his right shoulder and his parachute streaming behind him. He thought that he was going to fall to his death. Then the parachute opened with a severe jerk, damaging hiss neck and arms and blowing his helmet off. Strangely, he remembers looking at his watch and wondering how he could phone home to say he would be late for dinner.

Brand looked for his aircraft and spotted a huge fireball and pall of smoke coming from the crash site, 200 metres from a farmhouse. He inspected the canopy of his parachute and was horrified to notice a major rip in some of the right-hand panels. He realized this would increase his rate of descent, which could affect his landing. Nevertheless, he was in the parachute for seven minutes.

During this time Charl Marais circled Brand to confirm that he was conscious.

As he approached the ground, Brand noticed that he was drifting backwards towards high-tension cables. He pulled down on the parachute in an attempt to twist around and face the threat. However, this caused a severe pendulum movement to his body. He missed the wires and a large tree but hit the ground horizontally at the full extent of a pendulum motion. The board of inquiry came to the conclusion that he struck the ground at nine metres per second instead of the normal seven. For many weeks he could be seen sporting a neck brace, even at mess dinners.

## A treasured moment

Brigadier Mac van der Merwe, the base commander of AFB Hoedspruit, phoned me to ask if I would give a motivational talk to the Impala pilots on his base. I agreed and flew to Hoedspruit early in the morning of 28 June in the back of a Queen Air. While reading the morning paper, I realized that the pilot had transferred the radio transmissions from his headset to the cabin loudspeaker. Having spent many years in the Fleet Air Arm and the SAAF on interception training, I became aware from the transmissions that an interception was in progress. The longer I listened the more certain I became that the interceptors were being vectored onto the Queen Air.

Letting the newspaper fall and undoing my seat straps, I dropped on my knees in the rear cabin of the light transport aircraft. Straining my eyes, I eventually picked up two F1s in a hard-right turn passing down our right-hand side. Shouting instructions to the pilot, I instructed him in the art of combat flying. Breaking right into the Mirages we forced them to overshoot our tail, before reversing the turn to slot neatly in astern of the fighters. Eventually, we had to stop our manoeuvring to allow the Mirage F1AZs to fall into the escort position, one on either wingtip. I then understood that this was 1 Squadron, paying their respects to me because I was to retire from the SAAF two days later. It was a tribute I greatly value. Normally these marks of respect are afforded only to heads of state so I felt doubly honoured.

On 30 July, F1AZs intercepted and escorted an Air France 747 carrying President Mitterand into Cape Town on an official state visit to South Africa.

## Flying united

In mid-July 1994, 1 Squadron and 60 Squadron combined for a very successful night-refuelling programme. During two night sorties on 19 July, Alan Brand achieved the magnificent scores of 25/25 then 40/40 night refuelling plugs. The following night he took off at 22h35, flying Mirage 232. Meeting the Boeing 707 he achieved a score of 35/36. The majority of these were dry plugs but on occasions he did take on fuel which allowed him to stay in the air. He broke off from the exercise when his warning panel illuminated, indicating the aircraft had an ancillary hydraulic system failure. With the pressure down to zero he returned to the long runway at AFB Hoedspruit, where he landed without any problems at 01h10 off a flapless approach at 210 knots. Ironically, 1 Squadron probably had a greater plug-rate success at night than during the day. Firstly, initial attempts at plugging require a certain amount of training, which takes place during the day. Only experienced operators are allowed to plug at night. Secondly, at night there are far fewer distractions because you cannot see the tanker out of the corner of your eye, therefore your entire concentration is on the task. All this becomes fairly straightforward for experienced pilots, provided the Boeing remains straight and level. However, when the Boeing lifts its huge wing to go into a turn, even the most experienced pilot suffers from severe vertigo.

When 60 Squadron obtained a new type of 'panty' for its refuelling baskets, Piet Coetzer and Alan Brand carried out a series of tests to check for suitability. The Cheetahs, which were considerably more difficult to refuel than the F1s, had experienced leakage on coupling and uncoupling. The two AZ pilots were asked to plug centre-centre, on the left edge then the right edge and finally to plug while on a downward vector to simulate the Cheetah probes. That this was accomplished successfully was a token of the F1's ability and the undoubted skill of the pilots.

## Year end

During 1994, the F1AZ simulator achieved the 2,000-hour milestone. Over the years, both CZ and AZ simulators were worth their weight in gold. The realism and accuracy of the simulations allowed pilots to build confidence in their abilities to handle every possible emergency.

On 22 September 1994, Alan Brand and Chris Pretorius flew two brand-new South African flags at Mach 2, twice the speed of sound. On landing, with cockpits open, they taxiied back displaying the nation's new flags, which were then presented to Lieutenant-General James Kriel, Chief of the Air Force.

On 3 October, Major Victor Parkehmento of the Soviet Air Force went solo in an F1AZ. Later that month, during a weapons deployment at AFB Bloemspruit, 1 Squadron took part in an air-power demonstration. The guest of honour was Reverend Chabaku, the lady speaker of the Free State parliament. Major Nic Scheltema demonstrated the F1AZ, while Lieutenant-Colonel Dolf Prinsloo explained the workings of the squadron to her. Prinsloo had just joined the select few who had achieved 1,000 Mirage F1 flying hours

The year ended well when two new pilots, captains Flynn and Potgieter, were posted in and 1 Squadron was awarded the SAAF Operational Efficiency Award for 1994.

## Stay of execution

In November 1994, a decision was taken to extend the life of the F1AZ beyond the end of 1995. In Plan 2000, Commandant Dolf Prinsloo was supposed to close 1 Squadron down. However, the new decision necessitated a new officer commanding. He rang Commandant Jan Mienie to warn him, unofficially, that he was in line to take over 1 Squadron.

Mienie was delighted. After the closure of 3 Squadron he had completed the staff course, on the understanding that he would then assume command of 8 Squadron. However, in true air force style, the planning was changed. After staff course, he was appointed onto the directing staff of the college. Therefore, the chance of another flying posting at 1 Squadron came as a welcome surprise and all was forgiven.

# Chapter 19

# 1995–1997:
# End of an era

## The final lap

In January 1995, Commandant Jan Mienie took over command of 1 Squadron from Dolf Prinsloo. Mienie was delighted to find that the extension to the life of the squadron had filled all his personnel with new enthusiasm. With new pilot, Captain Jaco Smith, he was soon occupied with the technical conversion course—a refresher for Mienie who had first flown AZs in 1983/84.

Major Alan Brand achieved a personal milestone on 20 January 1995. During his 990th sortie he passed the magical 1,000-hour mark flying Mirage F1AZs. He became the third pilot to do so after Norman Minne (June 1989) and Dolf Prinsloo (October 1994). The sortie was a third-generation, all-aspect-ratio, two-versus-two ACM engagement. In between rounds, all the involved aircraft carried out in-flight refuelling from a 60 Squadron Boeing tanker, before continuing the fight. On landing, Brand was met by the ground crew who placed the traditional laurel wreath around his shoulders and opened a celebratory bottle of champagne.

After gaining an engineering degree from Stellenbosch University, Major Chris Skinner returned to fly the F1 in 1995 from his position as a project officer at headquarters. In February 1996, eight years after his last air-to-air refuelling practice, he plugged in eight out of nine attempts, illustrating how well the aircraft handles in this aspect.

## The original Billy Boy

The 3rd of February was a particularly sad day for 1 Squadron when it was announced that the original Billy Boy had passed away. Hannes Faure, a much respected and admired aviator, had been Officer Commanding 1 Squadron in the western desert during the Second World War. The squadron, attached to a

On landing at AFB Langebaan, the nose-wheel steering remained deflected fully left, despite actions from the pilot.

Royal Air Force wing, was easily recognizable over the radio by the strong South African accents of the pilots.

1 Squadron earned a wonderful reputation as ground-attack specialists, destroying hundreds of German and Italian armoured and logistic vehicles. Hannes Faure, invariably the leader during these attacks, had the habit of shouting, *"Jou bielie!"* (lit. you stout fellow) over the radio every time a vehicle exploded in front of his gun sight. Royal Air Force pilots, unused to the common Afrikaans expression of delight, thought he was calling the name Billy.

From that period on, 1 Squadron became known as 'The Billy Boys', and the officer commanding by the call sign 'Billy'. On being appointed to the squadron each new pilot was presented with a Billy Boy certificate, detailing the squadron's code and ethics. By preserving this tradition, the squadron has maintained the enviable reputation built by men like Hannes Faure.

On 8 February 1995, Commandant Jan Mienie landed in F1AZ 240 as No 2 in a formation touchdown at AFB Langebaan. On roll-out, he dropped back from the leader as the speed decreased below 110 knots before lowering his nose wheel onto the runway. Immediately, his aircraft began sliding uncontrollably to the left. He managed to stop the Mirage without damage, after it had turned through 120 degrees. Miraculously, the Michelin tyres remained intact despite the extreme loading that had been placed on them.

On investigation, it was found that the nose-wheel steering had jammed in

Jan Mienie looking at the defective nose-wheel steering.

the full-left deflection position. The exact cause was not positively established. Either the hydraulic fluid had been contaminated or there was a fault in the hydraulic distributor. Both fluid and distributor were changed and the problem never reoccurred.

## The new South Africa

After the successful national elections of 1994, the air force found itself in a most unaccustomed position. For many years, SAAF aircraft had been crossing international borders, usually without the authority of the controlling country. In the early 1980s, I can well remember Commandant Bertus Burger flying a Canberra photographic-reconnaissance sortie that violated five international borders in one flight. However, by 1995 the situation had normalized and the SAAF flew legally throughout sub-Saharan Africa.

Namibia, demonstrating her newly acquired independence, held an airshow in Windhoek on 23 March. The organizers invited the SAAF to participate and a C-130 Hercules duly landed in Windhoek carrying ground-support personnel and equipment, followed by two Mirage F1AZs. The aviation fans in Namibia welcomed the needle-nosed aircraft, but not so members of the SWAPO government. For too many years they had been on the receiving end of the Mirage F1s' sharp noses. To the acute embarrassment of the air display organizers, the SAAF contingent was told to leave. A last-minute intervention by

President Mandela saved the day and the F1AZs were allowed to perform.

In a rare display of solidarity, the entire southern African region welcomed the 'Rainbow Nation'. Mirage F1AZs performed at the Maputo Airshow in Mozambique on 4 July and at the Swaziland Airshow on 29 July.

On 28 August, international co-operation continued when a Royal Air Force VC-10 tanker aircraft arrived at AFB Hoedspruit. Commandant Mienie and 1 Squadron pilots carried out successful in-flight refuelling from the international visitor.

On 16 September, a huge Russian AN-124 transport aircraft and two MiG-29 fighters arrived at Hoedspruit, as part of a Russian export campaign. Despite language difficulties, the aircrew from both sides enjoyed the exchange of ideas and the thrill of flying, and fighting the magnificent MiGs.

These aircraft took part in the SAAF 75-Year Anniversary Airshow at AFB Waterkloof on 20 October. This wonderful airshow included flying displays by SU-31, SU-35, F-15, F-16 and Mirage 2000 aircraft and ended with a breathtaking performance by the Red Arrow aerobatic team.

For Captain Chris Pretorius, 29 September was an exciting day. While flying F1AZ 229 his engine suffered a high (8400) rev freeze. This almost full-power position required considerable skill on his behalf to land the aircraft safely. On inspection, it was found that a bolt had sheered off in the throttle cable.

Exercise *Suider Kruis* took place in October when ten AZs deployed to Upington. This airfield had been vital in the early years of South Africa's isolation. Airways B-707s, having to fly around the 'bulge' of West Africa, refuelled there before starting their long haul to Europe. Unfortunately, since those days, the airfield had assumed only minor importance.

Maintenance budgets had been reduced and sweeping of the extremely long runway occurred less and less frequently. Hard, flinty stones, blown onto the runway surface by the Kalahari winds, caused havoc among the fighters. The first casualty was a shredded nose-wheel tyre of an F1. Shortly afterwards a Cheetah-C, flown by Major John Erasmus, ran off the runway when the main-wheel tyres punctured. All flying was halted while pilots and ground crew walked the entire length of the runway, removing offensive material by hand.

From 16 to 18 November, an excellent pilot reunion was held at AFB Langebaanweg, unfortunately for a sad occasion. A 'wake' was held to mourn the final passing out from SAAF service of the venerable Harvard. For an unbelievable 50 years, all SAAF pilots had received their basic training on this legendary aircraft. The overwhelming feeling was that, though the replacement trainers were good aircraft, the Harvard 'put hairs on your chest'.

## 1996

During the first half of 1996, financial restrictions within the transforming South Africa were becoming noticeable at front-line level. Replacement pilot flow reduced to a trickle and flying hours were cut in an effort to reduce fuel bill costs. The spotlight of depression changed to one of celebration when General Willem Hechter, the first officer commanding of the Mirage F1AZ squadron, was appointed Chief of the Air Force on 1 May.

On 5 July, the 21st anniversary of the Mirage F1 in SAAF service was celebrated in fine style at AFB Hoedspruit. The gathering included CZ and AZ pilots, ground crew from both squadrons, together with personnel from Denel, Atlas, Air Logistics Command and the Test Flight Centre. The address by the current 'Billy', Lieutenant-Colonel Jan Mienie, included the following passage:

> All indications are that the F1AZ could see the year 2000 and if the need arises, still continue as required. May I take this opportunity to congratulate all F1 operators for a sterling job and absolute dedication in the past, as well as the present. It is with great pride that we accept the 'key of the door' and remain prepared for whatever is required in the future.

Despite the obvious enthusiasm and dedication of the personnel the signs of the times were ominous.

In an effort to attract worldwide attention to Cape Town's bid to hold the 2004 Olympic Games, South African Airways had Boeing 747 'Ndizani' painted in the colours of the new South African flag. A most successful photographic flight was carried out on 29 June and the results, which were published in newspapers, magazines and books, captured the imagination of the public. The success of the sortie was a direct result of the careful planning which preceded the flight.

Captain Laurie Kay, himself an ex-SAAF pilot, flew the B-747. Commandant Jan Mienie led the formation of F1AZs of 1 Squadron that accompanied the huge 747. The late Herman Potgieter, South Africa's world-renowned aviation photographer, flew in a civilian aircraft to capture the truly remarkable photographs. The backgrounds for each shot were carefully selected and the flight paths of the large formation meticulously planned. Air traffic authority for the entire flight was approved by the Department of Civil Aviation. 60 Squadron, AFB Waterkloof, provided a B-707 tanker which allowed the Mirage F1s to complete what turned out to be a long, involved mission.

The aircraft took off from their respective airfields and headed towards the Cape. After taking on fuel from the B-707 tanker over Vryburg in the northern Cape, the Mirages joined the B-747 as it descended into Cape Town. Herman Potgieter photographed the formation as it flew low-level for 45 minutes over the peninsula. On completion of the flight, the aircraft climbed to altitude and then repeated the performance over Gauteng. The four AZs again met the B-707 overhead Sutherland to top up their fuel tanks.

After completion of the 30-minute low-level display over Johannesburg and Pretoria, Jan Mienie, Patrick Flynn, Chris Pretorius and Philip Potgieter landed their Mirage F1s at AFB Hoedspruit after a five-hour round trip.

The shortage of pilots was beginning to be felt at squadron level. On 26 July 1997, a Mirage AZ was required to display at the Virginia Airshow in Durban. Chris Pretorius, the AZ display pilot, and Philip Potgieter were designated to fly but Pretorius was on staff course. Therefore, Commandant Jan Mienie elected to fly the Virginia display himself, using the display sequence he had formulated when flying the same airshow on 13 July 1991 in a Mirage F1CZ from 3 Squadron.

*****

Thankfully, after many turbulent years, the future for South Africa held the prospect of a welcome peace. Nevertheless, 1 Squadron determined to stay prepared for any eventuality. A successful sortie on the evening of 20 November 1996 highlighted the state of preparedness maintained by the squadron.

Commandant Jan Mienie, with Major Phillip Potgieter as No 2, took off at dusk from AFB Hoedspruit and headed west into the rapidly darkening sky. Each aircraft was loaded with four 120kg bombs and their task was to attack a target on the Lohatla live weapons range. A successful night rendezvous with a 60 Squadron B-707 tanker allowed both pilots to take on extra fuel.

A descent to low level, simulating an under-the-radar approach to the target was made. Accelerating at low level, the pilots passed over their selected initial point (IP) on heading and speed. At pull-up-point (PUP), the pilots pitched their aircraft into a *Nagup* release profile. This high-G profile required the aircraft to manoeuvre in all three planes, before and after bomb release, to prevent radar-guided anti-aircraft guns from gaining a firing solution on a predictable flight path. All such manoeuvres at high speed and high G close to the ground require considerable skill and nerves of steel.

After the attack, the pilots climbed back to altitude for another rendezvous with the tanker and a second night in-flight refuelling, before returning to AFB Hoedspruit in thunderstorm conditions.

## 1997

A welcome interlude occurred in January 1997 when 1 Squadron, Royal Air Force, paid a courtesy call to 1 Squadron, South African Air Force at AFB Hoedspruit.

Two new pilots, captains Stuart Spencer and Paul Williamson arrived to boost the hope that the life of the squadron would be extended. This expectation was short-lived as the aircraft were grounded during April and May.

When Commandant Jan Mienie had assumed command at the beginning of

1995, he resolved to keep 1 Squadron as the best fighter squadron and to focus on the reasons why it should stay open. Through factors outside his control he did not succeed. At the 1997 Fighter Conference he realized 1 Squadron was doomed. Pilot numbers had been decreasing steadily as the air force downsized and other needs of the fighter line dictated that the AZs should be taken out of service. 1 Squadron could not continue operating productively and it was with mixed feelings that General Hechter, the first Mirage 'Billy', reluctantly ordered them to be phased out late in 1997.

The squadron still participated in the supersonic ACM camp held at AFB Durban in June and July. In September, they took part in the annual force preparation *Golden Eagle* exercise that was curtailed when Major Keith Fryer ejected from a Cheetah at AFB Louis Trichardt.

All the time, squadron personnel worked flat out in the forlorn hope that the phase-out decision might be rescinded—but to no avail. As November approached the squadron experienced sad times. Equipment was removed and dispatched to other units. Liaisons, carefully nurtured and treasured throughout 1 Squadron's existence as a Mirage F1 operator, were to be severed. Associations with the F1 Support Group, Denel, Air Logistics Command and the Test Flight and Development Centre (TFDC) were sadly brought to a close. Despite all this, motivation remained high to the end, with the final focal point being the closing-down ceremonies.

## The final curtain

The demise of the F1AZ came sooner than anticipated. Downsizing and the necessity to incorporate many thousands of liberation force and former TBVC soldiers into the South African National Defence Force (SANDF) forced severe budgetary cuts on the military. The effect on the air force was dramatic. Closures of units, deactivation of squadrons and mothballing of aircraft became the order of the day. Senior personnel were encouraged to take severance packages, causing an alarming experience drain and a feeling of despondency in the dedicated personnel who were trying to hold the entire structure of the air force together.

Perhaps the heaviest blow to fall on the SAAF was the decision to close 1 Squadron. The most senior squadron of the air force, with a proud history built up over 50 years of service to South Africa, ceased flying their beloved Mirage F1AZs on 25 November 1997.

The final parade was held, fittingly, on the hardstanding outside the readiness shelter at AFB Hoedspruit where Colonel Pierre Gouws, the base commanding officer, had welcomed the squadron on 14 January 1981. Invited guests arrived from all over South Africa, by vehicles and aircraft. The SAAF band and members of the media were flown in by C-130. A Boeing 707 from 60 Squadron flew down from AFB Waterkloof carrying ex-squadron members representing the entire 22 years that the aircraft had been in service.

Shortly after take-off the Boeing was intercepted by two F1AZs, which then plugged into the in-flight refuelling hoses trailed by the 707, under the watchful and appreciative eyes of the experienced passengers. These plugs brought to the end an era of assistance which 24 Squadron Buccaneers had begun before the acquisition of the 707s. This in-flight refuelling ability had comprehensibly increased the capabilities of the Mirage F1AZ and given the SAAF an operational force-multiplier. As always, the plugs were neat and quick, ably displaying the man-machine balance which had made the Mirage such a potent weapon.

A King Air from 41 Squadron arrived shortly before 14h00 bringing the parade review officer, Major-General Roelf Beukes. Lieutenant-General Willem Hechter was unable to officiate at the ceremony. He had been summoned to a crucial financial meeting with President Mandela in Cape Town.

The parade began under a burning lowveld sun, with an immaculate five-aircraft flypast at precisely 14h00. In his address, General Beukes praised the squadron personnel and the aircraft for the contribution they had made to the defence of the country over close to a quarter of a century. On completion of the parade the five F1s carried out a slow-speed, dirty-configuration flypast. Before landing they thrilled the spectators with individual, high-speed, low-level runs. The five aircraft taxiied in to form a half circle around the saluting platform where they carried out a synchronized shut-down.

Lieutenant-Colonel Jan Mienie, the last 'Billy', then performed a scramble take-off from the readiness shelter before returning to give a low-level aerobatic display. His landing brought to an end the Mirage F1 era in the South African Air Force. He taxiied through the semi-circle and finally stopped with his Pitot tube almost touching the saluting base. The sudden silence as he cut his engine brought home the sad truth that the beloved Mirage F1 would no longer streak across the southern African skies. The aircraft, which had become the very symbol of our nation's strength, had performed its duties loyally until the very end.

The farewell function was held inside the tastefully decorated Base Servicing Unit. The ceilings were hung with parachutes and the walls covered in camouflage netting, giving the feel of an operational setting. As a backdrop, two aircraft took pride of place either side of the stage. The one was in a clean configuration sporting the green and brown paint scheme with which the Mirage began its career in the SAAF. The other aircraft, painted in air-supremacy blue, was configured for war. The 14-bomb configuration perhaps emphasized the growth and development the aircraft had undergone during its 22 years of service. At the other end of the hall the complete range of air-to-air missiles flanked a cutaway 9K50 engine that was internally illuminated to look as if the engine was running.

The supper guests were entertained throughout the meal, initially by a vivacious singer then by a superb video tribute to the Mirage F1 that was shown on a large screen. Finally, General Beukes gave an entertaining oration. He spoke about the introduction of the F1AZ and was ably assisted by Gawie Winterbach, André van der Heever and the irrepressible Mossie Basson relating humorous stories. In a nice gesture of appreciation, Herman Potgieter presented four of his superb photographs of the Mirage F1. They were auctioned by Rick Culpan and four very happy bidders came away with pictures that will fondly remind them of a great aeroplane.

The memorable evening and the Mirage F1 era were brought to a close with everyone singing the tribute Rick Culpan had written.

**The Mirage F1**
(to the tune of *Sixteen Tons*)

**Chorus**
Sixteen tons and what do you get?
A Mirage F1, she's a whole lot of jet!
Loaded with bombs and loaded with gun
You'll find none better than the Mirage F1

She was born in France on a rainy day
A mean machine that was here to stay
She flies real fast and she flies real low
A supersonic fighter with a lot of go

**Chorus**

The Billy Boys love her as a fighting ship
With six bombs each she can make any trip
3 Squadron loved her in the combat role
She's a graceful lady with a lot of soul

**Chorus**

The ground crew who work her say she's real tough
She can take quite a beating when the times get rough
She needs their attention and she needs their care
To keep her flying in the cold blue air

**Chorus** (with feeling)

# Glossary

**AAA** – anti-aircraft artillery. Triple A was the overall term used to describe the anti-aircraft guns that were employed in limited numbers by SWAPO, but extensively by the Angolan defence force. These guns covered the complete spectrum of Soviet-supplied weaponry and included the following:

- 12.7mm
- 14.5mm
- 20.0mm
- 23.0mm*
- 37.0mm
- 57.0mm**

*This included the towed, twin-barrelled version that was probably the most widely employed and effective gun used in the entire campaign by either side, both in the ground-to-air and ground-to-ground mode. The four-barrelled, tracked version (Shilka) was also encountered. The 23mm cannons used by 32 Battalion, Koevoet and the SAAF were some of the many captured in operations over the years. Ironically, Angola became probably the biggest arms supplier to South Africa throughout the difficult years of arms boycotts

**These radar-guided guns were originally equipped with the Fire-can radar system and later updated with the Flap-wheel version

**ACM** – air combat manoeuvring, modern name for old-fashioned dog-fighting

**Adhemar** – French word meaning angle of attack indicator (AAI), sometimes irreverently referred to as ADI (angle of dangle indicator); ADD in the Buccaneer

**AFB** – air force base

**ADF** – automatic direction-finding navigational instrument which locks onto an NDB

**AFCP** – air force command post. The SAAF uses a system of command posts to efficiently command and control all of the resources available to it. This includes aircraft, personnel, radars, air-defence systems and ground security squadron specialists with their dogs. An AFCP controls the air force involvement in its designated area of responsibility, which includes both ground and air battles. An FAC, forward air command post, is subservient to an AFCP but handles all the equivalent operations, except it does not control the air battle

**AGL** – above ground level, the height in feet that the aircraft flies above the ground

**AI** – air interception

# Glossary

**AK-47** – Automat Kalaschnikov type 47, the standard, and ubiquitous, Soviet-designed automatic assault rifle

**Alouette III** – single-engined light helicopter, the aerial workhorse of the border war. In the trooper role it could carry a crew of two plus four soldiers, or two stretchers when used in the casevac role. In the offensive role as a gunship it carried a 20mm cannon firing out of the port side

**Alpha bomb** – circular-shaped anti-personnel bomb weighing six kilograms that when dropped by the Canberra from level flight, gave a natural dispersion pattern. The bomb would strike the surface activating the fusing mechanism and then bounce into the air to detonate about six metres above the ground. This bomb was an improved version of that used by the Rhodesian Air Force, and 300 of them could be loaded into the bomb bay of a Canberra

**ANC** – African National Congress

**ATC** – Air Traffic Control

**ATCO** – Air Traffic Controller Officer

*avtur* – aviation turbine fuel used in helicopter and fixed-wing jet-turbine engines

*bakkie* – pick-up truck (Afrikaans)

*Bakkie* ops – SWAPO insurgents were known to utilize the vehicles of sympathizers for the conveyance of personnel, equipment and explosives throughout Owamboland. As these vehicles were usually of the light pick-up variety, operations launched to combat this illegal use of vehicles became known as *Bakkie* ops

**bandit** – an aircraft identified as hostile

**beacon** – the cut-line designating the border between Angola and Owamboland stretched in a straight line the 420kms from the Cunene River in the west to the Kavango River in the east. Every ten kilometres a concrete beacon was built to identify position in an otherwise featureless terrain. Beacon 16 was therefore 160km east of the Cunene River.

**blue job** – anybody serving in the air force (slang)

**BM-21** – 122mm 40-tube multiple rocket launcher, mounted on a Ural-375 truck, with a maximum range of 20,000 metres

*boere* – a general-usage, normally derogatory term used by both SWAPO and the Angolans to describe the South Africa/SWATF security forces (from the Afrikaans *boer* meaning farmer)

**bogey** – an unidentified aircraft

**bombshell** – guerrilla tactic of splitting up during flight (slang)

**Bosbok** – single-piston-engined, high-wing reconnaissance aircraft flown by two crew seated in tandem. In the bush war it was utilized in many roles, including visual and photographic reconnaissance, Skyshout, pamphlet dropping and Telstar

*braai* – barbecue (Afrikaans)

**brown job** – any soldier; variations were 'browns' or the more commonly used 'pongos' (slang)

**Buccaneer** – S-50 version of the British-built naval strike fighter; twin-engined, subsonic two-seater that could carry the full range of bombs plus AS-30 air-to-ground missiles

**C-130** – four-engined turboprop heavy transport aircraft otherwise known as the Hercules. Used extensively throughout the bush war to support the actions of both ground landing and air-dropping of personnel and freight (*see* Flossie)

**C-160** – twin-engined tactical transport aircraft. Although limited in payload when compared to the C-130, it had the decided advantage of a larger-dimensioned freight compartment, allowing easier and quicker transporting of helicopters to the battle area. Known by NATO as the Transall it had the dubious distinction of being probably the most difficult and expensive aircraft to maintain in the inventory of the SAAF, owing to the extreme difficulties imposed by the international arms embargo

**Canberra** – English Electric twin-engined, medium jet bomber, used as such and also in PR roles. Armament included Alpha bombs, World War II-vintage 500lb and 1,000lb general purpose (GP) bombs plus the South African-manufactured 120kg and 250kg GP and pre-fragmentation bombs

**CAP** – combat air patrol. The armed mission air-defence fighters fly to ensure safety of own aircraft in the battle area

**CAS** – close air support. Aircraft supporting the ground forces in close proximity to the immediate battle line are termed to be giving CAS

**casevac** – casualty evacuation

**Casspir** – mine-protected, armoured personnel carrier

**CEP** – centre of error probability. A mathematical method of determining the miss-distance of a number of weapons from the centre of a target

**Cessna 185** – A single-engined, four-seater tail-dragger used in the communication, Skyshout, pamphlet-dropping and Telstar roles, by day and night

**CFS** – Central Flying School

**clampers** – visibility and cloud base below the minimum required for safe flying operations (air force slang)

**COIN** – counter-insurgency

**coke** – the centre or bull's-eye of the target (air force slang)

**ComOps** – communications operations. The type of activity performed to influence our own and the enemy forces positively, as well as the local population. Although the members of our ComOps teams did sterling work, the successes they achieved with the enemy and the local population were negligible compared to the effort they put in

**contact** – a fire fight, i.e. when contact is made with the enemy

**CO** – commanding officer

*cuca* – small shop/stall in Owamboland, derived from a popular brand of beer, Cuca.

***Cuca* blitz** – security force raids on cuca shops. These raids were mostly carried out after the receipt of intelligence but ad hoc raids were also undertaken to keep the enemy guessing. Most raids were carried out by the ground forces alone, but joint air force, army and police raids were also mounted. These raids were generally unsuccessful but a few did

# Glossary

result in the arrest of important insurgents, and presumably kept SWAPO guessing.

**curfew** – within the military operational area of Sector 10, i.e. Owamboland, a curfew was imposed on all movements of people and vehicles between sundown and sunrise, to inhibit SWAPO's nightly activities

**cut-line** – the border between Angola and Owamboland, so named from the graded strip cut through the bush to indicate the international border

**D-30** – Soviet-built 122mm cannon with a range of 15,000 metres; also used in an anti-tank role

**Dayton** – the radio call sign of the radar station situated at AFB Ondangwa. All matters concerning air defence were the responsibility of Dayton

**density altitude** – aircraft aerodynamic and engine performance are adversely affected by high temperatures and low pressures. Because these criteria vary from airfield to airfield and on a daily basis, the term 'density altitude' is used to determine aircraft performance. At a sea-level airfield in Europe during winter, a jet aircraft will produce more thrust and lift than it will at AFB Waterkloof, 5,000ft AGL, during the 30°C-plus temperatures of summer

*dominee* – padre (Afrikaans)

**DR** – dead reckoning, when navigating without electronic aids

**DZ** – drop zone designated for any parachute delivery, whether personnel or supplies

**ECM/ECCM** – electronic counter measures/electronic counter counter measures, part of EW (*see* EW)

**ERU** – explosive release unit The device which ensures clean separation of bombs from the carrying aircraft

**EW** – electronic warfare; covers all aspects of warfare involving use of the electromagnetic spectrum

**FAC** – Forward Air Controller

**FAPA** – *Forças Aeria Popular de Angola*, People's Air Force of Angola

**FAPLA** – *Forças Armadas Populares de Libertação de Angola*, People's Armed Forces for the Liberation of Angola

**FFAR** – forward-firing air rockets

**Fireforce** – an airborne offensive force comprising combinations of the following:

- gunships
- offensive firepower
- troopers
- command and control
- Bosboks
- recce or Telstar
- Pumas
- insertion of stopper groups
- troops—usually highly trained Parabats

**Flossie** – C-130 Hercules used as the air link between South Africa and South West Africa during the border war. A term of endearment as this aircraft took the troops home. (SADF slang)

**FLOT** – forward line own troops. A very necessary requirement during close air support operations, which ensures safety of own forces

**FNLA** – *Frente Nacional para a Libertação de Angola,* National Front for the Liberation of Angola

**FTS** – Flying Training School

**G** – gravity. Under normal circumstances everything on earth is affected by the pull of gravity, called 1G. In tight turns or loops, centrifugal force effectively increases the pull of gravity. A G meter in the cockpit registers this increase. Readings of -2 to +7G are the usual range experienced during a typical fighter sortie. At =7G, the body's blood effectively becomes seven times heavier than normal and hastens the onset of blackout as blood drains towards the pilot's feet. At -G readings, blood is forced to the head, sometimes resulting in red-out as the capillary blood vessels in the eyes burst due to the increased pressure

**G-suit** – the inflatable garment, zipped around abdomen and legs that inhibits blood flow to the pilot's feet as aircraft G-loading is increased

*Gatup* – a high-G manoeuvre developed by 1 Squadron pilots which affords maximum safety for an aircraft in a hostile environment. A 4G pull-up is followed by 120–130° banked turn, as the pilot pulls the sight onto the target. Immediately thereafter he fires a laser shot to accurately measure range to the target. The pilot then pulls the nose skyward. The laser input allows the computer to predict an automatic release of the bombs during the pull-up. After bomb release the pilot reapplies G, over-banks and pulls the aircraft's nose down toward the ground. The escape from the target area is flown at low level. When this manoeuvre is performed at night it is termed *Nagup*

**GCA** – ground controlled approach. Radar talk-down used to guide pilots to a safe landing in bad weather or at night

**GCI** – ground controlled interception

**GIB** – guy in the back i.e. Buccaneer navigator (air force slang)

**GOC SWA** – General Officer Commanding South West Africa

**Grad-P** – single-shot 122mm Soviet rocket launcher. Mounted on a tripod and could fire a 46kg rocket with an 18.3kg warhead, a maximum distance of 11,000 metres. Much used by SWAPO for their stand-off bombardments

**Guns free** – the state prevailing when all guns are allowed to fire at designated targets as and when they are ready; only ordered when no own-forces' aircraft are in the area

**Guns tight** – the order given to cease own forces' artillery firing when own forces' aircraft are operating over a battlefield

**HAG** – *helikopter administrasie gebied,* Afrikaans for helicopter administration area (HAA). A designated area, planned and secured by ground forces, from where helicopters operated to expedite operations. Very often it was co-located with a forward headquarters where immediate tactical plans were co-ordinated. Fuel in drums or bladders was available to refuel the helicopters, with extra gunship ammunition available. The HAG could be stationary for two or three days depending on the area, but longer than that was considered dangerous, as SWAPO could be expected to locate the HAG in that time. On the border, the Afrikaans HAG was always used as the sound came more easily to the tongue.

# Glossary

**HC** – Honoris Crux. The highest decoration for military valour that could be awarded to members of the SADF. There were three classes, namely: HC Bronze, HCS Silver and HCG Gold

**HE** – high explosive

**HF** – high frequency (radio)

**hopper** – a high-frequency radio that has the facility for hopping from one frequency to another during broadcast, thus improving the security of messages and signals

**HQ** – headquarters

**HUD** – head-up display. The sighting system mounted in the front windscreen of a cockpit. Information displayed relieves the pilot of having to look inside the cockpit during critical manoeuvres

**IAS** – indicated air speed

**IEC** – Independent Electoral Committee

**IFR** – in-flight refuelling/instrument flight rules, when flying in bad weather or at night

**IMC** – instrument meteorological conditions. Used when it is mandatory to fly with sole reference to aircraft instrumentation

**Impala** – a single-engined, light jet ground-attack aircraft used very successfully throughout the bush war, by day and by night. Armed with 68mm rockets, bombs and 30mm cannon

**interdiction** – offensive mission flown with the aim of disrupting the enemy's logistical lines of communication

**IP** – initial point. A well-defined navigational position, from where navigation or attack profiles can be commenced with accuracy

**IRT** – Instrument Rating Test. An annual requirement for all pilots

**ITCZ** – Inter-Tropical Convergence Zone

**JARIC** – Joint Air Reconnaissance Intelligence Centre

**JPT** – jet-pipe temperature

**kill** – during simulated ACM, missile launch or gun firing is expressed as a 'kill'

**KIAS** – knots indicated air speed

*klap* – smack, hit (Afrikaans)

**kraal** – either a single hut or a complex of huts, used as dwellings. In Owamboland the kraal complex (village) was usually surrounded by a thorn-bush fence that offered security to the cattle and goats owned by the occupants

**kts** - knots

**Kudu** – a single-piston-engined, high-wing battlefield communication aircraft with capacity for six passengers (provided the temperature was not too high) or a limited quantity of freight

**LABS** – low altitude bombing system. The system was originally designed to 'throw' tactical nuclear weapons in a toss-type manoeuvre. The launch aircraft pulls up from low level at high speeds and releases the bomb as the nose passes 45° above the horizon. The aircraft continues in a looping manoeuvre to escape the detonation, while the bomb flies nearly five miles before exploding. Never a very accurate method of delivery but sufficient for a nuclear blast

**lemon** – a futile operation (military slang)

**LIP** – low intercept profile (later changed to UNCIP, *see* UNCIP)

**LMG** – light machine gun

**LP** – local population. A more common usage was PB, from the Afrikaans *plaaslike bevolking*

**LZ** – landing zone. An area designated and secured by ground forces for the landing of helicopters

**Mach** – as the speed of sound varies with temperature and altitude, Mach + number is used to refer to the aircraft's speed as a per centage of the speed of sound, e.g. Mach 1.0 = speed of sound and Mach 0.9 = 9/10ths of that speed (which also equates to 9nms per minute)

**MAOT** – mobile air operations team. The air force team usually comprised an OC (pilot), an operations officer, an intelligence officer, a radio operator and one or two clerks. The team plus their equipment could be airlifted into a tactical headquarters co-located with the army or police, or could move with the ground forces in mine-protected vehicles, as an integral part of the command headquarters. The OC of the team was often called 'the MAOT'

**Mayday** – international distress call

**medevac** – medical evacuation. Differs from casevac as the patient is already under medical supervision, being transported to a more suitable medical centre

**MF** – medium frequency (radio)

**MHz** – megahertz, to denote frequency band

**MiG** – Mikoyan-Gurevich, the Soviet-designed family of jet fighters. The Angolan Air Force (FAPA) was equipped with the delta-winged MiG-21 and later the swing-wing MiG-23 variety

**Military Region** – for military purposes the border areas inside South West Africa immediately adjacent to the Angolan border were divided into the Kaokoland, Sector 10 Owamboland, Sector 20 Kavango and Sector 70 Caprivi Strip. The Angolans, however, divided their country into military regions. The 5th Military Region faced Kaokoland and Sector 10, while the 6th Military Region faced Kavango and Caprivi

**Mirage** – French-built Dassault, the family of supersonic fighters used by the SAAF

**misrep** – mission report. These reports had to be completed by the intelligence staff after debriefing the aircrew after every mission. Often a source of irritation to the aircrew and the communications department who had to encode and decode all these documents, but possibly the best source of intelligence for the successful prosecution of operations

**MPLA** – *Movimento Popular de Libertação de Angola*, Popular Movement for the Liberation of Angola

# Glossary

**MRG** – master reference gyro. The main gyro which controls all the flying instruments in a Buccaneer. Failure of the 'master' can, under certain circumstances, cause the crew instant dyspepsia, hysteria and can be accompanied by uncontrollable tears

**MTBF** – mean time between failure. A term used to describe the time period, usually in flying hours, that a component could be expected to remain serviceable

*Nagup* – the night equivalent of *Gatup* (*see Gatup*)

**NDB** – non-directional beacon. A navigational aid which transmits a signal in all directions, except immediately overhead. Pilots using their ADF instrument can lock-on to the NDB to receive directional information from the beacon

**nms** – nautical miles

**notam** – notice to airmen. The standard form of warning message sent to all operators of aircraft, informing them of air-related information that could affect the safe passage of the aircraft

**OC** – officer commanding

**OC WAC** – Officer Commanding Western Air Command

**OCU** – Operational Conversion Unit

**Ops Co** – operations co-ordinator

**Ops normal** – a radio transmission made at regular intervals (usually 20 minutes), allowing command post staff to monitor the progress of low-level missions

**orbat** – order of battle, the force levels of protagonists

**panty** – the name given to the canvas spreader that surrounds an in-flight refuelling basket. A pilot who breaks this material while attempting to refuel earns the reputation of being a 'panty-ripper' (air force slang)

**Parabat** – Parachute Battalion soldier, qualified to wear the famous red beret

**PBI** – poor bloody infantry (British slang)

**PI** – photographic interpreter

**PLAN** – People's Liberation Army of Namibia, SWAPO's military wing

**PNR** – point of no return

**POMZ** – Soviet anti-personnel mine, commonly known as 'the widow-maker'

**pongo** – an infantryman, a brown job (SADF slang)

**PR** – photographic reconnaissance

**Pro-Patria** – general-service medal awarded to those who had been involved in the fight against terrorism

**Puff the Magic Dragon** – the gunship version of the Dakota, fitted with a 20mm cannon and Skyshout facilities. More commonly referred to as 'the Dragon' (US/Vietnam cer.)

**Puma** – a twin-engined transport helicopter that carried a crew of three and 16 lightly armed or 12 fully armed troops

**PUP** – pull-up point

**QFI** – qualified flying instructor

**R&R** – rest and recreation

**RAMS** – radio-activated marker system

**recce** – reconnaissance, as in ground recce, an airborne visual recce, a photographic recce or an EW (electronic) reconnaissance of a point or area

**Recce** – Reconnaissance Commandos or Special Forces

**Romeo Mike** – from the Afrikaans *Reaksie Mag*, the army's mobile reaction force. This force usually consisted of four Casspir fighting vehicles plus a fifth logistical back-up vehicle. This force could act independently while searching for spoor, but became most effective in follow-up operations when used in concert with additional RM teams that could be summoned by radio, when a contact was imminent. The RM concept was copied from the Zulu system expounded so effectively by the Police Koevoet units. 101 Battalion, the so-called Owambo Battalion based at Ondangwa, supplied the RM personnel

**RP** – rocket projectile

**RPG-7** – rocket-propelled grenade. An anti-tank, tube-launched grenade of Soviet origin, with a maximum effective range of 500 metres, and an explosive warhead weighing 2.4kg. It is robust, 'soldier-proof', easy to use and much favoured by insurgents worldwide

**RSA** – Republic of South Africa

**RV** – rendezvous. The chosen point was usually a grid reference on a map, an easily recognizable ground feature, or a bearing and distance from a navigational facility

**RWR/RWS** – radar warning receiver/system

**SAAF** – South African Air Force

**SADF** – South African Defence Force

**SAM** – surface-to-air missile. A missile, guided by infrared or radar, fired from a launcher on the ground at an airborne target. By the end of the war FAPLA had an array of missiles which included the following:

- SA-2 fixed site
- SA-3 fixed site
- SA-6 mobile, tracked
- SA-7 shoulder-launched*
- SA-8 mobile, wheeled
- SA-9 mobile, wheeled
- SA-13 mobile, tracked
- SA-14 shoulder-launched
- SA-16 shoulder-launched

*SWAPO used only the SA-7 but FAPLA was equipped with the entire range

**SAMS** – South African Medical Services

**SAP** – South African Police

# Glossary

**SAR** – search and rescue

**SATCO** – Senior Air Traffic Control Officer

**scramble** – traditional air force term used when fighter aircraft are ordered to take off immediately

**shona** – a shallow pan or an open area in the bush that fills with rain during the rainy season and is invariably dry during the winter months. Also *chana* in Angola

**Sir Ponsonby** – nickname given to the very sophisticated automatic pilot fitted in the Mirage F1. Abbreviated to Sir Pons and used in preference to the more common George

**SOP** – standard operating procedure. Common parlance for anything that is a standard, recognized drill

**Souties** – from *soutpiel*, a derogatory name for Englishmen, originating from the Afrikaans idea that English immigrants to South Africa had one leg in Africa and the other in Britain. The piece between, known as a *piel*, was said to dangle in the salty (*sout*) sea

**Spook** – nickname for the DC-4 Skymaster fitted with EW equipment used for intelligence-gathering purposes. The Dakota that was later fitted with an EW suite became known as 'Casper'—the friendly ghost

**sprog** – a new, or trainee, pilot. Also known variously as studs, shirt-tails, second lieuts or bicycles (air force slang)

**SSO Ops** – Senior Staff Officer Operations

**States** – military slang referring to the Republic of South Africa, probably originating from the pilot who, when asked what type of aircraft he flew, answered, "I fly Cans in the States." What he actually flew were Spamcans (Harvards) in the Orange Free State

**stonk** – to attack or bomb (military slang)

**Strela** – Soviet-made shoulder-launched SA-7 surface-to-air missile. Each SWAPO detachment was issued with three or four of these missiles as an integral part of its armament. Rough handling and extremes of temperature in the field ensured that these weapons were unreliable. However, because they were so freely distributed, cognizance had to be taken of their presence. All flying in the operational area was affected by the need to minimize the chance of taking a Strela hit

**SWA** – South West Africa, now Namibia

**SWAPO** – South West Africa People's Organization (a misnomer as the organization only represented the Owambo people)

**SWATF** – South West African Territory Force. Both the SADF and SWATF were commanded by GOC SWA

**Tacan** – tactical air navigation facility

**Tac HQ** – a tactical headquarters instituted for the running of an operation close to the combat zone, commanded by a subordinate commander with guidelines and limitations delegated by a sector headquarters

**tail-dragger** – any propeller-driven aircraft that has two main wheels and the third under the tail. This aircraft requires different techniques when approaching and taking off, than those used by the more usual tricycle-configured aircraft

**Tally ho!** – The fighter pilot's call used when the enemy has been spotted, usually the precursor to a few minutes of mayhem

**Telstar** – an aircraft flown at medium altitude to relay VHF messages from aircraft on low-flying operational missions

**THTC** – Tobias Hanyeko Training Camp, SWAPO's training base outside Lubango

**tiffie** – a mechanic, from the word artificer (military slang)

**terr** – a terrorist; also known as a freedom fighter in some circles (military slang)

**TOD** – top of descent

**top cover** – aerial cover. Aircraft were considered prestige targets by the SWAPO insurgents. Aircraft are at their most vulnerable when taking off or landing in the vicinity of airfields. At Ondangwa, therefore, an Alouette gunship was airborne for all movements of fixed-wing transport aircraft. The gunship carried out a wide left-hand orbit of the airfield to counter any attempt by terrorists to fire at the transport aircraft. The concept was also used in combat areas to cover own ground troops or to make-safe landing zones for troop-carrying helicopters in the bush

**TOT** – time on target

**transonic zone** – the speed band where the airflow over the aircraft alters from subsonic to supersonic flow, usually between Mach 0.9 to 1.1. As the aircraft transits through this zone, changes to the centre of pressure can affect stability

**Typhoon** – SWAPO's elite group of highly trained troops whose specific task was the deep infiltration of South West Africa. Although highly esteemed by SWAPO they did not achieve any more notable successes than the ordinary cadres. They were also referred to as Vulcan troops

**UNCIP** – unconventional interception profile

**Unimog** – a 2.5-litre 4x4 Mercedes Benz transport vehicle, that bore the brunt of bush operations until SWAPO mine-laying hastened the introduction of mine-protected vehicles

**UNITA** – *União Nacional para a Independência Total de Angola*, National Union for the Total Independence of Angola. The breakaway party led by Jonas Savimbi, supported by the western powers, including South Africa, in the fight against the communist-backed MPLA in Angola

**UNTAG** – United Nations Transitional Agreement Group

**Vergooi** – a long-toss bombing profile used by F1AZ aircraft. From a high speed, low-level approach, the pilot pitches-up the aircraft at the pull-up-point (PUP). At about 2,000ft AGL, when the aircraft's nose is at 45° above the horizon, the bombs are released according to settings pre-set on the intervalometer. The bombs then follow one another in a parabolic flight path, flying a distance of around 5nms. The bombs detonate in a stick, hopefully spread evenly through the target. The aircraft recovers to low level and escapes from the combat zone. The manoeuvre affords the enemy missile systems minimum time to lock-on and fire. Inaccurate against pinpoint targets but very suitable against enemy brigades spread out in the bush

**vertical manoeuvre** – flying an aircraft to rapidly change height, as in a loop

**VHF** – very high frequency (radio), limited to line-of-sight communication

***Visgraat!*** – the order to rapidly disperse convoy vehicles under threat from air attack (der. Afrikaans for herring bone)

***Vlammie*** – a South African jet-fighter pilot. From the Afrikaans *vlamgat*, literally flaming hole, the afterburner flame produced by a fighter

**Volcano** – SWAPO's training base for their specialist Typhoon troops, 14km north-east of Lubango

***Vrystaat!*** – the radio call made immediately prior to an attack, warning pilots to select their armament switches to the live or hot position (Afrikaans der. the Orange Free State)

**VT fuse** – variable time fuse that allows bombs to be detonated at selected heights above targets

**WAC** – Western Air Command

**white phos** – a grenade or shell containing phosphorus which, when detonated erupts in a distinctive white cloud, utilized mainly to identify positions on the ground, but also as a grenade in close-quarter combat

**Yati Strip** – one kilometre south of the cut-line another strip was graded through the bush parallel to the cut-line. This one-kilometre strip of land was known as the Yati Strip and was originally designed as a no-go area but was largely ignored

**Zulu call sign** – *see* Romeo Mike

# Appendix I

# A day on the flight line

*by* WOI W. J. 'Doep' du Plessis, Eng Tech (M)

The blade sticking out of the belly of the Mirage pretends to be some sort of navigational antenna, but is in fact a menacing weapon, poised to gash the unwary with its razor-sharp edge on the spine between the shoulder-blades where the nervous system that signals *pain* seems to meet.

This time, however, it strikes another nerve. Sagging to my knees on the blistering hot tarmac, I feel an overwhelming wave of rage and resentment pushing up inside me, clogging my throat. Hating this stupid aircraft, hating the half-naked, sweating fitter that lies sprawled against the main wheel, hating this futile war, resenting the air force and all the ignorant clowns in it.

**Five days, *Ondangs* boys ...**
Grab a few pairs of underpants, a clean *ovie*, a couple of rand (you can get plastered on a rand if you go steady with the mix), kiss the wife and kids goodbye. Be back next weekend for that promised trip to Tshipese. And now, 23 days later, I am groping for the electrical socket and limply crawling back to my vantage point beneath the wing in the shadow, from where I can see the pilot.

**Waiting**
Twenty-three days! How I hate this place ...

The aircraft on the line tremble in the shimmering heat that rises from the glaring cement, giving the whole scene an atmosphere of unreality. Nothing moves.

Twenty-three days of frantic activity, changing the configuration of the aircraft.

Bombs off, rockets on. Rockets off, bombs on. One sortie. Aborted.

What an abortion! Fly-clogged mess tents and sand in the food, mosquito-ridden tents and sand in the sleeping bags, overcrowded showers and then the drinking. Blissful oblivion, with sand between your teeth.

Late yesterday afternoon—"Fit rockets!" Armourers scurry about with cumbersome trolley jacks, scratched and bleeding hands in small access doors as they hang the heavy pylons. Port rockets not firing. Trace the snag through a myriad of switches, relays, electronic devices, with the meagre test equipment I brought along. All the other trades wait—armourers play bridge, fitters lounge in the canopy covers, instrument mac helpfully trails me from gunsight to radar to armament plug box and gets in the way. Where's the bloody snag! Wing plug (calculated guess). Remove the pylon. Good-natured grumbling—"*Platkop* sparkie!"—the armourers swing into action. Ten past eleven and four kites to go. Up at five and trudging out to the line in darkness. How can the nights be so cold and the days so incredibly hot?

Oxygen trolleys, hobarts, tractors, fuel bowsers, bomb trailers, ladders and chocks. Boswell circus on the move in the pre-dawn dusk. Checking, fitting, priming, pumping, testing …

**Tower, this is 809. Comscheck, doureadover?**
We crowd into the hut to sign the 700 and linger there for warmth and wait …

Where the hell are they? Why must the aircraft be ready at the crack of dawn and they don't pitch up?

Eventually they come, swaggering across the now-already-hot apron, G-suit tubes dangling obscenely—walking stiff-legged to conceal their anxiety.

Sandbag is with us. He blows his top about a small smudge on his windscreen. Does he realize how many men with greasy hands have climbed into that cockpit during the night—and how many times this *korpie* obligingly cleaned that windscreen? Again and again. He goes around the aircraft peeping into holes, juggling the control surfaces, feeling and checking. The morose fitter in his slipstream collects Pitot covers, safety pins, and closes up the inspection holes.

He climbs into the cockpit and the *korpie* straps him down tightly (extra tight?). And there he sits now, immobile except for the gloved fingers drumming on both sides of the windscreen, sweating profusely. Waiting.

**Time passes**
The sweat stings the small wound on my back and reminds me of my stupid negligence. How could I have forgotten about that blade? What else have I overlooked? What vital system will malfunction at the most critical instant, owing to my misguided resentments and complacency? I glance at the figure in the cockpit, sitting there sweating in the blistering sun underneath layers

of protective clothing, flying and G suit, helmeted and gloved, relying on my limited knowledge and integrity with his life!

**Are we fighting the same war?**
The thought hits me like a mallet where I lie beneath the wing and in spite of the 40°C heat, a chill runs through my body. Impulsively, I'm up and walking to the shade-netted aircraft shelter where this innovative lot, the armourers, run a mobile café. They sell cold drinks from a fridge mounted on a trolley. (Clandestine beer can be had at a price.)

*"Kolie-op-tick, seblief* **boys"**
My money is long gone and the S+T *'het noggiegekommie'* according to the clerk in the Nissan hut that serves as orderly room. Will this tepid peace offering I carry between thumb and forefinger buy away the guilt? I hold the can up to the figure in the cockpit. The ladder has been removed and I need not look him in the eye. A grunt, two gulps and the can is passed down empty. I toss it behind the seat and ignore the mumbling about *gatkruip* (guts ache) emanating from the fitter against the wheel.

Just then the radios crackle and the whole line is instantly active. The canopy slams shut and the fitter is on his feet, fully clad in one smooth movement. I slam the Hobart's throttle flat, engage the generator and wait for the revs to pick up before pressing the button that supplies the aircraft with life-giving energy. Do I detect a friendly little wiggle in the thumbs-up signal from the cockpit? As the pilot presses the starter button, the Hobart groans and shudders from the extra demand. I mentally follow the current to the electric starter, counting five–six–seven seconds, willing the next stage into life. In comes the small, high-pitched gas turbine mounted on the main engine. Fourteen seconds … come on! Slowly the main engine starts rotating, picking up speed … 21 … 22 ignite, dammit!

Don't let it wind down! Press again! With a deafening roar and shuddering intakes the engine ignites, spewing a three-metre flame from the exhaust and spilling blobs of burning fuel onto the tarmac. There is no need to look at the ammeter to know when to cut power. I sense the difference in the Hobart as the various aircraft systems independently come to life, relinquishing their energy-sapping hold on the generator. As I unplug the umbilical cord from this roaring monster above my head, I notice that the fierce blade is now strangely out of my path as if the trembling machine is not concerned with petty grievances, but straining at the chocks to do what it was designed for—*Death and Destruction*. In its anxiety to be away, the Mirage is oozing little dribbles of fluids—seemingly from every pore. There is no sense in trying to avoid it as with a practised flick-and-throw I see the heavy-duty cables fall neatly into the brackets on the side of the Hobart. *Lekker*!

The fitter *korpie* is now conducting this cacophony of sound with odd little gestures, causing the ailerons to wiggle and the airbrakes to open and close like the gills of a giant fish gasping for air. We all stand slightly to the left, anxiously waiting for the OK sign, instead of the usual thumbs-up signal, an American-like salute from the cockpit. With great relief, and as if on cue, every crew member immediately responds, each with his own elaborate salute.

### Smiles on the sweat-stained faces—all is forgiven
There is go-stop testing of the brakes, pressing the front wheel flat to the ground like the nose of a bloodhound sniffing for the spoor of its prey. We rush behind the Hobart, huddle-scrum together, eyes closed, hands over ears as the burning blast from the exhaust hits us with a force that rocks the Hobart. It tears at our clothing with scorching fingers, sandblasting every part of the body despite the overall, and drawing tiny specks of blood from exposed flesh. We wait for the mind-shattering noise to recede and rise together, shaking the sand from hair and clothes. Dazed.

This is the customary time to make some witty, degrading remark about the uncaring jock in the cockpit, but only the *korpie* softly says, "*Bring my êrie trug, heel!*" meaning of course, the safe return of the pilot as well.

### We wish him good luck—*old Sandbag*
We head for the strip of shade next to the hangar, through the thick, pungent smell of paraffin that hangs in the air like some Macbethian witch's perfume, burning the lungs and stinging the eyes. I wipe the mist from mine, not caused by the fumes as my friends might expect, but by a strange, proud swelling in my chest and throat. *Ondangs* is not so bad.

We flop down among all the others and start the most difficult task of any trip. *We wait.*

# Appendix II

# The Billy Boys' song

(To the tune of *Ghost Riders in the Sky*)

The Billy Boys were loading up
One dark and windy night
Six bombs each, Mark 82s
It was a fearsome sight
To strike at dawn, that was their task
Against the Swapo swine
To kill the commies in a group
Before they crossed the line

**Chorus**
AZs high, AZs low, AZs in the sky

The sun was rising in the east
The boys were on the go
Nav computers working well
They crossed the cutline low
The Swaps were stirring from their sleep
To make the morning meal
Just before the Billys dropped
Their load of burning steel

**Chorus**

They reached the IP in good time
Their final run began
They pitched-up in the early dawn
The bombs were right on line
The Swaps were taken by surprise
Death came so quick and fast
No more would they terrorize
They'd met their end at last

**Chorus**

The AZs pulled out from the dive
Their deadly load now gone
With engines screaming low they flew
Into the morning sun
The Billy Boys are known throughout
Wherever men may roam
The task complete, a job well done
The Billy Boys flew home

**Chorus**

*Note:* The words to this song were written by Rick Culpan during the dark days of the bush war. They reflected the sentiments of those who had been at risk from the enemy war machine.

# Appendix III

# Commanding officers

| 3 Squadron | Date | Remarks |
|---|---|---|
| Cmdt P. B. Huyser | 1975–1976 | Late Maj-Gen (Rtd) |
| Maj C. Lombard (Temp) | Jul 1975–Dec 1976 | Maj-Gen (Rtd) |
| Cmdt F. E. du Toit | 1977–1979 | Maj-Gen (Rtd) |
| Cmdt J. L. Gründling | 1980–1982 | Brig-Gen (Rtd) |
| Cmdt A. M. Wehmeyer | 1983–1985 | Col (Rtd) |
| Cmdt C. Gagiano | 1986–1988 | Brig-Gen |
| Cmdt W. J. Hartogh | 1989–1992 | Brig-Gen |

| 1 Squadron | | |
|---|---|---|
| Cmdt W. H. Hechter | 1977–Jun 1979 | Lt-Gen CAF |
| Cmdt D. J. Lewis | Jun 1979–Mar 1980 | Col (Rtd) |
| Maj T. A. Nel (Temp) | Mar 1980–Aug 1980 | Col (Rtd) |
| Cmdt R. S. Lord | Aug 1980–Dec 1982 | Brig-Gen (Rtd) |
| Cmdt J. G. Radloff | 1983–1985 | Col (Rtd) |
| Cmdt J. J. Rankin | 1986–1988 | Brig-Gen (Rtd) |
| Maj N. G. Minne (Temp) | Jan 1989–May 1989 | Maj |
| Cmdt N.G. Minne | May 1989–Dec 1991 | Col |
| Cmdt A. E. Prinsloo | 1992–1994 | Lt-Col (Rtd) |
| Lt-Col J. W. Mienie | 1995–1997 | Col |

# Appendix IV

# Technical and Intelligence officers

*Key*:
CTO – Chief Technical Officer
TO – Technical Officer
AO – Armament Officer
ELO – Electronics Officer
FSG – F1 Support Group

**1 Squadron Technical Officers**

| | | | |
|---|---|---|---|
| Maj | E. P. Smith | TO | 1978 |
| Capt | Frik Smith | AO | 1978 |
| Capt | Giel Pretorius | AO | 1979 |
| Mr | Dawie Uys | FSG | 1980 |
| Maj | Chris Venter | CTO | 1981 |
| Lt | Terry Crous | EO | 1981 |
| Mr | Johan Ferreira | FSG | 1983 |
| Lt | Desmond Arthur | EO | 1983 |
| Lt | M. Oelofse | EO | 1986 |
| Mr | Dieter Niebühr | FSG | 1987 |
| Lt | J. W. Spies | TO | 1988 |
| Capt | Frans Strydom | TO | 1989 |
| Capt | Tony Letcher | TO | 1989 |
| Maj | Gerrie Coetzee | ELO | 1992 |
| Capt | Bert Pretorius | EO | 1993 |
| Lt | Danie Sutherland | TO | 1994 |
| Lt | J. J. Briedenhann | TO | 1995 |

## 3 Squadron Technical Officers

| | | | |
|---|---|---|---|
| Cmdt | Daantjie Retief | CTO | 1975 |
| Maj | Jan Coetzee | CTO | 1975 |
| Maj | Frank O'Connor | AO | 1975 |
| Capt | 'Wassie' Wasserman | TO | 1975 |
| Capt | Gandi van Heerden | TO | 1975 |
| Maj | Alan Nelson | CTO | 1976 |
| Capt | H. A. Kitley | TO | 1976 |
| Lt | P. J. Roos | TO | 1977 |
| Capt | C. P. W. Warner | AO | 1976 |
| Maj | Eddie Dert | CTO | 1981 |
| Capt | J. H. Barnard | TO | 1989 |
| Capt | J. van Heerden | TO | 1987 |
| Maj | Mýk Lembisch | TO | 1987 |
| Capt | S. J. Bothma | TO | 1989 |
| Lt | A. J. Hechter | TO | 1992 |

## 1 Squadron Intelligence Officers

| | | |
|---|---|---|
| Lt | H. van Vuuren | 1983 |
| Sgt | R. Campbell | 1984 |
| 2/Lt | L. Woodward | 1986 |
| CO | L. Rossouw | 1986 |
| 2/Lt | H. van Vuuren | 1986 |
| Lt | L. Jordaan | 1990 |
| Sgt | L. Hains | 1995 |
| Lt | A. Cloete | 1995 |
| Capt | R. Coertzen | 1996 |

## 3 Squadron Intelligence Officers

*list incomplete*

| | | |
|---|---|---|
| Lt | J. Lubbe | 1986 |
| Sgt | D. Duncan | 1988 |
| Lt | L. van Vuuren | 1989 |
| 2/Lt | J. Zaayman | 1990 |
| Lt | A. Joubert | ? |
| Capt | P. Vosloo | ? |

# Appendix V

# Mirage F1 pilots and potted biographies

| Rank | Name | Date | Type | Remarks |
|---|---|---|---|---|
| Capt | Johan Ackerman | 1981 | CZ | |
| Capt | Piet Ackerman | 1989 | AZ | |
| Maj | 'Mossie' Basson | 1976 | CZ/AZ | |
| Cmdt | Des Barker | 1986 | CZ/AZ | TFDC test pilot |
| Capt | Leon Bath | 1989 | AZ | Ejected, F1AZ 221 |
| Lt | Les Bennett | 1978 | CZ | Ejected, F1CZ 208 |
| Capt | Trevor Bernberg | 1982 | AZ | |
| Maj | Roelf Beukes | 1976 | CZ/AZ | |
| Capt | J. H. Botha | 1984 | AZ | |
| Capt | Alan Brand | 1989 | AZ | Ejected, F1AZ 224 |
| Capt | F. Brand | 1993 | AZ | |
| Maj | Chris Brits | 1978 | CZ | Ejected, F1CZ 200 |
| Maj | 'Budgie' Burgers | 1981 | AZ | |
| Maj | Paddy Carolan | 1981 | AZ | |
| Capt | Mark Clulow | 1980 | AZ | |
| Capt | Billy Collier | 1980 | AZ | |
| Capt | Piet Coetzer | 1993 | AZ | |
| Capt | Frans Coetzee | 1980 | AZ | |
| Capt | Peter Cooke | 1976 | CZ/AZ | |
| Lt | Mark Crooks | 1978 | CZ | |
| Mr | Rick Culpan | 1993 | AZ | Atlas test pilot |
| Lt | Dirk de Villiers | 1978 | AZ | |
| Lt | Neil de Villiers | 1977 | AZ | |
| Capt | Rikus de Beer | 1983 | AZ | Landed F1AZ 221 into barrier |

| | | | | |
|---|---|---|---|---|
| Lt | Ed Deschamps | 1978 | AZ | |
| Capt | Jaco de Beer | 1986 | CZ | |
| Capt | I. C. du Plessis | 1977 | AZ | Hit by SA-3 F1AZ 237 |
| Lt | Johan du Plessis | 1980 | CZ | |
| Capt | Johan du Plessis | 1992 | AZ | |
| Capt | Kobus du Plessis | 1993 | AZ | |
| Lt | Louis du Plessis | 1988 | CZ | |
| Capt | Pierre du Plessis | 1978 | CZ | |
| Capt | Charl Durandt | 1992 | CZ | |
| Cmdt | Fred du Toit | 1976 | CZ/AZ | OC 13 then 3 Squadron |
| Maj | Mike Edwards | 1989 | CZ | |
| Capt | Bill Einkamerer | 1977 | AZ | |
| Capt | Ed Every | 1980 | AZ | Shot down, Angola F1AZ 245 |
| Capt | Patrick Flynn | 1995 | AZ | |
| Capt | Carlo Gagiano | 1976 | CZ | OC 3 Squadron |
| Capt | Nelis Genis | 1989 | AZ | |
| Maj | 'Spook' Geraghty | 1982 | AZ | |
| Maj | J. P. Gouws | 1986 | AZ | |
| Maj | Jack Gründling | 1976 | CZ | OC 3 Squadron |
| Cmdt | Willie Hartogh | 1989 | CZ | OC 3 Squadron |
| Cmdt | Willem Hechter | 1977 | CZ/AZ | OC 1 Squadron |
| Capt | Jan Henning | 1980 | AZ | Ejected, F1AZ 222 |
| Capt | Digby Holdsworth | 1984 | AZ | Ejected, F1AZ 228 |
| Cmdt | 'Bossie' Huyser | 1975 | CZ | OC 3 Squadron |
| Lt | John Inggs | 1976 | CZ | |
| Cmdt | Spyker Jacobs | 1980 | AZ | |
| Lt | 'Tinkie' Jones | 1978 | CZ | |
| Capt | 'Blokkies' Joubert | 1989 | AZ | |
| Capt | Louis Joubert | 1993 | AZ | Crashed into sea F1AZ 234 |
| Capt | Vic Kaiser | 1980 | AZ | |
| Maj | Jafta Keyter | 1983 | AZ | |
| Capt | Dawie Kleynhans | 1984 | AZ | |
| Lt | Dave Klopper | 1989 | CZ | |
| Capt | Ron Knott-Craig | 1980 | AZ | |
| Cmdt | Israel Krieger | 1982 | CZ | Israeli Air Force |
| Capt | Francois Lategan | 1985 | AZ | |
| Lt | Darryl Lee | 1977 | CZ | |
| Capt | Pietie le Roux | 1992 | CZ | |
| Maj | Tristan la Grange | 1982 | CZ | |

| Rank | Name | Year | Type | Notes |
|---|---|---|---|---|
| Cmdt | Joshi Lavi | 1983 | AZ/CZ | Israeli Air Force |
| Cmdt | Casey Lewis | 1979 | AZ | OC 1 Squadron |
| Maj | Chris Lombard | 1975 | CZ | First F1CZ pilot |
| Cmdt | Dick Lord | 1980 | AZ | OC 1 Squadron |
| Capt | Hennie Louw | 1979 | AZ/CZ | |
| Lt | Martin Louw | 1979 | CZ | |
| Cmdt | Jan Marais | 1977 | AZ/CZ | TFDC test pilot |
| Capt | Charl Marais | 1992 | AZ | |
| Capt | 'Mitz' Maritz | 1975 | CZ | |
| Capt | Anthony Mathers | 1989 | AZ | |
| Capt | Leon Meech-Noyes | 1989 | CZ | |
| Capt | Rudi Mes | 1986 | CZ | |
| Maj | Jan Mienie | 1983 | CZ/AZ | OC 1 Squadron |
| Lt | Norman Minne | 1978 | AZ | OC 1 Squadron |
| Capt | 'Moolies' Moolman | 1982 | AZ | |
| Lt | Thys Muller | 1977 | CZ/AZ | |
| Maj | Trompie Nel | 1988 | AZ | |
| Maj | Theo Nell | 1978 | AZ | Temp OC 1 Squadron |
| Capt | Attie Niemann | 1989 | CZ | |
| Maj | Johan Niewoudt | 1980 | AZ | |
| Maj | Nic Oosthuysen | 1982 | AZ | |
| Lt | Dieter Ortmann | 1978 | CZ | |
| Maj | V. Parkhomento | 1994 | AZ | Russian Air Force |
| Capt | Ivan Pentz | 1989 | AZ/CZ | |
| Capt | Arthur Piercy | 1986 | CZ | Shot by MiG-23 F1CZ 206 |
| Maj | Phillip Potgieter | 1995 | AZ | |
| Capt | Chris Pretorius | 1993 | AZ | |
| Maj | Frans Pretorius | 1979 | AZ | Hit by SA-3 F1AZ 244 |
| Lt | Dolf Prinsloo | 1978 | CZ/AZ | OC 1 Squadron |
| Maj | Gerrie Radloff | 1980 | CZ/AZ | OC 1 Squadron |
| Maj | Johan Rankin | 1980 | CZ/AZ | OC 1 Squadron |
| Lt | Mark Raymond | 1983 | CZ | |
| Cmdt | Zach Repsold | 1974 | | F1 Prototype—04 in France |
| Capt | W. Serfontein | 1992 | AZ | |
| Capt | Nic Scheltema | 1989 | AZ | |
| Capt | John Sinclair | 1986 | CZ | Ejected, F1CZ 215 |
| Capt | Chris Skinner | 1983 | AZ | |
| Capt | Wayne Smal | 1992 | AZ | |
| Capt | Jaco Smith | 1995 | AZ | |
| Capt | Stuart Spencer | 1996 | AZ | |

| Rank | Name | Year | Type | Notes |
|---|---|---|---|---|
| Lt | Des Steinhobel | 1977 | CZ | |
| Capt | John Stipp | 1991 | AZ | |
| Capt | Dave Stock | 1991 | AZ | |
| Capt | Cobus Toerien | 1981 | CZ | |
| Capt | Frank Tonkin | 1986 | CZ | |
| Maj | Paulus Truter | 1989 | AZ | |
| Lt | Piet J. Truter | 1978 | AZ | |
| Maj | Clive Turner | 1982 | CZ | |
| Capt | Willie van Coppenhagen | 1985 | AZ | Crashed, Angola F1AZ 223 |
| Capt | Reg van Eeden | 1985 | AZ | |
| Maj | André van der Heever | 1976 | CZ/AZ | |
| Maj | Schalk van Heerden | 1989 | AZ | |
| Lt | Ed van Ravenstein | 1976 | CZ | |
| Maj | Anton van Rensburg | 1986 | CZ | |
| Capt | Riaan van Tonder | 1989 | AZ | |
| Maj | John van Zyl | 1989 | AZ | |
| Capt | Drago Vasiljevic | 1996 | AZ | |
| Maj | 'Jeronkie' Venter | 1992 | CZ | |
| Capt | Giep Vermeulen | 1982 | AZ | |
| Capt | Frik Viljoen | 1979 | AZ | |
| Capt | 'Floors' Visser | 1983 | AZ | |
| Maj | Piet Vivier | 1978 | CZ | |
| Capt | Marcel von Gunten | 1991 | AZ | |
| Capt | Wassie Wasserman | 1977 | AZ | Ejected, F1AZ 246 |
| Capt | Glenn Watson | 1991 | AZ | |
| Capt | Wayne Westoby | 1989 | AZ | |
| Capt | Dries Wehmeyer | 1976 | CZ | OC 3 Squadron |
| Capt | Mike Weingartz | 1983 | CZ | |
| Capt | Kenny Williams | 1982 | CZ | |
| Capt | Paul Williamson | 1997 | AZ | |
| Maj | Gawie Winterbach | 1976 | CZ/AZ | First F1AZ pilot |

# Potted biographies

### Des Barker

Des was born in Pretoria. He attended Lyttelton Manor High School just outside the Waterkloof Air Base so was destined to join the SAAF which he did in 1968. He flew Canberras operationally in Angola and Mozambique. His was the voice that controlled air traffic over Maputo during the SAAF attack during Operation *Skerwe*—in retribution for the ANC bomb blast in Church Street, Pretoria in 1983.

He then qualified as a test pilot and eventually commanded the SAAF Test Flight Development Centre near Bredasdorp. He flew 655 hours in the Mirage F1, carrying out development trials to clear the F1AZ for the 16-bomb configuration, clearing V3C and V3P air-to-air missiles for the air-defence mission, launching close on 50 missiles in the process, including a V3C launch at M2.01.

Perhaps the highlight of his test career was his first flight in the F1AZ fitted with the Soviet MiG-29's RD-33 engine. The French had stated that it couldn't be done which made the first flight even more satisfying. Incidentally, it transformed the Mirage into a 'rocket'. On one test flight he carried out a level acceleration at 25,000 feet to M1.8 and then pulling up the nose into a 50° climb angle and charging past 50,000 feet still at M1.8—a sensation he described as "awesome".

However, test flying was not all plain sailing. While carrying out 'flutter tests' to clear the Laser-Guided Bomb (LGB) for SAAF operational service, he encountered a case of 'explosive flutter'. His aircraft was configured with V3C wingtip missiles and one LGB on pylons under each wing. On acceleration to 350 knots at 20,000 feet, without warning, large lateral forces occurred, as if someone was hammering the aircraft along the Y-axis at a relatively high frequency. He immediately applied airbrake and retarded the throttle to reduce the energy exciting the vibration. Both LGBs were oscillating on their pylons to about six centimetres each side of their normal axis. The oscillation was so severe that any second one or both bombs could have snapped off from their pylons, impacting the aircraft or causing catastrophic failure of the wing or even the fin.

Des recently retired from the SAAF as a major-general.

### Trevor Bernberg

Trevor was born in Kimberley, matriculated at CBC Boksburg and joined the SAAF in 1977. On his pupil pilot's course Moolies Moolman, Ed van Ravenstein and Giep Vermeulen also flew Mirage F1s.

He says that his entire F1 tour was a highlight because of all the advances that were made in tactics, attack profiles and skills. The *Gatup* profile, suggested by Josi Lavi, had an offset point of three nautical miles by three nautical miles from the target. The attack was entered at 600 knots at 50 feet AGL, with a 4G pull-up to 4,000 feet, followed by a continuous high-G roll onto the target for a laser shot. Once the shot was taken, the bomb button was pushed and the stick of bombs was released automatically.

After that it was a dive to low level, with flares deployed to avoid heat-seeking missiles. The egress was a mad scramble to get back into battle formation for the return to base. To this day he can still recall where to look for the target—what excellent training. This profile got them in and out of the target quickly and efficiently. Anti-aircraft gunners on the ground had to be very good to get a shot at the Mirages.

Ironically, it was this manoeuvre which caused his most exciting moment. On a *Golden Eagle* deployment to Upington, the formation made a dummy attack on a selected target en route. In the pitch Trevor had the target visual but entered cloud at the apex. Maintaining the image of the target in his mind's eye, he continued the high-G roll-in. When he broke cloud he saw the ground in very close proximity from a most unusual attitude. He pulled "a million Gs", the magnificent Mirage responded and he avoided the ground, albeit leaving a long dust-trail across the arid Northern Cape and with serious vortices streaming off his wingtips. The scariest part was how quickly it all happened.

Trevor is now a B-737 training captain on SAA.

## Alan Brand

Alan was born in Boksburg, completed his schooling at CBC Kimberley and entered the SAAF in 1981. By 1988 he had passed through various stages of the fighter line before ending up on 1 Squadron for a tour that lasted over six years—how lucky can you get!

The highlight of his tour was an ACM training sortie he flew on 20 January 1995 in Mirage F1AZ 236. This was a mission of 2v2 3rd generation ACM simulating all-aspect air-to-air missiles. On completion of the sortie, when all four aircraft were low on fuel, they carried out in-flight refuelling, followed by another 2v2—most satisfying sortie, enhanced by the knowledge that it completed his 1,000th hour on the Mirage F1AZ.

In a career as long as his there are bound to have been some exciting moments and Alan had his share. On 9 June 1994 he ejected from Mirage F1AZ 224 near Potchefstroom, an incident described in chapter 18. On another occasion he ferried an AZ from Atlas back to Hoedspruit after a burn-damage incident in Durban. En route he carried out the required maintenance test flight and during the mach run the fire warning sounded. He immediately cut the afterburner but this did not cancel the warning. He then drew the throttle back to idle but the warning remained. There was no visible trail of smoke; however, the aircraft had a history of burn damage, so Alan decided to cut the engine, which solved the problem. Unfortunately, it would not relight.

Alan broadcast an emergency message and all rescue services at Hoedspruit were activated. The entire lowveld was covered in a layer of low cloud so Alan was in a predicament. He took a deep, calming breath, glided the aircraft to within the recommended envelope, where it relit immediately. It had been an exciting few moments which had kept Mac van der Merwe, the base OC, on the hop.

Alan is presently a senior first officer with South African Airways where, on a flight to Cape Town, aviation history was made. Alan was co-pilot and the aircraft commander was Wassie Wasserman, both ex 1 Squadron F1AZ pilots. Just before start-up, they realized that Wassie was the first SAAF pilot to eject from an F1 and Alan the last to abandon an F1. In the interest of maintaining peace and calm in the cabin they decided not to tell the passengers that both pilots had had more take-offs than landings.

**Paddy Carolan**
Paddy was born in Pietermaritzburg, matriculated at King Edward High School, Matatiele and joined the SAAF in 1968. The highlight of his F1AZ career was how quickly it all began. The war in Angola had intensified and squadrons were expanding rapidly. Paddy's first formation flight in an AZ was flying close formation on the MiG-17 used during Lt Bomba's defection from Mozambique. On this flight however, the MiG was being flown by SAAF test pilot, Bob Masson.

Paddy then found himself at AFB Grootfontein with 1 Squadron, participating in Operation *Protea*. On only his 16th flight in an AZ he was dropping live bombs on the Angolan radar site at Chibemba. Later during the war, while carrying out a MAOT tour with 32 Battalion deep inside Angola, he witnessed the aerial fight between Carlo Gagiano, Arthur Piercy and two Mig-23s and he described the noise as unbelievable.

His most exciting moment occurred during *Protea* when he was led into a rocket attack against the enemy OP positioned on top of the Ongiva water tower. They had rolled into the briefed attack dive for a 'high' release to stay out of the envelope of the SA-7 missile. Norman Minne, the formation leader, missed the high-release altitude and, when prompted by Paddy over the radio, answered back, "Let's make it academic weapons release height."

They drew a lot of fire as they descended into the low centre of the battlefield and, as they broke off the attack after the low release, Paddy applied too much G for the V3A missiles on his wingtips and both heads promptly broke off just ahead of the warhead. He returned somewhat gingerly to Ondangwa after being warned by Mossie Basson, a MAOT listening on the same frequency, that a bird or even an insect strike could set off the proximity fuses. He landed safely and was told to taxi to the far end of the Ondangwa runway so that if the missiles exploded they wouldn't damage anything other than Paddy and his Mirage. Paddy watched anxiously as the armourers arrived to make-safe his aircraft. To his dismay, these men took one look at the damaged missiles and promptly fled into the distance. Paddy exited his cockpit via the aircraft spine and tail plane and joined the armourers in the distance. All's well that ends well.

Paddy is now in charge of the Ground School at 43 Air School, Port Alfred.

## Frans Coetzee

Frans was born in Blyvooruitzight and matriculated at Fochville High School in 1974. He received his conscription papers to join 4 SA Infantry Battalion in Middelburg, Transvaal in July 1975. During the six-month wait he worked underground in the world's deepest goldmine, Western Deep Levels. It was while sitting nearly three kilometres below ground that he decided that life in the sky was perhaps a far better option for him. He completed basics (basic training) in the army and then transferred to the SAAF to join Pilot Course 2/75, along with Glen Warden and Johan du Plessis who also volunteered for fast jets.

The highlight of his Mirage career was "to be trained as a fighter pilot and have the privilege to serve our country operationally during the Border War".

His service in 1 Squadron included a number of 'hairy' moments, one of which was the flight on which his best friend, Ed Every, was shot down. The pilots knew the risks involved, especially late in the war when enemy defences had increased with the introduction of advanced SAMs. Recovering from bomb-release he looked out on the beam to see Ed's aircraft engulfed in flames, with the cockpit pointing 80º nose-down, plunge into the ground. The formation did a 360º turn at low level to establish whether or not Ed had managed to eject. That turn, even though it was carried out as low as possible, provided a few very anxious moments as it was performed in the knowledge that there were more missiles in the area waiting to be launched.

The second exciting moment occurred during one of the fuel-stretched *Vergooi* sorties. The four-ship F1AZ formation took off in the early morning, maintaining radio silence. About 50 nautical miles out they noticed a layer of stratus above them but, as it looked high enough to continue, they did. They passed the checkpoint, concentrating on navigation, hit the IP and were committed into the pitch. Bomb release came as they flashed into the cloud at 600 knots. The cloud layer was thicker than expected so all pilots reverted to instruments to complete the escape manoeuvre. This difficult situation suddenly became extreme as they were illuminated by a SAM-8 warning on the RWS. They were inverted in the recovery manoeuvre, desperate to get back to low level with no ground visible. What followed was not taught in any training manual. With a slightly reduced dive-angle they dived out of the cloud and initiated a sharp pull-out to low level. Only once they were south of the cut-line did their breathing return to normal.

**Peter Cooke**

Peter Cooke was born in Durban, matriculated at Queen's College and entered the SAAF in 1967. From his earliest days at CFS Dunnottar it was obvious to all the instructors that Peter was a talented youngster with a flair for flying. After gaining his wings he entered the fighter fraternity and flew every single-engined jet in the SAAF's inventory, ending up on 3 Squadron, flying the Mirage F1CZ.

After ten years in the Permanent Force, Peter left to join South African Airways, and transferred to the Active Citizen Force of the SAAF. Apart from his duties with the airline, Peter flew a further 15 years in the SAAF, becoming the only Citizen Force pilot flying Mirages.

He also carried out numerous bush tours and flew 40 operational sorties in Impalas during the war. Included among these were the very hazardous night weaponry sorties under operations *Maanskyn* and *Donkermaan*. However, the nastiest incident of his Mirage career occurred during an ACM training exercise. He was engaged in a 2v2 dogfight when he pulled nose-high to enter a Hi Yo-Yo manoeuvre, keeping his eyes fixed on his target below. Suddenly his windscreen was filled by another F1 diving downwards. There was insufficient time to take avoiding action and fortunately the aircraft passed within metres of each another, miraculously without a collision. Peter could hear the engine in full afterburner as the other aircraft passed.

The highlight of his career was his final flight in the SAAF on 31 January 1992. He flew a Mirage F1CZ low level at an aerobatic show at AFB Waterkloof in front of invited guests, the OC of 3 Squadron, Willie Hartogh, and members of the press. He crowned a wonderful flying career by carrying out a fine performance. What was really remarkable about this flight was that Peter had just become a grandfather.

He flew Boeing 747s as a captain with South Africa Airways and later with Singapore Airlines.

### Dirk de Villiers

Dirk was born and raised in Standerton, matriculating at Standerton Hoërskool. He then entered the SAAF in the fighter line, moving through Impalas, Sabres, and Mirage IIIs before joining 1 Squadron to fly the F1AZ.

His 1,000th flight hour was carried out flying a strike on the SWAPO THDC training camp outside Lubango, as described in chapter 7.

Dirk did two operational tours on 1 Squadron. In between these tours he studied electronic engineering, making him an extremely useful member of the fighter fraternity. A sophisticated aircraft like the F1 requires pilots with engineering knowledge to extract maximum performance from the aircraft systems—particularly at a time when South Africa was isolated from world aviation developments. People like Dirk were invaluable to the SAAF.

Even on his first tour, as a very young man, Dirk became an expert on the involved navigation and weapon system of the F1AZ. As a consequence, he was sent to study the Israeli Kfir system which was later embodied in some respects in the South African-produced Cheetah. Returning to the squadron as an engineer allowed him to enhance the F1 with cost-effective upgrades. All this experience allowed him to eventually establish a military avionics capability in local industry—Project Neckwar, which was local South African avionics integrated into the Mirage F1. Ultimately this led to our aerospace industry winning a NATO contract to upgrade 55 Mirage F1s for the Spanish Air Force and, subsequently, the contract for the development and validation of the BAE Systems' Hawk Mk 120 navigation and weapon systems for the SAAF, currently being released into service.

After leaving the SAAF, Dirk entered the local aero industry and is currently Director Fixed Wing at Advanced Technologies Engineering.

### Louis du Plessis

Louis was born in Johannesburg, matriculated at Helpmekaar Boys' High and joined the SAAF in 1980. The highlight of his SAAF career was being appointed to 3 Squadron where he served under Carlo Gagiano and with another ex-Helpmekaar pupil, Martin Louw. He says the professionalism was par excellence. He fondly recalls his first solo in the F1CZ and particularly the wonderful solo party arranged by Cobus Toerien. However, his passion for the aircraft is tempered by the fact that it only had one seat and that no one else could experience the thrill of flying in it.

His scariest moment occurred on 22 May 1985, but not in an F1. He had to eject from a Mirage III D2Z at high speed in which his instructor, Major Jan Pen Wessels, lost his life. He left the SAAF in 1990 as a captain, a rank he still holds in South African Airways, flying Boeing 737s.

**Pierre du Plessis**

Pierre was born in Stellenbosch, matriculated at De Aar High School and joined the SAAF in 1971. He chose the fighter line and graduated through 85 ADFS at AFB Pietersburg, before being appointed to 3 Squadron.

The highlight of his eight-year F1 career was the day he reached his 1,000th hour on type—14 July 1986, his 34th birthday. He flew a sortie in formation with the SAAF Museum Spitfire, flown by Alan Lurie. The formation was filmed out of the back of an accompanying C-130. On completion of the formation, Pierre flew back to Waterkloof where he gave a short, low-level display. On climbing out of his aircraft he was met by General Bossie Huyser, the 'father' of the SAAF Mirage force, who placed a laurel around Pierre's shoulders and handed him a celebratory bottle of champagne.

At the other end of the scale was the air-to-air sortie he flew from AFB Langebaanweg. After completing his firing on the flag in the vicinity of Dassen Island, he experienced fluctuating JPT and engine surging when selecting afterburner. He declared an emergency and headed straight back to base with Anton van Rensburg, his wingman, following close behind. Pierre did a straight-in approach on runway 16 into a 30-knot southeaster. After landing he turned onto the taxiway and opened up power to check the engine. On reaching full power there was a loud bang from the engine and both 'fire' and 'overheat' lights illuminated. Pierre immediately shut down with Anton shouting over the radio, "Major, the aircraft is burning!" before making a tyre-squealing U-turn and getting his aircraft out of danger. Pierre needed no further encouragement to abandon his cockpit as fast as possible. As he dropped to the ground he could see burning fuel spewing out of the engine near the undercarriage wells. Fuel-tank explosions followed and the entire rear section of the aircraft was engulfed in flame, while Pierre ran so far from the aircraft the firemen couldn't find him!

They extinguished the fire but it had sustained Cat 4 damage.

Investigation revealed that the glow-plug, used during the engine-starting sequence, had lost its retaining circlip and dislodged, leaving a gaping hole in the combustion chamber. While airborne, airflow around the engine prevented a fire but not so when the aircraft was stationary. The front section of Pierre's Mirage 205 was mated with the rear section of Arthur Piercy's 206, and was known affectionately thereafter as Mirage 205 and a half.

During his career Pierre also led the Silver Falcons for three years with 100 displays. He is still serving in the SAAF as a brigadier-general and sports the French National Order of Merit (ChONM) among his medal ribbons.

## Carlo Gagiano

Carlo was born in Bonnievale, matriculated at Clanwilliam High School and entered the SAAF in 1968. He has had an exceptional career in the SAAF where he is presently still serving as Lieutenant-General, Chief of the Air Force.

The highlight of his F1 service was when he was commanding 3 Squadron during the latter stages of the Border War. At that stage The SAAF had to engage the enemy in his own backyard. The Mirage F1 was a wonderful aircraft but, by the late 1980s its air-to-air armament and navigation systems were inferior to those in the swing-wing MiG-23 that the enemy was flying. An additional, and perhaps even a greater handicap, was the lack of radar cover in the combat zone. Enemy radar could see from ground level upwards, whereas SAAF radar, positioned at Rundu, could only see aircraft flying above 20,000 feet AGL while all the fighting was being conducted at low level.

This perilous situation led to the encounter where Carlo and Arthur Piercy engaged a pair of Cuban-piloted MiG-23s. During this fight the enemy launched AA-8 front-sector missiles, which weren't in the SAAF inventory. Arthur's aircraft was damaged and, at one stage in the fight, Carlo had to revert to instruments as he flew through the smoke trail of these missiles fired at him from directly ahead. This was a very challenging situation for the SAAF pilots during the final seven months of the war.

## Chris Lombard

Chris was born in Pretoria, matriculated at Paarl Gymnasium and joined the SAAF in 1963. He instructed at CFS Dunnottar and at FTS Langebaanweg on the first Impala course. He spent 1970 as the aide de camp to the State President and then moved into the fighter line. He did the OTC on both Vampire and Sabre in

1971 and was appointed to 2 Squadron, flying Mirage IIIs in 1972. In 1974 he was part of the first SAAF group that went to France with Colonel Bossie Huyser. In 1975 he started 3 Squadron with Bossie. Between 1985 and 1988 he was OC AFB Hoedspruit, home base of 1 Squadron, so Chris has had a long association with the Mirage F1 force.

The highlight of his service with F1s was the training period he had in France. The SAAF contingent consisted of very experienced Mirage III technicians and pilots. The courses were presented in a strange mixture of English interpreted from rapidly spoken French. The weather conditions in Europe were vastly different to those in sunny South Africa and called for great concentration when flying a brand-new type of aircraft. Fortunately, the Mirage F1 turned out to be a lovely aircraft to fly.

It was in France on his first solo flight that Chris experienced his hairiest moment in the F1. It was at Mont de Marsan in southern France. The weather was awful with 8/8s cloud cover, streaming rain and a wet runway. It was a foreign country with the air traffic controllers speaking a peculiar language they called 'Eengleeesh'. He never saw the ground until breaking cloud on final approach to land—a most traumatic introduction to the F1. In addition to the difficulties he encountered during the flight, he had the nagging thought in the back of his mind of the reception he was going to receive from a very "pissed off" Bossie Huyser after landing. Bossie had led the two aircraft out on their first solo flights, his greatest desire to be able to claim that he was the pilot who first flew a SAAF Mirage F1. A slight instrumentation snag delayed his take-off and the controllers launched Chris to become our first F1 pilot. This story is documented in chapter 1.

Chris had a distinguished career before retiring as major-general from the position of C of AFS in 1998.

## Martin Louw

Martin was born in Bloemfontein in 1955. He was to matriculate at Helpmekaar High School in Johannesburg and entered the SAAF directly thereafter in 1973. He elected to enter the fighter line and completed various courses at 85 ADFS at AFB Pietersburg, flying Impalas and Mirage IIIs, before being appointed to 3 Squadron to fly the Mirage F1CZ.

The highlight of his career was performing a low-level aerobatic display at Upington at last light. What made this a special occasion was the audience—the entire SAAF fighter community. He received the nod of approval from all his peers as it was a great demonstration of flying skill.

His most alarming experience in the F1 was escorting Glen Warden on a low-level photo-reconnaissance over Lubango in Angola. Glen was flying a Mirage III R2Z fitted with two supersonic drop tanks. As his aircraft was unarmed speed was his best defence. As he approached the target he entered a valley south of Lubango and accelerated to 630 knots at a height of 50 feet. Martin's F1CZ was fitted with a 1,200-litre drop tank which was only cleared to 600 knots. Every time Martin banked to negotiate a bend in the valley, his aircraft would yaw wildly out of the turn. The mission was being flown under conditions of radio silence so he couldn't ask Glen to slow down. Martin described the situation as being far worse than when being shot at by FAPLA.

Martin is presently the Director of Flight Operations at Comair. In his spare time he still works at the SAAF Museum on Mirage F1 projects. He is co-author of the book, *The South African Air Force at War*.

### Jan Mienie

Jan was born in Umtali, Rhodesia but matriculated at Afrikaans Boys' High, Pretoria. He joined the SAAF in 1970 but, when Rhodesia was fighting its bush war he left to join the Rhodesian Air Force. Eventually he returned to the SAAF, did an operation tour on Mirage F1AZs before ending up as the last OC of 1 Squadron in 1995, before the Mirage was taken out of service.

Being appointed OC of this fine squadron was the top point in his flying career. The sortie he remembers particularly occurred during Operation *Askari* when he was one of the very few who delivered six 1,000lb bombs. This old fashioned, high-drag bomb was an extremely heavy load to lift in the hot and high conditions that existed up on the border. Throughout the war the Mirages usually carried the low-drag 500lb bombs.

Perhaps the most exciting moment of his career occurred in 1995 when landing at AFB Langebaanweg flying F1AZ 240. As he lowered his nose wheel onto the runway it deflected and stuck in the fully right position. Jan was fortunate to be flying the only aircraft that was testing the Michelin tyres, which proved to be more durable than the tyres normally used on the Mirage. After an exciting ride across the grass the aircraft came to a stop, none the worse for its offroad jaunt.

Jan is presently still serving and is the OC of AFB Langebaan. He retires in December 2009.

## Norman Minne

Norman was born in Port Elizabeth, matriculated at the Pearson High School and entered the SAAF immediately thereafter. The highlight of his Mirage flying occurred during 1987 when he returned to 1 Squadron for his second tour. He re-soloed on 31 January 1987, his 33rd birthday and then flew 240 hours on the F1AZ during the rest of that year. This included learning the updated EW system which included the RWS and the ACS EW pods; using the *Gatup* profile with auto-bomb release; learning the *Vergooi* profile; delivering Tiekie (cluster bomb) and Condib (anti-runway cratering bomb) for the first time; assisting in the establishment of the air-to-air refuelling capability with 60 Squadron B-707s (including participating in the planning and execution of the first non-stop bombing sortie from Hoedspruit to Langebaan and back); becoming operational in night operations (*Maanskyn* and *Donkermaan*) without ever having done previous night operations; flying unconventional intercept profiles in air-to-air (UNCIP, LIPS etc); participating in a number of camps (A-A firing, ground attack and *Golden Eagle* exercises) and, finally, flying from the opening of Oeration *Moduler* into 1988. Truly a year to remember.

His hairiest/scariest moment occurred during Operation *Smokeshell* in 1981 on the strike on THDC outside Lubango. He was No 3 in the third four-ship formation and his wingman was Tinkie Jones, a junior from 3 Squadron. Missiles were already crisscrossing the target area when Norman and Tinky pitched-up. Moments before release height he identified the target then saw three missiles coming straight for him. He shouted a radio warning, did a sort of wingover, released the bombs and continued straight down. He levelled at very low level and realized he was just about supersonic with a belly tank still attached. After a minute or so he started to climb, as he heard I. C. du Plessis call that he had been hit. Shortly thereafter he joined up with the front-runners on the way back to Ondangwa, landing No 3 after starting as No 11, with less than 200 litres of fuel and in a high state of stress.

Norman is still serving in the SAAF and gains a well-deserved promotion to brigadier-general on 1 October 2008.

## Johan Moolman

Johan ('Moolies' to his SAAF friends) grew up in Pretoria, matriculated at Afrikaans Boys' High then joined the SAAF in 1977, electing to enter the fighter line. In 1982 he was appointed to 1 Squadron and served until 1986 as a 'Billy Boy'. In the interest of stoking the fire of inter-squadron rivalry, the author quotes him verbatim: "I had the privilege to be part of the best squadron." The highlight of his Mirage F1 career was his first solo flight in the AZ.

His most tense flight occurred very early in his tour. In May 1982, when Moolies was still a 'new boy', the squadron was deployed to AFB Ondangwa. During one strike into Angola he was No 8 in a formation that rolled into a live attack. No 2 called that he was drawing flak. When Moolies rolled in he said "it looked like serious war down there". It was SOP to push the bomb-jettison button immediately the pilot began pulling out from his attack dive, to rid the aircraft of any bomb which may have 'hung up'. Moolies did this and at that precise moment he heard a loud bang, his radio failed and he assumed his Mirage had taken a hit. Unable to attract the attention of the rest of the formation he made his way cautiously back to land at Ondangwa, without further drama. After landing he discovered the jettison cartridge had exploded inside the pylon, causing the loud bang with the radio failure being purely coincidental. Those who have experienced a dive onto a hot target will appreciate the tension caused by any loud bang.

Johan is now a Boeing 738 captain with South African Airways.

**Theo Nell**

Theo was born in Warmbaths, matriculated at the Louis Trichardt High School and joined the SAAF in 1966. His flying career in the fighter line brought him through Mirage IIIs onto 1 Squadron where he flew the F1AZ. As a major he was appointed temporary OC and led the squadron in operations in Angola.

The 'longest day' of his F1 career occurred in June 1980. He led the formation that took off in the pre-dawn darkness at 05h00 from Upington to AFB Grootfontein. They landed, refuelled and bombed-up for the first strike of the day on a target inside Angola. On completion they landed at AFB Ondangwa to re-arm and prepare for a late-afternoon strike deep into Angola where he was to lead a formation of 16 Mirages. During this mission, in appalling visibility, the formation was fired at and hit by SA-2 and SA-3 missiles. Later that same night they ferried from AFB Ondangwa to AFB Grootfontein to be faced with a runway with only one set of runway lights. It was a day of adrenaline, drama, close shaves and offroad landings at Grootfontein. The full story is described in chapter 7.

Theo experienced another 'exciting' moment when leading a four-ship formation on a close-air-support strike over northeastern Angola, way out of own radar cover. Deep inside 'Injun territory' he had a complete communications failure due to a loose connection inside of his headset. On a straight leg of his flight he selected autopilot and removed his helmet to try and fix the problem. MiGs were ever present so Theo regularly checked the position of his formation before continuing with his electrical repair. On looking up a few seconds later he saw that his formation had already broken through 90 degrees. He then must have broken the world record for replacing his helmet, disengaging autopilot and breaking at max G. It turned out that his No 3 had spotted an 'enemy aircraft' and called the break. However, the enemy happened to be a SAAF Impala returning from another mission.

Theo left the SAAF as a colonel as the SSO Protection Services and is now an aviation consultant.

## Arthur Piercy

Arthur was born in Bulawayo, Rhodesia (now Zimbabwe). He matriculated at Clapham High School in Pretoria before joining the SAAF in 1977 on pilots' course 2/77.

He progressed through the various fighter courses at 85 ADFS at AFB Pietersburg before arriving at 3 Squadron. He was enthralled with the Mirage F1CZ from day one and places his first solo in the machine as the highlight of his F1 career. He particularly enjoyed not having an instructor in the backseat!

The most memorable flight was the one on which he was injured as there were numerous incidents during that eventful flight which will always be etched in his memory—the adrenaline rush as he entered the arena with Mig-23s; having a forward-sector missile fired at him; the clamour of the warning system in his headphones as all the lights on his panel illuminated after his aircraft was struck; the tense flight back to AFB Rundu in his seriously damaged F1; not being able to stop on the runway and then ploughing through sand as the aircraft sped into the bush, crashing violently and leaving him permanently disabled—all have left indelible memories.

Many Vlammies remember the morning he arrived very fast and extremely low over 32 Battalion Headquarters in Rundu—graphically described in chapter 14.

## Frans Pretorius

Frans Pretorius was born at the Kushke Farm School near Pietersburg, and matriculated from Potchefstroom Hoër Gimnasium in 1961. His one abiding memory of his childhood was the sight and sound of Sabre jets carrying out training exercises over the Northern Transvaal. As a consequence, he volunteered for military service in the SAAF Gymnasium in 1962 where he applied for pilot training. He failed due to an unexpected kidney complaint. He re-applied unsuccessfully in 1963 and 1964 with the same result. In desperation he applied again in 1965, this time using the advice given him by a sympathetic doctor on how to 'dope' the test. He was accepted, started flying training a few weeks later. He had to 'dope' his annual medical test for the remainder of his flying career—as his ex-commanding officer the author can say thank goodness he did as he truly became an asset to fighter-pilot fraternity.

The highlight of his Mirage F1 service occurred on the morning Frans and Hennie Louw were returning to land at AFB Hoedspruit after a training sortie. As a well-trained fighter pilot, Frans kept his lookout going even as they approached the airfield. Suddenly, out of the corner of his eye, he picked up an aircraft pulling up through the horizon in a threatening position in the rear of the Mirage F1 formation. At first glance Frans saw what he thought to be the silhouette of one of his beloved Sabres. Milliseconds later he realized it was a MiG-15. Reacting immediately he called the formation to counter towards the threat and within a few seconds they had the MiG out in front of them. Hennie moved into a shooting position and closed to 300 metres, with his aiming pipper trained on the MiG cockpit, with Frans covering Hennie's tail while looking for the rest of the MiG formation.

Moments before Hennie opened fire a radio message from ATC ordered both pilots to force the MIG to land on the long runway at Hoedspruit, which they did. However, what made this last sequence of events even more exciting was the fact that the Mirages were now below minimum fuel. After escorting the MiG safely onto the ground, Frans had to go around for his landing with less than 400 litres of fuel—way below safety limits. Frans and Hennie were both disappointed to find out afterwards that the defection of Lieutenant Bomba from the communist-aligned Mozambican Air Force had been set up beforehand, unbeknown to them.

The most exciting mission he flew was the strike on 7 June 1980, when he had to dodge three SAM-3 missiles over Lubango, as described in chapter 7. (His dodging was not entirely successful as his aircraft was damaged by an exploding missile. His 28-mile glide to a dead-stick landing at AFB Ondangwa was one of the great aviation exploits of the war.)

His other highlight concerns the author, so he includes the incident exactly as he wrote it: "One other highlight during my F1 tour, which I *must* tell you about, was on 28 April 1981, when I flew an ACM sortie in the vicinity of Phalaborwa, against my squadron commander (can't remember the chap's name, but he was a damn good pilot) and, after an aerial battle like I had never had before and with me absolutely soaked and drenched with sweat, but sticking to his six like a burr sticks to cloth, he throttled back, levelled his wings and congratulated me on my 'kill'. *I really appreciated that*! I never told any of the other squadron pilots about my 'kill' because he was my boss and I respected him way too much.

Frans retired from the SAAF in 1997 and presently works for Safair.

## Gerrie Radloff

Gerrie was born in Kroonstad, Orange Free State, completed his schooling at Afrikaans Boys' High in Pretoria and then entered the SAAF Gymnasium in 1964. His career path in the fighter line eventually led him to take over command of 1 Squadron from the author in January 1983.

One of the goals he set himself was to oversee the development of the *Vergooi* (long toss) and *Gatup* (dive toss) attack profiles. The squadron ground crew were tasked to improve the AZ systems to a standard technically better than specified, particularly the Doppler navigation system on which the accuracy of the attack profiles largely depended. At the same time flying tactics were focused on achieving the consistency to defeat the air defences (SAM-7, -8, -9, -13, -14 and -16) against which the squadron was required to operate by the mid and late 1980s. The profiles had to be executed within the minimum reaction time of the air defences which made it vital to achieve surprise on each attack. It was therefore necessary to ingress below 100 feet, below the enemy radar lobe, and at 600 knots to compress their time to react if their radar did acquire lock-on on our aircraft. Leading ten F1AZs on the first operational *Vergooi* mission during Operation *Weldmesh* in September 1985, after two years of perfecting the profile, was therefore a tremendous highlight for Gerrie and the entire squadron.

Earlier in his career, while serving on 3 Squadron during Operation *Daisy*, he had a 'post facto' hairy moment when flying with the late John Inggs. They were flying an armed patrol of the road up to Cassinga to prevent enemy reinforcements moving down to the Iona area. These patrols were flown at 15,000 feet AGL to stay beyond reach of the SAM-7 threat. The patrol took them to the limit of Dayton's radar coverage which was about 140 nautical miles at 15,000 feet. At that point Gerrie saw a vehicle leaving a town and verified over the radio with the SAAF MAOT that it was not one of our own vehicles (the MAOT was Pierre du Plessis, also a 3 Squadron pilot). The two pilots then dived down to low level and attacked the vehicle with cannon. John was in the better position to lead the attack while Gerrie covered his tail but no one was watching Gerrie's six. As they dived they lost line-of-sight radio contact with the radar controller. At that precise moment two MiGs, flying at near-supersonic speed, entered the radar coverage, heading directly for the two Mirages. The radar controller frantically shouted a warning to the Mirage formation which promptly disappeared off Dayton's radar screen without acknowledging the warning call. The vehicle was attacked and destroyed and following SOPs the Mirages remained at low level. At Pierre's insistence they even carried out a fast, low pass over the MAOT's position "so that he could just see an F1 again". After crossing the cut-line, they climbed back up to altitude and re-established contact with Dayton radar, blissfully unaware that they had been 'missing, presumably shot down', for 20 minutes.

Gerrie ended his career in the SAAF as SSO Electronic Warfare but continued to serve South Africa's aviation industry as the Senior Executive Airborne EW Systems at Avitronics.

**Mark Raymond**

Mark was born in Pretoria, matriculated at King Edward High School in Johannesburg and joined the SAAF in 1979.

Mark had difficulty identifying the highlight of his Mirage F1 service as there were so many, but he felt a thrill every time he climbed into the F1 cockpit and truly appreciates the privilege of having flown F1s at 3 Squadron. His daily highlights were walking back from the flight line, sweaty, tired but satisfied. Two possible career highlights were the periods in 1986 and 1987/88 when 3 Squadron operated from AB Rundu. The flying was intense and with purpose. It all seemed to culminate with the unfortunate incident with Arthur Piercy. The amazing camaraderie with fellow squadron members and other SAAF people was perhaps the icing on the cake.

His scariest moment was his infamous night 'spin' en route to Waterkloof from AFB Langebaan. He levelled off at 41,000 feet and engaged the autopilot, hoping to scrape over the top of a squall line of 'Charlie Bravos' on his track. The lightning flashed like disco lights below him as the aircraft jumped around more and more. The speed bled off and, in trying to maintain height, the angle of attack increased. He engaged afterburner too late and at approximately 210KIAS, the aircraft departed and entered a spin. The lightning in the cloud enveloped him and he was convinced his aircraft would be struck. A thought crossed his mind that if he had to eject he would be bobbing up and down between 20,000 and 40,000 feet in his parachute as the updrafts took hold of him. He recovered at 25,000 feet and, because of full backward trim on the elevators (applied by the autopilot when trying to maintain height), as he released forward pressure on the stick the nose came up, he stalled and entered another spin. He again applied instinctive spin-recovery actions and the aircraft finally levelled off at 14,000 feet as he broke cloud. On landing at Waterkloof he remembers with appreciation the calm and professional manner in which he was handled by his OC, Commandant Dries Wehmeyer. The ATCOs in Johannesburg Tower weren't quite so calm, having had to manage an F1 plummeting through all other aircraft safety heights.

Mark left the Permanent Force in November 1988 and served as a CF pilot until February 1989. He is presently living in Australia.

**Cobus Toerien**

Cobus Toerien is a born and bred 'Blue Bull' who matriculated at Pretoria North High School before joining the SAAF in 1974. For many years he was a 'single living out' officer so, according to the 'wise men' in the HQ career planning office, Cobus endured a career that included many moves—his record being four appointments in four years. However, he can't really complain because this allowed him to complete three tours on 3 Squadron where he totalled 1,226 F1 hours in over 1,500 sorties. These sorties included quite a few low-level aerobatic displays, operations over Angola and being John Rankin's wingman when the second MiG-21 was shot down on 5 October 1982.

His most exciting moment however, occurred on a test flight in Mirage F1CZ 204 on 6 September 1990. The aircraft required a test flight before night-flying commenced and Cobus, as the squadron 'hog', jumped at the chance to fly it. Full PC up to M1.4, then straight back down to initial at Waterkloof, doing 500 knots at full throttle. On breaking downwind he reduced throttle to flight idle for the first time on the quick flight, which resulted in a loud explosion, followed by severe vibration and abrupt power loss. He turned the aircraft to the southeast ejection area but realized that the vibration had declined with the airspeed. At this stage the Waterkloof air traffic officer shouted, "The circuit is yours" and, with speed in the turn, Cobus headed for the threshold of RWY 01. Turning base leg, Cobus realized that, because of the built-up area under the aircraft's approach path, he had no other option but to go for the landing. He made it with about ten knots to spare. Investigation revealed a 6mm screw had dislodged when power had been reduced below 7,400rpm, destroying most of the finely balanced compressor blades. Cobus appreciated that, had he closed the throttle anywhere in the general flying area, he probably would not have made it back to base.

He left the SAAF as a colonel, proudly wearing the Air Force Cross awarded to him for the forced landing. He is presently a flight safety specialist at South African Airways.

### Frank Tonkin

Frank was born in Nigel and grew up close to Dunnottar, hence his desire to fly. He matriculated at Potchefstroom Boys' High and was then called up for national service in the army. He did his 'basics' in Walvis Bay during 1975, followed by his corporal's course and then went off to war in Angola on Operation *Savannah*, taking part in the famous 'Bridge 14' battle. On release from the army he gained his PPL at Rand Airport and joined the SAAF in 1978. As an Impala pilot on 7 Squadron he did many bush tours before finally arriving on 3 Squadron in 1984.

He had always wanted to be a fighter pilot and places his first solo on the F1CZ as a real highlight, to be matched with flying Mach 2-plus and low-level supersonic 'dogfights' off Langebaan and Durban. Another exciting mission was being scrambled to intercept MiGs on 10 September 1987 and watching from 4,000 feet above, as a Matra 550 missile, fired by Anton van Rensburg, tracked a MiG-23. Anton and Frank were some of the very few F1CZ pilots to do the Moonshine course with Peter Cooke in 1988.

His 'hairiest' moment occurred on 27 September 1987 when Arthur Piercy's aeroplane was hit and damaged by 'head-on' missiles. Frank and John Sinclair had also been scrambled but for some reason were kept at low level. During the intercept and commotion that followed after Arthur was hit, Frank requested clearance to climb to assist but, as all communications were through an Impala Telstar, couldn't get approval. Fortunately he then heard Carlo Gagiano and Arthur talking on the radio as they made their way back to Rundu. At that stage Frank says his heart rate must have been 1,000 beats per minute.

Frank left the SAAF after a five-year tour on the Mirage F1CZ and is now flying for South African Airways. He wanted the author to include his favourite quote from Major Doyle 'Wahoo' Nicholson, USMC: "There are only two types of aircraft—fighters and targets."

### Paulus Truter

Paulus was born in Ceres, matriculated at Strand High and joined the SAAF in 1976. After completing all his fighter courses and time on Impalas he arrived on 1 Squadron in time for the 'big war' around Cuito Cuanavale in 1987/88. The high point in his F1 tour was participating in operations *Moduler*, *Hooper* and *Packer* over the entire seven-month period.

The most exciting mishap of his F1 career occurred during a buddy-buddy refuelling sortie with a

Buccaneer as the tanker. On trying to withdraw from the basket he discovered that the probe was stuck in the basket. His only option was to attempt to break the weak-link built into the F1 nozzle for this very eventuality. Unfortunately, the weak-link turned out to be quite a strong-link. Instead of the nozzle head breaking off, the whole refuelling pod tore off the Buccaneer's wing. Considering the position of the pod directly ahead of the pilot, this turned out to be quite an exciting moment for Paulus. He was immediately blinded by the escaping fuel but managed a safe breakaway, avoiding the tanker's pod. This incident occurred over the Eastern Transvaal under the watchful eye of Jan Henning.

Paulus left the SAAF in July 1996 from the position of chief instructor at CFS Langebaanweg where he was instrumental in presenting the first Pilatus Astra course. He is presently a training captain with Comair.

## Schalk van Heerden

Schalk was born in Montagu and matriculated at Clanwilliam High School, alma mater of Carlo Gagiano. He joined the SAAF in 1974 and eventually ended up as a 'Billy Boy' on 1 Squadron.

His most interesting take-off in the F1AZ occurred when Norman Minne led a three-ship, close-formation take-off with Schalk and Nick Scheltema on either side as wingmen. Nick and Schalk released brakes at mini PC+ with Norman still at idle. Norman then lit his PC and hit full power to catch up as Nick and Schalk cut PC and braked in order to slow down. Norman overtook his wingmen who then re-lit PC and caught up to be in perfect formation on lift-off! (Shades of the the classic Vampire take-off when the leader called, "Brakes off, brakes off. Go, go, go!" The one wingman released the hand brake on the first "brakes off", the second wingman on the first "go" and the leader, who got airborne last, on the last "go".)

Schalk's most exciting moment occurred while landing at Langebaanweg after a ferry flight from Hoedspruit on Bingo fuel. His drag-'chute failed, as did the brake on left wheel. He performed a high-speed snake down the runway, trying to brake with his right wheel and counter the swing by using full-left, nose-wheel steering. He called for the arrestor barrier to be raised and it came up two feet then stuck. He managed to bring the Mirage to a halt with the Pitot tube over the barrier, still holding the radio transmit down. Dolf Prinsloo says he has never heard anybody sucking oxygen like Schalk did over the final 1,000 metres.

Schalk is still in the SAAF, is a colonel and is presently our Air-Naval attaché in Washington, DC.

## Pete Vivier

Peter was born in Durban, matriculated at Christian Brothers' College, Pretoria and joined the SAAF in 1967. After a stint flying light aircraft he entered the fighter line and eventually became an instructor at 85 Advanced Flying School at AFB Pietersburg, teaching aerial warfare to aspirant fighter pilots. Eventually he was posted to 3 Squadron at AFB Waterkloof while he studied for a BSc Electronic Engineering degree at the University of Pretoria. During his vacation periods he would return to the squadron to keep up his competency on the Mirage. In this capacity he used to take his university vacations abroad—usually in the seat of an F1CZ over Angola.

Perhaps his most exciting moment occurred when flying as a member of a four-ship Mirage F1 formation at 20,000 feet which entered a large cumulo-nimbus thunderstorm. Formation flying in cloud is not usually a cause for concern. However, as each aircraft was carrying four, fully loaded 68mm rocket pods, they were in a high-drag configuration. At 20,000 feet they entered the most active, violent storm cell. The aircraft were tossed about like feathers and the pilots lost visual sighting with each other, making for a very tense few minutes.

Pete retired from the SAAF as a brigadier-general in 1998 as Director Air Force Acquisitions and is presently a director with Advanced Technologies Engineering Pty Ltd (ATE).

## Wayne Westoby

Wayne was born in Durban and attended Westville Boys' High before matriculating at Edenvale High in Johannesburg. He spent his formative years in the SAAF flying operationally in Angola in the Impala.

After joining 1 Squadron he became the solo display pilot between 1988 and 1990 which was the highlight of his F1 career. He described this opportunity in these words: "The vice-less handling characteristics and splendour of a Mirage F1AZ in flight allowed a display pilot the freedom to show off just how well the design team at Dassault Aviation got it right."

Display flying takes the aircraft to the limits of its performance envelope, leaving little margin for error—and, on one occasion, err he did. While practising for a display he came through the top of a low-level loop 200 feet too low. He had to 'unload' while accelerating vertically downwards in full PC, waiting for 'corner speed' to be able to make the pull-out. He never realized the acceleration from 120KIAS to 440KIAS could take so long—four seconds.

Wayne left the SAAF in 1990 as a captain and is presently still a captain in South African Airways, flying the Airbus A319.

**Paul Williamson**

Paul was born in Paarl, matriculated at Selborne College, East London and joined the SAAF in 1989. He came via 2 Squadron, where he'd flown Cheetahs, to 1 Squadron where every flight in an F1 was regarded as a highlight. What amazed him most was the fuel efficiency, range and carefree handling of the AZ compared to the Cheetah D. Professional rivalry between 1 and 2 Squadron is part of SAAF tradition. It was therefore a pleasure for Paul to fly a clean F1 to Louis Trichardt and complete a few circuits before 'setting heading' over 2 Squadron's crew room to return to Hoedspruit.

The 'cherry on the top' of his Mirage career was flying combined strikes to Lohatla range, the rendezvous with 60 Squadron's tanker and the comradeship on the tanking lane, and the pleasurable feeling of returning to Hoedspruit for a four-ship ops initial.

Life consists of both ups and downs and one of his downs was being short of fuel when near Lohatla and having to carry out low-level, air-to-air refuelling on a hot, bumpy summer's day. All's well that ends well, but everyone who has been in the same position can certainly empathize.

Paul left the SAAF Permanent Force in 1999 and the Citizen Force in 2005. He now resides in the UK where he is a training captain flying the Airbus A320 for EasyJet Airlines out of Gatwick.

# Appendix VI

# Honours and awards

**3 Squadron**
| | | | |
|---|---|---|---|
| Maj | C. B. Lombard | CSADF Commendation* | 1977 |
| Maj | J. L. Gründling | CSADF Commendation | 1977 |
| Sgt | J. Robertson | CSADF Commendation | 1977 |
| F/Sgt | S. H. G. Beeton | CSADF Commendation | 1979 |
| WOII | F. van der Walt | Pro Merito Medal | 1981 |
| Cmdt | J. L. Gründling | Southern Cross Medal | 1982 |
| Maj | E. H. Dert | Southern Cross Medal | 1982 |
| Maj | A. M. Wehmeyer | CSADF Commendation | 1982 |
| F/Sgt | A. T. Uys | CSADF Commendation | 1984 |
| WOII | J. H. Henning | CSADF Commendation | 1985 |
| Maj | P. du Plessis | CSADF Commendation | 1987 |
| WOII | A. R. de Wet | CSADF Commendation | 1987 |
| Maj | A. D. Piercy | Southern Cross Decoration | 1989 |

**1 Squadron**
| | | | |
|---|---|---|---|
| Capt | I. C. du Plessis | Honoris Crux | 07/06/80 |
| Maj | F. A. Pretorius | Southern Cross Medal | 07/06/80 |
| Cmdt | J. J. Rankin | Southern Cross Medal | 25/11/88 |
| Maj | E. R. Every | Southern Cross Medal (PH)** | 25/11/88 |
| Maj | J. W. van Coppenhagen | Southern Cross Medal (PH) | 25/11/88 |
| Maj | N. G. Minne | Southern Cross Medal | 25/11/88 |
| Maj | J. P. Truter | Southern Cross Medal | 25/11/88 |
| Maj | T. R. Nel | Southern Cross Medal | 25/11/88 |
| Capt | G. H. de Beer | Southern Cross Medal | 25/11/88 |

| Capt | D. Holdsworth | Southern Cross Medal | 25/11/88 |
| Capt | D. H. P. Kleynhans | Southern Cross Medal | 25/11/88 |
| Capt | C. W. Skinner | Southern Cross Medal | 25/11/88 |
| Maj | F. J. Coetzee | CSADF Commendation | 25/11/88 |
| Capt | I. R. van Eeden | CSADF Commendation | 25/11/88 |
| F/Sgt | G. C. de Lange | CSADF Commendation | 25/11/88 |
| WOI | C. F. J. Scheepers | Pro Merito Decoration | 25/11/88 |
| Sgt | G. J. du Toit | Pro Merito Medal | 25/11/88 |
| Sgt | C. Lourens | CSADF Commendation | 25/07/91 |
| Maj | P. F. Ackerman | CSADF Commendation | 03/09/92 |
| Lt-Col | A. E. Prinsloo | Military Merit Medal | 06/05/94 |
| Maj | A. D. Brand | Military Merit Medal | 03/02/95 |
| Maj | N. J. C. Scheltema | Military Merit Medal | 03/02/95 |
| Maj | P. F. Ackerman | Southern Cross Medal | 31/10/96 |
| Maj | P. J. Potgieter | Military Merit Medal | 31/10/96 |
| Capt | C. Pretorius | Ad Astra Decoration | 31/10/96 |
| Capt | C. Pretorius | Military Merit Medal | 31/10/96 |
| Sgt | G. Ferris | Military Merit Medal | 01/05/97 |
| Sgt | L. B. Hains | Military Merit Medal | 01/05/97 |
| Sgt | C. J. van Rensburg | Military Merit Medal | 01/05/97 |

*Note*: This list pertains only to honours and awards during the Mirage F1 period

*Commendation South African Defence Force, later changed to the more manageable Military Merit Medal (MMM)

**posthumous award

# Appendix VII

# "One of our aircraft is missing"— SAAF aircraft and crew losses to enemy action during the bush war

---

**Date**         14 August 1974
**Aircraft**    Alouette III      Side number 111
**Crew**       Pilot            Lt Ray Houghton
               F/Eng          Sgt Ray Wernich

Aircraft was struck by an RPG and crashed in the Madziwa Tribal Trust area of Rhodesia. 111 was the leader of two Alouette helicopters landing in a bush LZ. As the wheels touched the ground an RPG, fired from no more than 20 metres, exploded as it struck the aircraft. The pilot and flight engineer fell out of the wreckage, suffering from minor shrapnel wounds. Lt Erasmus, flying the second helicopter, dropped his troops and then returned to evacuate the downed. crewmen

**Date**         25 November 1975
**Aircraft**    Cessna 185      Side number 739
**Crew**       Pilot            2/Lt K. W. Williamson (KIA)
               Pax             2/Lt E. B. Thompson (KIA)
               Pax             Capt D. J. Taljaard SA Army (KIA)

Aircraft failed to return from a reconnaissance flight for Task Force Foxbat during Operation *Savannah*. On 27 November an intercepted enemy radio message indicated that the aircraft had been shot down north of Ebo. Three months later a correspondent of the London *Times* reported that he had seen the wreck of the aircraft north of Ebo.

| | | |
|---|---|---|
| **Date** | 22 December 1975 | |
| **Aircraft** | Puma | Side number 134 |
| **Crew** | Pilot | Capt John Millbank |
| | Co-pilot | Maj Chris Hartzenberg |
| | F/Eng | F/Sgt Piet O'Neill du Toit |
| | Pax | Medic cpl |

During Operation *Savannah*, the Puma was hit by Cuban AAA from a hillside 18 kilometres north-west of Cela. The pilots carried out a forced landing fewer than three kilometres from the AAA site. The crew then evaded capture for 22 hours before returning safely.

| | | |
|---|---|---|
| **Date** | 22 February 1977 | |
| **Aircraft** | Alouette III | |
| **Crew** | Pilot | Lt Neil Liddell (KIA) |
| | F/Eng | Sgt Flip Pretorius |

Operating out of AFB Mpacha, Lt Liddell's helicopter was struck by enemy small-arms fire as it overflew a SWAPO detachment operating in Zambia. A bullet entered the floor of the aircraft and wounded the pilot after passing through the bottom of the pilot's seat. Lt Liddell made a forced landing and the flight engineer ran off to get aid. Lt Liddell succumbed to his wound before help arrived.

| | | |
|---|---|---|
| **Date** | 14 March 1979 | |
| **Aircraft** | Canberra | Side number 452 |
| **Crew** | Pilot | Lt Dewald Marais (KIA) |
| | Navigator | 2/Lt Owen Doyle (KIA) |

A formation of four Canberra bombers attacked a target close to Cahama in Angola. Immediately after bomb release, the Canberras descended from 500 feet to low level. It was noticed that Lt Wally Marais' aircraft remained with bomb doors open. Radio calls failed to establish contact with either occupant. Detaching from the formation, Capt Roly Jones closed in on 452. He could see no outward sign of damage to the aircraft. Flying above 452 he noticed the pilot slumped over the controls. 452 climbed slowly up to 2,000 feet while decreasing speed to around 200 knots. The aircraft then banked gently to port before adopting a 10° nose-down attitude. It descended to extremely low level before suddenly pitching up into an almost vertical attitude. The aircraft stalled before plunging into the ground.

| | | |
|---|---|---|
| **Date** | 6 July 1979 | |
| **Aircraft** | Mirage III R2Z | Side number 856 |
| **Crew** | Pilot | Capt Otto Schür |

Capt Schür, flying a reconnaissance aircraft, was tasked to take post-strike damage-assessment photography of a target near the Angolan town of Omapande. At 600 knots and 190 feet above the ground, he began his filming run. Seconds later he was struck by AAA that caused a total electrical failure. Clearing the target, he zoomed to gain altitude as he turned back towards base. Passing 8,000 feet and 500 knots, the Mirage flicked into a high-G, right-hand descending spiral, from which he could not recover. He ejected, evaded capture and was recovered to AFB Ondangwa.

| | | |
|---|---|---|
| **Date** | 6 September 1979 | |
| **Aircraft** | Puma | Side Number 164 (?) |
| **Crew** | Pilot | Capt Paul Vellerman (KIA) |
| | Co-pilot | Lt Nigel Osborne (KIA) |
| | F/Eng | F/Sgt Dick Retief (KIA) |
| | Pax | 14 Rhodesian troops (KIA) |

Capt Vellerman was flying as No 4 in a formation of Rhodesian Air Force helicopters during Operation *Uric* in Mocambique. His helicopter was struck by AAA as the formation circled over a terrorist camp, whose position was unknown before the operation. Without a radio call the helicopter crashed killing all the occupants.

| | | |
|---|---|---|
| **Date** | 18 October 1979 | |
| **Aircraft** | Impala Mk II | Side number 1033 |
| **Crew** | Pilot | Maj Aubrey Bell |

On an armed reconnaissance mission near Omapande in Angola, Aubrey Bell's Impala was hit by AAA slightly below and behind the cockpit. The aircraft started buffeting, warning lights began flashing and the smoke in the cockpit persuaded him to eject close to the town. After a combined rescue mission involving Impala jets, Puma helicopters and Parabats, the pilot was recovered. Maj Polla Kruger's rescue Puma returned with 22 bullet holes.

| | | |
|---|---|---|
| **Date** | 24 January 1980 | |
| **Aircraft** | Impala Mk II | Side number 1056 |
| **Crew** | Pilot | Capt Leon Burger |

During an armed reconnaissance mission near Aanhanca in Angola, Capt Burger's Impala was struck by a SA-7 missile while at low level. The missile entered the jet pipe from the lower right-hand side and detonated against the bottom of the vertical tail fin. Despite the loss of the entire vertical fin, Capt Burger managed to fly the aircraft back to AFB Ondangwa. As night had fallen by the time he arrived overhead, he was ordered to eject rather than attempt a landing. The airfield was packed with aircraft and it was decided not to risk landing the Impala with severely reduced directional control.

| | | |
|---|---|---|
| **Date** | 23 March 1980 | |
| **Aircraft** | Impala Mk II | Side number 1050 |
| **Crew** | Pilot | Capt Sarel Smal |

With fuel filters blocked with very fine white powder, suspected to be an accumulation of Ondangwa sand, Capt Smal's engine lost power while he was on a mission in Angola. Smal ejected at very low level. Angola propaganda claimed they had shot down this aircraft. They produced publicity photographs demonstrating their skill, with pictures of their soldiers standing on the tail and near the cockpit in victorious poses. They claimed that they had killed the pilot, Capt J. H. Henning. Capt Henning's name was painted on the aircraft but he is still very much alive.

| | | |
|---|---|---|
| **Date** | 25 April 1980 | |
| **Aircraft** | Impala Mk II | Side number 1029 |
| **Crew** | Pilot | Lt Pete Hollis (KIA) |

A pair of Impala aircraft on an armed reconnaissance mission in Angola found and attacked an enemy target. While pulling out from the attack, Impala 1029 was struck by ground fire and flames were seen coming from the tail section as Lt Hollis ejected. His neck broke on ejection. The Board of Inquiry found that the pilot's head struck the canopy before the canopy breaker on the seat, causing the fatal injuries. The ejection seat had not been lowered prior to the ejection.

| | | |
|---|---|---|
| **Date** | 20 June 1980 | |
| **Aircraft** | Impala Mk II | Side number 1037 |
| **Crew** | Pilot | Lt Neil Thomas |

On an army support mission during Operation *Smokeshell* Lt Thomas's aircraft was struck by a 23mm shell in the region of the cannon barrel. Debris passed through the engine compressor and with 98 per cent power selected minimal thrust was produced. The aircraft descended until it was striking the treetops when Lt Thomas ejected. He was rescued by Lt André Hattingh and flown to the HAG near Evale in Angola. En route the Alouette red fuel-warning light illuminated, indicating a fuel-filter blockage. After a forced landing in enemy territory, the crew cleared the filter before the rescue mission was completed. The aircraft was recovered by Frelon helicopter and returned to Atlas Aircraft Company. It was repaired and returned to service with the same side number.

| | | |
|---|---|---|
| **Date** | 23 June 1980 | |
| **Aircraft** | Alouette III | Side number 24 |
| **Crew** | Pilot | Capt Thinus van Rensburg |
| | F/Eng | Sgt Koos Celliers (KIA) |

Aircraft was struck by enemy fire while providing top cover for landing Pumas and crashed 12 kilometres east of Xangongo in Angola. After exiting the burning wreckage Sgt Celliers was shot by Swapo terrorists. He was confirmed dead by Capt van Rensburg. No pulse could be found. Capt van Rensburg managed to escape and evade capture and reached safety by foot. He was found by ground forces near Cuamato, suffering from compression fractures of the vertebrae, superficial scratches and dehydration. Radio intercepts indicated that SWAPO had taken the body of Sgt Celliers to Lubango.

| | | |
|---|---|---|
| **Date** | 10 October 1980 | |
| **Aircraft** | Impala Mk II | Side number 1042 |
| **Crew** | Pilot | Capt Steve Volkerz (KIA) |

Lt Volkerz, a Mirage III pilot on 2 Squadron, was still current on Impalas and volunteered to do an operational tour on Impalas at AFB Ondangwa. During a mission 20 kilometres south-west of Mupa in Angola, Lt Skinner, the other pilot in the formation, saw Impala 1042 hit by two SA-7 heat-seeking missiles. He saw Lt Volkerz eject and the aircraft explode as it hit the ground. Circling the scene, he saw Lt Volkerz land in his parachute, stand up and wave to indicate that he was uninjured. Radio messages intercepted from the enemy the next day, indicated that Lt Volkerz had been shot and killed by SWAPO.

| | | |
|---|---|---|
| **Date** | 25 August 1981 | |
| **Aircraft** | Alouette III | Side number 48 |
| **Crew** | Pilot | Lt Bertus Roos (KIA) |
| | F/Eng | Sgt Clifton Stacey (KIA) |

During Operation *Protea*, Alouette 48 was involved in a CAS (close air support) mission with the ground forces 20 kilometres NNW of Cuamato in Angola. The aircraft was struck by 14.5mm anti-aircraft fire. Smoke was observed coming from the helicopter as it crashed, killing the crew.

| | | |
|---|---|---|
| **Date** | 29 December 1981 | |
| **Aircraft** | Alouette III | Side number 30 |
| **Crew** | Pilot | Lt Serge Bovy |
| | F/Eng | Sgt A. J. Janse van Rensburg |

Alouettes were operating with the ground forces during Operation *Vlinder* near Evale in Angola. On 29 December, ground forces were in contact with the enemy who were armed with SA-7s and RPGs. A serious casevac from an enemy 82mm mortar blast needed to be picked up. Lt Arthur Walker led a two-ship Alouette formation to the scene. He provided top cover to Lt Serge Bovy's helicopter that was to carry out the pick-up. After calling for the ground troops to mark the LZ with 'white phos', Lt Bovy approached to land. During the approach he saw Lt Walker's helicopter veer sharply as it drew heavy AAA fire. Lt Bovy also drew tracers as he flared to land. On touch-down, two troops loaded the casevac into the helicopter while the rest of the platoon formed a defensive semi-circle around the helicopter. On lift-off, because of the extra weight, it took a long time for the Alouette to pass through the transition from vertical to forward speed. As Bovy started to bank away from the enemy positions he saw two 14.5mm AA guns firing at him from a little over 100 metres away. His aircraft was hit with rounds going through the door, another removing the top part of the instrument panel and one passing through his flying overall but missing his leg. Turning away from the AA site, Bovy tried to fly below tree level, barely keeping his rotors clear of the branches. There was a smell of burning and several electrical sparks in the cockpit. The AAA continued and further hits were felt in the port forward door and the co-pilot's seat. Bovy's armoured seat was also hit and he was bounced briskly forward several times. The engine started losing power, causing the rotor blades to slow down. Realizing they were about to crash when the controls stiffened up, he flared harshly to dig the tail in. Looking up, he realized that the helicopter was going to hit a big tree so he deflected the cyclic and rudder to the right. After impact the helicopter came to rest. Dolf van Rensburg, the flight engineer, was lying in the small space between Bovy's chair and the door. Although a lot of blood was streaming from his mouth, he indicated that he was otherwise fine. Bovy unstrapped and, apart from a very sore back, was able to exit the helicopter by punching out the window. The casevac showed no signs of life and was trapped in the wreckage. Seconds later, mortars started falling around them and the two men ran off in a northerly direction. During their escape Bovy noticed a terrorist with an AK-47 about 50 metres away. Dolf wanted to make a stand but Bovy persuaded him to keep silent as the terrorist hadn't seen them. He was looking up at the gunship helicopter firing from above. Soon AK-47 rounds and other larger-calibre shells started bouncing off the trees around the two men. It sounded as if the terrorists were running on the aircrew's spoor. Sgt Botes in the overhead gunship spotted the escapees and, despite heavy AAA, Arthur Walker landed in a confined LZ. The two airmen jumped aboard as Arthur pulled all the instrument panel needles into the red to get the heavily loaded helicopter into the air and on track for base.

| **Date** | 5 January 1982 | |
|---|---|---|
| **Aircraft** | Puma | Side number 168 |
| **Crew** | Pilot | Capt John Robinson (KIA) |
| | Co-pilot | Lt Michael Earp (KIA) |
| | F/Eng | Sgt Kenny Dalgleish (KIA) |

While trooping, the helicopter was struck by small-arms fire. All hydraulic pressures were probably lost and the helicopter struck the ground inverted.

| **Date** | 1 June 1982 | |
|---|---|---|
| **Aircraft** | Impala Mk II | Side number 1052 |
| **Crew** | Pilot | T/Maj Gene Kotze (SD) (KIA) |

Diving to attack an enemy target, Maj Kotze's aircraft was hit by AAA and crashed.

| **Date** | 9 August 1982 | |
|---|---|---|
| **Aircraft** | Puma | Side number 132 |
| **Crew** | Pilot | Capt John Twaddle (KIA) |
| | Co-pilot | Lt Chris Pietersen (KIA) |
| | F/Eng | Sgt 'Grobbies' Grobler (KIA) |

At 13h20 on 9 August, eight Pumas took off from a HAG, trooping a company of 32 Battalion for a follow-up operation. The formation, flying at very low level, came under heavy AAA and small-arms fire as it crossed an open *shona*. Puma 132, the fifth Puma in the formation, had its tail shot off. The helicopter inverted and crashed into the ground, killing all the occupants.

| | |
|---|---|
| **Date** | 3 September 1987 |
| **Aircraft** | Bosbok　　　Side number 934 |
| **Crew** | Pilot　　　　Lt Richard Glynn (KIA) |
| | Pax　　　　　1 (KIA) |

During operation *Moduler*, Lt Glynn was tasked to fly a night artillery-spotting mission south of the Lomba River in Angola. The aircraft was struck by a missile, presumed to be an SA-8, and crashed, killing both occupants.

| | |
|---|---|
| **Date** | 20 February 1988 |
| **Aircraft** | Mirage F1AZ　　Side number 245 |
| **Crew** | Pilot　　　　　　Maj Ed Every (KIA) |

During a *Vergooi* bombing mission near Cuito Cuanavale, Maj Every's aircraft was struck by a SA-13 missile as the pilot was levelling out at low level. The aircraft was seen to crash into the trees.

**Unmanned remotely piloted vehicles/aircraft (RPVs)**

Operation *Askari*: November 1984 to January 1985
The Scout system was deployed to Xangongo in southern Angola and flew missions in the Cahama area in an attempt to locate SA-8 batteries located in that region. During one mission, three SA-8 missiles were captured on video as they were fired at the RPV. Shrapnel from the third missile damaged the camera's protective dome. Approximately 250 rounds of 23mm AAA were also fired at the drone, but it was recovered safely.

Operation *Moduler*: September 1987
The system was transported to Mavinga where a runway was graded and compacted for the deployment. The poor quality of the runway resulted in damage to four propellers before the runway was improved. On the second operational mission, 16 SA-8 missiles were fired at the drone before it was finally shot down. UNITA soldiers witnessed the shooting and found the wreckage. They then spent three days searching for the pilot, not knowing that it was an unmanned aircraft. Two more RPVs were lost to missile fire before the deployment was curtailed.

**Summary**
During 15 years of bush war between 1974 and 1989, the South African Air Force lost 22 aircraft as a direct result of enemy action. This period included operations in Rhodesia, Mozambique, Angola, South West Africa and Namibia.

Lost were:

| | |
|---|---|
| 1 x Mirage F1AZ | No 245 |
| 1 x Mirage III R2Z | No 856 |
| 1 x Canberra | No 452 |
| 5 x Impalas Mk II | Nos 1056, 1029, 1042, 1052, 1033 |
| 1 x Bosbok | No 934 |
| 1 x Cessna 185 | No 739 |
| 4 x Pumas | Nos 134, Vellerman, 168, 132 |
| 5 x Alouette IIIs | Liddell, 111, 24, 48, 30 |
| 3 x RPVs (RPAs) | |

During this time many aircraft were struck by hostile fire but all landed safely, were repaired and returned to service. The list includes:

- Two F1AZs hit by SA-3 missiles near Lubango (Majs du Plessis and Pretorius)
- A Mirage F1CZ struck by AA-8 missiles in combat near Cuito Cuanavale (Capt Piercy)
- A Mirage III hit in the tailpipe by an SA-7 over Ongiva (Capt Keet)
- An Impala struck by a SA-7 over Mulondo (Lt Meintjies)
- An Impala had its starboard rear tail plane removed by an SA-9 over Cuvelai (Capt van den Berg)
- A DC-3 Dakota's entire tail section was shredded by a strike from an SA-7 missile (Capt Green)
- A DC-4 Skymaster's fuselage was punctured by small-arms fire north of Ruacana (Maj Rybicki)
- The helicopter fleet, flying close to the fire fights, naturally received the greatest attention from enemy small arms-fire, 12.7mm, 14.5mm and 23mm AAA, as well as RPG and SA-7 missiles. Many helicopters were hit, often suffering multiple strikes, but apart from those listed as destroyed, all returned to service. Perhaps the record belongs to Maj Polla Kruger whose Puma returned to AFB Ondangwa sporting 22 bullet holes after he had rescued a downed Impala pilot.

Other aircraft destroyed in the operational areas as a result of maintenance and aircrew errors but not enemy fire. The list includes:

- Two Impalas that impacted the ground while pulling out after firing at enemy targets (1074 and 1024)
- An Impala that crashed after take-off on a night mission after the canopy blew off (1096)

- A Mirage F1AZ that crashed while returning from a night mission inside Angola (223)
- A Puma that spiralled into the Cunene River after a mechanical failure (135)
- A Puma that crashed while landing in thick dust at night at Oshakati (174)
- A Puma that crashed after take-off while trooping near Cassinga (155)
- A Kudu, with engine trouble, that forced-landed in an enemy-infested area of Rhodesia (975)
- An Alouette that crashed into high-tension cables in Rhodesia
- An Alouette that crashed into Lake Kariba after an engine cut. The aircraft was salvaged from the lake and placed onto a low-bed truck for transportation back to a repair depot. The truck was destroyed en route when it detonated a landmine
- An Alouette that crashed at Okankolo at night after striking an antenna (43)
- A Cessna 185 that crashed on take-off from Impalela Island in the Caprivi Strip (743)

# Appendix VIII

# Mirage F1 losses

---

**F1AZ 246**
15/2/79
Capt 'Wassie' Wasserman
Pilot ejected safely after repeated engine flame-outs. Aircraft crashed near Cullinan, South Africa.

**F1CZ 200**
15/2/79
Maj Chris Brits
Aircraft crashed after a slow flypast of the crash scene of F1AZ 246. Pilot ejected but seat failed to deploy in time. Pilot killed.

**F1AZ 244**
7/6/80
Maj Frans Pretorius
Aircraft damaged by SA-3 missile over target near Lubango, Angola. Pilot recovered the aircraft successfully at AFB Ondangwa after engine flamed out 28 miles from base. Pilot carried out a dead-stick landing.

**F1AZ 237**
7/6/80
Capt I. C. du Plessis
Aircraft damaged by SA-3 missile in the same raid. Pilot recovered to forward airfield at Ruacana and landed without nose-wheel.

**F1CZ 208**
4/11/80
Capt Les Bennett
Pilot ejected successfully after experiencing full upwards runaway trim during a night interception mission near Groblersdal, South Africa.

**F1CZ 209**
5/7/84
Cmdt Joshi Lavi
Pilot landed heavily. Having flown the F1AZ at AFB Hoedspruit, pilot possibly misjudged the difference in density altitude when landing at AFB Waterkloof. Damaged undercarriage and bumped the tail cone.

**F1AZ 228**
13/3/84
Capt Digby Holdsworth
Pilot lost in bad weather with malfunctioning instruments. Pilot ejected successfully. Aircraft crashed near Lydenburg, South Africa.

**F1CZ 205**
8/2/85
Capt Pierre du Plessis
During air-to-air sortie pilot experienced severe engine fluctuations. Landed safely at AFB Langebaan. Turning off runway fuselage erupted in ball of fire. Pilot evacuated safely. Fire extinguished by fire department. Fire caused by faulty ignitor jet.

**F1AZ 222**
4/4/85
Maj Jan Henning
Aircraft crashed at AFB Hoedspruit. Pilot ejected safely.

**F1AZ 221**
23/7/85
Capt Rikus de Beer
Aircraft suffered fuel pipe problems, severely reducing thrust. Pilot attempted a forced landing and aircraft crashed onto threshold.

**F1CZ 215**
1986
Capt John Sinclair
Aircraft struck mountain ridge on low-level navigation sortie. Pilot ejected safely.

**F1CZ 206**
27/9/88
Capt Arthur Piercy
Aircraft hit by AA-7 or AA-8 missiles in dogfight with Angolan MiG-23s. Pilot landed damaged aircraft successfully at AFB Rundu, but aircraft overshot the runway. Pilot inadvertently ejected during over-run.

**F1AZ 245**
20/2/88
Maj Ed Every
Aircraft hit by SA-13 missile and crashed in Angola. Pilot killed.

**F1AZ 223**
19/3/88
Capt Willie van Coppenhagen
Aircraft crashed during low-level night operation in Angola. Pilot killed.

**F1AZ 224**
20/2/93
Cmdt Dolf Prinsloo
Engine fire on start-up. Engine and fuselage damaged.

**F1AZ 221**
5/2/92
Maj Leon Bath
Pilot ejected successfully after bird ingestion into engine. Aircraft crashed one nautical mile short of runway at AFB Hoedspruit.

**F1AZ 234**
23/11/93
Capt Louis Joubert
Aircraft crashed into sea off Cape Point during maritime shipping strike. Pilot ejected at extremely low level but was lost at sea.

**F1AZ 224**
9/6/94
Maj Alan Brand
During a 4-ship low-level bombing sortie on Potchefstroom range, aircraft suffered shrapnel damage. Pilot ejected successfully.

**F1CZ 214** was intentionally broken up during fitting of the Soviet engine.

**F1CZ 205** had tail section of F1CZ 206 fitted and returned to service as F1CZ 205.

# Appendix IX

# V3 air-to-air missiles

**1973: V3A**
First local air-to-air missile. Built in three sections, which was found to be a poor technique. Based on Sidewinder D. Solid state. Limited to 30° angle off firing under low G conditions. Integrated on the F1CZ before the aircraft left France.

**1977: V3B**
Improved version. Went into production and was carried operationally on the F1. Same category as Sidewinder J. Gimbal limits 34°. No bias ahead of the plume—like the Matra 550, it tended to detonate on the plume. Used an I/R detector fuse, which could be triggered by decoy flares or hot patches on the ground. There was, therefore, a low-level limitation. Fired in anger during the bush war but did not achieve a kill because it detonated on the enemy aircraft's heat plume.

**1986: V3C**
Greatly improved version. Category similar to Sidewinder L. Gimbal limits 55°. Short reaction time. Laser fuse. 17kg tungsten cube warhead. Lead bias optimized from 20°–160° using a colour guidance system to distinguish between aircraft and decoy flare. The bush war ended before it could be used operationally.

**1988: V3S**
Acquired as an interim measure but not used operationally.

**1992: V3P**
Successful integration trials completed but missile not brought into SAAF inventory. Combination of helmet sight and missile gave lock-on up to 75° with a keep-lock ability up to 80°. Missile lock-on was achieved on a 180° pass. Turning diameter at sea level with a Mach 0.9 launch speed was 200 metres. Not in SAAF inventory owing to budgetary constraints.

# Bibliography

Steenkamp, W., (1989) *South Africa's border war*, Gibraltar: Ashanti Publishers
Spies, Prof. F. J. du Toit, (1989) *Angola Operasie Savannah 1975–1976*. Pretoria: SADF
*Nyala* – South African Air Force Aviation Safety Magazine
*Ad Astra* – South African Air Force Magazine
*Paratus* – Official monthly periodical of the SADF
*Salut* – Official monthly periodical of the SANDF
*Roll of Honour* – South African Air Force

# Index

Aanhanca 297
Ackerman, Capt Piet 220, 267, 293
African National Congress (ANC) 146, 147, 271
ANC *see* African National Congress
Anderson, Capt Harry 139
Angolan Air Force (FAPA) 90, 152, 190
Armscor 27
Atlas Aircraft Corporation 14, 33, 34, 43, 52, 54, 77, 78, 80, 104, 136, 155, 165, 209, 221, 227, 229, 241, 267, 273, 298

Barker, Maj Des 173, 174, 222, 267, 271
Basson, Cmdt 'Mossie' 42, 46, 47, 50, 85, 186, 245, 267, 274
Bath, Maj Leon 217-219, 221, 224-226, 228, 267, 306
Bekker, Sgt Dolf 127
Bell, Maj Aubrey 296
Beneke, Lt Daantjie 69
Bennett, Capt Les 56, 86, 98-100, 114, 135, 171, 267, 305
Beretta, Val 143
Beretta, Wendy 143
Bernberg, Capt Trevor 147, 148, 267, 271, 272
Beukes, Capt Roelf 42, 46, 47, 50, 56, 63, 244, 245, 267
Billy Boy *see* Faure, H
Blaauw, Brig Jan 24, 39
Blignaut, Steve 104
Bolton, Maj-Gen Frikkie 27, 74, 198
Bomba, Lt (MAF) 273, 284
Bordeaux, France 29-31, 33
Botes, Sgt 300
Botha, Capt Johan 156, 267

Botha, Col Koos 195
Botha, Pik 70, 137, 212
Botha, PW 24
Botha, Sgt Willem 103, 128
Boyd, WO Geoff 29
Brand, Capt Alan 214, 216, 218, 219, 222, 224, 226, 227, 229-231, 233-235, 237, 267, 272, 273, 293, 306
Brand, Capt Francois 224, 229, 267
Brits, Maj Chris 62, 68, 69, 267, 304
Bronkhorstpruit 45
Bruton, Capt Norman 73, 74, 107
Buissoin, JC 82
Burger, Capt Leon 117, 182, 297
Burger, Col Bertus 139, 239
Burgers, Capt 'Budgie' 89, 90, 136, 267
Byleveldt, Deon 128
Byleveldt, Riaan 104
Byleveldt, Rita 104

Cahama, Angola 71, 110, 111, 113, 115, 116, 119, 121, 132, 134, 137, 139, 178, 295, 301
Caiundo, Angola 150
Calonga River, Angola 139
Campbell, Sgt R 266
Cape Town 46, 81, 82, 180, 184, 200, 212, 229, 231, 234, 241, 244, 273
Caprivi Strip 63, 64, 72, 166, 172, 303
Carolan, Capt Paddy 96, 107, 121, 131, 132, 143, 267, 273, 274
Cassinga, Angola 63, 111, 119, 121, 132, 285, 303
Cazaux, France 26
Cazombo, Angola 166
Cela, Angola 295

309

Celliers, Sgt Koos 298
Central Flying School (CFS) 45, 275, 278, 289
CFS *see* Central Flying School
Chabaku, Rev 235
Chambinga, Angola 188, 201
Chibembe, Angola 111
Church, Maj John 195
Claridge, Alf 127
Cloete, Lt A 266
Clulow, Capt Mark 81, 90, 103,267
Coetzee, Brig Gerrie 205, 265
Coetzee, Capt Frans 95, 103, 153, 155, 196, 197, 199-201, 214, 223, 267, 274, 293
Coetzee, Maj Jan 34, 266
Collier, Capt Billy 95-97, 103, 147, 267,
Conradie, Capt Frans 139
Cook, Capt HP 199
Cooke, Maj Peter 43, 45, 50, 173, 175, 206, 207, 209, 211, 267, 275, 288
Crooks, Capt Mark 73, 74, 267
Crous, Lt Terry 119, 128, 265
Cuamato, Angola 298, 299
Cuito Cuanavale, Angola 166, 168, 180-182, 187, 189, 190, 196, 199, 201, 202, 288, 301, 302
Cuito River, Angola 181, 190, 194
Culpan, Rick 227, 245, 263, 267
Cunuene Province, Angola 110, 117
Cunene River, Angola/SWA 113, 122, 130, 247, 303
Cuvelai, Angola 138, 139, 151, 152, 302

Dalgleish, Sgt Kenny 126, 300
Dar es Salaam, Tanzania 146
Dassault Aviation 24, 25, 28, 33, 36-38, 55, 65, 82, 104, 176, 224, 290
Dassault, Marcel 37
Dassault, Serge 37
Dayton radar station *see* 70 MRU
de Beer, Capt Jaco 182, 185
de Beer, Capt Rikus 174, 175, 180
de Klerk, FW 220
de Lange, Sgt Chris 103, 214, 293
de Villiers, Maj Dirk 65, 81, 86, 88, 100, 214, 221, 267, 276
de Villiers, Cmdt 'Div' 119, 204
de Villiers, Lt Neil 55, 267
de Wet, WOI 'Tubby' 79, 209, 292

Delport, Maj 'Dellies' 98, 99, 179
Deschamps, Lt Ed 57, 67, 268
Devon radar centre 34, 98, 99, 152, 173, 179
Dillon, F/Sgt Alan 128
Dodds, Capt Lyle 156
Doyle, Lt Owen 71, 295
du Plessis, Capt IC 55, 67, 72, 87, 89, 90, 91, 100, 198, 268, 281, 292, 304
du Plessis, Lt Johan 98, 100, 114, 122, 124, 268, 274
du Plessis, Capt Kobus 224, 268
du Plessis, Lt Louis 268, 276, 277
du Plessis, Capt Pierre 42, 47, 67, 73, 74, 77, 78, 85, 87, 124, 182, 185, 192, 268, 277, 278, 284, 292, 305
du Plessis, WOI WJ 'Doep' 13, 258-261
du Preez, Mariette 210
du Toit, Cmdt Fred 42, 43, 45, 46, 52, 62, 67, 72, 78, 79, 264, 268
du Toit, Sgt GJ 293
du Toit, Cmdt Thinus 182, 199
Durandt, Capt Charl 208, 268
Durban 42, 43, 48-50, 56, 82, 83, 117, 144, 146, 147, 149, 176, 209, 229, 242, 243, 273, 275, 288, 290

Earp, Brig Dennis 198, 201, 202
Earp, Lt Michael 127, 300
Ebenezer Dam 36
Ebo, Angola 294
Edwards, Maj Mike 158, 159, 206, 207, 212, 268
Einkamerer, Capt Bill 55, 64, 100, 268
Eksteen, F/Sgt Mike 214
Ellis, Capt Neall 139
Engela, Cmdt Tom 67, 71
Erasmus, Capt 'Rassie' 294
Erasmus, Maj John 240
Estherhuise, Eric 27
Etosha Pan 129, 202
Every, Capt Ed 95, 97, 148, 151, 154, 155, 196, 197, 199, 201, 247, 268, 274, 292, 301, 306

Facer, Maj Marsh 122
FAPA – *see* Angolan Air Force
FAPLA (Forças Armadas Populares de Libertação de Angola) *see* People's

Armed Forces for the Liberation of Angola
Faure, Hannes 237, 238
Ferreira, Cmdt Deon 114, 115
Ferreira, Johan 265
Ferreira, Maj Steve 63
Flying Training School (FTS) 278
Flynn, Capt Patrick 234, 242, 268
Foote, Maj Dudley 119
Forças Aeria Popular de Angola (People's Air Force of Angola) *see* Angolan Air Force
Fourie, WOI Daantjie 128
Fourie, Sgt Gerhard 215
Fryer, Maj Keith 243
FTS *see* Flying Training School

Gagiano, Cmdt Carlo 42, 43, 45, 53, 62, 67, 73, 74, 79, 171, 172, 174, 180, 182, 183, 185, 186, 192, 264, 268, 272, 276, 278, 288, 289
Geldenhuys, Lt-Gen Jannie 180
Genis, Capt Nelis 202, 203, 216, 268
Geraghty, Capt 'Spook' 131, 132, 142, 143, 147-149, 165, 268
Gerhard, Capt Dieter (SAN) 74
Glynn, Lt Richard 301
Golden Eagle exercise 165, 176, 178, 201, 202, 219, 222, 228, 243, 272, 281
Gouws, Capt JP 173, 268
Gouws, Col Pierre 102, 103, 243
Green, Capt 302
Griesel, Sgt Deon 208
Grobler, Sgt 'Grobbies' 300
Groblersdal 69, 100, 305
Gründling, Cmdt Jack 27, 28, 31, 34, 36-38, 44, 45, 50, 71, 73, 74, 79, 80, 83, 84, 121, 135, 137, 264, 268, 292

Hammanskraal telemetry range 228
Hart, Maj Errol 89
Hartebeespoort 43, 97, 135
Hartogh, Maj 'Skilly' 79, 205, 206, 208, 209, 211, 212, 264, 268, 275
Hartzenberg, Maj Chris 295
Hattingh, Capt André 298
Hauptfleisch, Lt Bart 74
Hechter, Lt AJ 266
Hechter, Lt Braam 210, 212

Hechter, Lt-Gen Willem 51-56, 64, 68, 74, 117, 189, 214, 243, 244, 264, 268
Henning, Capt Jan 95, 136, 159-161, 169, 216, 268, 289, 292, 296, 305
Henning, WOI 'Poen' 79
Hippo Pools 179
Holdsworth, Capt Digby 152-155, 162, 163, 174, 187, 268, 293, 305
Hollis, Lt Pete 297
Holmes, Cmdt Ollie 80, 87, 211
Hougaard, Cmdt Jan 130
Houghton, Cadet Ray 294
Humbe, Angola 74, 113
Huyser, Brig 'Bossie' 12, 25-31, 33-38, 52, 82, 92, 93, 95, 112, 113, 264, 268. 277, 279

Inggs, Capt John 88, 124, 268, 285
Ionde, Angola 119, 137

Jacanin, Lt Jake (USN) 142
Jacobs, Col 'Spyker' 65, 128, 268
Jamba, Angola 132, 166
Janse van Rensburg, Sgt AJ 299
Johannesburg 28, 33, 44, 93, 149, 218, 242, 276, 279, 286, 287, 290
Jones, Capt Ian 158, 219
Jones, Capt Roly 295
Jones, Lt 'Tinkie' 56, 67, 70, 71, 73, 74. 135, 268, 280
Joubert, Lt A 266
Joubert, Capt 'Blokkies' 268
Joubert, Dawie 104
Joubert, Brig 'Joep'
Joubert, Capt Louis 229-231, 268, 305
Joubert, Capt Pierre 192

Kaiser, Capt Vic 81, 268
Kaokoland 130, 201, 215, 252
Katima Mulilo 64
Kavango 108, 131, 144, 166, 247, 252
Kay, Capt Laurie 241
Keet, Capt Rynier 114, 217, 302
Kentron missile factory 199, 201, 202
Kimberley 55, 148, 158, 232, 271, 272
Kirkland, Cmdt Derek 66
Klaserie Game Reserve 143, 156
Kleynhans, Capt Dawid 156, 197, 200, 201, 268, 293

Knobel, F/Sgt Quintus 107
Knott-Craig, Capt Alan 95, 103, 147-149, 160, 169, 268
Koevoet (SAP), 215
Koop Pan Suid 52
Kotze, Maj Gene 300
Krieger, Capt Israel 137, 268
Kriel, Gen James 230, 235
Kruger, Cmdt Martin 161, 230
Kruger, Maj 'Polla' 160, 161, 296, 302
Kuruman 52, 72

la Grange, Capt Tristan 268
Labuschagne, Capt 'Lappies' 190
Lategan, Capt Francois 268
Lavi, Cmdt Joshi 152, 156, 269, 272, 305
le Guen, Col 34
le Roux, Capt Pietie 212, 268
Lee, Capt Darryl 38, 51, 53, 67, 70-73, 85-87, 91, 92, 117, 118, 135, 268
Lewis, Cmdt Casey 74, 75, 81, 82, 264, 269
Liddell, Lt Neil 295, 302
Lohatla live weapons range 242, 291
Lombard, Col Wouter 161
Lombard, Maj Chris 26, 28, 30, 31, 33, 36-39, 42, 43, 45, 264, 269, 278, 279, 292
Lomberg, Capt Les 139, 140
Lord, Cmdt Dick 92, 103, 111, 136, 264, 269
Loskop Dam 179
Lourens, Sgt C 293
Louw, Capt Hennie 74, 81, 86, 103, 136, 158, 269, 284
Louw, Capt Martin 205, 207, 212, 269, 276, 279, 280
Lubango, Angola 67, 75, 78, 85, 87, 91, 121, 148, 178, 183, 195, 196, 201, 276, 280, 281, 284, 298, 302, 304
Lydenburg 93, 152, 154, 155, 305

Macatamney, Mac 95, 170, 231
Madimbo 179
Mafeking 96, 97
Magaliesberg 135
Malan, Gen Magnus 137
Mandela, Nelson 232, 240, 244
Maputo, Mozambique 146, 147, 240, 271
Marais, Capt Charl 233, 234, 269

Marais, Lt Dewald 'Wally' 71, 295
Marais, Cmdt Jan 51, 56, 209, 269
Mariepskop 154, 173
Maritz, Maj 'Mitz' 27-29, 31, 34, 36-39, 41, 42, 46, 50, 119, 269
Masson, Cmdt Bob 51, 273
Mathers, Capt Anthony 217, 269
Mavinga, Angola 166, 176, 180, 181, 187, 301
McCarthy, Maj Mac 215, 231
Meech-Noyes, Capt Leon 211, 212, 269
Meintjies, Lt Neels 302
Meiring, Maj-Gen Georg 184
Menonque, Angola 78, 116, 121, 148, 168, 173, 181-183, 187-189, 190, 196
Mes, Capt Rudi 171, 172, 182, 185, 192, 206-208, 210-212, 269
Meyer, Maj Willie 110
Mienie, Lt-Col Jan 147, 154, 206, 236-242, 244, 269, 280
Millbank, Capt John 295
Miller, Maj Richard 219
Minne, Capt Norman 65, 72, 76, 83, 85, 87, 101, 103, 139, 178, 183, 187, 195-197, 200, 201, 214-224, 237, 264, 269, 273, 281, 289, 292
Mitterand, Francois 234
Mongua, Angola 70, 117
Moolman, Lt Johan 148, 159, 176, 269, 271, 281, 282
MPLA (Movimento Popular de Libertação de Angola) *see* Popular Movement for the Liberation of Angola
Muller, Lt-Gen Mike 43, 137
Muller, Lt Thys 51, 53, 56, 62, 67, 74, 269
Mulondo, Angola 132, 302
Mupa, Angola 114, 137, 298

Nairobi, Kenya 146
Namibe, Angola 67, 121, 178, 200
National Union for the Total Independence of Angola (UNITA) 117, 148, 166-168, 181, 301
Nel, Col Gert 104
Nel, Capt 'Trompie' 178, 196-198, 264, 269, 292
Nell, Maj Theo 64, 66, 75, 76, 82, 83, 85, 86, 103, 115, 269, 282, 283
Nelson, Maj Alan 30

Nelspruit 153
Nichols, Richard 04
Niemann, Capt Attie 205, 210, 269
Niewoudt, Maj Johan 269
Norrie, Lt Alan 42, 52
Nujoma, Sam 134, 215

O'Neill du Toit, F/Sgt Piet 295
O'Regan, John 209
OCU *see* Operational Conversion Unit
Omapande, Angola 296
Ombalantu 86
Oncocua, Angola 70, 201
Ondangwa 16-18, 66, 67, 70, 71, 74, 75, 77, 78, 84-92, 111-117, 119, 124, 126, 128, 129, 131, 132, 137-139, 148, 150, 151, 172, 178, 180, 189, 195, 196, 202, 204, 215, 274, 281, 282, 284, 296-298, 302, 304
Ongiva, Angola 71, 101, 110, 111, 114, 117, 119, 137, 179, 273, 302
Oosthuizen, WOI 'Oosie' 79, 209
Oosthuysen, Capt Nic 154, 156, 162, 163, 175, 176, 269
Operational Conversion Unit (OCU) 35
OPERATIONS
  Askari 17, 149-151, 280, 301
  Bellombra 179-186
  Daisy 13, 118-127, 131, 285
  Donkermaan 275, 281
  Hooper 181, 187-195, 216, 288
  Knife 112-114
  Konyn 110-112
  Maanskyn 275, 281
  Magneto 166
  Meebos 136-139
  Merlyn 215
  Moduler 180-188, 194, 205, 214, 216, 281, 288, 301
  Packer 181, 188, 216, 288
  Phoenix 144
  Protea 110-112, 116-119, 131, 166, 204, 273, 299
  Reeftan 231
  Rekstok 70, 74, 75
  Rekstok II 75
  Rekstok III 131
  Saamwerk 144-146
  Saffraan 72
  Savannah 288, 294-295
  Sceptic 83, 84
  Second Congress (FAPLA) 166-169
  Skerwe 146, 271
  Smokeshell (QFL) 83-85, 281, 298
  Super 130
  Uric (Rhodesian) 296
  Valknes 159,160
  Vlinder 299
  Wallpaper 166
  Weldmesh 166, 170, 176, 181, 285
  Wishbone 100, 101
Orr, Capt John 73, 74, 107
Ortmann, Lt Dieter 56, 269
Osborne, Lt Nigel 296
Oshakati 117, 138, 143, 195, 303
Oshikango 179
Owamboland 89, 108, 130, 131, 144, 149, 166

Page, Capt Keith 117, 182
Palela 101
Parkhomento, Maj V 227, 269
Penhall, Maj Rod 119, 121
Pentz, Capt Ivan 202, 212, 222, 269
People's Armed Forces for the Liberation of Angola (FAPLA) 13, 85, 110, 111, 113, 114, 117, 131, 166, 167, 173, 176, 180, 181, 188, 204, 215, 280
Phalaborwa 179, 284
Pienaar, Gen Ed 28, 33, 43, 102
Piercy, Capt Arthur 152, 158, 182, 184-186, 192, 202, 269, 273, 278, 283, 286, 288, 292, 302, 306
Piet Gouws Dam 179
Pietersen, Lt Chris 300
Popular Movement for the Liberation of Angola (MPLA) 252, 256
Port Elizabeth 83, 127, 281
Port, Maj Billy 226
Potchefstroom 63, 64, 219, 232, 233, 272, 283, 288, 306
Potgieter, Col PP 34
Potgieter, Herman 241, 245
Potgieter, Maj Phillip 235, 242, 269, 293
Potgieter, Sgt Francois 29
Pretoria 24, 35, 43, 44, 50, 53, 54, 65, 58, 81-84, 93, 100, 102, 105, 106, 119, 126, 128, 135, 146, 150, 166, 201, 202, 205, 209, 219, 228, 242, 271, 278, 280, 281,

313

283, 285-287, 290
Pretorius, Capt Bert 265
Pretorius, Capt Chris 229, 235, 240, 242, 269, 293
Pretorius, Capt Giel 265
Pretorius, Sgt Flip 295
Pretorius, Maj Frans 74, 77, 85, 87-89, 97, 269, 283, 284, 292, 302, 304
Prinsloo, Cmdt Dolf 79, 217, 224, 228-230, 235-237, 264, 269, 289, 293, 306
Project *Dikvel* 73, 74
Punda Milia 176

Quiteve, Angola 122

Radloff, Cmdt Gerrie 80, 81, 91, 113, 122, 124, 143, 148, 156, 169, 221, 264, 269, 285, 286
Rankin, Maj Johan 121, 122, 124, 139, 140, 142, 173-176, 178, 180, 183, 187, 195-199, 204, 214, 264, 269, 287, 292
Rautenbach, WOI Bachus 20
Raymond, Capt Mark 158, 159, 182, 192, 269, 286, 287
Reboul, Capt 30,
Red Arrow aerobatic team 64, 240
Repsold, Cmdt Zach 25, 26, 35, 269
Retief, Cmdt Daantjie 29, 30, 34, 227, 266
Retief, Sgt Dick 296
RhAF *see* Rhodesian Air Force
Rheims, France 28
Rhodesian Air Force (RhAF) 77, 247, 280, 296
Robinson, Capt John 127, 300
Rochat, Cmdt Graham 46, 73, 74, 162
Rogers, Gen Bob 31, 33, 43, 78
Roodewal bombing range 53, 54, 57, 82, 127, 148, 165, 174, 175, 208, 215, 220, 229
Roos, Lt Bertus 117, 299
Roos, Lt PJ 266
Roy, Cmdt Sandy 216
Ruacana 90, 112, 132, 178, 302, 304
Rudnick, Capt Charlie 229
Rutsch, Col Martin 222
Rybicki, Maj 302

SAAF Museum 210, 277, 280
Sakkers, 'Onno' 104
SAN *see* South African Navy
Savimbi, Jonas 166, 256
Scheepers, WOI 'Skippy' 128, 210, 293
Scheltema, Capt Nic 217, 228, 233, 235, 269, 289, 293
Schür, Capt Otto 78, 85, 117, 296
Serfontein, Capt W 224, 230, 231, 233, 269
Siebrits, Cmdt 'Pikkie' 190, 217
Silver Falcon aerobatic team 39, 81, 229, 279
Sinclair, Capt John 171, 173, 182, 192, 269, 288, 305
Skinner, Capt Chris 147, 155, 174, 180, 189, 197, 200, 202, 236, 269, 293, 299
Slade, Capt Alan 215
Smal, Capt Sarel 224, 297
Smal, Capt Wayne 168, 269
Smith, Capt Frik 265
Smith, Capt Jaco 237, 269
Smith, Maj EP 102, 265
Snecma, France 29, 227
Snyman, Capt 'Toekie' 46
SOUTH AFRICAN AIR FORCE (SAAF) BASES
Bloemspruit 62, 64, 129, 148, 176, 202
Eros, Windhoek 5
Grootfontein 75, 84, 90, 112, 115, 117, 119, 120, 144, 150, 167-169, 180, 183, 184, 187-191, 194-196, 198, 200, 201, 205, 214, 273, 282
Hoedspruit 13, 20, 32, 37, 38, 56, 60, 68, 82, 84, 92-95, 100, 102-106, 110, 118, 127-129, 131, 139, 142, 143, 145, 148-152, 154-156, 159, 163, 169, 173, 175-178, 180, 197, 199, 200, 205, 210, 215-222, 224, 225, 228, 229, 233-235, 240-243, 273, 279, 281, 284, 289, 291
Mpacha 63, 72, 172, 295
Ondangwa 16-18, 66, 67, 70, 71, 74, 75, 77, 78, 84-86, 88-91, 111-114, 117, 119, 124, 126, 128, 129, 131, 1322, 137-139, 148, 150, 151, 156, 173, 179, 180, 189, 195, 196, 202, 204, 215, 274, 281, 282, 284, 296-298, 302, 304
Pietersburg 26, 35-37, 41, 45-47, 49, 51, 66, 80, 92, 102, 178, 209, 217, 219, 223, 228, 277, 279, 283, 290
Rundu 108, 167, 168, 177, 181-184, 186-

189, 194, 198, 278, 283, 286, 288, 306
Swartkop 233
Waterkloof 14, 24, 25, 27, 28, 33, 34, 36-39, 41-43, 45-47, 51, 52, 54, 57, 60, 61, 64, 65, 67, 69, 70, 72, 73, 77, 81-84, 91, 93, 95, 98, 99, 102, 103, 135, 156, 158, 159, 171-173, 180, 204, 208-211, 216, 231, 240, 241, 243, 271, 275, 277, 286, 287, 290, 305
Ysterplaat 39, 81, 200

SOUTH AFRICAN AIR FORCE (SAAF) SQUADRONS
1 Squadron: Hoedspruit (Mirage F1AZ) 5, 36, 42, 43, 47, 51-53, 55-57, 60, 61, 65, 67, 68, 72, 74-77, 81-85, 92-96, 98, 102-107, 110, 112, 118, 119, 127-129, 131, 136, 143, 146-148, 152, 156, 169, 170, 172-174, 176, 178, 180, 183, 186, 190, 194, 197, 199, 201, 203, 214-217, 219-222, 224, 227-230, 234-238, 240-243, 264-266, 272-274, 276, 279-282, 285, 288-292
2 Squadron: Waterkloof (Mirage III CZ & R2Z) 24-28, 31, 32, 36, 43, 49, 56, 60, 63, 67, 68, 70, 74, 85, 107, 108, 173, 178, 179, 205, 279, 291, 298
3 Squadron: Waterkloof (Mirage F1CZ) 31, 33-39, 41-46, 50-53, 55-57, 60, 62, 65, 67, 68, 70-74, 76-81, 84, 85, 98, 105, 113, 119, 122, 131, 135-137, 139, 144-146, 150, 152, 156, 158, 171-173, 176, 207, 210-212, 217, 219, 228, 236, 242, 244, 264, 266, 275-279, 281, 283, 285-288, 290, 292
4 Squadron: Swartkop (Impala) 50, 53
8 Squadron: Bloemspruit (Impala) 236
12 Squadron: Waterkloof (Canberra) 70, 71, 101, 139, 172, 173
17 Squadron: Swartkop (Alouette) 126
24 Squadron: Waterkloof (Buccaneer) 46, 47, 50, 86, 97, 148, 173, 194
28 Squadron: Waterkloof (C-130 & C-160) 53, 73, 84
41 Squadron: Swartkop (Cessna185) 244
60 Squadron: Waterkloof (Boeing-707) 174, 178, 180, 216, 217, 228, 234, 235, 237, 241-243, 281, 291
85 Advanced Flying School (Impala, Sabre & Mirage III) 26, 35, 37, 47, 49, 51, 56, 68, 74, 92, 145, 171, 172, 277, 279, 283, 290

SOUTH AFRICAN AIR FORCE (SAAF) UNITS
310 AFCP Oshakati 138, 195
70 MRU (Mobile Radar Group), 'Dayton', Ondangwa 49, 67, 71, 88, 122, 124, 126, 139, 179, 285, 286
70 MRU (Mobile Radar Group), 'Sunset', Rundu 182
AFCP (Air Force Command Post), Pretoria 5, 147, 219
SAAF HQ Pretoria 5, 25, 31, 37, 81. 83, 102, 110, 146, 147, 167, 224
WAC (Western Air Command), Bastion, Windhoek 112
SOUTH AFRICAN ARMY UNITS
32 Battalion 130, 196, 273, 282, 300
44 Parachute Brigade 63, 120, 126, 139, 197, 296
61 Mechanized Battalion 111, 119
South African Navy (SAN) 24, 51
South West Africa People's Organization (SWAPO) 60, 63, 64, 70, 72, 74, 84-87, 91, 100, 108, 110, 111, 114, 115, 117, 119, 120, 126, 130-132, 134, 137-139, 144, 149-152, 166, 195, 215, 239, 276, 295, 298
Spencer, Capt Stuart 242
Spies, Lt Jimmy 198, 215, 265
Sproul, Capt Rob 200
St Lucia 63
Stacey, Sgt Clifton 117, 299
Steinhobel, Lt Des 44, 51, 270
Steyn, F/Sgt 215
Steyn, Capt Barrie 202
Stipp, Capt John 217, 219, 221, 222, 270
Stock, Capt Dave 197, 270
Strydom, Capt Frans 265
SWAPO *see* South West Africa People's Organization

Taljaard, Capt DJ 294
Terblanche, Sandra 104
Tetchamutete, Angola 124, 138
Thackwray, Brig 'Thack' 184
Thatcher, Margaret 215
Thomas, Lt Neil 298
Thompson, 2/Lt EB 294
Thoyandou 179
THTC *see* Tobias Haneko Training Camp

Tobias Haneko Training Camp (THTC), SWAPO base 85
Toerien, Maj Cobus 139, 142, 204, 206, 212, 219, 270, 277, 287
Tonkin, Capt Frank 182, 185, 192, 270, 288
Tooth Rock range 77, 207, 217
Truter, Lt Piet 57, 67, 270
Truter, Maj Paulus 173, 174, 187, 203, 270, 288, 289, 292
Turner, Maj Clive 172, 270
Twaddle, Capt John 300

Umhlanga Rocks 50
UNITA (União Nacional para a Independência Total de Angola) *see* National Union for the Total Independence of Angola
United Nations (UN) 70, 151, 166, 215
United Nations Transitional Agreement Group (UNTAG) 70, 215
UNTAG *see* United Nations Transitional Agreement Group
Upington 64, 72, 73, 75, 76, 84, 112, 178, 201, 202, 216, 219, 240, 273, 279, 282
Uys, Dawie 104, 105, 127, 265

van Coppenhagen, Maj Willie 180, 195-197, 199, 200, 270, 292, 306
van der Heever, Maj André 34-36, 43-45, 47, 52, 53, 56, 57, 62, 67, 69, 77, 245, 270
van der Merwe, Cmdt Mac 73, 107, 108, 228, 234, 273
van Eeden, Capt Reg 176, 184, 196, 197, 270, 293
van Heerden, Capt Gandi 34, 266
van Heerden, Maj Schalk 223, 270, 289
van Rensburg, Maj Anton 171-173, 182, 183, 192, 270, 276, 277, 288
van Rensburg, Sgt CJ 293
van Rensburg, Sgt Dolf 299
van Rensburg, Capt Thinus 298
van Schalkwyk, Cmdt Piet 217
van Straaten, F/Sgt Kenny 78
van Tonder, Capt Riaan 214, 270
van Zyl, Capt Nick 214
van Zyl, Maj John 202, 270
van Zyl, Lt Piet 117
Vellerman, Capt Paul 296, 302
Venter, Hennie 107

Venter, Capt 'Jeronkie' 108, 205, 209, 211, 212, 270
Venter, Col Steyn 215, 221, 228
Venter, Maj Chris 102, 103, 110, 119, 128, 265
Venter, Rika 102
Vereeniging 55
Vergottini, Capt Mario 215
Vermeulen, Capt Giep 146, 147, 217, 219, 221, 270, 271
Viljoen, Capt Frik 74, 270
Viljoen, Col Eddie 184
Visser, Capt 'Vissie' 163, 164
Vissers, Capt 'Floors' 148, 270
Vivier, Maj Pete 146, 270, 290
Volcano, SWAPO base/troops 144
Volker, Maj Carl 155
Volkerz, Capt Steve 298
von Gunten, Capt Marcel 220, 270
Vorster, John 60, 65

Waldheim, Kurt 70
Walker, Capt Arthur 299, 300
Warden, Capt Glen 117, 274, 280
Warnke, Cmdt Dick 214
Wasserman, Capt 'Wassie' 42, 54-57, 61, 66, 68-70, 74, 81, 83, 91, 92, 98, 100, 266, 270, 273, 304
Wehmeyer, Cmdt Dries 42, 46, 49, 50, 70, 71, 144, 145, 158, 264, 270, 287, 292
Weingartz, Capt Mike 152, 158, 270
Wen-Soo Chang, Capt 206, 212
Wernich, Sgt Ray 294
Wessels, Capt Carel 192
Wessels, Maj JP 277
Westoby, Capt Wayne 201, 270, 290, 291
Williams, Capt Kenny 270
Williamson, 2/Lt KW 294
Williamson, Capt Paul 242, 270, 291
Windhoek 156, 215, 239
Winterbach, Cmdt Gawie 34, 36, 37, 43-45, 47, 50, 55, 118, 121, 122, 216

Xangongo, Angola 101, 110, 111, 113, 117, 119, 137, 298, 301

Yati Strip 257

Zimmer, Lt-Col Hans 227